ICONS OF LATINO AMERICA

**Recent Titles in
Greenwood Icons**

Icons of Horror and the Supernatural: An Encyclopedia of
Our Worst Nightmares
Edited by S.T. Joshi

Icons of Business: An Encyclopedia of Mavericks, Movers, and Shakers
Kateri Drexler

Icons of Hip Hop: An Encyclopedia of the Movement, Music, and Culture
Edited by Mickey Hess

Icons of Evolution: An Encyclopedia of People, Evidence, and Controversies
Edited by Brian Regal

Icons of Rock: An Encyclopedia of the Legends Who Changed Music Forever
Scott Schinder and Andy Schwartz

Icons of R&B and Soul: An Encyclopedia of the Artists Who Revolutionized Rhythm
Bob Gulla

African American Icons of Sport: Triumph, Courage, and Excellence
Matthew C. Whitaker

Icons of the American West: From Cowgirls to Silicon Valley
Edited by Gordon Morris Bakken

ICONS OF LATINO AMERICA

Latino Contributions to American Culture

VOLUME 1

Roger Bruns

Foreword by Ilan Stavans

Greenwood Icons

GREENWOOD PRESS
Westport, Connecticut · London

Library of Congress Cataloging-in-Publication Data

Bruns, Roger
  Icons of Latino America : Latino contributions to American culture/Roger Bruns.
    p. cm. — (Greenwood icons)
  Includes bibliographical references and indexes.
    ISBN 978-0-313-34086-4 (set : alk. paper) — ISBN 978-0-313-34087-1 (v. 1 : alk.
  paper) — ISBN 978-0-313-34088-8 (v. 2 : alk. paper)
    1. Hispanic Americans—Biography. 2. Hispanic American celebrities—Biography.
  3. United States—Civilization—Hispanic influences. I. Title.
    E184.S75B78 2008
    920′.009468073—dc22   2008013646

British Library Cataloguing in Publication Data is available.

Library of Congress Catalog Card Number: 2008013646
ISBN: 978-0-313-34086-4 (set)
       978-0-313-34087-1 (vol. 1)
       978-0-313-34088-8 (vol. 2)

First published in 2008

Greenwood Press, 88 Post Road West, Westport, CT 06881
An imprint of Greenwood Publishing Group, Inc.
www.greenwood.com

Printed in the United States of America

∞™

The paper used in this book complies with the
Permanent Paper Standard issued by the National
Information Standards Organization (Z39.48–1984).

10 9 8 7 6 5 4 3 2 1

Contents

Volume 2

Photos

Desi Arnaz, 1958 (page 1). Courtesy of Library of Congress.

Ruben Blades (left) and Mickey Rourke in *Once Upon a Time in Mexico*, 2003 (page 25). Courtesy of Columbia Pictures Corporation/Photofest. © Columbia Pictures Corporation.

Fabiola Cabeza de Baca Gilbert in front of rural New Mexico schoolhouse (page 49). Fabiola Cabeza de Baca Gilbert Pictorial Collection, Center for Southwest Research, University Libraries, The University of New Mexico.

Cesar Chavez, 1966 (page 71). Courtesy of Library of Congress.

Woman removing chile peppers from stove, Taos, New Mexico, 1939 (page 101). Courtesy of Library of Congress.

Sandra Cisneros, 1991 (page 121). AP Photo/Dana Tynan.

Baseball player Roberto Clemente (page 145) of the Pittsburgh Pirates vs. the Mets at Shea Stadium, 1966. Courtesy of Photofest.

Celia Cruz, 1962 (page 167). Courtesy of Library of Congress.

Placido Domingo, 1970 (page 189). Courtesy of Photofest.

Jaime Escalante (page 213) teaching math at Garfield High School, in California, 1988. AP Photo.

Thirteen-frame comic strip by Gus Arriola (page 237). Gordo and his young nephew Pepito wish to return home to their friends and relatives after assisting some Mayan archaeologists. Having killed Japanese troops who were trying to sabotage their excavations by posing as Mayan ghosts, the archaeologists arrange for Gordo and Pepito to go home. August 13, 1945. Courtesy of Library of Congress.

Speedy Gonzalez (right) with Yosemite Sam in *Pancho's Hideaway*, 1964 (page 242). Courtesy of Warner Bros./Photofest. © Warner Bros.

Dora the Explorer with Monkey Boots (page 248). Courtesy of CBS/Photofest. © CBS.

Carlos Castellanos displays his Baldo comic strip (page 252) in 2000 at home in West Palm Beach, Florida. AP Photo/Terry Renna.

Comic strips of "La Cucaracha" (page 255), by artist Lalo Alcaraz at his studio in Whittier, California. AP Photo/Damian Dovarganes.

Dolores Huerta (page 261), co-founder of the United Farm Workers and founding board member of the Feminist Majority Foundation, during a symposium, 2000, in Baltimore. AP Photo/Dave Hammond.

Jennifer Lopez at the 2003 Academy Awards (page 285). Courtesy of AMPAS/ABC/Photofest. © AMPAS/ABC Photo: Craig Sjodin.

Rita Moreno in *West Side Story*, 1961 (page 309). Courtesy of Library of Congress.

Edward James Olmos in *My Family*, 1995 (page 333). Courtesy of New Line Cinema/Photofest. © New Line Cinema.

Tito Puente (page 357). Courtesy of Library of Congress.

Ruben Salazar first-class postage stamp (page 381).

Carlos Santana (page 405). Courtesy of Photofest.

Cristina Saralegui addresses her audience during the taping of her show in 2001 (page 429), at the Blue Dolphin Studio in Miami. AP Photo/Tony Gutierrez.

Selena (page 451). Courtesy of Photofest.

Golfer Lee Trevino (page 475) from Dallas, Texas, blasts from the sand trap on the first hole during the Canadian Open in Oakville, Ontario, 1989. AP Photo/Hans Deryk.

Author/director Luis Valdez (right) standing with Cesar Chavez (page 499) outside the Winter Garden Theatre in New York where *Zoot Suit* is playing, 1979. © Bettmann/Corbis.

Ritchie Valens (page 525). Courtesy of Photofest.

Poster for the film *Don Q, Son of Zorro* (page 547), showing Douglas Fairbanks in the role of Don Cesar De Vega, holding whip. Courtesy of Library of Congress.

Series Foreword

Worshipped and cursed. Loved and loathed. Obsessed about the world over. What does it take to become an icon? Regardless of subject, culture, or era, the requisite qualifications are the same: (1) challenge the status quo, (2) influence millions, and (3) impact history.

Using these criteria, Greenwood Press introduces a new reference format and approach to popular culture. Spanning a wide range of subjects, volumes in the *Greenwood Icons* series provide students and general readers a port of entry into the most fascinating and influential topics of the day. Every title offers an in-depth look at approximately 24 iconic figures, each of which captures the essence of a broad subject. These icons typically embody a group of values, elicit strong reactions, reflect the essence of a particular time and place, and link different traditions and periods. Among those featured are artists and activists, superheroes and spies, inventors and athletes—the legends and mythmakers of entire generations. Yet icons can also come from unexpected places: as the heroine who transcends the pages of a novel or as the revolutionary idea that shatters our previously held beliefs. Whether people, places, or things, such icons serve as a bridge between the past and the present, the canonical and the contemporary. By focusing on icons central to popular culture, this series encourages students to appreciate cultural diversity and critically analyze issues of enduring significance.

Most importantly, these books are as entertaining as they are provocative. Is Disneyland a more influential icon of the American West than Las Vegas? How do ghosts and ghouls reflect our collective psyche? Is Barry Bonds an inspiring or deplorable icon of baseball? Designed to foster debate, the series serves as a unique resource that is ideal for paper writing or report purposes. Insightful, in-depth entries provide far more information than conventional reference articles but are less intimidating and more accessible than a book-length biography. The most revered and reviled icons of American and world history are brought to life with related sidebars, timelines, fact boxes, and quotations. Authoritative entries are accompanied by bibliographies, making these titles an ideal starting point for further research. Spanning a wide range of popular topics, including business, literature, civil rights, politics, music, and more, books in the *Greenwood Icons* series provide fresh insights for the student and popular reader into the power and influence of icons, a topic of as vital interest today as in any previous era.

Foreword

Ours is a society defined by the cult of personality. The famous make a constant demand on our attention. They want to be admired, imitated, and eulogized. Their life serves as a collective mirror. Through them, we measure our own qualities. Do we have the same stamina? Are we also capable of battling adversity like they do? What makes their place in the world unique?

Of the almost 50 million Latinos in the United States, less than two dozen are profiled in the following pages. The ratio is crunched: exactly one icon is selected for every two million people. Still, the percentage is standard. By definition, the number of celebrities at any given period in history is small. Our interest evaporates easily. We get tired rather quickly of the same old faces.

Are the stars in this set the best endowed? The answer, of course, is relative. Every society has the luminaries it deserves.

What makes them representative? Through a Darwinian law of evolution, they have been embraced by the environment as the most salient—and the most symbolic. Cesar Chavez overcame poverty to become a fundamental Civil Rights leader. Celia Cruz sang her way—¡azúcar!—from the Havana slums to Madison Square Garden. Roberto Clemente was a slugger with a philanthropic heart. And Ruben Salazar used the pen and the microphone to remind others of the unfinished quest for Chicano self-realization.

These chosen ones are role models. Yet they are unlikely to stand the passing of time in equal measure. In a decade or so, the list of role models will be different. With other needs to satisfy, some figures now eclipsed will be revamped while others currently basking in the sunlight will be forgotten. This is as it should be. Every community has the icons it deserves.

Roger Bruns' selection is a thermometer of our health. It includes one teacher, one playwright, two journalists, two writers, and two labor activists. Aside from mice and myths like Speedy Gonzalez and Zorro, the rest are actors, musicians, and athletes. No Nobel Prize-winning physicists, chemists, economists, and medical researchers. No philosophers. No inventors. And no U.S. presidents.

This is not necessarily bad news. It ought to serve as a reminder for Latinos of where improvement is needed.

Ilan Stavans

Preface

Icons of Latino America focuses on men and women with Latin American or Hispanic cultural roots who have made important contributions to American society and who are either U.S. citizens or who have spent much of their lives in the United States. This two-volume set includes essays on some of the most significant exemplars of the Latino experience, whose lives and careers have pushed cultural boundaries, effected social change, and expanded artistic expression in the larger U.S. culture. It also includes, in a few cases, inanimate Latino icons that have also had a strong cultural impact.

When we think of the word "icon," we think of individuals whose names can be identified in the public mind by a single thought or one name. When we think of farm workers, we think of Cesar Chavez. When we think of Tejano music, we think of Selena. We think of people whose names can be seen on T-shirts in barrios; whose images appear on walls in simple home shrines; whose lives have been celebrated in corridos, poetry, folk songs, and murals; whose identity sparks emulation and loyalty; and whose work inspires followers. The figures selected in this work are mostly individuals not only of achievement but of inspiration, of legendary proportion. Some of the individuals gained this status through long, productive careers; others gained it in the space of a few years cut short by premature death. In many cases, their iconic status resulted not only from their own personal activities and accomplishments but also from circumstance. Icons from a wide range of fields are included: sports, entertainment, journalism, music, education, labor, and literature. Most figures made their mark in the latter part of the twentieth century, and many continue to add to their iconic stature through new work. Family background, schooling, career trajectory, and further contributions to society are discussed. The few non-human Latino icons profiled include fictional and cartoon or comic characters and representative Latino food.

A Latino here is defined as a person in the United States with heritage going back to any of the Spanish-speaking cultures of the Western Hemisphere. The terms Latino and Latina include many aspects of cultural and linguistic identity. A Latino may be an immigrant or someone born in the United States; may be fair-skinned or dark-skinned; and may speak Spanish only, English only, or both.

Readers will find that a number of the icons profiled were influenced by or may have an important connection to other profiled icons. For example, Tito Puente and Celia Cruz performed together for many years. Actress Jennifer Lopez portrayed the singer Selena in a biographical film. Edward James Olmos portrayed teacher Jaime Escalante in the film *Stand and Deliver*. Cesar Chavez and Dolores Huerta together made the United Farm Workers union a reality. Furthermore, in telling the story of an icon, each essay relates many of the historical and social issues of the times. Thus, reading these essays gives students and other readers a good sense of recent Latino and Latin American history and progress.

The biographical profiles are presented in alphabetical order. Each essay concludes with suggested reading, including websites, and a list of relevant movies, recordings, or books. All profiles are accompanied by a sidebar that further illuminates the icon. A timeline of events provides a framework for the lives, contributions, and places of the icons in history.

Timeline

Icons profiled in volumes 1 and 2 are indicated with bold text.

7500 B.C.	Chile peppers are likely used in the diets of native Americans.
1941	Hundreds of thousands of Latino Americans serve in armed forces during World War II.
	Cartoonist Gus Arriola introduces the character **Gordo** in his nationally syndicated cartoon strip.
1943	The U.S. government forges an agreement with the Mexican government to supply temporary workers, known as *braceros*, for American agricultural work.
	The so-called Zoot Suit riots take place in southern California. Bands of sailors, marines, and other soldiers in southern California range the Hispanic neighborhoods, assaulting Latino youth who were wearing a teenage fashion called a zoot suit. The incident would later be made the subject of a play and film by the writer **Luis Valdez.**
1944	The Puerto Rican government begins Operation Bootstrap, a program to help meet U.S. labor demands caused by World War II. The program begins a wave of worker migration to the United States.
1951	In October, the "I Love Lucy" show begins an unprecedented run on national television. Starring Lucille Ball and Cuban bandleader **Desi Arnaz**, the situational comedy is the most-watched television show in four of its six seasons. Arnaz not only stars in the series but establishes one of the most successful entertainment production companies, Desi-Lu Productions.
1954	In the landmark case of *Hernandez v. Texas*, the U.S. Supreme Court recognizes Hispanic Americans as a separate class of people suffering profound discrimination, paving the way for

Hispanic Americans to use legal means to battle all types of discrimination throughout the United States. It is also the first U.S. Supreme Court case to be argued and briefed by Mexican-American attorneys.

1954–1958 Operation Wetback, a government effort to locate and deport undocumented workers, results in the deportation of 3.8 million persons. Few are allowed deportation hearings. Thousands of U.S. citizens of Mexican descent are also arrested and detained.

In the early 1950s, Latinos buy time on local television stations for Spanish-language programs in such cities as New York, San Antonio, Corpus Christi, and Harlingen, Texas. The first Spanish-language television station in the United States is San Antonio's KCOR-TV in San Antonio.

1956 Social worker and teacher **Fabiola Cabeza de Baca** publishes *Historic Cookery*. Formerly published in 1939 in pamphlet form by the New Mexico State University Extension Service, the work, which is the story of the cultural evolution of cuisine in the southwest, is as much about cultural icons such as chili as it is a cookbook. Many credit *Historic Cookery* as being the first critical influence in introducing Latino food preparation to a wider Anglo audience. In 1983, *Historic Cookery* appears in a hardcover edition from the Museum of New Mexico Press.

1959 Fidel Castro's Cuban Revolution overthrows the repressive regime of Fulgencio Batista. As Castro moves the country toward a communist state, Cuban immigration to the United States increases sharply. A number of entertainers are among those who choose to live in the United States, including famed salsa singer **Celia Cruz** and talk show personality **Cristina Saralegui**.

Young Latino rock and roll singer **Ritchie Valens**, along with Buddy Holly and the Big Bopper, is killed in a winter plane crash in Iowa during a music tour. Because of the circumstances of his death, Valens, considered to be the first Latino rock and roll star, would become an almost mythic figure.

1960s Young Mexican Americans throughout the United States become caught up in the struggle for civil rights and seek to create a new identity for themselves. These efforts become known as the Chicano Movement. The movement sparks a renaissance in the arts among Mexican Americans.

1961 In April, anti-Communist Cuban exiles, trained and armed by the United States, attempt a foray into Cuba that is doomed from the beginning. The so-called Bay of Pigs fiasco embitters thousands of exiled Cubans while strengthening Fidel Castro's position at home.

The movie *West Side Story*, loosely based on Shakespeare's play "Romeo and Juliet," opens to rave reviews. The story of street gangs—one made up of Puerto Rican youths and the other of European immigrants—at war in New York showcases the tensions of modern life in the big cities. Although the film was notable for the performance of **Rita Moreno**, a Puerto Rican actress playing a Puerto Rican character, the leading stars were Anglos playing Puerto Ricans. The film featured music by Leonard Bernstein and choreography by Jerome Robbins.

1964   The Civil Rights Act of 1964 establishes affirmative action programs. Title VII of the Act prohibits discrimination on the basis of gender, creed, race, or ethnic background, "to achieve equality of employment opportunities and remove barriers that have operated in the past." Discrimination is prohibited in advertising, recruitment, hiring, job classification, promotion, discharge, wages and salaries, and other terms and conditions of employment.

The *bracero* program ends. After a brief decline in immigration, numbers of workers from Mexico increase, either under the auspices of the Immigration and Nationality Act of 1952 and for family unification purposes, or as undocumented workers.

In October, the United States blocks a Soviet plan to establish missile bases in Cuba. Soviet Premier Khrushchev agrees to withdraw the missiles with the proviso that the United States declare publicly that it will not invade Cuba.

1965   The end of the *bracero* program in 1964 had forced many Mexicans to return to Mexico. To provide jobs for them, the Mexican and U.S. governments begin border industrialization programs, allowing foreign corporations to build and operate assembly plants on the border. These plants are known as *maquiladoras*.

A farmworkers union organized by **Cesar Chavez** engages in the successful Delano, California, grape strike and first national boycott. It becomes part of the American Federation of Labor and Congress of Industrial Organizations (AFL-CIO) in 1966 and later changes its name to the United Farmworkers of America.

For the first time, the United States enacts a law placing a cap on immigration from the Western Hemisphere, becoming effective in 1968.

Fidel Castro announces that Cubans can leave the island nation if they have relatives in the United States. He stipulates, however, that Cubans already in Florida have to come and get their relatives. Nautical crafts of all types systematically leave Miami, returning laden with anxious Cubans eager to rejoin their families on the mainland.

1966   A program is started to airlift Cubans to the United States. More than 250,000 Cubans are airlifted to the United States before the program is halted by Castro in 1973. About 10 percent of the island's population emigrates to the United States between 1966 and 1973.

1968   Chicano student organizations spring up throughout the nation, as do barrio groups such as the Brown Berets. Thousands of young Chicanos pledge their loyalty and time to such groups as the United Farmworkers Organizing Committee, which, under Cesar Chavez and **Dolores Huerta**, has been a great inspiration for Chicanos throughout the nation. An offshoot of both the farm worker and the student movements is the La Raza Unida party in Texas, an organization formed in 1968 to obtain control of community governments where Chicanos are the majority.

A Chicano Moratorium organizes in Los Angeles to protest the Vietnam War. More than 20,000 Chicanos and supporters draw attention to the disproportionately high number of Chicano casualties in the war. Conflicts erupt between police and demonstrators; journalist **Ruben Salazar** is killed by police.

In June, at the Oak Hill Golf Club in Rochester, New York, a short, stocky, jovial Mexican American accepts the trophy for one of the most prestigious tournaments in golf: **Lee Trevino** wins the United States Open.

1969   In August, an estimated 400,000 young people turn up for a three-day event to hear big-name bands play in an open-air venue near the town of Woodstock, New York. The name "Woodstock" would become emblematic of the anti-Vietnam war movement and the youthful, hippie drug culture of the 1960s. **Carlos Santana**, a young Latino guitarist destined for a long and celebrated career, makes his national debut.

1970s–   The rise in politically motivated violence in Central America
early 1980s spurs a massive increase in undocumented immigration to the United States.

1972   On December 31, New Year's Eve, famed baseball player **Roberto Clemente**, along with four other men, takes off from his native Puerto Rico on a mission to deliver supplies to hurricane-racked victims in Nicaragua. He, along with the others, is lost in the storm and never found. Clemente becomes the first Latino player ever inducted into baseball's Hall of Fame.

1973	The right of the Puerto Rican people to decide their own future as a nation is approved by the United Nations.
1974	Congress passes the Equal Educational Opportunity Act. One aspect of the law makes bilingual education available to Hispanic youth. According to the framers of the act, equal education means more than equal facilities and equal access to teachers; students who have trouble with the English language must be provided with access to programs to help them learn English.
1975	The Voting Rights Act Amendments extend the provisions of the original Voting Rights Act of 1965 and make permanent the national ban on literacy tests. Critical for Latinos, the amendments make bilingual ballots a requirement in certain areas.
1978	The United Nations recognizes Puerto Rico as a colony of the United States.
1979	Political upheaval and civil wars in Nicaragua, El Salvador, and Guatemala contribute to large immigrations of refugees to the United States.
1980s	The rates of immigration to the United States approach the levels of the early 1900s. During the first decade of the century the number of immigrants was approximately 8.8 million; during the 1980s, 6.3 million immigrants are granted permanent residence.
1980	Fidel Castro, reacting to negative worldwide press, announces that anyone who wants to leave Cuba should go to the Peruvian embassy. Ten thousand Cubans descend upon the embassy grounds and receive exit visas. Cuban Americans in Florida organize a fleet of boats to pick up the Cuban exiles at Mariel Harbor. The Mariel Boatlift continues from April through September. By the end of the year, more than 125,000 "Marielitos" arrive in the United States.
1982	A class of students at Garfield High School in a barrio of Los Angeles passes an Advanced Placement calculus examination under the tutelage of Bolivian-born teacher **Jaime Escalante**. So incredulous are testing officials that this group of students from a low socioeconomic background had passed the exam that the students are forced to take the exam again. They again pass. Their experience leads to a 1988 movie called *Stand and Deliver*. The part of Escalante is played by veteran actor and political activist **Edward James Olmos.**
1983	**Sandra Cisneros'** novel *The House on Mango Street* bursts on the international literary scene.

1986	After more than a decade of debate, Congress enacts the Immigration Reform and Control Act (IRCA), creating a process through which illegal aliens could become legal immigrants by giving legal status to applicants who had been in the United States illegally since January 1, 1982.
1989	Immigration to the United States from Central and South America increases from 44.3 percent in 1964 to 61.4 percent. Of the major countries of immigrant origin, Mexico accounts for 37.1 percent of total documented immigration to the United States; the next highest proportion of immigrants comes from El Salvador, 5.3 percent.
1991	Musician and actor **Ruben Blades**, a native of Panama, returns to Panama for a time to found the *Movemiento Papa Egoró*, which translates roughly into Mother Earth Party or Motherland Party in the language of the local Choco Indians. The party promises to fight drugs, hunger, and unemployment and expresses concern for ecology and the environment. Blades would return to Panama in 1994 to run for the presidency of Panama, an unprecedented move by a U.S. Latino; Blades garners 18 percent of the popular vote in 1994 but fails in his bid for the Panamanian presidency.
1994	The North American Free Trade Agreement (NAFTA) takes effect, eliminating tariffs between trading partners Canada, Mexico, and the United States within fifteen years from the date.
	In November, Californians pass Proposition 187 with 59 percent of the vote. The initiative bans undocumented immigrants from receiving public education and public benefits such as welfare and subsidized health care, except in emergency circumstances; makes it a felony to manufacture, distribute, sell, or use false citizenship or residence documents; and requires teachers, physicians, and other city, county, and state officials to report suspected and apparent illegal aliens to the California attorney general and the Immigration and Naturalization Service (INS). California Federal District Court Judge William Matthew Byrne, Jr., temporarily blocks the enforcement of Proposition 187, stating that it raises serious constitutional questions. Judge Byrne exempts the provisions that increase penalties for manufacturing or using false immigration documents.
1995	A nationwide boycott of ABC-TV by Hispanic Americans is held in Los Angeles, New York, Chicago, Houston, San Francisco, and Fresno, in protest of the network's failure to provide Latino-themed programming in its 1994 line-up.

Selena, age 23, a young Tejana music star murdered by her fan club president and boutique manager, is laid to rest on April 3. Six hundred people attend her private funeral. Before the funeral, thousands view her casket at the Bayfront Plaza Convention Center in Corpus Christi. In Los Angeles, four thousand people gather at the Sports Arena Memorial to honor the slain singer. Mourners also gather in San Antonio. The gravesite services were broadcast live by San Antonio and Corpus Christi radio stations. Her death by gunshot at the hands of her boutique manager makes her a Latino heroine.

1996   Proposition 209, introduced as a ballot initiative, is passed by California voters. The initiative bars preferential treatment on the basis of race or gender, virtually eliminating affirmative action in state hiring, public contracts, and education. Although challenged in court, the U.S. Supreme Court refused to hear the appeal, and Proposition 209 eventually takes effect in California.

Placido Domingo is named artistic director of the Washington Opera.

1997   Bandleader and musician **Tito Puente,** called "King of the Mambo" or usually "El Rey," receives a National Medal of Arts from President Bill Clinton. At the ceremony the President says, "Just hearing Tito Puente's name makes you want to get up and dance. With his finger on the pulse of the Latin American musical tradition and his hands on the timbales, he has probably gotten more people out of their seats and onto the dance floor than any other living artist."

1998   California voters pass Proposition 227, which bans bilingual classroom education and English as a second language programs, replacing them with a one-year intensive English immersion program.

Four years after Proposition 187, the growing Latino electorate helps make Lieutenant Governor Cruz M. Bustamante the first Hispanic statewide official in California in more than a century.

In *The Mark of Zorro*, Antonio Banderas becomes the first Latino actor to star in a major film based on the famed Latino character.

2001   Antonio Villaraigosa, former speaker of the California State Assembly, wins a commanding first-place primary finish in the race to succeed Republican Richard J. Riordan as mayor of the country's second largest city, Los Angeles.

2003   Hispanics are pronounced the nation's largest minority group—surpassing African Americans—after new U.S. Census figures are released that show the U.S. Hispanic population at 37.1 million as of July 2001.

2006   Thousands of people join rallies in cities across the country to protest proposed immigration reform. The protests, organized by labor, civil rights, community, and religious interests, culminate on April 10 in a "National Day of Action."

2007   Univision, the most-watched Spanish language broadcast television network in the country, is sold for a reported $13.7 billion.

In 2007, film and recording star **Jennifer Lopez**, known popularly as J-Lo, stars in a film called *El Cantante* about salsa legend Hector Lavoe.

2008   Cartoon series such as **"Baldo"** and **"La Cucaracha"** continue to inform and entertain American audiences.

Latino population in the United States surpasses 40 million individuals.

Desi Arnaz

In the grainy black-and-white era of early television, a Latino character gained a prominent place in the hearts of the viewing public for the first time. Ricky Ricardo, played by Desi Arnaz, was a bandleader and the husband of the dizzy but lovable Lucy, played by Lucille Ball in the hit series *I Love Lucy*. Ricky Ricardo's accent was new to many Americans, but his charm was infectious. As Desi Arnaz's stature and popularity soared over the years, fans began to learn more about the life, the cultural heritage, and the remarkable achievements and career, both on-screen and off, of the man who played Ricky.

CHILD OF PRIVILEGE

Desi Arnaz was born in Santiago de Cuba, Cuba, on March 2, 1917, the son of Desiderio Arnaz and Dolores de Acha. This boy's family was no ordinary family. His paternal great-grandfather had served as the mayor of Santiago de Cuba, appointed by the queen of Spain. His paternal grandfather, Don Desiderio, was a Cuban doctor who had aided the forces of Teddy Roosevelt's Rough Riders when they charged up San Juan Hill during the Spanish-American War. His maternal grandfather was Alberto de Acha, one of the founders of the Bacardi rum company.

In 1923, when the boy was six years old, his father won election as mayor of Santiago de Cuba, following in the footsteps of the boy's great-grandfather. One of Desi's uncles was the chief of police at the time.

An only child, Desi luxuriated in the trappings of wealth at a mansion in Santiago de Cuba, at three farms run by his father, and at a beach house at Cayo. While attending Colegio de Dolores, a Jesuit school, Desi helped on the farms, rode horses, and learned to fish. By the time he was ten years old, Desi owned his own Tennessee walking horse and, long before he was of legal age to drive, he had been given not only a car but also a speedboat. "The world was my oyster," he wrote later. "What I wanted I only needed to ask for. Ambition, incentive, opportunity, self-reliance, and appreciation of what I had meant little to me. I had a fast-swelling case of what, in a language I couldn't speak at all then, is called a fat head."[1]

In 1932, when Desi was fifteen, his father took another step up the political ladder. Elected to the Cuban congress to represent Oriente province, Desiderio Arnaz traveled to Havana in January 1933 to begin his term. He planned to move the family at a later time to Havana, where his son would complete his final year of high school and then, if plans worked out, attend the University of Notre Dame in the United States in preparation for a career in law and politics.

CUBAN REVOLT

Cuba had slowly been caught up in a divisive, potentially catastrophic, political whirlwind of change. As Desiderio Arnaz began his service in the

Cuban congress, the corrupt political party run by General Gerardo Machado, under pressure from students, writers, journalists, and left-wing supporters, had responded with a series of orders to put down dissent and free speech. There was a growing sense that the government was losing control of the country. A puppet of the United States government and business interests, the Machado regime increasingly resorted to a horrifying rampage of violence against its opponents. The bodies of government opponents appeared on the Cuban streets; others simply disappeared.

On September 4, 1933, a year after Desiderio Arnaz joined the Cuban congress, Fulgencio Batista y Zaldívar and military supporters, who saw the Machado regime as weak and unable to withstand growing political opposition, overthrew the government in an uprising that became known as the Revolt of the Sergeants. The military coup marked the beginning of a long period in Cuba in which the army was the organized force that ran the government. Batista himself emerged from the overthrow as the self-appointed head of the armed forces and actual leader of the new Cuban government.

After Machado fled to Miami, the various members of his government, including Desiderio Arnaz, were arrested and jailed. Mobs of rioting looters soon began to sack the homes of the imprisoned officials. Fortuitously, Dolores Arnaz escaped the carnage with her son and went into hiding with relatives in Havana. Through the next weeks of turmoil and chaos, however, their main home was destroyed along with their farms and beach house, and their other possessions were carried off or ruined—even the animals were massacred. Except for a few hundred dollars that Dolores Arnaz carried from the home, the family lost everything.

Batista appointed figurehead supporters as official presidents of Cuba, but the power rested entirely in his hands in the form of the armed forces. Although the United States had sent an ambassador to Cuba in 1933 to mediate differences between the political parties, Batista also won his support to run the country. The United States, seeing Batista's rule as a stabilizing force, formally recognized the Cuban government under his rule in early 1934.

FLEEING TO THE UNITED STATES

The Arnaz family lost everything but their lives in the government overthrow. After six months in prison, Desiderio was released but advised to leave the country. He acted swiftly to save himself and his family from further humiliation and ruin. After borrowing a small amount of money from his relatives, he left for the United States in April 1934. He would start his life over again with little money and no position. Three months later, Desi's mother sent the boy ahead to meet up with his father. She planned to join them when her husband had found his financial footing in the new country.

In the fall of 1934, Desi enrolled in Saint Patrick's High School in Miami and began to learn the English language. Although he had studied English in Cuba, he had never tried to use it outside the classroom. Among his new friends at the school was Al Capone, Jr., whose infamous crime boss father was serving time in Alcatraz.

Desiderio attempted to start a few small businesses, including importing bananas. To save money, he and his son moved from a boarding house and lived in the banana warehouse for a time. They kept baseball bats by their beds to fend off rats. For a family that had not so long ago enjoyed the benefits of wealth, this was an extraordinary and improbable change of fortunes.

With some of the money he earned cleaning canary cages, Desi went to a pawn shop and bought a guitar and began to experiment with it. Music, he realized, was a deep part of his make-up, from the rhythms and beats of the Cuban music he had heard as a small boy to the other sounds he was hearing while growing up in Miami.

When his mother was able to join the family in Miami, life for the boy seemed more complete. In December 1936, Desi left behind the days of the canary cages—invited to sing and play the guitar with a rumba band in Miami called the Siboney Septet, he eagerly accepted.

WITH THE RUMBA KING

A group that played between sets of major bands at Miami's elegant Roney Plaza Hotel, the Siboney Septet featured the rumba. Although only in his senior year of high school, Arnaz was able to maintain a routine of seven nights a week and a Sunday afternoon tea dance. His natural affinity for the guitar and the hours he privately worked on his style over the years yielded immediate dividends. He not only fit in with the group but made it better.

It was during one of his performances at the Roney Plaza that Arnaz caught the eye of a musical legend—Xavier Cugat. Cugat would forever change the life of the young Cuban musician and singer.

Cugat was a pioneer of Latin American dance music. During a career that would span eight decades, he helped popularize the tango, the mambo, and, especially, the rumba. Born in Genoa, Spain, Cugat moved with his family to Cuba in 1905. Trained as a classical violinist, he played with the Orchestra of the Teatro Nacional in Havana before he was a teenager. When his family immigrated to the United States, he joined a popular dance band and then, in 1920, formed his own group, calling it The Latin American Band.

Cugat asked Arnaz to audition for his orchestra. When the young singer belted out his rendition of "Para Vigo Me Voy" ("Say Si Si"), Cugat not only hired him but made Arnaz his featured vocalist. After finishing his high school studies, Arnaz joined the Cugat orchestra. It was the beginning of what would be a unique and remarkable professional career in entertainment.

At first, Arnaz drew a salary of twenty-five dollars a week. When it became clear that the young talent was making an immediate favorable impression on the audiences, Cugat raised his salary to thirty-five dollars.

After six months traveling from venue to venue on a grueling schedule, the young performer decided that this was not the kind of musician's life he saw in his future. He wanted to settle down in one place with his own band, and he wanted to return to Miami. Besides, he said, he figured that six months learning was all he needed.

Arnaz did learn much from Cugat about showmanship, style, and elegance, as well as how to incorporate the various Latin dances into the productions while instructing and involving the audience in the dance numbers. Later, Arnaz wrote, "During my internship with Cugie I learned not only about how the music should be played, how it should be presented, what the American people liked to dance to, but also how to handle the band, the rehearsals, the salaries, and all the angles of the band business."[2]

Arnaz made Cugat a proposal. If Arnaz returned to Miami and put together his own set of musicians, he still wanted to be able to capitalize on the Cugat name. If Cugat would let him call the band "Desi Arnaz and his Xavier Cugat Orchestra direct from the Starlight Room of the Waldorf-Astoria in New York City," he would pay a royalty for the use of the name. Cugat asked how much. "The same as you paid me when I started, twenty-five dollars a week," Arnaz suggested. "And like you told me then, if we do good, we'll renegotiate." Cugat agreed.[3]

BANDLEADER

After securing a location for a small band at the Park Central Restaurant in Miami Beach, Arnaz persuaded Cugat to arrange for five musicians to travel from New York. When Arnaz and the band members got together for the first time, he realized he had a rather unique assortment. For a Cuban band, he had a Jewish man at piano, another Jewish man on saxophone, an Italian on violin, another Italian on bass, and a Spaniard on drums who had little more in his musical repertoire than bullfight marches. None of them knew many Latin pieces.

Instead of throwing up his arms in total frustration at a seemingly lost cause, Arnaz worked quickly. On December 30, 1937, he gave the downbeat to his first band at the Park Central.

Most everyone agreed the performance was a disaster. The owner of the club quipped sarcastically that he would have been better off hiring a Salvation Army Band. Here was a so-called Latin band without a trumpet, bongos, maracas, or conga drum.

In desperation, Arnaz remembered the carnivals he had seen in Santiago, Cuba, with thousands of people in the streets, and the singing and dancing and the rhythms filling the air, the beat of conga drums, along with other improvised instruments, even frying pans. The simple beat, the glorious participation of masses of people—all of it gave Arnaz an inspiration. He would turn this infant nothing of a band into a conga group.

Conga reputedly was brought from Africa by slaves to Cuba and the sugar plantations of the West Indies. By 1936 the music and the dance, in which participants would line up and place their hands on the hips of the individual in front and move in rhythm and step, had gained much popularity in France. Ironically, during the Machado dictatorship in Cuba, of which Arnaz's father was a supporter, peasants were forbidden to dance the conga because rival groups would often dance with such fervor that, in their excitement, they created outbreaks of street fighting.

But Arnaz had seen the conga many times as a child and remembered its technical musical components; he taught this to his band. Within a few weeks, the dance had become so popular that the club filled night after night. Ecstatic about the turn of events, the owners decided to change the name of the establishment. It now became La Conga Café.

The establishment began to draw big names in show business, from Eddie Cantor to Sonja Henie, the Olympic ice-skating champion whom Arnaz taught to conga on skates at a local ice arena. The comedian Joe E. Lewis, who was playing at a club near La Conga Café, became a regular visitor. One evening, an inspired Arnaz led his usual boisterous conga line of cast and audience out of La Conga Café, down the street, and, much to the comedian's delight, into Joe E. Lewis' own club.

PLAYING BROADWAY

Although Miami was a significant stepping-stone in the career of Arnaz, the location itself was seasonal. Only in the winter months did the city and the club thrive. Soon, Arnaz was in New York, attempting to capitalize on his building reputation and success. Arnaz's move to New York coincided with the opening of a new club at Broadway and 51st Street in the Times Square area. It was also called La Conga. The club, in its own garish way, was made to look like a tropical paradise, replete with fake palm trees, bluish-green lighting, and other similar touches. Arnaz and the new club could not have made a better fit.

On August 5, 1939, columnist Malcolm Johnson reviewed Arnaz's act for a New York paper:

> Desi Arnaz is a young man with a drum. He is a new type of Pied Piper who leads enthusiastic, uninhibited followers in the sinuous, serpentine conga dance every night at La Conga, the night club dedicated to torrid Cuban music

and entertainment. Two or three times each night, Arnaz steps down from the bandstand, his tall, goat-skin drum slung across his shoulders, and begins beating out the wild, savage rhythm which lures dancers on to the floor and behind him in the conga line. Arnaz, a youthful, handsome Cuban (he is barely 22 years old), has headed his rumba band at La Conga for two months now and is an established success.[4]

At one of his performances, two of the great names in Broadway show business were in the audience—Richard Rogers and Larry Hart, the songwriting team that for over a decade had been enormously successful, especially after the production of *A Connecticut Yankee* in 1927. Always on the lookout for new talent, the duo had heard about the Cuban sensation at La Conga and came to see for the show for themselves. They met Arnaz after the show that night and pledged to introduce him to George Abbott, one of the premier directors of the Broadway stage.

Abbott came to La Conga the next evening. This was the beginning of a collaboration that would launch Arnaz into a new field. Two days later, Arnaz was at a Broadway theater reading lines for Abbott and his production and writing team; the piece was a college-musical romp called *Too Many Girls*. So unfamiliar was Arnaz with theater that when the team began speaking to him about the script the singer did not even know what the word script meant.

His first attempt was miserable; too much waving of hands and contrived emoting. Besides, most of the individuals on the set had no idea of the identity of this young Cuban. When someone called him "Dizzy," Desi, with some embarrassment, had to correct him.

Despite the awkward beginning, Abbott hired Arnaz for the part, principally because he fit the character in the play so well—a young Latino football player who was supposed to be the best prospect ever to come out of Latin America but who was clueless about the United States and somewhat bumbling with its language.

The play follows the fortunes of a rich American heiress who has just returned to the United States from a series of scandalous adventures abroad. When Connie Casey decides to return to college at her father's alma mater, Pottawatomie College in New Mexico, her father hires four football players to be her guardians. Through romance and misadventure, the play ends as Connie finds that one of the players with whom she has fallen love is actually in the employ of her father. Will love prevail over deceit?

The songs included "I Didn't Know What Time It Was," "Love Never Went to College," "Shake the Maracas," and "Give it Back to the Indians." Arnaz sang the title song, "Too Many Girls." He would later say that it was often suggested to him that the message in the song was the story of his life.

George Abbott was director and librettist, as he was to a number of other Rodgers and Hart hits over the years. Like the other collaborations, *Too*

Many Girls was fast-paced and witty. It was the perfect vehicle for Arnaz who had a natural comic sense.

The musical opened in New Haven, Connecticut, in late September 1939, moved on to Boston, and then to Broadway at the Imperial Theatre. It opened on October 18, and ran for 249 performances. The cast included Marcy Westcott, a new comic named Eddie Bracken, dancer Hal LeRoy, and a newcomer named Van Johnson. It played on Broadway throughout the 1939–1940 season, which is when the producers of the play became acquainted with La Conga. So charmed were the producers with Arnaz's conga line that they changed the finale of the play to end with the entire cast joining in their own conga line. Arnaz shuttled between performances at the club and the theater night after night at a frantic pace to keep the two jobs.

Matinee days, Wednesday and Saturday, were especially hectic. Arnaz would arrive at the theater at 2:00 P.M. for the play, have dinner after the performance, take a cab to La Conga for the early show at 7:30 P.M., then go back to the theater for the evening performance, and, finally, run back to La Conga for a midnight show and then another show at 2:30 A.M.

In 1939, his breakthrough year in show business, Desi's parents divorced. The long periods of separation after the revolution in Cuba had deeply affected their relationship. Arnaz's father remarried; his mother did not. For a time, from the early part of 1940, his mother stayed with Arnaz at his home at 60 Central Park West, the same apartment complex in which Broadway star Ethel Merman lived at the time.

In just a few years, Desi had come from the aristocratic heights of the Cuban social and political elite, to a life of a penniless refugee living with his father in a warehouse fending off rats with a baseball bat, to a penthouse next to Central Park. And he was not yet twenty-five years old.

Arnaz was also quickly gaining a well-earned reputation as a fast-moving ladies' man. Flirtatious, handsome, and engaging, he found time to move from one admirer to another with extraordinary aplomb. The well-known columnist Walter Winchell once joked that the conga line in his New York club could have been called the "Desi chain" because of all the female hearts the Cuban entertainer had broken.

HOLLYWOOD AND LUCILLE BALL

The success of *Too Many Girls* on Broadway stirred the interest of RKO Films. Arnaz, along with several of the other performers, was asked to play his stage role on screen. The leads would be well-known actors already under contract by RKO, Richard Carlson and Lucille Ball.

Lucille Ball was born on August 6, 1911, in the small town of Celeron, New York. Her father, Henry Ball, was a telephone lineman for the Bell

Company. Because her father's job required frequent transfers, she and her mother, Désirée, were shuttled to Anaconda, Montana, and then to Wyandotte, Michigan. In 1915, while her mother was pregnant with their second child, Frederick, Henry Ball contracted typhoid fever and died.

After the death of her father, Lucille, Frederick, and Désirée lived with Désirée's parents. Lucille's grandfather, Fred Hunt, was an aficionado of the theatre and often took the family to local vaudeville shows. "He loved the three-a-day vaudeville that played in Jamestown," Lucille remembered. "In the summer, we went to the silent flickers that were shown outdoors at Celoron Park. I loved the Pearl White serials and couldn't wait until the following week for the next episode. Wow! I knew I had to be a part of it."[5]

When the young girl began to show an increasingly special interest in acting, her grandfather encouraged her to take part in local and school plays. At the age of fifteen, Lucille dropped out of school and enrolled in the John Murray Anderson/Robert Milton School of the Theater in New York City.

Naturally shy and intimidated by her surroundings among aspiring actors and actresses in New York, Lucillee returned to Celeron for a time until she felt ready to again take on New York City. Despite a bout of potentially crippling rheumatoid arthritis, the naturally glamorous-looking teenager with long, chestnut-colored hair took a job as a model with dress designer Hattie Carnegie. The first hint of fame came with her selection by the company of Liggett and Myers to promote cigarettes. She became "The Chesterfield Girl."

After a chance encounter with a local theatrical agent, Ball made the most of an audition to play one of the "Goldwyn Girls" in a new film starring Eddie Cantor. It was called *Roman Scandals* (1933) and was produced by Samuel Goldwyn. Her career as an actress in so-called B movies was under way. After a number of bit parts, she progressed to lead roles in minor films. Through the late 1930s, Ball played in both drama and comedy in roles as a dancer, college student, even a flower clerk. Her hair now dyed blond, she moved up to classier films such as *Stage Door*, in which she played in the same cast with Katherine Hepburn and Ginger Rogers.

For a time, Buster Keaton, the renowned silent comedian, worked with Ball on stunts that she showed off in films like *DuBarry Was a Lady* opposite Red Skelton. Nevertheless, she appeared in so many minor films that she became known by some as "Queen of the B's."

And now, on the Hollywood set for *Too Many Girls*, Ball, playing the lead role, met the young Cuban, Arnaz. The repartee and attraction between the two was electric. "I saw this girl come in," he wrote. "She was dressed in a pair of tight-fitting beige slacks and a yellow sweater, with beautiful blond hair and big blue eyes." Arnaz recalled that, after exchanging a few words, he used one of his most successful lines to pick up women: "Do you know how to rumba, Lucille?"[6]

Ball later recalled her first impression of the Latin entertainer and lover of whom she had already heard much. "Desi was in greasy makeup and old clothes," she said, "and I thought he wasn't so hot." It did not take long for that first impression to be changed forever. Eddie Bracken said later, "You could tell the sparks were flying with Lucy. It happened so fast it seemed it wouldn't last. Everybody on the set made bets about how long it would last." But Ball's friend, actress Maureen O'Hara recalled, "She talked about Desi all the time. I said, 'Go ahead and marry him if you love him.'"[7]

It only took six months. Lucy said later, "We were in love almost immediately. We spent a great deal of time talking about our pasts, what we'd done with our lives, and our goals for the future. Some of it was very painful; neither of us were angels, but it had to be faced before we became involved."[8]

They married on November 30, 1940, in Greenwich, Connecticut, while Desi was on a four-week engagement at the Roxy Theatre in New York.

The couple settled down on a five-acre ranch in the Chatsworth area of the San Fernando Valley in California, which they fondly named the Desilu Ranch. In 1941, Arnaz continued his acting career, appearing in a film called *Four Jacks and a Jill* along with Ray Bolger and Eddie Foy, Jr. Even from the perspective of his very limited theatrical experience, Arnaz knew from the beginning that the musical comedy seemed aimless, its humor lost in a chaotic mess of a script and terrible direction.

In 1941, Arnaz appeared in *Father Takes a Wife* opposite Adolphe Menjou and Gloria Swanson. One of the songs in the film was "Perfidia," a popular old Mexican song about love and betrayal written by Mexican composer/arranger Alberto Domínguez. Charles Koerner, the president of RKO pictures, had heard Arnaz perform the song at a benefit in San Francisco accompanied only by a guitar, and he wanted it included in the film. During the filming of the movie, however, the producer decided that Arnaz should sing it in the form of an operatic aria with a large orchestra.

Because Arnaz's singing abilities were not equal to that kind of production, the filmmakers dubbed his voice with that of an Italian tenor backed by a symphony orchestra. For months afterward, Arnaz recalled, he received letters from Cuba, Latin America, and even Spain asking why he ruined the beautiful old song with that rendition. Like *Four Jacks and a Jill*, *Father Takes a Wife* was also a less than mediocre product that did not fare well at the box office.

Also in 1941, Arnaz joined movie stars like Clark Gable and Bing Crosby to kick off President Franklin Roosevelt's Good Neighbor Policy in Mexico. Because of Arnaz's Latino background, many in the group relied heavily on Arnaz to present the key points of the policy to Mexican officials. The phrase "good neighbor," used by the Roosevelt in his first inaugural address, was meant to convey the principle that the United States would no longer intervene in Latin America to protect private American property interests. Secretary of State Cornell Hull's reciprocal trade program, which resulted in several agreements with Latin American republics, did lower some trade barriers and was popular in many Central and South American nations. For Arnaz, however, trying to explain the sudden interest in the United States to pursue such a collegial relationship with a country that it consistently ignored was not easy. Most of the Mexican officials with whom he spoke were skeptical. Arnaz said later that the United States had consistently shown such disregard for Latin American countries that ambassadors and other officials assigned to those countries could not even speak their language.

After the bombing of Pearl Harbor in December 1941, Arnaz received a commission as a lieutenant in the Cuban army. He resigned the Cuban commission and instead toured with Hollywood stars in 1942 as part of the Army and Navy Relief operation.

Ironically, before the tour, Arnaz appeared in his last RKO picture *The Navy Comes Through* opposite Pat O'Brien, George Murphy, Jane Wyatt, and Jackie Cooper. Arnaz played a Cuban sailor aboard a U.S. Merchant Marine freighter that was used to attack both Nazi U-boats and fighter planes. Both the picture and Arnaz received critical praise for the film.

In 1942, Louis B. Mayer, the feisty, cigar-chomping czar of Metro-Goldwyn Mayer, offered to put Arnaz under contract. Arnaz readily accepted. Before appearing in any MGM production, Arnaz joined other performers in a tour of the Caribbean with the United Service Organizations (USO). During a stop in Guantanamo Bay, Cuba, Arnaz persuaded a pilot to fly him for a short visit to Santiago to visit his relatives. On the return flight, they encountered severe weather. If it had not been for Arnaz's knowledge of the topography, which enabled the pilot to weave through the storm at a low altitude, the men would have likely perished.

Arnaz made a brief appearance in MGM's 1943 war film *Bataan*. The story of a handful of men who defended a bridge to allow General Douglas MacArthur's escape from the Philippines, the film featured Robert Taylor, George Murphy, and other talented actors. Playing a soldier who dies of malaria, Arnaz recited the *Mea Culpa*, part of the Catholic Mass where sinners acknowledge their failings before God. Arnaz, at his own suggestion, spoke the words in Latin, as he had been taught when he was a young boy in a Jesuit school. The part won him recognition as one of *Photoplay* magazine's "Best Performances of the Month," the first time he had garnered any such award for his professional acting.

In May 1943, Arnaz received a draft notice and was set to join the United States Air Force bombardier school when he tore cartilage in his knee playing in a baseball game. Unable to join the Air Force because of his leg, he was assigned to the United States Army Medical Corps, and he entertained hospitalized servicemen until his discharge in November 1945.

Returning home to California, Arnaz assembled a rumba band and opened at Ciro's nightclub in Hollywood in January 1946. It was there that he introduced the conga song "Babalu," a song that would become something of a trademark.

In 1946, Arnaz appeared in Universal's *Cuban Pete*, directed by Jean Yarbrough. The film starred Desi, who basically played himself. It also showcased many numbers of Cuban music and dance, including the song "Cuban Pete." He was Cuban Pete; he was king of the rumba beat; he played maracas; and the sound was "chick chickky boom."[9]

By this time in their marriage, Arnaz's womanizing had become frequent and public when he was away from Lucille. As she continued her own career in the early 1940's, appearing in several films for MGM, Ball felt that the relationship with Arnaz had become so strained and stormy that she filed for divorce. After a single appearance in court, only a few days after filing, she withdrew from the divorce proceedings. Despite the constant tensions, jealousies, and misunderstandings, the two remained very much emotionally attached.

Yet, even when both were in Hollywood at the same time, it often seemed as if they were thousands of miles apart. For a time, Desi was musical director for the band accompanying Bob Hope's radio show at the same time that he had recording sessions and club dates. Lucy spent most of her time at the MGM studios. She worked mostly during the day and he at night.

"Most of the time," she said, "we would meet at the top of Coldwater Canyon about five-thirty in the morning as I was driving to the studio and Desi was returning to the ranch from one of his nightclub engagements. The same thing would happen in reverse about seven o'clock at night. That's married life?" Desi said that often, if they were in a hurry, they just waved as their cars passed each other. "If we had a few moments to spare, we'd park and sit in Lucy's car, talking and stealing a few kisses before we went on our separate ways again."[10]

In the early years of their marriage, she suffered, on more than one occasion, a miscarriage. Both partners felt that a baby would strengthen their relationship and both suffered much anxiety on these occasions. It would not be until July 17, 1951, that she would give birth to a girl they named Lucie Desiree Arnaz. The child bore a striking resemblance to her father.

Ball later said that having the baby at the age of forty and after ten years of marriage transformed their lives together. Little Lucie, she said, was their lucky charm.

Through all the arguments and extreme tension, they stayed married. Arnaz later wrote, "I'm convinced that the reason we survived this constant arguing, fighting, and accusations for so many years was because we had something extra-special going for us."[11]

I LOVE LUCY BEGINS

Beginning in 1948, Lucille Ball starred in a radio series for CBS called *My Favorite Husband*, a situation comedy about a scatterbrained housewife and her banker husband. Its modest success prompted executives to approach Ball two years later about converting the radio show to a new medium—television.

This was the beginning of a new age. Suddenly, all across America, television sets began to appear in the windows of department stores or in emerging businesses ready to sell the new-fangled technological wonders. In 1948 only one American in ten had ever seen a television set, but it was clear to everyone that television's time had come. So quickly did the phenomenon catch on that radio comedian Fred Allen joked that within two years television "threatened to change Americans into creatures with eyeballs as big as cantaloupes and no brain at all."[12]

Television programming was initially controlled by a small number of network stations that were located in major cities and were affiliated with existing radio stations. Three of these networks—the National Broadcasting Company (NBC, the broadcasting arm of RCA), CBS (originally the Columbia Broadcasting System), and the American Broadcasting Company (ABC)—dominated television broadcasting for more than 30 years. In the late 1940s, radio and movie producers, stars, and executives jockeyed to adapt their companies and careers to the emerging medium. New stars, such as Milton Berle, Arthur Godfrey, Sid Caesar, and Red Skelton, became familiar faces to the burgeoning number of Americans who had acquired television sets.

When CBS executives began to discuss with Ball the possibility of converting *My Favorite Husband* to television, the actress responded with much interest. After negotiations were under way, she agreed to do the series under one condition, and it was a condition that she insisted was not negotiable. The husband in the series, she said, would be her own real-life husband, Arnaz.

A number of the CBS brass seemed flabbergasted at the prospect. Arnaz wrote, "The network, the agencies, everybody involved said nobody was going to believe that a Latin bandleader with a Cuban Pete conga-drum Babalu image could ever be married to a typical redheaded girl (by now she was a redhead)."[13]

After much quibbling and numerous questions by executives about how the public would respond to what amounted to a mixed marriage, Ball responded quite simply: The public would accept the two as a married couple, she pointed out, because they were a married couple.

To prove their compatibility as a performance team, the two briefly went on the road to a number of cities across the United States with a vaudeville routine that was mildly successful.

On the issue of Arnaz joining Ball on the television comedy, all the arguments mounted by senior Hollywood executives could not persuade her to change her mind. In addition to her confidence that the pairing would work on the television screen, Ball had another motive for her demand. Working together, she reasoned, would bring the two closer together. Despite the misgivings of CBS management about the casting, plans for the *I Love Lucy* show progressed. After the new team for the show produced a pilot, Philip Morris agreed to be its sponsor.

Before these discussions with CBS with regard to the television show, Arnaz and Ball had formed a company they called Desilu Productions to coordinate all of their activities in music, radio, motion pictures, personal appearances, and recordings. Now, Desilu Productions negotiated details for the proposed new television show—and Arnaz proved to be a tough negotiator.

His exterior was carefree and loose; on the inside was a shrewd business sense. Madelyn Pugh Davis, who along with Bob Carroll made up Lucy's longest-running comedy-writing team, said, "Desi was a charmer. We used to call him the Cuban Arm because he'd put his arm around you and say, 'Listen, amigo...' And you were done for."[14]

As Philip Morris and CBS worked with Arnaz over the arrangement, Arnaz finally agreed that he and Ball would work for a lower salary than originally discussed but that Desilu Productions would have sole ownership. In 1951, almost all television shows were broadcast live and were not preserved on film, and therefore were relatively worthless beyond their original performances. When Arnaz negotiated for the rights, CBS executives figured they were not giving up very much. They were very wrong.

Arnaz decided to shoot the new series on 35-mm film rather than merely air the episodes live on television. His decision to film the series was mostly based on the couple's desire to remain in California and not to move to New York, where all the television shows were being produced. However, the decision to film also made it possible to have a high-quality print of each episode available for endless rebroadcasts. Although Arnaz at the time was not fully aware of the far-reaching implications of the decisions he made at the beginning of the series, his instincts proved to be prescient. Rights to re-run episodes from the series, sold to independent stations and translated into many languages for foreign distribution, set the pattern for the future of television. It also would make the Arnaz family wealthy.

In addition to his decision to film the episodes, Arnaz also suggested that the performances be filmed live in front of a studio audience. Arnaz hated laugh tracks and he, along with studio executives, had seen during the vaudeville tour how Ball's sense of comedy seemed to thrive before audiences. Filming a show before a live audience had never before been attempted on television—but it all seemed to make sense, as did Arnaz's suggestion that three cameras be used simultaneously to allow for editing of the finished product.

Many programs in the infant industry of television had suffered because of inadvertent mistakes by actors, producers, and film equipment. Filming would guarantee a better product; filming before an audience would preserve comedic spontaneity.

Arnaz and Ball began the show in a converted motion picture sound stage and added bleachers that seated approximately 300 people. The site included four sets: bedroom, living room, kitchen, and nightclub. After two weeks of work, they were ready to start what Ball called a "three-act play before an audience, filming it like it was a movie, recording it like radio, and releasing it on television."[15]

The series went forward with the same team that had produced the *My Favorite Husband* radio series. Producer Jess Oppenheimer and his writers, Bob Carroll and Madelyn Pugh, had worked together for four years. In addition, Arnaz persuaded Oscar-winning cinematographer Karl Freund, who had first developed the moving camera and other production innovations in Hollywood, to leave Washington, D.C., and return to California to work on the series.

Arnaz and Ball were risking two careers with all of their demands about casting and production methods. Nevertheless, in October 1951, it all came together on national television.

The situational premise of *I Love Lucy* was relatively simple, not especially different from earlier comedies. Lucy, an eccentric, wacky wife, gets gnarled in outlandish situations, leaving her husband Ricky often bewildered and dismayed. They were the Ricardos. Lucy, whose maiden name was MacGillicudy, was of Scottish ancestry and sported the reddest hair on the planet. Ricky, a Cuban bandleader, led the band at the Tropicana Club in Manhattan. The apartment building in which the Ricardos resided, located in a middle-class neighborhood on the East Side, was also the building that housed their landlords and friends, the Mertzes, Fred and Ethel. The address sometimes mentioned in the show placed its location in the East River. Naïve but loving, Lucy is ambitious, yearning to be more than a housewife, fascinated by the professional life of her husband and his world of entertainment. She wants to be a part of it, wants a show business life of her own, and is obsessed with finding ways to show off her imagined talent. After all, Fred and Ethel were both former vaudevillians and they did not seem to have any show business acumen. Lucy's resolve to prove herself as a performer even though she cannot play an instrument or carry a tune leads her, often with the reluctant, sometimes unwitting, conspiratorial assistance of Ethel, into a series of convoluted and embarrasing schemes. The exasperated Latino Ricky endures the consequences, his broken English often degenerating into unrecognizable Spanish exhortations.

I Love Lucy was the perfect vehicle for the evolving talents of Lucille Ball. She soon established herself as the medium's premier physical comedian and brought a sympathetic poignancy to even her most outlandish schemes. As the bored housewife, she hoped for more in life, a universal yearning that began to touch an audience that grew astonishingly large in a very short time.

I Love Lucy – First Season, Episode Thirty

"Lucy Does a Television Commercial"

When Ricky is given the opportunity to host a television show, he needs to find a young woman to do a commercial spot for one of their sponsors. Lucy wants the role, but Ricky refuses to try her out for the part. Nevertheless, when Ricky returns home after band rehearsal, Fred stands by the television set that is covered by a sheet and asks Ricky to watch the program. When the sheet is uncovered, Lucy's head is inside the television box. As she tries to do a mock commerical, Ricky walks behind the television to put the plug into the socket and finds that the entire set has been dismantled. Lucy had taken out each part piece by piece rather than removing the whole of the chassis.

The following morning Lucy avoids Ricky. Noticing her behavior, Ricky asks Fred to wait for a call from the woman who was hired to do the commericial. Fred is to tell the woman when and where she is to show up for the screening. Overhearing the conversation, Lucy then tells Fred that she will answer the call and deliver the message. Naturally, she had no intention of telling the woman any such thing; when the woman calls, Lucy tells her that she is not needed.

Later that day, Lucy shows up at the television studio in place of the woman. Not knowing her identity, the director tells her that the sales pitch is for a health tonic called "Vitameatavegamin." Lucy is unaware that the tonic contains 23% alcohol and is not meant to be taken more than once a day. Lucy decides to rehearse. Shuddering at the first taste, she presses on, trying to perfect the sales pitch.

By the end of her rehearsals, she can no longer spoon out the liquid and begins to swig it from the bottle. When the commercial finally begins, Lucy is totally tipsy! She introduces herself as the vida-vida-vigee-vat girl and asks, "Do you pop out at parties? Are you unpoopular? . . . The answer to all your problems is in this little old bottle. Vitameatavegamin contains vitamins and meat and megetables and vinerals. So why don't you join the thousands of happy, peppy people and get a great big bottle of vita-veedee-vidi-meanie-minie-moe-amin." The episode can be viewed online at http://www.kaneva.com/asset/assetDetails.aspx?assetId=3929136&communityId=0].

When the regular part of the television show begins, Ricky comes out and starts singing a number. Lucy staggers toward Ricky, swaying and waving to the camera. She starts to sing along with Ricky and begins her sales pitch in the middle of his singing. Ricky desperately carries her off the stage.

Jack Gould, radio and television editor of the *New York Times*, wrote of Ball's comic genius: "First and foremost is her sense of timing; in this respect she is the distaff equivalent of Jack Benny. Maybe it is the roll of her big eyes. Maybe it is the sublime shrug which housewives the world over will understand. Maybe it is the superb hollow laugh. Maybe it is the masterly double take that tops the gag line. Whatever it is, it comes at the split-second instant that spells the difference between a guffaw and a smile."[16]

If Ball's performance as Lucy was nothing less than comic genius, the on-screen relationships were also pivotal to the show's immediate success. The real-life tempestuous relationship of Ball and Arnaz seemed to add resonance to the fictional duo. In addition, against all screen renditions ever presented on radio or motion picture, in this situation it was the Latino who was more reasoned and grounded, more intelligent and comically aggrieved.

Also crucial was the casting of Fred and Ethel. The series creators turned to William Frawley, a veteran of vaudeville and motion pictures who had appeared with such comedy legends as Joe E. Brown, Harold Lloyd, and Charlie Chaplin, to play the irascible and constantly agitated Fred.

As his frumpy if quick-witted wife, they selected Vivian Vance, a 39-year-old actress whose career was primarily in the theater where she had appeared in thirty-eight stage productions. Arnaz saw Vance perform at the La Jolla Playhouse and immediately saw her as Ethel Mertz.

From the early productions, Vance and Frawley had personality conflicts off-screen. As the series progressed, each seemed a constant annoyance to the other. Ironically, the hostility, which they were able to conceal from the public, seemed to add to their effectiveness as a team playing a long-married couple barely able to continue the relationship.

LUCY, DESI, ETHEL, AND FRED

On the evening of October 15, 1951, immediately after the usual showing of Arthur Godfrey's *Talent Scouts*, television audiences were introduced to the Ricardos and the Mertzes. The first episode was titled "The Girls Want to Go to a Nightclub."

To celebrate the Mertzes' eighteenth wedding anniversary, Ethel suggests they go to the Copacabana nightclub; Fred and Ricky instead want the group to go to a prizefight. When Lucy threatens to find two other escorts to go to the club, the battle of the sexes ensues. When the men decide to call the women's bluff, Lucy and Ethel follow through with the threat. They get dressed up and head off for the club. Would they find escorts? Before the men opt to attend the boxing match, Ricky worries. He persuades Fred to go with him and two other women to go the Copacabana spy on the wives. Ricky calls his friend Ginny Jones, a singer at the Starlight Roof, and asks her to arrange dates for Fred and himself. Coincidentally, Lucy, very soon thereafter, calls Ginny Jones herself and asks her to arrange dates for her and Ethel. When Ginny spills the boys' plan to Lucy, Lucy decides that she and Ethel will impersonate their husbands' blind dates. Dressed as hillbillies, Lucy and Ethel arrive at the Ricardo apartment. After Ricky sings a chorus of "Guadalajara," Lucy gives herself away by reaching for some cigarettes that she knew were hidden in a desk drawer. All four see the nonsense in their behavior and all make amends. The two couples kiss and make up—all is forgiven.

Episode by episode, unprecedented numbers of viewers gathered around their television sets on Monday nights to see the series. *I Love Lucy* began to sweep away the competition. People began talking about episodes in casual conversations, and articles in newspapers and magazines began analyzing the show's appeal. By early 1952 the American Research Bureau had announced that *I Love Lucy* was the first show in TV history to reach 10 million homes and was the number one show in television.

At the time of the premiere of *I Love Lucy*, there were few female comedy stars. Gracie Allen performed alongside her husband George Allen; Martha Raye and Imogene Coca starred in variety shows. The advent of the *I Love Lucy* series gave women viewers a new female star, wacky and wonderful, with whom to identify.

The immediate success of the series put to rest the quiet unease that surrounded the pairing of Ball's character with a Cuban bandleader. Not only did the studio not see evidence that the ethnic mix was hurting the show, it became clear that the match was a novelty that piqued the interest of viewers. Most television viewers in the early 1950s were in cities where large immigrant populations resided. Many were immigrants themselves or worked with immigrants. Here again, this was new television ground, innovative and thought-provoking.

Many Americans began to see the marriage not as an aberration but as a growing contemporary situation. Not only Latinos but blacks gravitated toward the show. Black comedian Eddie Murphy often recalled the lack of television characters with whom he could identify as a child. The exception, Murphy said, was Ricky Ricardo. Murphy could identify with his comic Spanish tirades. Later, in his own on-stage comedy, Murphy used the Arnaz model as the model for one of his own characters.

Some of the episodes were instant classics. There was the show in which Lucy, trying to bake bread, was pinned to the far wall of her kitchen when the loaf, into the mix of which she had thrown two packages of yeast, was released from the oven. In another episode, while on a trip to Europe, an Italian producer offered Lucy a minor role in a film called *Bitter Grapes*. In an effort to absorb the atmosphere of the land and its people, and presuming that the film had something to do with the grape processing industry, she ends up stomping around in a vat of unpressed grapes and, in the process, getting into a fight with a professional grape stomper.

During the second season, Ball was pregnant with the couple's second child. Instead of working around the incidence of the pregnancy, Ball and Arnaz embraced the situation and made the pregnancy a part of the series itself. At a time when the words "pregnant" and "pregnancy" were not allowed to be uttered on television, *I Love Lucy* used them as a theme. During the weeks of the pregnancy, the character of Lucy experienced urges to eat exotic foods in the middle of the night and to be a sculptress; Ricky experienced sympathetic labor pains, and they argued over baby names.

On December 8, 1952, Lucy announced to Ethel, "I am going to have a baby." Through subsequent shows, the expectations and plans mounted for both the Ricardos on television and the Arnazes. On January 19, 1953, the most viewers in the history of television tuned in to watch as Lucy gave birth to little Ricky, Jr. That morning, remarkably, Lucille Ball had delivered Desiderio Alberto Arnaz IV by cesarean section. So caught up in both the fictional birth and the actual birth was the public that the Arnazes received nearly 28,000 letters from across the country and the world, along with more than 3,000 telegrams and many gifts.

The Arnaz family was riding high. Desi negotiated a new contract for two more years for the number one series in television. The contract for $8 million was the largest in television history. *I Love Lucy* sustained its popularity. One of the most memorable episodes derived from a scene in Charlie Chaplin's historic comedy *Modern Times*. Lucy and Ethel get jobs in a chocolate factory wrapping bonbons as they move along a converyor belt. Frantic to keep up with their wrapping responsibilities as the belt gains speed, the two start suffing chocolcates everywhere—in their mouths, inside their puffy hats, down the fronts of their uniforms. While they have successfully concealed their wrapping failures from the supervisor upon inspection, they receive congratulations along with an order to the converyor belt operator to "speed it up a little."

So enamored did American viewing audiences become with *I Love Lucy* that department stores changed their once-popular Monday night shopping hours to accommodate the series. Nothing, not even shopping, could compete. In several cities, police departments reported a drop in crime during Monday shows. At the height of the Lucy craze, fans could purchase Lucy jewelry, clothing, and pajamas; Desi smoking jackets and sports shirts; Lucy and Desi dolls; even a life-size, twenty-one-inch vinyl replica of Ricky, Jr., not to mention Ricky Jr. bonnets, booties, and waterproof diaper bags identical to the one used on the television show. From all of this, Desilu reaped five percent of the gross.

Over the years, *I Love Lucy* attracted film stars who had never appeared on television. Considering it an honor to play a cameo role on the show, a distinguished list of stars lined up. They included Harpo Marx, Orson Welles, Bob Hope, John Wayne, William Holden, and Charles Boyer.

As the show progressed, Ricky Ricardo became increasingly successful in his entertainment career. A movie offer led to a cross-country trip by car with the Mertzes. Later, also with the Mertzes, they took a trip to Europe. By the start of the 1956–1957 season, Ricky had opened his own club called the Ricky Ricardo Babalu Club.

BUILDING DESILU PRODUCTIONS

I Love Lucy set the standard for "sitcom" productions. Playing the part of Ricky, Arnaz often said, was the least of the challenges he personally faced in producing the series. He suggested and helped develop filming techniques. During production, he spent several hours a day assisting in the editing. He negotiated deals for Desilu Productions in all sorts of areas, from purchasing and leasing to arranging production schedules; he created, developed, and sold new pilot productions. Although he surrounded himself with an excellent team, his enterprising ideas and forward thinking were at the heart of the company's success.

The rumba bandleader, whom the entertainment industry had never seen as a heavyweight, became a Hollywood giant. Milton Berle said at the time: "I was so struck by the way he handled everything on his own show that I asked him to direct a show for me. He's got a tremendous flair for comedy; there's almost nobody like him around."[17]

Arnaz's business savvy and natural professional instincts not only helped propel *I Love Lucy* and his company to the heights of the profession, but his innovations proved lasting. The large syndication deals being made well into the twenty-first century are an extension of the arrangements he made in the 1950s.

In 1954, Arnaz and Ball took time to star in an MGM film that capitalized on the husband-wife team that had made such an historic impact in television. The film was called the *Long, Long Trailer*. The two characters were newlyweds, Tacy and Nicky Collini. Because Nicky's job requires much travel, Tacy convinces her husband that they should purchase a mobile home, a 3-ton, 28-foot behemoth, almost impossible to maneuver through congested city streets and on narrow highways. As the couple heads west with the large beast in tow, all sorts of predicaments and perils await. At one point, the trailer nearly tips off a mountainside precipice.

In 1956, Arnaz negotiated the purchase of RKO Studios, a move that expanded the Desilu facilities to allow for increased production. The company now had thirty-five soundstages and several hundred employees.

Desilu produced such shows as *Our Miss Brooks* with Eve Arden, *The Loretta Young Show, The Danny Thomas Show, Ray Bolger Show, December Bride* with Spring Byington, *Those Whiting Girls, Sheriff of Cochise,* and the *Red Skelton Show*. By the end of 1956, Desilu was a major production company, filming nearly 300 half-hour shows a year.

THE FAMED SERIES ENDS

Success took its toll. Fatigued by the hectic pace of running Desilu and beset with progressing alcoholism and serious bouts with diverticulitis—an often very painful and debilitating stomach condition—and troubled by the feverish imbalance of love and overwhelming mistrust and jealousy in his marriage because of his continued womanizing, Arnaz, by the close of the 1950s, faced personal and professional crises.

At the end of the 1956–1957 season of *I Love Lucy*, Arnaz and Ball decided to end the series even though it was still the number one show in television. As a gradual way to ease out of the grueling pace of weekly shows, Arnaz produced a few hour-long specials featuring the cast and characters from *I Love Lucy* and called it *The Lucy-Desi Comedy Hour*. Featuring a great deal of music and dancing that was integrated into the plot lines, the series of one-hour productions was, just as the *I Love Lucy* half-hour series had been, enormously successful.

The last episode of *I Love Lucy* aired on May 6, 1957; thirty-five million people watched. For many, it was as if there had been a death in the family—Monday night at 9:00 P.M. would never again be the same.

Arnaz continued to head Desilu, serving as executive producer until he sold his portion of the company to Ball, who eventually sold the studio to Gulf & Western. With the original show out of production, prime-time reruns of the series aired for several more years on CBS; syndicated reruns have been running continuously ever since.

Shortly after the conclusion of the *I Love Lucy* series on television ended the saga of the Ricardos, Arnaz and Ball divorced; she was 49 years old, and he was 43.

Comedian Jack Carter said later, "Lucy loved Desi till the day she died ... He was the father of her kids." Carter said, even late in life she would "... still run these lovely home movies of her and Desi and the kids when they were little. Everybody was in them, smiling by the pool, running up real fast, waving hello, Lucy walking knock-kneed and doing her Lucy faces. She'd sit there giving commentaries. She loved watching those movies."[18]

Director William Asher said, "Maybe I'm the romantic, but there was a great, great love there, there really was. Desi was very unhappy about the break up, and I think she was too. I don't think either one of them ever got over it."[19]

Throughout the rest of his life, Arnaz and Ball would talk often on the phone. He continued to send her flowers every year on their anniversary. In 1961, she married a vaudeville and nightclub comedian named Gary Morton.

Increasingly beset with illness and with battles to overcome alcoholism and depression, Arnaz went into semi-retirement and pursued his interests in raising racehorses. He also built a vacation hideaway in Las Cruces on the Pacific coast of Baja, Mexico, just below the United States border.

In March 1963, he married Edith McSkiming Hirsch, a long-time friend and horseracing aficionado. It was a union that lasted until her death in 1983. In 1966, in a brief return to television, Arnaz formed Desi Arnaz Productions Incorporated and developed the series *The Mothers-in-Law* starring Eve Arden. Arnaz assumed the role of the show's director and also appeared in four of the episodes as Señor Raphael Del Gado, a Spanish matador. The show ran for three seasons.

In 1972, he was a visiting professor at San Diego State University and taught classes in studio production and acting. He made a few appearances on television in such shows as *The Men from Shilo* and *Bonanza*.

On February 21, 1976, Arnaz acted as the host on the comedy show *Saturday Night Live*. Accompanied by his son, Desi, Jr., Arnaz played the drums and sang, read Lewis Carroll's poem "Jabberwocky" in a heavy Cuban accent that made the title sound like "Habberwocky," shared with Desi, Jr., some of the initial ideas that were proposed before *I Love Lucy* was picked up by the network, played a Cuban acupuncture doctor who used cigars on his patients instead of needles, and finshed the show by leading the entire cast in a conga line through the studio.

Although his health was seriously failing in 1982, he agreed to appear in a feature film for Warner Brothers/Zoetrope. In *The Escape Artist*, which starred Raul Julia, Joan Hackett, and Jackie Coogan and was produced by Francis Ford Coppola, Arnaz played a corrupt politician like the ones who had run his family out of Cuba so many years ago.

In 1976, Arnaz published his autobiography titled *The Book*, which chronicled his life up until his divorce from Lucille Ball. In the epilogue of *The Book*, Arnaz wrote: "I want to thank the United States of America and her people. I cannot think of another country in the world in which a young man of sixteen, broke and unable to speak the language, could have been given the chances to accomplish what I did, or the welcome, *carino*, praise and honor which were given to me."[20]

On December 2, 1986, Desi Arnaz succumbed to lung cancer.

A PIONEER ENTERTAINER

Arnaz celebrated his Latino heritage. In the *I Love Lucy* series, the Latino character was for the first time not portrayed on the screen as a stereotype. He was not lazy or dishonest; his character was solid in his footing, a talented professional and entrepreneur.

In his own professional career, Arnaz was a leader and an innovator. Along with Xavier Cugat, Arnaz was among the first to introduce the Cuban conga to the United States; he was the first Latino to appear in a musical on New York's Broadway and also the first Latino to appear on television and a Hollywood film. Arnaz blazed the trail for eminent figures in Cuban music, such as Mario Bauza, Machito, Panchito Riset, and many others. Tito Puente, a legendary figure in music and popularly known as "King of the Mambo" once said, "You have to divide Latino music in the U.S. into two periods: before and after Desi Arnaz."[21]

Arnaz was an astute and innovative business executive. Through Desilu Productions, Arnaz set new standards in television management and production.

He was the living image of a victorious Latino, says actor Danny Pino, who played Arnaz in a CBS television film about Lucille Ball. Pino said of the role, "That was an opportunity to play a character that was so influential as an American icon and as a Cuban-American icon … he was the first Latino and the first Cuban in Hollywood to make it as a comedian, actor and as a producer."[22]

He was, in other words, a Latino pioneer.

SELECTED RECORDED MUSIC

Arnaz, Desi. *The Best of Desi Arnaz: The Mambo King*. RCA, 1992. CD.
Arnaz, Desi. *Babalu*. RCA, 1996. CD.
Arnaz, Desi. *1937–1947*. Harlequin Records, 1998. CD.
Arnaz, Desi. *Conga!* Sony Music Special Products, 1999. CD.
Arnaz, Desi. *Cuban Originals*. RCA, 1999. Original recording remastered, CD.

SELECTED MOVIES

Too Many Girls. Directed by George Abbott. RKO Radio Pictures, 1940.
Father Takes a Wife. Directed by Jack Hively. RKO Radio Pictures, 1941.
Four Jacks and a Jill. Directed by Jack Hively. RKO Radio Pictures, 1942.
The Navy Comes Through. Directed by A. Edward Sutherland. RKO Radio Picutres, 1942.
Bataan. Directed by Tay Garnett. Metro-Goldwyn-Mayer, 1943.
Cuban Pete. Directed by Jean Yarbrough. Universal Pictures, 1946.
Holiday in Havana. Directed by Jean Yarbrough. Columbia Pictures Corporation, 1949.
The Long, Long Trailer. Directed by Vincente Minnelli. Metro-Goldwyn-Mayer, 1954.
Forever Darling. Directed by Alexander Hall. Zanra Productions, 1956.
Salsa. Directed by Leon Gast. Documentary, 1976.
The Escape Artist. Directed by Caleb Deschanel. Zoetrope Studios, 1982.

NOTES

1. Warren G. Harris, *Lucy and Desi: The Legendary Love Story of Television's Most Famous Couple* (New York: Simon & Schuster, 1991), 38.
2. Desi Arnaz, *A Book* (New York: Warner Books, 1976), 57.
3. John Steele Gordon, "What Desi Wrought," *American Heritage*, December 1998, 20.
4. "They Called Him Cuban Pete," ttp://www.lucyfan.com/desidiscography.html.
5. Harris, 22.
6. Arnaz, 126.
7. "Lucille Ball and Desi Arnaz," *People Weekly*, February 12, 1996, 74.
8. Harris, 17–18.
9. Desi Arnaz, "Cuban Pete," http://www.lyricsbox.com/desi-arnaz-lyrics-cuban-pete-gsrh1hb.html.
10. Harris, 133.
11. Arnaz, 206.
12. "Early Years of TV, Time Magazine," http://www.time.com/time/archive/collections/0,21428,c_television_history,00.shtml.
13. Arnaz, 229.
14. Susan Schindehette, "The Real Story of Desi and Lucy," *People Weekly*, February 18, 1991, 84.
15. "TV Team," *Newsweek,* February 18, 1952, 67.
16. Jack Gould, "Why Millions Love Lucy," *New York Times,* March 1, 1953, 8.
17. Wes Gehring, "*I Love Lucy* Turns 50," *USA Today Magazine*, September, 2001, 68
18. Schindehette, "The Real Story of Desi and Lucy," 1991.
19. ——. 1991.
20. Arnaz, 379.
21. Rafael Lam, "Desi Arnaz:The Victorious Cuban," http://www.cubanow.net/global/loader.php?secc=6&cont=people/num25/02.htm.
22. Douglas McGrath. "The Good, the Bad, the Lucy: A Legacy of Laughs; the Man behind the Throne; Making the Case for Desi," *The New York Times*, October 14, 2001, 30.

FURTHER READING

Anderson, Christopher. *Hollywood/TV*. Austin, Texas: The University of Texas Press, 1994.
Andrews, Bart. *The "I Love Lucy" Book*. New York: Doubleday, 1985.
Andrews, Bart, and Thomas J. Watson. *Loving Lucy*. New York: St. Martin's, 1980.
Arnaz, Desi. *A Book*. New York: Warner Books, 1976.
Brady, Kathleen. *Lucille: The Life of Lucille Ball*. New York: Hyperion, 1994.
Firmat, Gustavo Perez. *Life On the Hyphen: The Cuban-American Way*. Austin, Texas: University of Texas Press, 1994.
Harris, Warren G. *Lucy and Desi: The Legendary Love Story of Television's Most Famous Couple*. New York: Simon & Schuster, 1991.
Sanders, Coyne Steven, and Tom Gilbert. *Desilu: The Story of Lucille Ball and Desi Arnaz*. New York: Morrow 1993.

Ruben Blades

To say that Ruben Blades is a Renaissance man, a man of varied interests and accomplishments, is not overstatement or hype. Singer, songwriter, screenwriter, jazz musician, stage and screen actor, lawyer, political figure, and activist, Blades grew up in Panama City, Panama, and immigrated to New York in 1974 with only $100 in his pocket. During the next two decades, he earned a law degree from Harvard University, became an entertainer of international acclaim, and even returned to Panama to run for president.

In an interview with *Time* magazine in 1990, Blades reflected on his cross-cultural interests and career and also on difficulties in breaking down perceived barriers between Anglos and Latinos. Ignorance and fear are at the root of the gulf that persists between the cultures, Blades said. "It implies an acceptance of a barrier," he said, "and I refuse to acknowledge a barrier. I think the barriers are in the mind and in the heart. People tell me, 'You close your eyes and you're too idealistic,' and I have to say no. In all honesty, I never saw the barrier."[1]

SON OF PANAMA AND MUSIC

Ruben's father, Ruben Blades, Sr., who was born in Colombia and later moved to Panama, was a conga player who was recruited to play on the National Secret Police's basketball team. The association with the team led to his enlistment with the Secret Police, where he served as a detective. Ruben's mother, Anoland Bellido de Luna, was a nightclub singer and piano player, as well as a radio performer. She met Blades, Sr., when she moved from her native Cuba to Panama to perform in the clubs and landed a job singing with the band in which he was playing.

Ruben Blades, Jr., the second of five children, was born on July 16, 1948, in Panama City, Panama, in a working-class neighborhood called San Felipe, close to the Canal Zone, the ten-mile by fifty-mile strip of land occupied by the United States.

The American military and other American citizens who lived in the Zone and in relative prosperity had a powerful impact on the poor neighboring communities occupied by Panamanians. The tensions between the two groups had been longstanding.

In a treaty signed in 1901, the United States was granted authority to build and operate a canal crossing through a narrow part of eastern Panama. The Panama Canal, completed in 1914, thus connected the Atlantic and Pacific Oceans and provided an invaluable route for ships that now did not have to sail around all of South America.

From the beginning, Panamanian residents resented a relationship that seemed to benefit only the Americans. They also resented the racial and cultural slights that seemed unrelenting.

On the other hand, many Panamanians held up the American example as a goal. Many youngsters saw themselves as someday being soldiers like the ones they saw controlling the Canal. They felt a kinship to American culture. One of those youngsters was Ruben Blades.

Looking back on his earliest years, Blades said, "I grew up in Panama. My grandfather on my father's side was English. That is why my last name is Blades. When people ask me, 'How is your name pronounced?' I say Blades. If people want to pronounce it Blá-des, I don't have a problem with that, as long as they don't think that I am ashamed of my name or that I'm trying to Anglicize my name to get over or that kind of stupid thing. But if somebody says Blá-des, you know, I'm fine with it. ... My grandmother on my mother's side was from Galicia in Spain, and on my father's side, she was from Colombia."[2]

Ruben's paternal grandmother, Emma, played a special part in the young boy's life, encouraging his love of books and telling him many stories reflecting on his Latino roots. She was one of the few women in Panama who had completed high school. So culturally aware was Emma that she introduced such subjects as Picasso and cubism to the boy by the time he was six years old. Also, she often took him to a local air-conditioned theater to escape the heat of summer. There, they watched Bob Hope and Bing Crosby and other Hollywood greats.

Although the family lived in a small, two-room house and did not have the money to buy a piano or other expensive musical instruments, Ruben saw his mother on occasion playing and singing at the radio studio where she worked and it impressed him greatly.

Many children in Panama in the 1950s grew up listening to radio recordings of American rock and roll stars such as Elvis Presley, the Platters, and Chuck Berry. As he reached his early teens, Blades idolized Frankie Lymon and the Teenagers, who recorded the hit "Why Do Fools Fall in Love?" Lymon was only fourteen years old when he led the group. "Rock and roll in the mid-fifties was a turning point for many of us." Blades recalled. He remembered seeing Lymon's group in the movie *Rock, Rock, Rock*. "They were kids who looked like guys that might have hung out on our corner. We were flabbergasted that kids could do those things.... For me it was a revelation to realize that I didn't have to wait til I was twenty-five to be a musician."[3]

At one point Blades even wrote a letter to Lymon, asking to join the group. Blades' mother, who wanted her son to concentrate on his education, did not send it. When the youngster learned that she had thrown the letter away, he was furious and hurt. Now realizing the extent of his dreams to be in entertainment, she went to a local store and bought him a cheap guitar with a decal of Elvis Presley emblazoned on it. It was the first musical instrument the young Blades owned. He would learn to play it on his own.

Although basically shy, Ruben began to sing with friends in the neighborhood as they tried to imitate various rock and roll groups. They hung out at an old vacant building called Audisio that had a great echo on the second floor. Sometimes, he would go there alone and belt out a number or two.

At the age of fifteen, Blades made his first appearance on stage. His older brother, Luis, was in a band called The Saints. One night, Luis was informed that the lead singer would not be able to make a gig, and he asked Ruben to act as his replacement. Luis knew that Ruben was familiar with the rock and roll hits that the band played and knew that his brother was also quite talented. Although his mother protested, Ruben, overcoming his shyness and his mother's protests, went along with the band. The crowd loved him.

In 1964, when Blades was not yet sixteen, the uneasy political situation surrounding the U.S. occupation of the Canal Zone erupted. The tension between the U.S. citizens and local Panamanians flared over a disagreement regarding the flying of the flag of Panama. Although U.S. and Panamanian officials had agreed that both the U.S. and Panama flags should fly together in the Canal Zone, some U.S. citizens refused to comply. At one high school, only the U.S. flag was hoisted every morning.

A group of protestors, led by Panamanian students, marched to the school and set off a full-scale riot. The fighting resulted in the deaths of twenty-two Panamanians and four U.S. soldiers and the wounding of more than 500 Panamaniancitizens. One Panamanian later remembered: "I was eight years old on January 9, 1964. Up to this date, I can still hear the shots from the U.S. army against the Panamanian nationals. Those of us that lived those years will always remember that, as well as the apartheid-driven Canal Zone…. I lived about one mile from the site, and remember hearing the shots as if it was yesterday. I also remember crawling on the floor, in case a bullet went through a window."[4]

For Ruben Blades the riots changed his heart. In the early years of his childhood and adolescence, his aspirations and interests had been pro-American. He loved the music. The images of the United States he saw with his grandmother on the local movie screen on those hot summer days had seemed almost idyllic. Most of the films had happy endings.

But now his adulation of the United States was shaken. "The Army that we all had wanted to be a part of as kids came with tanks," Blades remembered. "There was so much brutality, it was so unfair, that it created a reaction of outrage." His sense of awe and respect for the U.S. withered before what he saw as bullying arrogance and a disregard for the lives of average Panamanians. After all, he said, the Americans were supposed to be the good guys.[5]

The riots so close to home affected him deeply. He began to question many of his previous assumptions, began reading some history, and began to think about political causes. He began to appreciate more fully many of those Latino cultural roots about which his grandmother had frequently talked. He started playing some Latin music and studying its foundations. He decided to write and sing in Spanish. He listened to such musicians as Puerto Rican salsa singer Ismael Rivera, Puerto Rican percussionist Rafael Cortijo, and, especially, a young singer from Argentina named Piero.

Unlike rock and roll that had dominated his interests up to this time, the music of Piero was of social problems and themes, stories of city life and the effects of poverty, and the need to champion reform. It was in this direction that Blades would take his own music. When the Argentine singer visited Panama, Blades and a friend managed to visit him at his hotel. Blades gave him a song he had written called "Pablo Pueblo," a piece about a factory worker whose life was fueled by hope. Blades played his guitar and sang the music in the room and asked Piero if he would sing it. The Argentine praised the work but declined, saying the song was written by Blades and was for Blades. The Panamanian promised to carry on with this music with a social message and a vision.

But the teenager was gifted in other ways besides music. Blades had a strong intellect and much curiosity. His parents hoped that he would not follow their steps into show business but would, instead, discover a professional life in the law or other arena that would take full advantage of his intellectual strengths. When he graduated from high school, they strongly encouraged him to enroll in law school at the University of Panama. Blades agreed.

As Blades began his studies at the University of Panama, he continued experimenting with his music. In 1968 he briefly joined an Afro-Cuban group called Bush and the Magnificos. The team made an album that did not sell many copies but did pique the interest of a music producer in New York named Pancho Cristal. So impressed was Cristal with the singing talents of Blades that he asked the youngster to come to New York. Although mightily tempted, Blades decided to continue his education.

As Blades settled into his classroom routine at the university, he worked at a shipping agency to help keep him financially afloat. Although the university did not require tuition payments, his low salary at the job made it difficult to keep going. But he studied diligently, worked, played occasionally with local bands, and moved toward his degree until, once again, the seemingly never-ending political turmoil in Panama escalated into crisis.

In 1968, Anulfo Arias, a right-wing politician, was elected for the third time in his career as President of Panama. Although he had a strong national following, he also had determined opponents, including members of the country's National Guard who were intent on keeping him from office. They attacked him for election fraud and raided his headquarters. Only ten days after he had taken office, Arias' government was overthrown by a military coup.

The coup was led by Colonel Omar Torrijos, a charismatic leader who, upon taking over the reins of government, announced that he was "maximum chief." He abolished all political parties and dissolved the national legislature. But Torrijos was able to unite a large portion of the country behind him by actively supporting social needs programs to help the lower and middle classes, students, and others. He also justified his overarching takeover by stressing the need to unify the country behind the effort to negotiate a treaty with the United States that would ultimately give control of the Panama Canal to Panama.

Despite Torrijos' support, many within the university reacted defiantly against this arrogant assumption of power. Students, faculty, and school administrators issued a protest attacking the military coup. They held a public march and confronted the Panamanian army. Many student leaders and other supporters were herded off to jail. In response to the university protest, the Torrijos government occupied the campus and closed down its operations for one year.

When the university closed its doors, Blades decided to travel to New York to take a look at the music scene. This was 1969, a time when artists such as Tito Puente had already brought Afro-Cuban and other Latin sounds to New York. The Palladium Ballroom at Broadway and 53rd Street had become the American center of the mambo dance craze, followed by the cha-cha-cha and other dance music.

In the 1960s, the first Latino-owned record label, Alegre, recorded much of the new Latin jazz. Other Latino artists such as Dominican-born flutist Johnny Pacheco and American-born conga player and bandleader Joe Cuba made an impact with a fusion of new sounds and new dances. Willie Colon, trombonist and singer, and his friend and collaborator, Hector Lavoe, moved toward a more hard-edged, urban sound.

By the late 1960s, the Dominican *merengue,* Colombian *cumbia,* and Puerto Rican *plena* and *jibaro* styles had become part of the New York music scene. Excitement swirled around the new *salsa* beat, the dynamic combination of rhythms from Africa, the Caribbean, Spain, and the United States, a rich fusion of Spanish guitar, rock and roll, rhythm and blues, and jazz. New York was a melting pot of sounds that made up *salsa*; the word itself means a sauce.

All of this excited Blades—he wanted to be a part of it.

"My brother, Luis, was working at Pan American," Blades said, "And if you work at an airline, your dependents can travel for very little money, and I got to come to New York for, like, twenty dollars. But I had also made a connection with a producer here, Pancho Cristal. They were producing, like, The Joe Cuba Sextet and Richie Ray and Bobby Cruz.... And, he'd seen me in Panama, and he talked about maybe doing something in New York...."[6]

Pete Rodriguez, another of New York's young Latin Jazz musicians, worked with Blades on an album. It was called *De Panama a Nueva York: Pete Rodriguez Presenta a Rubén Blades* (From Panama to New York: Pete Rodriguez Presents Ruben Blades). Blades wrote almost all of the songs. Although the album did not sell well, Blades had made his first serious effort to break into the recording scene.

When the university reopened in Panama, Blades left New York to return to his studies. In 1972 he earned degrees in both political science and the law and then worked as an attorney for a time with the Banco Nacional de Panama, the national bank of Panama.

Ruben's sense of activism and community service always keen, he also volunteered some of his time counseling prisoners. And, although the University did not allow its law students to perform music outside the academic setting, he did begin again to write songs, many of them infused with political overtones and calls for justice.

From the time he was a young boy in Panama, the political upheavals and tensions surrounding him and his family had played a crucial role in determining his future. The political struggles had not only defined his evolving views of democracy and human rights and the simple struggles of people trying to make their lives worthwhile. Politics had also determined, to a large extent, where he had moved and lived.

In 1973, the twenty-five-year-old Blades found himself again in the middle of a family crisis brought about by Panamanian politics. Blades' father, a member of Panama's Secret Police, was accused by General Manuel Antonio Noriega, the head of the spy service, of providing information to the United States Central Intelligence Agency. Although he strongly denounced the charges, Blades, Sr., decided to leave Panama, to become an exile. Accompanied by his wife and four of his children, he moved to Miami, Florida, into the center of a growing Latino community.

At first, Blades, Jr., decided to stay. For a time, he continued his job as a bank attorney while, at the same time, joining a few small music groups. It did not take long, however, for him to make a critical decision. He was uneasy continuing to practice law under a military regime. He felt strongly that he could make a difference with his music. He chose to return to New York.

"I felt that popular music would play an important role in Latin America," he said. "I felt it was an effective way of stating cases, of presenting the truth, the people's side, because they all had sounds, and those sounds were as important as anything I could do in a court of law."[7]

NEW YORK AND SALSA

After living for a short time with his exiled parents in Miami, Blades arrived in New York with less than $100 in his pocket. He soon headed for the offices of Fania Records, the principal recording studio in New York for salsa music. Few other American labels were interested in recording Latin music. As Blades said later, Fania was the only game in town.

Although a number of artists had heard Blades perform in Panama and recommended him to executives at Fania Records, the studio was not yet ready to sign him to a contract. He persisted in asking whether there was any work available at the record company. They told him there was a vacancy in the mailroom. He took it.

He rented a tiny apartment on East 61 Street, within walking distance of Fania Records, for $175 a month. He was now physically where he wanted to be, in the heart of New York's salsa scene. He would now bide his time and wait for an opportunity to show off his talent, wait for an opportunity to break out of the mailroom and into the recording studio.

He swept floors. He pushed a cart filled with mail each day from 57th Street all the way to 52nd Street to the post office. He did numerous other necessary chores. And he wrote songs, played guitar, and began making whatever contacts he could make to open doors.

Soon he was practicing with salseros Ray Barretto and Larry Harlow and trombonist and bandleader Willie Colón. It was Barretto who gave Blades his first big break.

Son of a financially strapped Puerto Rican family in Brooklyn, conga player Ray Barretto played with "El Maestro"—Tito Puente—in the famous Palladium Ballroom and other venues. In the sixties, Barretto formed his own salsa ensemble that produced a national hit record and later signed with Fania Records.

Barretto needed a backup singer for his group at Fania and he did not have to look farther than the mailroom. At the historic Madison Square Garden, Blades made his New York debut in 1974 singing with Barretto's group. Nervous and not at his best, Blades nevertheless made a solid impression on the crowd in the Garden. His New York music career was now launched.

In 1976, Blades began to work with one of the big names of the salsa world, Willie Colon. For seven years, Colón had worked with singer Héctor Lavoe in a collaboration that produced ten albums full of vibrant songs that spoke the language of the street and gave salsa music a higher place as a musical genre. In 1976, the two went their separate ways. It was then that Colón began to team with Blades.

With Colón as arranger for Blades' songs, they released in 1977 *Willie Colón Presents Rubén Blades*. A year later, they released the album *Siembra*, a triumph that has been considered the most popular salsa production in history. It sold over three million copies. The hit single from the album, "Pedro Navaja," became the biggest-selling single in salsa history. The song is about a criminal—the word *navaja* in Spanish means knife or razor, and the main character, according to Blades, was inspired by the song "Mack the Knife," a Kurt Weil number that was made popular by trumpeter Louis Armstrong and then, in rock and roll circles, by Bobby Darin. "Pedro Navaja" is a darkly humorous story of the shadowy side of Latino culture and deals with the hard issues of life and sudden death.

In explaining the success of *Siembra*, Blades said, "The people who bought it weren't just the dancers. They identified with the stories as much as the rhythm."[8]

The emphasis of salsa music had traditionally been on the dance rhythms, not on the lyrics. Blades saw music as a way of communicating the realities of the urban cities. With Blades writing the music and Colón working on the productions, the new albums became a sudden innovation in the music field.

Not only did the dancers now buy the records, but so did many others. "The grandmother, the mother, the worker, the student, the intellectual, the professional, the unemployed, everybody identified with the songs because they were descriptions of life in the city," said Blades. "So that where you sold 20,000, all of a sudden we were selling 350,000 records. So it was a big, huge impact that was caused by the fact of the lyrics and that is why *Siembra* became the first million seller." The album earned a Grammy Award nomination and was listed on *Time* magazine's list of the year's top ten rock albums.[9]

Blades' lyrics replaced lightness with social commentary. He confronted issues in what had traditionally been a musical form of dance moves. Although many fans of salsa did not quite know what to make of the experiment, they liked what they heard.

Some of the songs tended to give disc jockeys programming problems because they were much longer than the usual three minutes. Songs such as "Pedro Navaja," for example, lasted about six minutes.

Some of Blades' work stirred controversy. In 1980 he wrote "Tiburon" (Shark), a song that condemned the world's superpowers for interfering with the political affairs of smaller countries. Many understood the lyrics as a direct attack against those who wielded political power in the United States, those who continued the policies that made the Canal Zone an occupied territory. Some Latinos in Miami were so offended by the song that they refused to play it on the air. When Blades made an appearance in Miami, he wore a bulletproof vest.

Nevertheless, when Blades, Colón, and the group went on the road, especially to Latin America, they were often greeted like heroes. In Venezuela, large groups turned out to hear them perform. Whenever they played, Blades remembered, people's attention was not on dancing but on listening. Often, he thought, some of the clubs in which they performed seemed at least during their performances like theaters. The Latin crowds seemed more sensitive to what the group was trying to accomplish than the crowds in New York. Nevertheless, wherever Blades and Colón took their music, the venues filled up.

The music became known as *salsa conciente*, salsa with a message. Other bands and individuals would follow, creating music that demanded justice and accountability to the established power structure and rights for minorities.

During the nearly six years of their collaboration, Blades and Colón produced a series of memorable albums, including *Siembra*. The years had been refreshingly creative for both artists. They had taken the music to many countries around the world. In 1982, however, Blades decided once again to strike out on his own. His last concert with Colón was in Berlin at the Waldune Auditorium.

A NEW GROUP

"After I left the band and Willie in '82, I gave him a whole year's notice," Blades said. "I wanted to go in a different direction. I wasn't sure exactly what it was that I wanted to do. I was thinking about going back to school and getting a post-graduate degree. I wasn't sure where nor when. I wanted to explore film. I wanted to go to Panamá, I mean, there were so many things that I wanted to do. And I also wanted to move away from what we had done up till that time."[10]

He decided to form a small group. There would be, he promised, more fusion and experimentation, a greater attempt to explore ways in which his ideas and beliefs could be part of a new kind of musical force.

He called the new group Seis del Solar (Six from the Hood). Blades created an unusual blend of traditional salsa and jazz, doo-wop, rock and roll, and various Latin sounds. Most salsa bands have more than ten musicians and singers. Using a synthesizer instead of the usual horns, he was able to keep the band much smaller. Also, he incorporated the kind of drum set used in rock and roll. The entire effect was to enhance the lyrics. It also was a change that a number of music critics called "crossover," moving from Latin music toward American pop.

Blades did not like the characterization. "I find the whole idea of crossover dangerous, because it implies the abandonment of one base for another. I'd rather talk about convergence—the idea of two sides meeting in the middle of a bridge. Some people in the music industry feel that because of the language barrier the songs won't ever be accepted by English-speaking North Americans, but I refuse to believe it."[11]

Whatever definition Blades wished to give the word "crossover," his recording in 1984 of an album called *Buscando America* (Searching for America) broke into new markets around the world. Much of the reason had to do with the language barrier that Latino music had always carried as baggage in records stores and radio stations around the world, including the United States.

For this album, produced by Elektra/Asylum/None records, Blades provided translations of the lyrics into whatever foreign language was spoken wherever the album was being sold. Purchasers in the United States could read the words in English; buyers in Germany could read the words in German. Blades was fond of pointing out that, in the year in which the record appeared in Germany, it outsold such artists as Prince. The album sold 300,000 copies in the first five months and was nominated for a Grammy Award.

Now listeners could appreciate the innovative sounds of Blades' brand of salsa and, at the same time, understand his messages, many of them filled with literary and cultural references and most of them intended to make political or social points. One of Elektra's vice presidents told a *New York*

Times reporter that the contract Blades signed with the company included the provision that translations be included. The purpose, said the executive, was to make sure he was understood.

On *Buscando America,* Blades sang about kidnappings in such countries in South America as Chile, Argentina, and El Salvador. The song was called "Desapariciones" (Disappeared), and it sorrowfully recounted how citizens had been rounded up for expressing political beliefs challenging the leadership.

In "GDBD" he described the everyday activities of a man getting ready for work. Only at the end of the song does Blades reveal what the man does for a living. He is a secret police officer who hunts down the government's political opponents.

In other songs, Blades lamented the murder of human rights advocate Archbishop Oscar Arnulfo Romero of El Salvador and attacked the emerging dictatorship of General Manuel Antonio Noriega of Panama, who had taken over the Panamanian government in 1981 after a mysterious plane crash killed President Omar Torrijos.

Once again, Blades' lyrics provoked censorship. "Decisiones" (Decisions) from the *Buscando* album was banned by Panama's censors for allegedly promoting abortion. When Blades gave a performance in Panama, he was prohibited from playing the song.

The *Buscando* album featured mythical characters well known to Latinos including Pablo Pueblo, a factory worker, and Ligia Elena, a society girl. Most Latin songs, Blades said, were about love themes; about, for example, a love affair in which a guy betrayed his best friend, or about a guy whose woman left him, or simply about partying. Although not critical of the genre, he was out to change it.

After hearing a Blades performance, *New York Times* reporter Anthony DePalma wrote: "The words he sings are not of partying, but of protest, of indignance against greed, corruption, and spiritual sloth.... He sings of the 'disappeared ones' of Argentina and of the working men in the barrios of New York. His call is not salsa's usual 'Let's Dance,' but a rallying cry urging all Latinos in North and South America to 'Get Moving.'"[12]

Blades made waves in 1984 when he put his career on hold and headed north to Harvard University, where he spent the year earning a master's degree in international law. "My music fans were stunned," says Blades. "One guy in Colombia even wrote a letter to a newspaper. He wanted to know why I was going to this school, the cradle of capitalism, and why I just didn't stay with music. Everyone is entitled to their opinion, but I don't see why I can't go there and learn and utilize what I've learned for something constructive."[13]

In 1986, many Americans who had not known of the work of Ruben Blades, despite his artistic success, were given a unique introduction. He became the subject of filmmaker Robert Mugge's documentary *The Return of Ruben Blades*, a film that debuted at the Denver Film Festival. Chronicling the life, music, and philosophy of Blades, Mugge captured his intelligence, passion, and talent at a number of locales: at New York City's famed club S.O.B.'s, where Blades and Seis del Solar often performed; at a political discussion with journalist Pete Hamill of the New York *Daily News;* and at a recording session with singer Linda Ronstadt.

While attending Harvard, Blades had met an aspiring actress named Lisa Lebenzon, a native Californian and Sarah Lawrence-educated actress. They married in December 1986 but later divorced.

Blades won his first Grammy Award for the album *Escenas*, released in 1985. Unlike *Buscando America*, this album was more personal, more an exercise in exploring personal relationships, things he had both seen and felt in his own life. The album included a duet with Linda Ronstadt called "Silencios," describing a couple's loss of love. But the album was also a call to Latinos to move forward, not just in their own lives, but for good of all. One of the pieces, a sprightly song called "Muevete," is a plea to Latinos everywhere to join forces.

Constantly experimenting with music and lyrics, Blades moved in an unusual direction in 1986. Earlier, while on a trip to Mexico, Blades had befriended Colombian novelist Gabriel García Márquez, who had won the Nobel Prize for Literature in 1982, "for his novels and short stories, in which the fantastic and the realistic are combined in a richly composed world of imagination, reflecting a continent's life and conflicts."[14]

Blades struck up a long-distance collaboration after meeting the novelist in person. He admired Garcia Márquez's novels and short stories, with their extraordinary depth of feeling and appreciation of the culture of Latin America and its people. He admired the crusading spirit of the work and the call to throw off the yoke of oppression and darkness from the masses. "I love him not because of his skills but because he is an intellectual who likes salsa music," Blades said. "He has kept one foot in the popular culture."[15]

In 1987 Seis del Solar recorded *Agua de Luna*, with songs inspired by the works of the great novelist. The songs created by Blades for the album were not direct quotations from Garcia Márquez's work but adaptations, emotional reactions of Blades to the stories and the feelings he had for the work. Garcia Márquez was quite pleased with the association with Blades; some of the novelist's fans were disappointed that Blades had not simply set the literature to music. Nevertheless, the album represented yet another novel experiment by Blades, a testament to his innovative and creative impulses.

Garcia Márquez said, "What Ruben did, to use a word that is a bit common but has a lot of worth, was to become inspired by my stories." Blades, said the novelist, had become a forceful voice of an emerging Latino self-awareness.[16]

A year after *Agua de Luna*, Blades recorded his first record in English. The album, called *Nothing but the Truth,* demonstrated just how influential

Blades had become in American music circles. Artists such as Elvis Costello, Sting, Lou Reed, and Eric Clapton joined him not only in the music but also in writing many of the songs. Most of the album confronted major social issues such as the AIDS epidemic and the political upheavals in Latin America. The album also was novel in that it included various blends of sounds and lyrics in the songs. He later said that the idea for the record came to him when he thought of his early days as a child listening to the radio in Panama, hearing on different stations everything from Latin mariachi music to rock and roll, jazz, and classical music.

By the end of the 1980s, Blades had already made substantial contributions in the world of music. But, as always, the creative urges took Blades into other areas. He decided to take on the challenges of acting.

BLADES THE ACTOR

In 1982, Blades and his musical partner Willie Colón had teamed up with former Oakland Raider football star-turned-actor, Fred "The Hammer" Williamson in a film written by Williamson called *The Last Fight*. The plot involves a singer turned boxer named Andy "Kid" Clave (Blades) who signs a contract with a shady boxing promoter named Joaquin Vargas (Colón). But The Kid turns against Vargas when the promoter's thugs kill Clave's girlfriend when he thinks about backing out of a contract. Although Clave learns he has a blood clot in his head, he aims for revenge.

The film was mediocre at best. It was poor vehicle for Blades to begin an acting career. But in 1985, Blades tried again, this time on a project for which he had much emotional investment. Its title was *Crossover Dreams*.

When a small, independent company named Max Mambru Films contacted Blades about the film, he knew the story was both promising and appropriate both for him to move forward in the acting world but also to make an important contribution for the Latino community. The story involved a small-time salsa singer from East Harlem named Rudy Veloz who wants to cross over into the American pop market. In his quest he will do anything to get ahead, including abandoning his friends and culture. When he fails, he is left with nothing. The film was created, produced, and performed by Latinos.

Blades told a reporter after the production of the film that the experience with the people of East Harlem had been rewarding beyond anything he could have expected. They welcomed the actors into their homes, fed them, and did anything they could to cooperate. It was a Latino effort, Blades said, "done by ourselves to help ourselves."

Blades talked about the lack of opportunities for Latinos—in the entertainment industry, in politics, and in most areas in which individuals are entrusted with power and influence. "We really don't get that many opportunities because of the way things are structured," Blades said. "We don't have the political clout in this country. So we really don't get that much consideration.... When you look at the majority of films, they revolve around the white experience, and the second most important segment is the English-speaking black experience. When you look at the Latino community, we are not there. We are pretty much in the position blacks used to be in the 50s—we are stereotyped."[17]

For many years, Latino stereotypes had dominated the silver screen. As early as such films as *Toney the Greaser* (1911) and *Rio Grande* (1919), the image of the Latino as an amoral, stupid, violent character was so familiar that for a time some countries, including Mexico, banned such films.

Later, when portrayals of Latinos became softened somewhat and, in some cases, were given a heroic edge, the actors were never Latinos but

Acting Parts that Ruben Blades Would Not Take

In 1984 NBC began a series that became one of the most successful in television history—*Miami Vice.* Innovative and powerful, the series focused on the Miami police department's battle against illicit drugs, prostitution, and other crimes of the underworld. Produced by Michael Mann, the series featured Don Johnson as Detective James "Sonny" Crockett and Philip Michael Thomas as Detective Ricardo Tubbs. For a time the admired Latino actor Edward James Olmos appeared in a supporting role as a detective. Unlike almost all other roles given to Latino actors in Hollywood, Olmos' character portrayed a Latino character in a positive light.

At one time during the series, the producers of Miami Vice approached Ruben Blades about portraying a drug dealer. He refused. So concerned was Blades about the continuing negative roles given to Latino actors and the stereotypes that television and Hollywood were creating about Latino culture and people that he wrote an essay in *The New York Times.* "If you happen to find a Latin character in television nowadays," Blades wrote, "he or she is likely to be a drug dealer, guerilla, pimp, whore, maid, or that perennial favorite, the Latin lover."[1]

Over the course of one six-month period during his career, Blades read fifteen scripts for different shows and turned down all of them. In half of them, he said, they wanted him to be a Colombian coke dealer. In the other half, they wanted him to play a Cuban coke dealer, he said, only half joking. He called on Latino actors and Latino groups to come together to discourage negative stereotyping and to demand respectful portrayals of the Latino community.

---

[1]Ruben Blades, "The Politics behind the Latino's Legacy," *New York Times,* April 19, 1992, p. H31.

Anglos. Paul Muni played the President of Mexico Benito Juarez in 1939; Tyrone Power played Latinos in several films; and in 1952 Marlon Brando played Mexican rebel Emiliano Zapata in *Viva Zapata*.

Blades hoped that such films as *Crossover Dreams* would begin to make a difference in Hollywood, that other mainstream films would begin to portray Latinos in a less demeaning manner, and that Latino actors and actresses themselves would be given greater opportunities in serious roles.

Crossover Dreams appeared at the same time as critical acclaim for *Buscando America* was having a great impact in the music field. The one–two punch of good reviews for both the film and the album fueled Blades' career. Suddenly, he was the subject of newspaper, magazine, radio, and television interviews. The attention gave him increasingly strong platforms to express his views on many subjects, especially the impact of Latino culture, the need for mutual appreciation and cooperation between English- and Spanish-speaking communities, and the obligation of society to help those suffering from discrimination, injustice, and poverty.

While continuing his recording career and concert touring, Blades appeared in director Robert Redford's *The Milagro Beanfield War* (1988), a film based on the award-winning novel by John Nichols.

The story centers on a small agricultural community in northern New Mexico that has fallen victim to the evils of backroom deals between the state government and agribusiness interests. To enable developers to persuade small landowners in Milagro to sell their property, the water for crops has been diverted by an irrigation ditch to the properties of big agricultural interests. When one of the farmers kicks out a valve on the pipeline allowing water to wash over his drought-ridden beanfield, the "war" is under way.

Blades played the part of Sheriff Bernie Montoya, a Latino who tries to keep order but eventually takes a principled stand. Director Redford chose Blades, he said, over about two thousand other actors.

In 1989 Blades wrote the song "Tu y Yo" for Spike Lee's *Do the Right Thing*. A year later he played a hard-nosed bookie of another of Lee's films, *Mo' Better Blues*.

In almost all of the films in which he appeared, Blades played the part of a Latino. In a film directed by and starring Jack Nicholson called *The Two Jakes*, Blades played the character of Michael "Mickey Nice" Weisskopf, a Jewish tough guy who is not quite the unsavory character he would like to think. So convinced was Nicholson that Blades was the right actor for the part that he planned the film's shooting schedule around the musician's touring dates.

Blades delivered a number of impressive performances on television including the part of a death row inmate in HBO's *Dead Man Out*; a part alongside Anthony Hopkins in *One Man's War* (HBO, 1991), a film about repression in Paraguay; and a part as Pepito Abatino, the Sicilian-born gigolo and friend of Josephine Baker in HBO's *The Josephine Baker Story*, a role that garnered him an Emmy nomination.

If for all of his professional life Blades had remained exclusively in the field of music and had accomplished what he had done before the age of forty-five, he still would have been regarded as a singer, songwriter, and bandleader who made an enormous impact. If he had simply been a movie actor, his career would have impressed film historians and the public as worthy of admiration. But in the early 1990s, already a star in both music and acting, Blades took a decidedly different direction.

THE POLITICIAN

Possessed both of a searching intellect and also a driving ambition to make a personal difference in matters of social reform, Blades turned his attention again to the political situation in his native Panama.

In 1989, relations between the United States and Panama had once again exploded into violence. Charging Panamanian leader Manuel Noriega with numerous crimes, such as corruption, drug trafficking, and complicity in the murder of a U.S. Marine officer, U.S. President George Bush, on December 15, 1989, ordered a military strike. For Ruben Blades, this brought back again the memories of seeing U.S. soldiers herding his Panamanian countrymen like cattle in an earlier invasion.

Mainly aimed at Noriega's headquarters in Panama City, the invasion was swift and deadly, with U.S. troops killing more than 200 Panamanian soldiers. Some 300 civilians and 23 U.S. soldiers also lost their lives. Noriega surrendered and was transported to Miami, Florida, where he later stood trial on a host of charges and was sent to prison.

Although he had little use for Noriega, Blades lamented what he saw as an arrogant use of U.S. power against a much smaller nation in its hemisphere. The United States must not be the arbiter of Latin American governments, Blades insisted. He decided to attempt to make a difference in Panamanian affairs.

He decided to use his considerable popularity and fame to help found a new independent political party, one that would speak out for those Panamanians wishful of neither a dictator such as Noriega nor a puppet government established by the United States. "What I propose," Blades said, "is to create what up to this point has been a mythical place: a Latin America that respects and loves itself, is incorruptible, romantic, nationalistic and has a human perception of the needs of the world at large."[18]

He told a reporter that when he was writing songs early in his career in Panama he was not making fifty dollars a month. On the other hand, Blades in the 1990s could make twenty thousand dollars in one concert. "And I started to confront that contradiction and say, 'You know, I'm living better than the people I sing about.' And they made it possible for me to live the way I live, they made it possible for me and my family to escape the dire conditions that most of these people continue to be mired in. So the only way that I found to underscore the sincerity of the work, and to face the responsibility that I felt, was to take to the streets. I mean, you're gonna change the world in the streets. And so abandon the commodity that wealth and fame or whatever gave you and go to the streets now with the people that you claim to care for and try to change something."[19]

In 1991 Blades traveled to Panama and founded the Movemiento Papa Egoró, which translates roughly into Mother Earth Party, or Motherland Party, in the language of the local Choco Indians. The party promised to fight drugs, hunger, and unemployment and expressed concern for ecology and the environment.

Although it had been eighteen years since Blades had resided in Panama, he had kept in touch with friends and associates and had visited the country two or three times a year. So strongly did Blades speak out about political matters in Panama that many of his friends were not surprised at his decision to become so closely and personally involved in politics. A number said that his law degree in Panama and his master's degree from Harvard revealed over the years his ultimate intent of moving into the political arena.

With a number of parties vying for power in Panama, Blades sought to establish a base of support mostly around the young people who not only shared his love of music but the messages in the music. He wrote a campaign song called "The Good Seed," which spoke of the coming change. T-shirts suddenly appeared in Panama featuring crossed maracas and the slogan "The Sound of Triumph." Early in the organization of the party, he told a friend that if the vote were left totally to the kids the party would win handily.

In November 1993, the party nominated Blades to run as the candidate for president. He accepted. For four months Blades, with little money compared with his main rival, Ernesto Balladares, campaigned as hard as he could across the country. At most of the campaign stops, he would deliver a speech encouraging the crowds to restore decent government to Panama; then, on some occasions, he would perform some songs. Two weeks before the election, polls showed Blades running second in a field of seven candidates—and closing the gap.

Some Panamanian politicians charged that Blades had no business returning to interfere in their government. Blades responded to his critics: "A country is not abandoned because we are far from its territory," he said, "a country is abandoned when we remove it from our heart."[20]

He hosted a free concert in Panama City that drew an enormous crowd. He participated in a national television debate, the first ever organized in Panama, and a majority of the observers felt he had won.

Ultimately, the party lacked organizational skills and money. Also, Blades drew cheap political charges that he was a CIA agent, that he was a Communist, that he was a drug addict, and several other attacks, none of which were anything close to the truth. Opponents, including popular Panama boxer Roberto Duran, blasted Blades for his long absence from the country and the idea that an entertainer should take over as the head of the government. He also had to defend the fact that his wife was not a Latino and that the next first lady of Panama if Blades were elected would be a foreigner. Lisa Blades remained in California for most of the campaign.

As Election Day approached, Blades said, "My wife and I understand each other's needs and spaces and silences.... It's very difficult to be here by myself. We used to drink coffee together, work crossword puzzles, walk. I miss our routine." To the complaints that she was a blond, blue-eyed North-American "gringo," Blades said in a speech, "Love is international." "Hearts don't ask for visas."[21]

By the time of the election on May 8, 1994, Blades' popularity could not overcome the many obstacles to his campaign. He came in third in the voting in a field of seven candidates. The Papa Egoró party did manage to win several seats in the national legislature.

RESUMING HIS ENTERTAINMENT CAREER

It did not take long for Blades to move forward after the election. In Panama in 1995, he recorded an album entitled *La Rosa de los Vientos* (The Rose of the Winds)—a nautical term for the intersection of the four points of the compass. "Everything meets there," he said of Panama, "the north and the south and both oceans.[22]

For *La Rosa de los Vientos*, Blades drew on the work of other Panamanian songwriters representing rock, salsa, and other musical forms. Among his songs was one he wrote after reading an anthology of Mayan documents that included a fragment of a priest's invocation. Another was based on a poem he wrote when he was seventeen after stumbling upon a peasant funeral procession. "The father walked up front with a crown of flowers and a small box," Blades recalled, "meaning it was a child. I never forgot that. I've saved it for almost thirty years."[23]

Returning to the United States, Blades was determined to dispel some of the myths and misunderstandings of Latinos long fueled by the movies. He blamed the entertainment industry directly for many of the stereotypes that portrayed Latinos in a consistently menial if not hostile light. "The woman with the fruit on her head, the bum, the drug addict, and the lowlife. All of that I can help change," said Blades, "because I don't fit any of those categories."[24]

In 1997 he found a role that he regarded as a chance to display a character of more substance than the usual Latino on film. The film *The Devil's Own* starred Brad Pitt as an Irish Republican Army terrorist who has traveled to America to purchase weapons. Harrison Ford is a Irish New York cop named Tom O'Meara; Blades plays his partner, Eddie Diaz.

In January 1998, Blades starred on Broadway in Paul Simon's musical, *The Capeman*. The musical was based on an event in New York City history involving a Puerto Rican teenager named Salvador Agron—known as "The Capeman" because of the cape he wore—who was convicted in 1959 and sentenced to death for killing two white members of a rival gang.

Blades remembered the case well from newspaper accounts. At the age of sixteen, Agron was sentenced to the electric chair. The governor of New York at the time, Nelson Rockefeller, commuted the sentence to life imprisonment. While in prison, Agron found religion, poetry, and education and turned into a model prisoner. He was eventually paroled.

Despite a large budget and praise for its moving score and magnificent sets, the play closed within two months. New York's Latino community lauded its fair treatment of the subject, a tribute not only to the producers of the show but to Blades as well. But the subject matter was apparently too controversial, too much anchored in the city's fears and strains, to attract a large number of theatergoers anxious for a pleasant musical night at the theater.

Blades enjoyed immensely his role as Mexican artist Diego Rivera in *Cradle Will Rock* (1999), which pitted his character's communist sensibilities against those of New York Governor Nelson Rockefeller. Directed by Tim Robbins, *Cradle Will Rock* was a film woven of several stories. The principal story involves Governor Nelson Rockefeller, played by John Cusack, who commissions Mexican artist Diego Rivera (Blades) to paint a mural in the lobby of Rockefeller Center in New York.

This was a role particularly rooted in Blades' own personality and inclinations, the kind of role that enabled him to concentrate on a multi-talented Latino figure. He determined to get into the mind and spirit of Rivera, to study extensively the life of the famous and politically controversial painter. "Right before I started shooting, I figured out how to physically portray Rivera," says Blades. "It was something I did that had to do with the position of my head and something I did with my face. It was important to find the balance of the character. There are some scenes where Rivera is very funny, and others where his seriousness comes through and he's very upset at what's being done. Rivera was a very complex person and it was a lot of fun to play him that way."[25]

Asked about his appreciation of Rivera, Blades said, "The strongest similarity between Rivera and I is that we were both artists and politically involved. We both believed in the necessity to work without any censorship and defended the idea of giving opportunities to the disenfranchised."[26]

Blades's later records became more world-inspired, exploring Celtic, Arabic, and Hindu musical influences. On *Tiempos*, released in 1999, Blades collaborated with the Costa Rican jazz group Editus. The album resulted in a Latin sound that was filled out with classical European music.

For his album called *Mundo*, Blades won a Latin Grammy Award for Best Contemporary Tropical Album in 2002. The album was something of a journey. There were songs about the Caribbean, songs with African beats, a Brazilian piece that moved from a ballad to the swing of a samba, American jazz, and even, in a tribute to victims of the September 11 tragedy, his rendition of Ireland's beloved "Danny Boy." He originally conceived of the work as a way to marry Irish and Latin sounds, but ended up making "a kind of map, where I began in the Northeast part of Africa, from Ethiopia, and I took that path to Asia Minor," he is quoted as saying in Billboard. "I crossed part of Turkey, what today are independent Russian republics. I crossed toward Europe and then I jumped to America. During that voyage, I integrated these sounds." After the release of *Tiempos*, Blades performed in sold-out venues all over the world.[27]

Editor and writer Richard Byrne wrote, "Since its explosion as a Latin musical force in the 1970s, salsa has become the sound sensation that conquered listeners all over the world." Blades's album, Byrne wrote, "is a musical excursion that combines his salsa roots and concerns for justice with a willingness to seek out new influences and sounds.... On *Mundo*, Ruben Blades's willingness to take the listener to new and exotic locales results in a wonderful record that can truly be labeled as 'global.'"[28]

In September 2004, the life of Ruben Blades once again veered sharply. He accepted a cabinet-level position as minister of tourism in the new Panamanian government led by President Martin Torrijos. In his campaign, Torrijos, who was educated in the United States, appealed to younger Panamanians to promote a strengthening of democracy, human rights, and a freer association with the United States. Blades saw in Torrijos' campaign much of the same enthusiasm for change for which he had stood in his own run for the presidency of Panama. And so, with Torrijos' victory, Blades became a suit-wearing government employee. Not surprisingly, he made the most of it.

"The bureaucracy drives me crazy," he admitted. "I didn't have a boss for, like, thirty years. But I feel that I am trying my best to help my country ... I'm also very down to earth so that people feel that they are accessible to me. I mean, it's very interesting, people call me by my first name when they meet me. Or even people when we've never been introduced. They say, "Hey, Ruben, como esta? How are you, Ruben?" Whether it is the doorman down there, or the cab driver. So that is, I think, the best. The sense of access to the world. That is the best. And that, to me, is the most important thing because anything else is ... you know, you're not going to take that. The material stuff, you're not going to take with you."[29]

A number of initiatives he pursued as Minister of Tourism reflected his personal commitment to civil rights and social justice. He launched one program to train young gang members from the streets of the neighborhood where he grew up in the historic center of Panama City.

As he steered Panama's $1.2 billion tourism industry and wrestled with negotiations, contracts, and legislation, he never lost any of his passion for music. He had new ideas for songs, for new approaches.

He also remarried. His new wife was Luba Mason, a native New Yorker of Slovakian descent, whom he had met in 1998 on the set of *The Capeman*.

In 2007, El Ministro, as he became known in Panama, performed on stage in public for the first time since his appointment. The occasion was Panama's reenergized carnival celebration, which featured an international summit of salsa groups Blades helped organize.

As he completed his position in the Panamanian government, Blades prepared for another return to his entertainment career, one that had, by 2007, included some thirty-two films, twenty albums, seven Grammys, and hundreds of songs. Once again, he looked forward to new discoveries in his cultural and artistic journey.

He talked about his 1978 song "Buscando Guayaba" (Looking for the Guava), which is about life as an endless search. "We're never satisfied," he says, "but to feel dissatisfied you have to have a notion of what you want and what you can attain. As long as you feel restless, you're never going to reach it. That's the problem of the creative spirit. So I hope to always feel restless, because the day I stop will be the day my creativity runs out."[30]

SELECTED RECORDED MUSIC

Blades, Ruben. *Buscando América*. Elektra, 1984. CD.
Blades, Ruben. *Escenas*. Elektra, 1985. CD.
Blades, Ruben. *Nothing but the Truth*. Elektra, 1988. CD.
Blades, Ruben. *Rubén Blades y Seis del Solar ... Live!* Asylum, 1990. CD.
Blades, Ruben. *Caminando*. Discos CBS International, 1991. CD.
Blades, Ruben. *The Best*. Fania, 2001. CD.
Blades, Ruben. *Mundo*. Sony BMG, 2002. CD.
Blades, Ruben. *The Best of Ruben Blades*. Snapper UK, 2004. CD.
Blades, Ruben. *Cali Concert*. Immortal, 2006. DVD.
Blades, Ruben. *Live! In Concert*. Via Sonido, 2006. DVD.
Blades, Ruben and Son del Solar. *Amor y Control*. Discos CBS International, 1992. CD.
Colón, Willie, and Blades, Ruben. *Siembra*. Fania, 1978. CD.

SELECTED MOVIES AND TELEVISION

The Last Fight. Directed by Fred Williamson. Best Film & Video Corp., 1983.
Crossover Dreams. Directed by Leon Ichaso. CF Inc., 1985.
Homeboy. Directed by Michael Seresin. Twentieth Century-Fox, 1988.
The Milagro Beanfield War. Directed by Robert Redford. Esparza, 1988.

Heart of the Deal. Directed by Marina Levikova and Yuri Neyman. Chanticleer Films, 1990.
Mo' Better Blues. Directed by Spike Lee. 40 Acres & A Mule Filmworks, 1990.
The Two Jakes. Directed by Jack Nicholson. 88 Productions, 1990.
Crazy from the Heart. Directed by Thomas Schlamme. De Mann Entertainment, 1991.
One Man's War. Directed by Sergio Toledo. Channel 4 Television, 1991.
The Super. Directed by Rod Daniel. JVC Entertainment, 1991.
Miracle on Interstate 880. Directed by Robert Iscove. Columbia Pictures, 1993.
Color of Night. Directed by Richard Rush. Cinergi Pictures, 1994.
The Devil's Own. Directed by Alan J. Pakula. Columbia Pictures, 1997.
Cradle Will Rock. Directed by Tim Robbins. Cradle Productions, 1999.
All the Pretty Horses. Directed by Billie Bob Thornton. Columbia Pictures, 2000.
"Gideon's Crossing," ABC television series (2000–2001).
Assassination Tango. Directed by Robert Duvall. American Zoetrope, 2002.
Imagining Argentina. Directed by Christopher Hampton. Multivideo, 2003.
The Maldonado Miracle. Directed by Salma Hayek. Showtime Networks, 2003.
Once Upon a Time in Mexico. Directed by Robert Rodriguez. Columbia Pictures, 2003.
Secuestro Express. Directed by Jonathan Jacubowicz. Miramax, 2005.

NOTES

1. Guy Garcia, "Singer, Actor, Politico," *Time,* January 29, 1990, http://www.time.com/time/magazine/article/0,9171,969275-1,00.html.
2. Bruce Polin, "Interview: A Visit with Ruben Blades, Part 1," 1996, http://www.descarga.com/cgi-bin/db/archives/Interview6.
3. Stephen Holden, "Ruben Blades Turns His Talents to Movies," *New York Times*, August 18, 1965, H16.
4. "The 'Day of the Martyrs'—January 9, 1964," http://www.maestravida.com/january9/january9.html.
5. Anthony DePalma, "Ruben Blades: Up From Salsa," *New York Times Magazine,* June 21, 1987, 30.
6. Polin.
7. Robert A. Parker, "The Vision of Ruben Blades," *Americas,* English Edition, March-April 1985, 16.
8. "Hispanic Heritage: Ruben Blades," http://www.gale.com/freeresources/chh/bio/blades_r.htm.
9. Polin.
10. Polin.
11. Holden.
12. DePalma.
13. Garcia.
14. "The Nobel Prize for Literature, 1982," http://nobelprize.org/nobel_prizes/literature/laureates/1982/.
15. DePalma.

16. DePalma.

17. Robin Davies: "Ruben Blades: "Musician and Man for the People," http:// www.salsasf.com/features/articles/blades00.html.

18. Garcia.

19. Bruce Polin, "Interview: A Visit with Ruben Blades, Part 2," 1996, http:// www. descarga.com/cgi-bin/db/archives/Interview7.

20. Ruben Blades, Updated September 2005. "Ruben Blades," *Contemporary Hispanic Biography*, Volume 3. Gale Group, 2003, http://gale.cengage.com/free_ resources/chh/bio/blades_r.htm.

21. Meg Grant. "Panama's favorite son: salsa's Ruben Blades is a man with a plan—to be president." *People Weekly,* May 9, 1994.

22. Sean Mitchell, "Crossover candidate," *Los Angeles Magazine,* September 1995, 145.

23. Mitchell.

24. Garcia.

25. Elizabeth Hunter, "Ruben Blades in 'Cradle Will Rock,'" *La Prenza, San Diego,* December 17, 1999, http://www.laprensa-sandiego.org/archieve/dec17/ cradle.htm.

26. Hunter.

27. "Ruben Blades, Updated …"

28. Richard Byrne, "Salsa Conquistador," *The Globalist,* November 2, 2002. http://www.theglobalist.com/DBWeb/StoryId.aspx?StoryId=2826

29. Polin interview, Part 2.

30. Agustin Gurza, "Ending his Tour of Political Duty; Ruben Blades Returns to Music after a Trying Mission in Panama," *Los Angeles Times,* March 4, 2007, F12.

FURTHER READING

DePalma, Anthony. "Ruben Blades: Up from salsa." *New York Times Magazine*, June 21, 1987, 24–31.

Free Resources: Hispanic Heritage: Biographies: Rubén Blades. Available at http:// gale.cengage.com/free_resources/chh/bio/blades_r.htm.

Garcia, Guy. "Singer, Actor, Politico." *Time*, January 29, 1990, 70–72 Available at http://www.time.com/time/magazine/article/0,9171,969275-1,00.html.

Garza, Agustin. "Ending his tour of political duty; Ruben Blades returns to music after a trying mission in Panama." *Los Angeles Times,* March 4, 2007, p. F12.

Mitchell, Sean. "Crossover candidate." *Los Angeles Magazine,* September 1995, 145.

Polin, Bruce, "Interview: A visit with Ruben Blades, Parts 1 and 2," 1996 Available at http://www.descarga.com/cgi-bin/db/archives/Interview6; http://www.descarga. com/cgi-bin/db/archives/Interview7.

Fabiola Cabeza de Baca

The plains of northeastern New Mexico and northwestern Texas are called the Llano or great plateau. Hispanic ranchers and homesteaders settled the land for many generations before New Mexico became a state in 1912. They herded sheep and cattle, hunted buffalo, established small communities, built churches and schools, traded with and fought Indians, and left a rich cultural heritage.

One of the most prominent and well-respected families on the Llano had the surname of Cabeza de Baca. The family was one of those that had acquired grants of land from the Spanish government, those that represented the aristocracy on the Spanish frontier in America. Many amassed fortunes, lived in haciendas similar to plantations in the American south, and owned slaves. In the 1870s, three of the Cabeza de Baca brothers, from an area known as Upper Las Vegas, owned sheep herds that totaled more than half a million head.

Origin of the Name Cabeza de Baca

The Cabeza de Baca family produced a wealth of notable figures. The most well known of the individuals through the centuries was Alvar Nuñez Cabeza de Vaca, a famous Spanish explorer who sailed to North America in 1527. Part of an expedition of nearly 300 men, Cabeza de Vaca was only one of four who survived hurricanes, battles with Native Americans, and enslavement. For ten years he wandered from west Florida to the Colorado River and eventually to Mexico City, returning to Spain in 1537.

The unusual name, which, in its early form, meant "Head of Cow," has been the subject of much genealogical research. The most accepted story is traced to the year 1212 and a man by the name of Alhaja, a peasant shepherd. A few days before the critical battle of Las Navas de Tolosa in Andalusia on July 11, 1212, in which the kings of Castile, Aragon, and Navarro fought off the Moors, Alhaja offered to show the Christian forces a path through the mountainous region held by the Moors. To indicate the path, he placed at the entrance the skull of a cow.

After the victory, King Alfonso VIII rewarded Alhaja with a coat of arms that included cow skulls in its design. His name was now Cabeza de Vaca. Generations later, after Alva Cabeza de Vaca's adventures in North America, another gentleman of the family, Luis Maria Baca, one of whose lineal descendants was Fabiola Cabeza de Baca, was awarded a large grant of land in what is now New Mexico.

By the time of the land grants, the name had been changed from Cabeza de Vaca to Cabeza de Baca. The spelling change, genealogists and historians surmise, occurred because the descendants wanted to rid the family name of the reference to cows.

A girl named Fabiola Cabeza de Baca was born into one of the families in 1894. Unlike many of her aristocratic friends and neighbors, she was hardly content to live out her life on the riches of the family.

She became a teacher in small schools among the poor of New Mexico. For more than thirty years she worked as an agricultural extension agent for the federal government, teaching and assisting poor families trying to make a life on the frontier. Along the way, she roamed the mountains, valleys, and plains of the Llano, eagerly collecting folklore from the Latino culture—from food recipes to language to music.

She became a respected writer, providing insight and sensitivity to the mores and life experiences of her own family and of those less fortunate. She wrote the first definitive description of Indian-Hispanic cooking techniques in the upper Rio Grande. She recorded oral narratives, family histories, and poetry, and she left a remarkable account of the early Spanish influence in the American southwest.

Among Latinos at the time, from those who used her cookbooks to those who treasured the stories of her Spanish heritage, she was an important link to their own cultural past. She became a beloved figure. She became, as some historians have said, "virtually a legend in her own lifetime."[1]

ARISTOCRACY ON THE FRONTIER

The Cabeza de Baca family can trace its ancestry back to Alvar Nuñez Cabeza de Vaca, who explored New Mexico in the 1530s. Fabiola's paternal great-grandfather, Don Luis Maria Cabeza de Baca, held title to the Las Vegas Grandes land grant of a half million acres, which he acquired in 1823.

In the eighteenth century, the Llano had been a formidable natural barrier that separated the Spanish settlements along the Rio Grande River from the French settlements along the tributaries of the Mississippi River. Although buffalo hunters and Indian traders ventured into the Llano in these early years, it was not until the sheep herders and cattle drivers appeared in the rugged land that the vast isolation began to yield to a coming migration. It was this place and this era that shaped the young girl's life.

Fabiola's father, Graciano Cabeza de Baca, was born on December 18, 1867, to Tomas Cabeza de Baca and Estefana Delgado. Fabiola's mother, Indalecia, married Graciano Cabeza de Baca on January 28, 1892, at San Ysidro Labrador de Chaperito. Indalecia died in December 1898 at the age of twenty-four, leaving four small children: Luis Maria, Fabiola, Guadalupe, and Virginia.

After her mother's death, Fabiola, now age four, was brought up on the family ranch. "As a child," she wrote, "I lived with my paternal grandparents on their hacienda across the Gallinas river from the village of La

Liendre, eighteen miles southeast of Las Vegas. This, our ancestral home, was the stopping place for all who made the trips into the Ceja and the Llano to oversee their large sheep and cattle holdings. In this environment, the history of the country was imprinted on my mind from early childhood."[2]

As the primary market for the cattlemen and sheepherders from the Llano country, Las Vegas was the most prominent town in the territory. In her youth, Fabiola recalled, Santa Fe and Albuquerque were mere villages.

Fabiola described the house of her childhood: "Our home at La Liendre was a modern two-story structure. Every room had a fireplace with ornate black moulding. The house was built on a hill and below it were the orchard, the well, which supplied us with domestic water, a large cottonwood and poplar park, with the Gallinas River running close by. The village was across the river and most of the men worked for grandfather on the farm and others were on the Ceja (ridge) with the sheep and cattle."[3]

Fabiola's grandfather, Tomas Cabeza de Baca, and his family grazed 15,000 head of sheep and 2,000 head of cattle. They had large holdings of horses, hired teams of men to hunt buffalo, and hauled trading goods over the Santa Fe Trail. In addition to the large herds of sheep and cattle, the family farm produced a variety of fruits and vegetables—apples, peaches, pears, alfalfa, wheat, corn, barley, and beans.

Fabiola remembered her grandfather as a generous and kind gentleman, not given to pretension or power. She remembered him eating with his workers and greeting travelers and friends with graciousness. She remembered traveling with Tomas on his trips to Las Vegas in a large carriage drawn by two horses. Fabiola also remembered winter evenings around the fireplace, when Tomas read aloud or discussed everything from *Don Quixote* to *Les Miserables* while her grandmother Estefana quilted.

Fabiola remembered the strong influence in her early years of her grandmother. Stern, religious, and industrious, she taught her granddaughters to cook and sew. She was a tough pioneer. Her grandmother was also a *curandera*, or healer. Although not officially a doctor, she was often called upon by local families to treat family members. She grew some medicinal herbs and gathered others on the prairie land. There were no formally trained doctors within two hundred miles of the Cabeza de Baca hacienda during Fabiola's childhood. She later wrote that her grandmother, like other women throughout the prairies, often filled that role. "Every village had its *curandera* or *medica* versed in the curative powers of plants and in midwifery," she said. Knowledge of plant medicine had been handed down by the Moors in Spain and brought to New Mexico by the Spanish settlers through the generations. Fabiola's grandmother had been given that information from her family members; she passed much of it along to Fabiola. At an early age, the young girl learned the names of "herbs, weeds, and plants that have curative potency."[4] During the occasional yet widespread outbreaks of deadly smallpox, Estefana traveled from ranch to ranch attempting to convince wary farmers and ranchers to have their families vaccinated. Every year, she procured vaccine from her cousin, a doctor in El Paso.

The Cabeza de Bacas belonged to a wealthy Spanish elite class. Women did not perform manual labor. Estefana spent much of her time engaging in charity work and supervising the house servants who cooked and cleaned. Doña Estefana was also a gifted storyteller, Fabiola recalled, who held the rapt attention of all friends and family members as she reminisced about the early days of the family on the Llano.

Fiercely independent and energetic, Fabiola tried as much as possible to escape the aristocratic roles that she felt were constantly holding her back. Often as a young child, she, in a limited way, went missing, chased around the ranch with her grandmother and others in hot pursuit. Her father did allow her to ride the range on occasion and help during branding time. Nevertheless, although she had her own pony, she longed for greater freedom.

"True to my aristocratic rearing," she wrote, "I had to lead a ladylike life and should not resemble that of our uncouth neighbors whose women were able to do men's work. I always envied any woman who could ride a bronco, but in my society it was not done. How skillfully they saddled a horse! I often watched them catch a pony out in the pasture, just as the men did on our range, but it never was my privilege to have to do it. When I arose each morning, my horse was already saddled and tied to a hitching post, waiting for me if I cared to ride.[5]

When the children were of school age, Estefana insisted that the family move into town. "Grandmother had never been happy at the hacienda," Fabiola recalled. "She was a very tired person.... For grandfather it was a hard decision but grandmother did not give him time to change his mind. She started disposing of furniture and other possessions." Fabiola's father continued to run the ranch.[6]

Estefana and the children took up residence in a large stone mansion in Las Vegas. Estefana enrolled Fabiola in the Loretto Academy, a Catholic school run by the Sisters of Loretto. Fabiola's education at Loretto did not last. During her first year, the rambunctious youngster on one occasion slapped one of the nuns—Fabiola left the school for a time.

In 1906, when she was twelve, the family decided to send her for a year to Spain to study Spanish and history at the Centro de Estudios Historicos. It was the first of several visits to Spain that she would make during her lifetime. She finished high school in 1913. True to the spirit of independence that had marked her personality from her earliest days, Fabiola Cabeza de Baca wanted desperately to break out of the traditional mold of women within the aristocratic class. At the age of 21, she became a schoolteacher.

ONE-ROOM SCHOOLS

As remote areas of the American West began slowly to fill up with home-steaders and other pioneer families, small, one-room schoolhouses began to dot the prairie landscape. Those schools desperately needed teachers.

In 1916, Fabiola left the homestead and took a job in a one-room school in rural Guadalupe County, just six miles from the family but several hours ride on horseback from the closest town. She boarded with a local family who gave her a room and meals for twelve dollars a month.

She was now among people who had to scrape and fight for existence on the plains. Children in the area mostly worked on the farms or ranches to help their parents earn subsistence wages. If they were fortunate, the children would attend school for half a year. Most of the teachers did not even have an eighth grade education; many had not completed grammar school.

"When one of the school directors came to solicit me to teach school in our school district," Cabeza de Baca wrote, "I felt privileged. Papa was not so sure that it was the proper thing for me to do and it took a great deal of pleading to gain his consent. In giving it, he stressed that if I signed a contract I had to live up to it and, whether I liked it or not, I had to stay the full seven months. He was certain that after I found out what the environment held for me I would repent, but I was determined to keep my word."[7]

She was one a number of young Latina women who began to teach school in rural New Mexico. All of them were bilingual and had at least an eighth grade education. They became a cadre of newly independent female professionals who began to break away from their prescribed roles on the frontier. The talent of improvising was critical for teachers on the frontier, and Fabiola proved more than adequate. She was eager and able to succeed in this atmosphere, one so foreign to her own background and upbringing. Those six miles from the Cabeza de Baca homestead might as well have been hundreds of miles.

The school in Guadalupe amounted to little more than four rock walls with four narrow windows and some desks, an oilcloth black board, some older books very much out of date, and a few supplies. The teacher's desk, she noticed, was held together by bailing wire. The schoolhouse had neither a bathroom nor running water.

On one of her trips home, Cabeza de Baca mentioned to her father that the school did not even have a privy. When her father told one of the school directors that he would pay for a privy, the director told him it was not nec-essary—there were enough juniper trees close by the school.

The children came to school mostly on foot, some from several miles dis-tant. A few rode horseback or buggies. On one of her first days at the school, the children helped clean out the building, wash the desks, and remove debris from the schoolyard. During that normal routine at the be-ginning of the school year, the group encountered a sound that even the most hardened western pioneer had to take seriously—the distinctive rattle of a rattlesnake. A well-aimed blow with a hoe took care of the snake. The blow was administered not by the teacher, who later said she had had the fright of her life, but by one of the students. This teaching assignment was, indeed, the beginning of a new experience for the daughter of a wealthy rancher. But, as her life unfolded, Fabiola Cabeza de Baca was never one to turn away from challenges.

Along with other teachers in the early nineteenth century, Fabiola confronted the problems associated with classrooms made up of a distinct division of students who spoke separate languages. Educators would wrestle with the problem for generations—should all students be expected to speak English or should teachers accommodate the Spanish-speaking students with bilingual texts and presentations?

Fabiola disagreed with the notion that teachers should attempt to suppress the native tongue of Spanish-speaking students. She saw the effort to enforce English-only classes as a nefarious, misguided, and lazy way to address the problem, and a sure way to rob young people of their valuable cultural heritage. "It was a mixed school," she recalled. "There were the children of the homesteaders, the children of parents of Spanish extraction and children with Indian blood but of the Spanish tongue.... We had bilingual readers for the primary grades. These were adopted texts of that day. In this way, the English-speaking children and the Spanish-speaking learned English."[8] Her students sang folk songs in Spanish and cowboy ballads in English. Americanization of the students, she believed, should instill the traditions and joys of a variety of lands and cultures.

As teachers across the United States have always found, the school materials furnished for their use were not sufficient. For a teacher on the frontier, the supplies did not come close to meeting the needs. In her case, Fabiola used her own money to purchase most of the school materials.

At first, Fabiola had fifteen students. As word about the new teacher spread to outlying areas, however, a number of other parents decided they could spare the work of the youngsters on the ranches for periods of time. They took the opportunity to provide the children with a quality educational experience, and soon other children began to arrive at the schoolhouse with the bilingual teacher who had at least a high school education.

If the children were receiving the best possible grammar school learning experience that the New Mexico frontier could offer, their teacher was also learning a bounty of information that would become invaluable to her as her life and career progressed. From the youngsters she learned food habits, customs, religious practices, medical needs, folkways, and family traditions. She learned much valuable information about the cultural mores and beliefs of people who had come from very different circumstances—Anglos, Latinos, and many with mixed blood or mestizo backgrounds. She learned how the homesteaders faced the drought years on the plains and how they tried to deal with their own poverty. She learned how few of the children had been exposed to books and how little they knew about the world outside of the life on the Llano.

Fabiola recognized early on that the children in this rural setting desperately needed basic information about history and geography, about the lives of people far away and long ago, about opportunities and sights beyond the lonely horizon of their plateau in northwestern New Mexico. She was determined to locate for them this spot on the globe, at this time in history and with all the culture and tradition surrounding it, especially its historical relationship to the Spanish explorers and settlers. By the end of the first year, she believed, the sixth graders in her school likely knew more about Mexico and Central and South America than the average high school graduate in the United States.

At the end of her first year, Fabiola looked back with a great sense of accomplishment. "We had only one more week of school after Easter and it was with deep regret that I bade goodbye to the children. As I look back to my first year of teaching, I know I have never been happier and I have never been among people who were more hospitable, genuine, and wholesome than those who lived on the Ceja."[9]

Fabiola taught school for the next ten years in various small towns in New Mexico, including Santa Rosa, the county seat of Guadalupe County, and at a Spanish-language school started in El Rita by Venceslao Jaramillo, a wealthy land- and storeowner and later state senator from Rio Arriba County. Fabiola began taking summer classes at New Mexico Normal (later New Mexico Highlands) in Las Vegas. She earned a Bachelor of Arts degree in Pedagogy and minored in Romance languages.

While pursuing her degree at New Mexico Normal, Fabiola also absorbed considerable information about home economics, or what was then called "domestic science." Many years later, she spoke to a group of graduates in home economics at New Mexico Highlands and said that the introduction she received had been invaluable. It encompassed "foods, clothing, home management, art appreciation, house planning, home nursing, child care, interior decoration, chemistry of food and nutrition, textiles, and perhaps some others." Fabiola would later pursue the subject in even more detail at another university, and it would eventually form the basis for much of her later career.[10]

Few American women in the early part of the twentieth century, of any part of the country or from any ethnic group, became college graduates. For a bilingual Latina woman to achieve such academic success, especially in the American West, was very rare. After her graduation from college, Fabiola spent another year in Spain engaging in genealogical work at El Centro de Estudios Historicos in Madrid. Here she traced much of the prodigious records of her prominent family's origins. She would pass on this extraordinarily valuable information to historians, genealogists, and family members.

When Fabiola returned from Spain, she again taught at the school in El Rita and was assigned the course in home economics. As she had read much literature on the subject and after her years of working with students whose families mostly worked the land, she began to see the potential to assist families in New Mexico to embrace newer methods of home economics, including various advances in efficiency and food preservation. To bolster her background in these subjects, Fabiola returned again to New Mexico Normal to take additional classes in food, clothing, and chemistry. In 1927 she moved to Las Cruces, New Mexico, and entered New Mexico State University. In 1929 Fabiola earned a second Bachelor of Arts degree, this time in home economics.

A new career now lay ahead. For Fabiola the academic credentials were anything but a dilettantish exercise undertaken to pass the time and make impressions. Since the days when she completed her high school education, her path had been sharply distinctive, aimed at a purpose—to prepare her to make a special contribution to the lives of those born into much less favored circumstances.

ON THE ROAD TO TEACH FARMERS

In 1914, the United States Congress passed the Smith-Lever Act and President Woodrow Wilson signed it into law. The law established the Cooperative Extension Service, an agency dedicated to teach small farmers in rural areas the latest agricultural technology and to teach home economics to women and girls.

In the American South, the boll weevil infestation and generations of agricultural practices that left much of the land eroded and unfertile had taken their toll. Through a cadre of "Home Extension Agents," the Service was a means by which the federal government could make a positive impact on the often isolated communities they served, many of which lacked telephones, electrical services, or even mail delivery. The Extension Service hired agents to work in rural areas across the country. Many of those agents were women. They organized clubs that provided training in nutrition, hygiene, and child rearing.

This was not the first time that the U.S. government, cooperating with county and state governments, had made efforts to bring the latest technology and methods to rural America. As early as 1862, President Abraham Lincoln, in establishing both the United States Department of Agriculture and the land grant college system, provided for instruction in agricultural and home economics through those colleges. By the end of the nineteenth century, the Department of Agriculture and the land grant colleges were working together to establish programs for agricultural research and guidance. Also, the government provided annual federal funding for agricultural experiment stations in all states. Through these efforts, the government sought to improve the productivity of the farms, build the economy, and help local communities.

Fabiola Cabeza de Baca joined the Extension Service in New Mexico in 1929. She began to work among farm families at the age of thirty-five. In addition to working with Hispanic families, her responsibilities included Indian pueblos such as Chimayo and Ildefonso. She was the first demonstration agent assigned to such Native American villages.

First, Fabiola took a two-month orientation course, traveling with veteran agents in San Miguel County. The experience, she said, gave her a concept of the vastness of the territory for which she would have responsibility. It also was a sobering introduction to the overall needs of the people and gave her a sense of what might be accomplished. Even as she looked ahead ten years, she said, the challenges seemed so great that she feared how little could be accomplished in relation to the problems.

Early on, Fabiola believed that the extension work would be an exchange in which she learned as well as taught, just as in her first years of working as a schoolteacher on the plains. Through her studies, Fabiola had gained a sizable amount of book learning and laboratory instruction in the arts and sciences of home economics. Nevertheless, she lacked experience in the normal, everyday activities of women working on farms and ranches.

"My qualifications as a home demonstration agent were anything but adequate," she recalled. "My father had always had a home garden, yet I had never as much as gathered a vegetable. I learned ranch cooking from the men, but horseback riding was more interesting." She recalled, with some amusement, that at one time in her youth, the ranch hands had left her to do the breakfast dishes, and she had decided instead to go for a ride. When she returned, someone had set the dirty plates and flatware and cooking utensils in a line, leading through the yard out to the well. "The poor dishes were thirsty and started out for relief," her brother told her.[11]

Although Fabiola humorously mocked her own skills and knowledge that she brought to the Extension Service, those who sought her employment had far different views. Not a single one of their agents spoke Spanish. Sixty percent of New Mexico's population was Spanish; more than half of the entire population and most rural women spoke no English. Fabiola brought an entirely new dimension as one of New Mexico's agents.

Before she set out for her first forays as an extension agent, there was one crucial skill that she needed to master. She had to learn to drive a car. For this necessity she turned to her father. He bought her a car and for several weeks taught her to drive. The roads she would traverse in driving from farm to farm had not been created for automobiles but for horses or carriages. In New Mexico, especially, she faced rough terrain. Also, the distances were daunting. When she began her work with the Extension Service, the entire state of New Mexico had not yet reached a million people. Some of the counties in the state were larger in area than many of the entire states in the East. In New Mexico, she joked, people talked about so many miles to a person rather than so many persons to a mile. "The roads which I had to travel were country wagon trails," she wrote. "There were arroyos to cross, no bridges. When it rained, often I had to wait hours for the water to subside in order to cross them. Many times I had to walk miles to get help when my car had stuck in the mud or slipped on ice into a rut. Cars could not travel over thirty-five miles an hour, which meant starting at sun up to make the communities in which work had been planned."[12]

She began her post in Rio Arriba and Santa Fe Counties. From dawn until midnight, she drove from farm to farm armed with an ever-increasing store of knowledge and a pressure cooker. When she arrived in Rio Arriba in 1929, the many women she visited on her rounds had long grown fruit, vegetables, and meats. They preserved meats by drying techniques that had been handed down for generations. Farmers also grew nutritious beans and chili peppers, and in early spring they gathered from the hillsides edible plants such as pigweed, waco, and chimaja. But they had never been introduced to the art of canning.

By all accounts, the practice of canning proved critical to the survival of many families when a severe drought hit the area in the mid-1930s. J. W. Ramirez, one of Fabiola's fellow extension agents, reported that the year 1934 "would have been one of the worst calamities ever experienced had it not been for timely financial aid from the Agricultural Drought Service and the food preservation program." More than 90 percent of the families in Rio Arriba had preserved enough food the previous year to survive in 1934. The survival of Rio Arriba County, along with neighboring Santa Fe and Taos, was a success story built on the cooperative work of state and federal agencies in providing crucial services.[13]

None of the families she visited had pressure cookers either. Gradually, with the instruction she offered, families began to set aside money for the utensil and began to preserve food. By 1935, thousands of pressure cookers sat in the kitchens of farm families in Rio Arriba. Fabiola also helped families acquire sewing machines. She made information available to families who spoke little English. With increasing visits to Pueblo Indians and other Native Americans, she began to learn enough of the Tewa and Towa dialects to communicate effectively with them.

Fabiola saw her job as one of reaching out to those in need while at the same time respecting their cultural values and incorporating those traditions in adapting to an increasingly Anglo world in rural New Mexico. It was Fabiola, many people remembered years later, who first taught them that beans and tortillas are not just "poor people's food" but ancient and nutritional staples of the New World. As her experiences with people on the frontier increased, the American-trained nutritionist was able to connect scientific principles with the cultural values and traditions of regional ethnic cuisine.

Fabiola founded a number of associations and clubs for women and children. She wrote of her experiences in trying to organize women in Rio

Arriba to join together for social events. "Outside of dances, church festivals, and weddings, they never get together for social activities ... they may not have accomplished very much materially, but they have gained much spiritually. It has started them to think along the social side of life." One of women with whom Fabiola worked said, "If we have an excuse to leave our work for one day a month, we ought to take advantage of it even if it is only to get away from the work."[14]

A devout Catholic, Fabiola once wrote that in Spanish New Mexican society marriage was as much a matter of obeying the wishes of parents as it was a matter of personal preference. Although the practice of arranged marriages was a thing of the past in aristocratic circles, children would not consider marrying someone not preferred by the father and mother. In 1931, Fabiola again showed her fierce independence. She eloped with a man named Carlos Gilbert, an insurance agent and political activist in the League of United Latin American Citizens (LULAC). A divorced father of two, Gilbert would have been an unacceptable choice for Fabiola's family.

The LULAC was formed in 1929 in Corpus Christi, Texas, a merger of three organizations devoted to the protection of the rights of Mexican Americans. In Texas and in other states in the Southwest, it was not uncommon to see signs with the words "We Serve Whites Only—No Spanish or Mexicans." Like the treatment meted out to American blacks, it was not unusual to read of murders of Mexican-American citizens that went unpunished. It was not uncommon to see signs at water fountains that prohibited their use by Latinos.

Early in the 1920s, men and women began organizing in Texas, filing suits to have Mexican Americans placed on jury rosters. They started to champion Mexican-American rights of self-determination and equal justice. Some of the members of these early organizations called for the violent overthrow of the system. They were branded as socialists and communists. The formation of the LULAC was a victory for those activists who wished to work within the system for peaceable change. The LULAC would become the largest Mexican-American self-help organization in the United States. It would still be active in the twenty-first century. The LULAC, from its earliest days, encouraged the participation of women in its activities. It also quickly spread to other states in the Southwest. In 1938, its president was from New Mexico.

After her marriage, Fabiola increasingly identified with Hispanic civil rights. She served as a trustee for the LULAC and as president of the Santa Fe Ladies Council of a local chapter of the group. In 1939, she was the director of Junior LULACs for the New Mexico region. Along with her husband Carlos, she served in many leadership positions in the LULAC.

Although Carlos and Fabiola shared the same passionate views about the rights of Latinos, their marriage struggled. Much of the difficulty arose from the nature of Fabiola's work and the long, difficult periods on the road. The time they spent together was severely limited. They would eventually separate. They had no children.

In 1932, Cabeza de Baca suffered an accident that for many individuals would have been career ending. While on one of her assignments for the Extension Service, she accidentally drove her car onto the tracks of an oncoming train. Although the collusion was not a direct hit, the force of the impact severely injured her right leg. The injury was so severe that the leg could not be saved with surgery, and she was forced to have it amputated because of the onset of gangrene. Although devastated by the accident that nearly took her life, Fabiola was determined to resume her career. Her convalescence lasted nearly two years, but her fighting spirit and confidence won out. Even while she was recovering, she continued with the help of friends to see many of the rural clients in the county. She also wrote extension circulars on canning and food preparation. She wrote bulletins for other extension agents focusing on cross-cultural nutrition and the need for agents to respect the ways of indigenous people.

In 1934, with the best wooden leg that medical science had in the 1930s, Fabiola returned to the road. With vigor and determination, she was back on those treacherous, unpaved paths in New Mexico's most rural outposts, working with groups of women, men, and children in homes and homesteads. She organized sewing groups, explained the latest gardening and poultry-raising techniques, and even helped explain, courtesy of a stream of federal government circulars, tips on everything from home repair to land conservation. She taught rural women new gardening techniques and new ways to prepare vegetables and fruits. She translated government bulletins.

So effective did Fabiola become at her work that the Extension Service encouraged her participation in as large an area in northern New Mexico as she could range. She later wrote, "I have not been interested in statistics. I did not keep count of the homes which I visited.... There were thousands."[15]

In those thousands of remote households, she was both helper and student, making her own suggestions and sharing the latest scientific nutritional knowledge, but also taking copious notes on recipes and family and neighborhood traditions that had been handed down through generations in both Latino and Native American communities.

In the mid-1930s, using the astonishing array of materials that she had collected from women in northwest New Mexico and combining it with her own academic and professional studies, Fabiola began to write pamphlets in Spanish on food preparation. In 1934, she published *Los Alimentos y su Preparation,* a pamphlet that was twice reprinted, and in 1935 she authored *Boletin de Conservar,* which was also twice reprinted. The pamphlets became the groundwork for a unique, two-volume cookbook called *Historic Cookery.*

The work was groundbreaking, a dazzling array of heirloom recipes gleaned from Fabiola's own family, mostly relayed to her from her grandmother, as well as recipes from Latino and Native American women and men with whom she had come in contact on the frontier. Published in 1939 in pamphlet form by the New Mexico State University Extension Service and reissued in 1956, the work was as much about cultural icons, such as the chili, as it was a cookbook.

Throughout the book Fabiola talks about the cultural evolution of cuisine in the southwest—why Mexican chili peppers do not have the same taste as New Mexican peppers; why women on the Llano are so skilled at preparing tortillas, shaping them by hand; why certain meats are not common on the tables of Latino families; why hamburger is never used in making chili; that frontier New Mexican families make cheese in the home almost every day; that certain vegetables through generations of trial and error in the remote areas of the plain have been found to be edible, even extraordinarily tasteful; that certain ancient methods of food preparation such as drying corn and chili peppers remain the preferred methods; and that many aspects of native diets have proven to be rich in nutritional value.

Many credited *Historic Cookery* as being the first critical influence in introducing Latino food preparation to a wider Anglo audience. Here were the keys for the non-native that unlocked the magical properties of various chili and corn dishes, passed from generation to generation. In 1983, *Historic Cookery* appeared in a hardcover edition from the Museum of New Mexico Press. It became a bestseller.

Overcoming enormous odds, Fabiola continued to work on the road after her divorce and despite her challenging physical disability. For thirty years, she traveled the rough roads of the plains visiting ranches, Indian pueblos, and Mexican-American villages. From her work in the Taos and Espanola valleys, she increasingly gained an intimate knowledge of indigenous cultures and traditions.

In addition to her tireless efforts on the road, Fabiola Cabeza de Baca Gilbert increasingly devoted a great deal of additional time providing the public with much of the unique information that she gathered in her work—those copious notes she constantly jotted down while on her travels, the wealth of recipes, herbal remedies, religious rituals, and agricultural techniques. She wrote numerous articles for the County Extension Service and a series of vignettes for a local magazine.

The vignettes offered her unique perspective on the folkloric traditions of the various cultures mixing in New Mexico's pioneer families. She had often said that she learned more from the individuals she had met on the road than they had learned from her. She now took advantage of every opportunity possible to relate that knowledge to others. Fabiola prepared bilingual newsletters, pamphlets, and bulletins, and she translated others. She composed in Spanish a weekly homemakers' column for Santa Fe's *El*

Nuevo Mexicano. She began appearing on weekly radio broadcasts on both English and Spanish stations. During World War II, she helped organize food canteens and victory gardens in New Mexico. She also began to arrange, in various towns and along outlying roads, small markets and roadside stands where Native American women could sell their rugs, baskets, pottery, and other handicrafts. For the first time, not only local New Mexico residents but also visitors from other states and countries could have access to objects of art and other goods that were before isolated and relatively unavailable.

By the 1950s, when automobile traffic westward increased dramatically, visitors to New Mexico could begin to stop along the road and buy canned delicacies, carved wooden figures, and decorative pots fired in stoves in villages far distant from normal traffic patterns. In popularizing the work of local women artists and artisans, Fabiola made laudable efforts in providing outlets for their creative work. For many of those women, selling their artistic creations was no less than a liberating experience. Her ideas of popularizing native work served as a model for others around the country.

In 1949, Fabiola followed her first book, *Historic Cookery*, with another classic work on traditional Hispanic New Mexico life and cooking. It was called *The Good Life*. Unlike her first book, *The Good Life* is a novel portraying the yearly cycle of seasons and festivals in a fictitious Hispanic village in New Mexico. Through the lives of those in the Turrieta family, she shows the rituals of the autumn harvest, the collection of herbs, Christmas traditions, and the frontier observances for marriage and death. Fabiola lamented that much of the cultural richness she witnessed on the frontier was vanishing. Writing *The Good* Life, she believed, was a way of preserving a part of it for her readers.As with most of her writings, figures of strong women dominate the pages. In *The Good Life*, she writes of the *curandera* of the village, a figure not unlike her own grandmother. She was called Martina, and she was mysterious; little was known about her past. "The medicine woman seemed so old and wrinkled to Dona Paula," Fabiola wrote, "and she wondered how old she was. She had not wanted her freedom, yet she had always been free. She had never married, but she had several sons and daughters."[16]

By the early 1950s, Fabiola's work among in the Extension Service had gained the attention of the United Nations. In 1951 the United Nations Educational, Scientific, and Cultural Organization (UNESCO) asked her to accept a mission to the Mexican state of Michoacán to establish a home economics program among the Tarascan Indians and to instruct agents from other Latin American countries in her techniques. She accepted.

Her assignment was new; however, the work was in many ways the same. She traveled to remote Mexican villages and trained workers in the techniques she had acquired working in Pueblo and Hispanic villages in New

Mexico and Texas. She established a kind of home economics program among the Tarascan Indians. She also set up nutrition and modern hygiene demonstration centers in the northwestern Lake Pátzcuaro region of Mexico in the mountains of Michoacan. Some of the fish-drying techniques she introduced in the Lake Pátzcuaro region are still in use today.

GENEALOGY AND FOLKLORE

Fabiola was a child of the Llano who never left. Through her childhood and schooling and in her careers in teaching and extension work, she was a product and prophet of the changing culture of the Hispanic frontier. Because of her deep respect for the values and traditions among those in her own family and in those whose lives she touched, she spent much of her life recording those practices and impressions for others to read and understand.

In 1954, the University of New Mexico Press published Fabiola's *We Fed Them Cactus* (1954), a chronicle of life on the Llano, the grasslands of eastern New Mexico, at the turn of the nineteenth century. Her first publication without a culinary theme, the book was a valuable contribution in tracing the cultural and historical themes of her own ancestors and others who established a foothold in a remote American landscape. The title of the book was a carefully considered symbol. It not only referred to the method of keeping cattle alive during a drought, but also to the nature of the cactus plant itself, with its ability to hold water in reserve and to overcome even the most severe threats to its survival. It is a metaphor for the Latinos themselves in the southwest who weathered innumerable misfortunes and survived.

Through four generations of her family to the disastrous drought of 1918 and the loss of her father, she explored the history of settlers on the plains, from the building of ranches and communities to the arrival of homesteaders in the 1880s to the period of her own youth. Using archival material, her own notes and memories and interviews with a variety of individuals, Fabiola offered folklore about herbal medicine, rituals surrounding the buffalo hunt, and an area in time and place unlike that envisioned by most Americans when they thought of the American West. In *We Fed Them Cactus*, she also paid tribute to the bravery and determination displayed by women on the frontier. Throughout the book, Fabiola emphasized that the voices and storytellers were of the whole community. Abiding by the oral tradition of her own culture, she attributed the authorship of the book not to herself but to the people whose voices were in it. The book was a *recuerdo*, a memory.

To explore the early days, for example, she recalls the voice of a ranch cook who could still remember the disappearance of the buffalo, the struggles over land, the coming of the longhorns and barbed wire. She uses other voices to recall the songs and stories and even little known nuggets of folk wisdom such as *las cabanuelas,* the old-time system of predicting the weather.

Book critic Charles Poore of the *New York* Times declared in December 1954 that the hero of the year in American literature had been Billy the Kid. He reported that a number of books had appeared in which Billy was either the central figure or a subject of critical analysis. Poore wrote, "Fifty million Americans may do no wrong, live and die, and never get into any books at all. But a juvenile delinquent puts on some chaps and shooting irons, goes in for a brief, bullet-inspired career of al fresco murder and is assured immortality."[17] Readers in the 1950s tended to think of the Old West of the nineteenth century as a place of train robberies and six shooters and horses and gunfights in dust-blown streets of no-account towns. They thought of the revered legends, the heroes of 10-cent, pulp novels and the romantic, misunderstood loners of the silver screen—they thought of Billy the Kid. From novelists and journalists, from historians and writers of folk songs, from screenwriters and movie actors, Americans have been showered with images. Most of them are overdrawn; many are simply fictitious. But Americans revel in all of it. Americans tell the old stories again and again, and each time the deeds seem to become even more astonishing, the figures even more heroic, more romantic. In the case of Fabiola's book, *We Fed Them Cactus,* Poore said Billy was not a figure of glamour, not heroic, but just an afterthought. And that is how it should have been.

Fabiola's literary endeavors were not those of classic prose or sophisticated technique. Indeed, her writing skills were quite ordinary. A few Chicano critics claimed that her work merely promoted her personal, romanticized view of the *rico* class, many of whom were corrupt. Other critics, however, point to the enormous value of the books in preserving rich details of life and culture on the frontier with unvarnished insight and depth.

At the end of the book, with the terrible drought drying out almost every growing plant except the cactus, with the winds raking across the sand like an evil force wiping away the livelihood of thousands, with the passing of her father as a symbol of the end of an era, Fabiola paid tribute: "Although our ancestors were adventurers who left their mother country in quest of new lands, yet those of us descended from them are of a stable nature. It takes more than droughts and other hardships to move us." And the people persevered and the land returned; she wrote, "It has come back. The grass is growing again and those living on his land are wiser. They are following practices of soil and water conservation which were not available to Papa. But each generation must profit by the trials and errors of those before them; otherwise everything would perish."[18]

When the second edition of *We Fed Them Cactus* printed in 1994, a reviewer in the *Dallas Times-Herald* wrote, "...this modern forward-looking

lady of the Llano, being a close observer, a patient listener and fully apprecia-
tive of her own rich heritage, has shown us life as seen from the early Hispanic New Mexico point of view.... The chapters on the fiesta and chapels
carry a peculiar flavor that could come only from Hispanic origin. Buffalo
hunts, rodeos...and outlaw episodes make magic-like appearances as if
mirages across the long vista of time."[19]

In her own work as a teacher and as an extension agent, and in everything she wrote, Fabiola believed in the transforming nature of progress, the
melding of cultural values and certain truths of the past with discovery and
invention. In 1958 Fabiola helped found a short-lived magazine called *Santa
Fe Scene*, for which she was a columnist and editorial board member. She
retired from the Extension Service in 1959. After her retirement Fabiola
worked as a trainer and consultant for the Peace Corps and was active on
the lecture circuit. She continued to write articles on folk life and food preparation for newspapers and magazines.

In her later years, Fabiola devoted much time to La Sociedad Folklorica
of Santa Fe, an organization of Hispanic women involved in preserving
Spanish culture, traditions, and folklore. The Society was founded by Cleo-
fas M. Jaramillo, a prominent author and chronicler of early New Mexican
society. The Society's archives, to which Fabiola made numerous contributions, included collections of documents on songs, sayings, food recipes,
folk remedies, superstitions, genealogical studies, and many other cultural
materials. In those frequent meetings of the Society and in all parts of her
life, the subject of food was not far from the conversation when Fabiola
was present. One of her fellow society members wrote, "These were occasions when I would see Fabiola, and I noted even then that many deferred
to her as an expert. This was in the late 30s and 40s. Once she and my
mother co-hosted a meeting of the society and she provided a great treat.
It was a cookie from an old recipe that required time and expertise. The
flavor was a cross between a *yema* and *suspiros*. It required dozens of
whipped egg yolks, a scant amount of flour, brandy, brown sugar, and an-
ise. The cookies were baked overnight in a warm oven. They were very
light and crisp."[20]

In her work with the Society and for her own enjoyment, Fabiola began
not only to enhance her grasp of the history of early Spanish settlers in New
Mexico but also undertook even more elaborate genealogical research on
her own family's descendants as well as others in the region. From historical
records and local documents, she tracked the winding family links back
through a Spanish heritage rich in history—the intersecting connections of
such names as Cabeza de Baca, Delgado, Salazar, Romero, Armijo, and
many others. She translated historical materials. She constructed elaborate
genealogical charts. She wrote some narrative histories that she shared with
La Sociedad. She paid particular attention to women's legal and property
rights.

Throughout her life, Fabiola Cabeza de Baca Gilbert worked on behalf of numerous community organizations including the Red Cross, the Girl Scouts, the International Relations Women's Board, and the School of American Research.

In 1957, the United States Department of Agriculture honored Fabiola with its Superior Service Award for her many unique and valuable contributions to the quality of life in New Mexico. The National Home Demonstration Agents Association honored her with its Distinguished Award for Meritorious Service. In 1976, the American Association of University Women honored her by including her works in the Museum of New Mexico Bicentennial Exhibit. The attention sparked a new wave of interest in her writing and led to new published editions of her writings. When a major work titled *The Hispanic 100: A Ranking of the Latino Men and Women Who Have Most Influenced American Thought and Culture,* authored by Himilce Novas, appeared in 1995, Fabiola Cabeza de Baca Gilbert's name was listed as number fifteen.

Fabiola's pioneering works on the merging cultures of the Hispanic Southwest have contributed mightily to the awareness and appreciation of how various communities influenced everything from cuisine to folklore. If she had not made those wide-ranging visits to the homes of Native Americans, Mexicans, and others in her area of the Southwest, many of the small details would have been lost to history—and the accumulation of those small details adds up to a major contribution.

Fabiola valued the lives of the so-called poor and ordinary people she saw on the frontier. She considered their lives and their struggles extraordinary. She gloried both in their progress and in their traditions. "Farm families in most communities can now afford electricity and modern plumbing in their homes," she wrote at the end of her time on the road. "Boys through the GI Bill have gone to college, many already have master *[sic]* degrees and some PhDs. More girls are going to college every year and it is gratifying that education is available to all who desire it. [Yet] the call of the land still persists in the Hispano's life. Let there be a fiesta in their villages and they manage to get there, PhDs and all."[21]

Adelina Ortiz de Hill, one of Fabiola's friends in her later years, wrote, "Often she would call my mother and ask her to send me over to her house to pick up some delicious gift from her kitchen. She loved to cook. She had been injured and barely survived an automobile accident. She had a disfiguring facial scar that despite a pleasant face made her look stern. She also had a leg amputated and wore an old-fashioned wooden leg. She rarely wore it on weekends and used crutches. A married couple lived in a guesthouse on her property and did housekeeping and drove her around. The last time I saw her was in the 80s, when she had an apartment in the Presbyterian retirement home on Peralta. I took my mother over for a pleasant visit. She was still walking and though more frail and elderly she was alert and cordial. She remains a legendary person in the Española Valley...."[22]

Fabiola Cabeza de Baca Gilbert died in Albuquerque, New Mexico on October 14, 1991. She was buried on the Llano at the family ranch near Newkirk, New Mexico.

Fabiola Cabeza de Baca Gilbert's influence on Latino culture in the Southwest and across the country was profound. More than a half century after she wrote her cookbooks, they remain in print, still selling, still passing on to new generations the secrets of chili peppers, chili cooking, the drying of beef, and the delicate sauces that her own ancestors and the ancestors of others on the frontier spread over their tamales and fry bread. More than half a century after she wrote her narratives about life on the frontier, they also are still conveying to historians and general readers alike the sense of time and place and the blending of cultures on the frontier.

NOTES

1. Matt Meier, Concita Serri, and Richard A. Garcia, *Notable Latino Americans* (Westport, Connecticut: Greenwood Press, 1997), 171.
2. Fabiola Cabeza de Baca, *We Fed them Cactus* (Albuquerque: University of New Mexico Press, 1994), 51.
3. *We Fed Them Cactus*, 52.
4. Linda Peary and Ursula Smith, *Pioneer Women: the Lives of Women on the Frontier* (Norman, Oklahoma: University of Oklahoma Press, 1998), 80.
5. *We Fed Them Cactus*, 129.
6. Virginia Scharff, *Twenty Thousand Roads: Women, Movement, and the West.* (Berkeley: University of California Press, 2002), 121.
7. *We Fed them Cactus*, 154–155.
8. *We Fed them Cactus*, 156, 161.
9. *We Fed them Cactus*, 170.
10. Scharff, 127
11. Scharff, 127–128
12. Scharff, 128.
13. Joan Jensen and Darlis Miller, *New Mexico Women* (Albuquerque: University of New Mexico Press, 1986), 243.
14. Jensen and Miller, 250.
15. Scharff, 128.
16. Fabiola Cabeza de Baca, *The Good Life: New Mexico Traditions and Food* (Santa Fe: Museum of New Mexico Press, 1986), 14.
17. Charles Poore, "Books of the Times," *New York Times*, December 23, 1954, 17.
18. *We Fed Them Cactus,* 176, 178.
19. University of New Mexico Press, "We Fed Them Cactus," http://www.unmpress.com/Book.php?id=1147.
20. Adelina Ortiz de Hill, "My Memories of Fabiola C. de Baca Gilbert" "Fabiola Cabeza de Baca y Delgado y Delgado de Gilbert (1898-1991)," http://perso.orange.fr/rancho.pancho/Fabiola.htm.

21. Scharff, 134.
22. Adelina Ortiz de Hill.

FURTHER READING

Cabeza de Baca, Fabiola, *The Good Life: New Mexico Traditions and Food.* Santa Fe: Museum of New Mexico Press, 1986.

Cabeza de Baca, Fabiola. *We Fed them Cactus.* Albuquerque, University of New Mexico Press, 1994.

Jensen, Joan, and Darlis Miller. *New Mexico Women.* Albuquerque, University of New Mexico Press, 1986.

Scharff, Virginia. *Twenty Thousand Roads: Women, Movement, and the West.* Berkeley, University of California Press, 2002.

Sullivan, Michael Ann. "Fabiola Cabeza de Baca (1894–1991)," New Mexico Office of the State Historian, http://www.newmexicohistory.org/people.php?Category Level_1=48&CategoryLevel_2=50&CategoryLevel_3=83&fileID=547#.

Courtesy of Library of Congress

Cesar Chavez

Cesar Chavez was an unlikely hero. His dream was to found a labor union of farm workers, but he had no money, no political connections, and no experience. He was not a particularly dynamic personality and had no special talent as a public speaker. Nevertheless, through determination, grit, and a dogged will to win, he forged a movement that successfully challenged powerful, entrenched economic and political interests and helped communities of Latinos achieve a new cultural self-awareness. When his life and career were over, people around the world hailed his achievements.

MIGRANT WORKERS

Stooped over in the intense sun along the rows of crops, Latino migrant laborers in California and in other western states worked from early morning till nearly dark. In the lettuce fields and the pea fields, in the grape orchards and cherry groves, they harvested—men and women alongside young boys and girls, day after day, their bodies contorted in painful routine. At night, they returned to the housing camps, dirty, cramped, rundown shacks, converted chicken coops, and storage sheds, none with running water or electricity, almost all of them infested with mosquitoes. Dozens of families shared a single outhouse. Water came from nearby irrigation ditches. They never had enough food. Children went to school only when they were not needed in the fields. In 1965 grape pickers in California made an average of less than a dollar an hour. Many workers suffered injury or death from disease or accident. The average life expectancy of a farm worker was forty-nine years.

One boy of Mexican descent who grew up with a migrant worker family in California remembered the constant traveling. Most winters they spent around Brawley, California, where they worked the fields harvesting carrots, peas, and mustard greens. In the broccoli fields, he remembered, the workers waded in water and mud that rose to the level of the youngsters' necks. Their hands, he said, were often numb with cold. "In late May," he said, "we had two or three options: Oxnard for beans, Beaumont for cherries, or the Hemet area for apricots. I think we did all at one time or another. From there we worked in corn and chili peppers, and picked fresh lima beans for fifty cents a basket. Then in August through part of October, we had grapes, prunes, and tomatoes. We would go before those crops started and wait in a camp until they were ready. Then we did cotton from October through Christmas. It was hard work, but there was nothing else."[1]

The boy's name was Cesar Chavez. Unlike anyone before him, he would make a difference for migrant workers.

Chavez was born near Yuma, Arizona, on March 31, 1927, the second of six children of Librado and Juana Chavez. His fraternal grandfather, Cesario "Papa Chayo," had crossed the border into Arizona from Mexico in 1888, settling on a farm along the Colorado River in the North Gila Valley desert.

Born an indentured servant in Chihuahua, Mexico, Cesario fled the hacienda (plantation). After crossing the border, he found work as a mule skinner in Arizona. He was illiterate. His wife, Dorotea, "Mama Tella," could read both Spanish and Latin, a skill she learned as an orphan in a Mexican convent. Cesario and Dorotea had fifteen children. One of their sons, Librado, was two years old when the family fled to the United States. In 1924, Librado married Juana Estrada, whose family had also migrated north from Chihuahua. For a time, Librado opened a small automobile repair shop and, later, a poolroom. He supplemented his income by driving stagecoaches and twenty-mule teams. Local residents also elected him to be a postmaster.

The family worked the land, cared for horses and cows, and opened a small grocery store. Living in their small adobe house, the family, although not wealthy, lived comfortably. Aunts and uncles surrounded young Cesar in the community. He was particularly close to his brother Richard, two years younger than himself, and his cousin, Manuel. He had an older sister, Rita, born in 1925, and two younger sisters, Helena (who died very young) and Vicky (1933). His youngest brother, Lenny, was born in 1934.

Cesar always remembered a loving family that surrounded him, centered in a Roman Catholic faith that played a central role throughout his life. Guided by Mama Tella, the Chavez children learned the rituals and trappings of the Catholic Church. All his life, Cesar would look to those teachings and his own religious impulses for guidance.

Although his mother could neither read nor write, she taught through stories and proverbs lessons about honesty and nonviolence, about sacrifice and obedience, stories that Cesar would absorb as his own moral compass. His father taught him that it was honorable to fight for the rights of others and to value labor and personal responsibility. When migrant workers began to organize unions to fight for better working conditions in the fields, Librado was always an enthusiastic leader.

ON THE ROAD LOOKING FOR WORK

During the upheaval of the Great Depression and its massive unemployment, the Chavez family faced the troubled times with little or no financial resources to fall back on. Unable to make payments for property taxes on their beloved farm, they were forced off the land in 1937. The relative stability he and the others had experienced on the farm was about to be shattered. Cesar was ten years old.

Librado and Juana, with their three sons and two daughters, loaded their few possessions in their car and joined the thousands of other Depression-era families on the road to California and its vast harvest lands where the dispossessed and poverty-wracked might find temporary work. Cesar would attend more than fifty different schools by the time he finished the eighth grade.

They continued moving from valley to valley, from harvest to harvest, trying to keep afloat. Increasingly, the work left them physically debilitated and relatively powerless. Nevertheless, they kept going, kept trying to keep their spirits high, and kept looking forward to better days.

For a time, Brawley, California, became a home base. As they traveled northward each spring from job to job, they gained greater knowledge about the rotation of crops and the successive harvests, and better insight into the location of the more reliable jobs. They learned what to expect from the weather, where to camp when no housing was available, how to find the areas that provided shelter from the winter fog and rain and from the heat of summer. They picked peas, lettuce, tomatoes, figs, prunes, grapes, and apricots.

FACING INTOLERANCE

Like most Mexican-American children first thrust into the local school systems, Cesar faced enormous challenges. Simple human relationships between culturally diverse children in school were frustrating. The phrase "dirty Mexican," Cesar remembered later, often rolled easily off the tongues of fellow classmates. Fights between whites and Mexican-American students usually favored the whites because of their numbers and also because of the tendency of teachers to decide disputes in favor of the Anglo students. Before he was ten years old, Cesar had learned hard lessons of prejudice and injustice.

In Brawley, the residents were segregated and Mexican Americans were told at an early age not to go into the Anglo section of town. More than once the family members were turned away from establishments by dispiriting signs announcing "We don't sell to Mexicans." Cesar later remembered the humiliation of seeing other signs on stores that read "No Dogs or Mexicans Allowed." From his earliest childhood days, Cesar, as did other Hispanic children in the United States, learned limitations rather than possibilities.

In June 1939 the twelve-year-old Cesar saw his father join an infant union in the dried-fruit industry. Although the strike was quickly broken, Librado walked a picket line. Even at such a young age, in seeing these early, halting attempts at organizing workers, Chavez felt a stirring motivation to become an active union leader himself.

FIGHTING BACK AGAINST INJUSTICE

In 1942, when Cesar was fifteen years old, his father was seriously injured in an automobile accident. The boy dropped any ideas about high school. It was now important for the family's survival that he become the primary money earner. For a time, with his brother and sister, he thinned lettuce and beets with short-handled hoes, a tool notoriously hard to use for any lengthy period of time because of the backbreaking posture in which the users were forced to work. He was now dealing with the injustices that were part of the migrant worker's experience and began to see, in a more first-hand, personal way, the suffering and cultural prejudices under which they labored.

Isolated in the fields, the workers had no choice but to stay in those shacks and no choice but to buy food and other supplies from makeshift stores owned by the companies that also charged outrageous prices. He saw unscrupulous labor contractors hired by the companies skim a portion of their salaries for the opportunity to work. He saw contractors make payroll deductions for Social Security and then pocket the money.

In 1943, the Chavez family settled in Delano, California, in the center of the crop-rich San Joaquin Valley. It was in Delano that the young teenager began to display, as did many other Mexican-American youngsters, the *pachuco* or *zoot suit* look. The style was from Los Angeles, and it spoke of the rebelliousness, sense of anger, and frustration of Mexican-American youth. The look was sleek—a long suit coat with tapered pants, a low-hanging watch chain, and a wide-brimmed hat, covering long ducktail haircuts.

On a day in 1943 Chavez walked into a malt shop in Delano and met Helen Fabela, a pretty, dark-haired girl about his own age, who worked as a clerk in a grocery store patronized by migrant workers. Fifteen years old and shy, she had already experienced the tough work in the grape and berry fields of California. She had lost her father a few years earlier, and the family, like most migrant families, was under severe financial burden. As had Chavez, she dropped out of high school to help the family pay bills. The two began to ride around Delano in his clunky, gas-guzzling car and occasionally attend the movies. It was the beginning of a life-long bond.

In 1944, at age seventeen, Chavez left his life in the fields and joined the Navy. "I was doing sugar-beet thinning, the worst backbreaking job," he said, "and I remember telling my father, 'Dad, I've had it.' Neither my mother or father wanted me to go, but I joined up anyway." Chavez was sent to the Mariana Islands and then to Guam. He served two years as a deckhand and painter on a destroyer escort.[2]

He remembered the experience as two of the worst years of his life. It was not only the war experience itself, with its death and destruction, but also the discrimination within the military against non-whites that became a lasting memory. After his stint in the Navy, Chavez returned to the United States in 1946. He saw no alternative but to return to work in the fields of California.

The members of the Chavez family joined the National Farm Labor Union, a branch union affiliated with the American Federation of Labor (AFL). Organized by Ernesto Galarza, a Mexican-American sociologist,

Outlawing the Short-Handled Hoe

Farm worker Roberto Acuna remembered the particular problems using a short-handled hoe in the fields of Arizona and California. "The hardest work would be thinning and hoeing with a short-handled hoe," he said. "The fields would be about a half a mile long. You would be bending and stooping all day. Sometimes I wouldn't have dinner or anything. I'd just go home and fall asleep and wake up just in time to go out to the fields again. There were times when I felt I couldn't take it any more. It was 105° in the shade and I'd see endless rows of lettuce and I felt my back hurting. I felt the frustration of not being able to get out of the fields."[1]

In 1969 Cesar Chavez, who had also worked with the short-handled hoe, said, "Growers look at human beings as implements. But if they had any consideration for the torture that people go through, they would give up the short-handled hoe."[2]

Chavez himself suffered debilitating back pain throughout his life, largely because of the twisted posture that use of the tool demanded. In those early days in the lettuce fields and in weeding sugar-beet fields along the Sacramento River, row after row in the searing heat, alone with the hoe, the bag, and the grinding succession of hours hunched in an unforgiving shape, Chavez learned to despise the short-handled hoe as an extension of those who made him use it. It was, he believed, the growers' weapon.

California's lettuce growers, insisting that the implement was the fastest and most efficient for the work, continued to require workers to use it. Get rid of the short-handled hoe, the growers argued, and the thinning and weeding would not be done properly, the growers would suffer crop losses, and many of them would go bankrupt. Even when evidence mounted that the tool caused ruptured spinal disks, arthritis, and other serious back injuries, the lettuce growers would not allow other equipment. To the laborers it was known as *la herramienta del Diablo* (the Devil's instrument).

Through the work of Chavez's union, Civil Rights attorney Mo Jourdane, and the support of California Governor Jerry Brown and others in his administration, the short-handled hoe was finally outlawed. New generations of field workers would never again face what Jourdane called "a flat-out symbol of oppression—a way to keep control of workers and make them live humbled, stooped-over lives."[3]

---

[1]Studs Terkel, *Working* (New York: Avon Books, 1974), 34–37.
[2]Susan Ferris and Ricardo Sandoval, "The Death of the Short-Handled Hoe," http://www.pbs.org/itvs/fightfields/book1.html.
[3]"Latino Attorney Honored by Farm Workers' Rights Group," November 21, 2001, http://www.laprensasandiego.org/achieve/november21/lawyer.htm.

author, and labor organizer, the infant union organized a number of strikes across California in the 1940s. Although the strikes netted few gains for the workers who joined him, Galarza's pioneering efforts drew admiring notice from Chavez.

This refusal to suffer indignity and injustice without a fight burned hotly in young Chavez. His family had fought; he would fight on. "I don't want to suggest that we were radical," he said later, "but I know we were probably one of the strikingest families in California, the first ones to leave the fields if anybody shouted '*Huelga!*' ('Strike!')."[3]

MARRIAGE AND CHILDREN

On October 22, 1948, Chavez married Helen Fabela. They honeymooned on the coast of California and visited historic Spanish missions from Sonoma to San Diego. When they returned to Delano, they continued working in the fields.

Thin, five feet, six inches tall, with jet-black hair, Cesar was twenty-one years old at the time of his wedding. It had been a hard youth. His body was muscled but already suffering the toll of years in the fields. Throughout his life, he would experience extensive back pain, a condition experienced by most migrant field laborers.

In 1949, Helen gave birth to Fernando, the first of their eight children. Sylvia, their second child, arrived a year later. To support the growing family, Chavez took a series of jobs in the fields. Soon, however, he managed to land a full-time job in a lumberyard in Crescent City, California, close to the Oregon border. Along with his brother Richard and his cousin Manuel, Cesar and Helen packed their belongings and took their families to the damp pinewoods, where Richard had built a shack for them. Although the constant drizzling weather and the muddy conditions in the woods began to weigh on all of them, the job was a breakthrough for Chavez, an experience that he was able to use to get a job in another lumber mill back in familiar territory in San Jose. In 1952, along with Richard and the others, Chavez moved into a barrio in southeast San Jose called Sal Si Puedes ("Get Out if You Can"). In California's agricultural areas, new Mexican-American barrios grew as seasonal migratory laborers such as the Chavez family became settled. Sal Si Puedes was one of those barrios.

NEW WORLD OF LEARNING

When a young Catholic priest named Father Donald McDonnell traveled to Sal Si Puedes to help establish a community organization among the farm laborers, he and Chavez soon became close friends. They were nearly the same age, both brimming with enthusiasm for changing the social order.

Chavez began to accompany McDonnell to the labor camps to help with mass and even to the city jail to spend time with the prisoners. McDonnell became to Chavez a tutor, friend, and fellow social worker.

It was coming together, now, the lessons from his father about not accepting as fate the conditions in which you found yourself and about working with others in unions to improve those conditions; the teachings of his grandmother about spirituality; and the example of his mother, who, on many occasions, asked her children to go out by the railroad tracks and ask a hobo to come for dinner. The road for the Latino field workers was not to passively accept conditions as they were, but to band themselves together as a family to work as a force for change.

Chavez read biographies of labor organizers such as John L. Lewis and Eugene V. Debs. He read about the organization of unions and about strikes. He also read about Mahatma Gandhi, the Indian politician and spiritual leader who had passed away in 1948. This exposure to the life and teachings of Gandhi opened Cesar's eyes to the ways in which the poor in all countries and cultures can work together to improve their lives. The ideas of Gandhi, who preached and practiced the philosophy of nonviolent social change, would change Chavez's life.

Chavez was particularly struck by the power strategically unleashed by Gandhi's nonviolent protests. Repeatedly, Gandhi organized campaigns of civil disobedience; many times he was arrested. In response to his arrests, he often fasted. Through Gandhi, Chavez would come to see nonviolence as both the philosophical and theological basis of his own commitment to social change. He would urge migrant workers to unleash the power of nonviolent resistance.

COMMUNITY SERVICE ORGANIZER

In the spring of 1952, Chavez met Fred Ross. A friend of Father McDonnell, Ross was in Sal Si Puedes representing the Community Service Organization (CSO), a social service group that promoted self-reliance and provided a variety of services including low-cost medical care and job referral; the CSO was also active in encouraging Mexican Americans to vote.

Ross explained to Chavez that the CSO was organizing chapters in a number of other California localities, including San Jose. The CSO, Ross predicted, would soon be a forceful Mexican-American civil rights organization in California. When Ross asked Chavez to join in the work, he accepted. That night in his journal Ross wrote, "I think I found the guy I'm looking for."[4]

Chavez was both enthusiastic and wary. Although he captured the loyalty of friends and small of groups of people with whom he associated, he had no experience speaking publicly to groups, was unsure about his organizing abilities, and was somewhat frightened about the responsibilities that were to become his. Nevertheless, he leaped into the work with a dedication that was infectious.

During the day, Chavez would pick apricots; at night, he conducted house meetings, talked with fellow migrants about their constitutional rights, and showed them how to register to vote. Instead of relying mostly on college students to serve as registrars for the voting drive campaign, Chavez recruited friends from the barrio. By the end of the campaign he had produced several thousand new voters.

Besides the organizing experience he gained in the voter registration drive in San Jose, Chavez also got a rough dose of the vicious, partisan politics of the early 1950s. The new voters that Chavez and his team had signed up threatened influence enjoyed by the local Republican committee. Fearing this new Mexican-American voting bloc rising in its midst, the Republican central committee decided to challenge first-time Mexican-American voters at the polls. The Republicans showed up on election day questioning whether the voters were illegal aliens or whether they had criminal backgrounds.

The tactics so infuriated Ross that he wired the United States Attorney General in Washington. Chavez added his name to the letter. For the Federal Bureau of Investigation, this letter presented a new target of investigation. The target, unhappily for the CSO, was not the possible voter intimidation but the CSO itself. Could this new organization in San Jose and its leaders, including Cesar Chavez, be tied in some way to an anti-American conspiracy?

In Bakersfield, California, a young congressman from California organized hearings concerning labor walkouts. This congressman believed that the labor protestors were connected to a communist plot. Chavez was so interested in the subject that he managed to attend some of the deliberations. The congressman was future president Richard Nixon. And now a few of the nation's defenders turned their attention to San Jose, California, and saw a young Mexican-American farm worker who had just turned organizer. Who was this new face in the protester ranks? What were his links to the international communist menace?

"The FBI agents took me in their car for a meeting with members of the Republican Central Committee, which turned into a shouting match," Chavez later remembered. "That's the first time I started shouting at Anglos, shouting back at them." The confrontation became the subject of a newspaper story, and suddenly Chavez was the talk of the area.[5]

Over the years, the file on Cesar Chavez at the FBI would grow larger. It filled up with information about his movements, his friends, his correspondence, his speeches, his philosophy, and his family. In the continuing intensive surveillance of Chavez, the FBI would find no evidence of his being implicated in communist activities. Instead, the file swelled with evidence of the remarkably active work and strong commitment of Chavez on behalf of Latinos.

After the highly successful drive in San Jose, Ross and the other leaders of the CSO decided to hire Chavez as a full-time organizer. His pay was $35 a week. In his entire career, he would never earn more than $6,000 in a year. Chavez's single-minded purpose soon became evident to all of the small groups of people he gathered in house meetings and to those fellow workers whom he recruited and who stayed with him over years of work. Helen encouraged him, remaining steadfastly behind the cause that drove them both, even though his immersion in his work left little time to help raise their eight children. Their third child, Linda, was born in 1951, Eloise in 1952, Anna in 1953, Paul in 1957, Elizabeth in 1958, and Anthony in 1958.

Throughout the 1950s, Chavez would organize more than twenty new CSO chapters in such California towns as Madera, Bakersfield, and Hanford. His years with the CSO brought the young organizer into contact with a whole range of public and private authorities who were involved with labor issues, immigration, and social problems involving Mexican Americans. They came to him singly or in groups, and Chavez listened to their problems. He wrote letters to government agencies for them; he intervened for them in misunderstandings with the police or with physicians or with welfare departments.

In the mid-1950s, Chavez befriended Dolores Huerta, a vigorous, attractive associate of Fred Ross and mother of seven children. At the Los Angeles headquarters, Huerta had heard of the organizing skills of Chavez but after meeting him briefly she seemed unimpressed, remembering mostly his shyness. In 1957, they met again at a CSO meeting in Stockton. This time, she marveled at the way he answered questions directly, precisely, and without pretension. He was, she concluded, a special messenger and activist for the cause of the workers. Huerta would become a pivotal ally for Chavez in the coming years.

In August 1958, Chavez traveled to Oxnard, a leading citrus-growing region north of Los Angeles, to establish a local office of the CSO. It was in Oxnard that Chavez worked against the *bracero* program, a federally funded effort to bring laborers directly from Mexico to California to work in the fields during labor shortages. Under the bracero program, growers were permitted under federal regulations to use Mexican workers only after exhausting the available pool of local farm workers. Because of the financial advantages that the bracero program afforded the growers, they often ignored those regulations. Thus, many of the local California Mexican-American workers and other migrant laborers frequently went without jobs while growers brought in growing numbers of braceros. By the late 1950s, Mexican-American field workers had been to a large extent replaced by the braceros. The signs declaring "No Pickers Wanted" increasingly greeted those looking for work.

Although Chavez sympathized with the plight of the Mexican workers brought in to the United States in the harvest seasons and then sent back, he also saw the larger labor issues involved. Mexican-American workers could not protest wages or working conditions for fear of losing jobs to braceros. The braceros, on the other hand, could not protest for fear of being returned immediately to Mexico. For thirteen months, Chavez and the CSO fought against these practices. He used many of the nonviolent but aggressive tactics used by Martin Luther King, Jr., and others in the Black Civil Rights movement that was now gaining momentum in the American South. Civil rights organizers had used "sit-ins" at lunch counters to protest discrimination against blacks. In Oxnard, Chavez organized a sit-down strike in the fields to challenge the hiring practices.

At a tomato ranch, ten carloads of workers and their families gathered, singing and carrying pictures of the Virgin of Guadalupe, whose image, it is said in Mexican culture, appeared on the cloak of an Aztec named Juan Diego in 1531. The Virgin of Guadalulpe, the patron and symbol of Mexico, representing the fusion of the Aztec and Spanish cultures, often appeared on flags carried by Chavez marchers.

Chavez also put together a boycott of merchants who sold the products grown by the farmers who used bracero workers extensively. Workers under Chavez's leadership picketed and filed complaints with the federal and state governments. They rallied the community so convincingly that, by the end of 1959, they had managed to set up at a local CSO headquarters a "hiring hall" through which most of the growers, weary from the struggle against Chavez and his lieutenants, had agreed to find workers. Chavez had essentially turned the local CSO in Oxnard into a union hall. It was in Oxnard that Chavez began to see clearly in his mind the exciting potential of organizing the farm workers of California into a union.

Chavez had gathered to his cause in Oxnard more than 1,500 workers, most of them farm laborers. He saw the group that he had assembled there in the year and a half of work as the nucleus of a union that could use all the tools—the boycotts, marches, and strikes—he had used against the bracero program. With seemingly limitless energy, he had given his all for the CSO. He wanted to take the gains, the resources, and the experience of Oxnard and turn the CSO into a farm workers' union. With no formal union contracts, Chavez knew, the growers in future years could return to the system that had so hurt Mexican-American farm laborers. Encouraged by the backing of the 1,500 workers at Oxnard, he proposed to the CSO that they found a union. The proposal was turned down. The organization, the CSO Board of Directors insisted, was by nature a social service program organization, not a union. Despite the setback, Chavez had achieved such respect and support among the management of the CSO that he was promoted to be its executive director in 1959.

Chavez continued to work for the CSO until 1962. Three months before its annual convention in the spring of 1962, Chavez once again asked CSO's board members if he could establish a pilot project to organize a union of farm workers. He would take no salary from the CSO itself but would accept funds from the workers. When his proposal was presented at the convention to the full membership for vote, it was a moment of high tension. Most of the members voted not to support Chavez in his effort to make a fundamental change of direction in the organization. Although the members had great respect for Chavez and what he had accomplished, they did not want to turn the organization into a union. When the vote was announced, Chavez quietly rose in the hall and said that he had an announcement. It was two words: "I resign."

Although his resignation turned the convention into near bedlam and although several shaken members tried to persuade Chavez to reconsider, he did not retreat from his decision. "It took me six months to get over leaving CSO," he said later.[6]

On March 31, 1962, his thirty-fifth birthday, Chavez cleared out his desk at the CSO headquarters in Los Angeles. With Helen and the children, he drove to the small beach town of Carpinteria, near Santa Barbara. While the children frolicked in the sand, the two talked of their plans. They would go to Delano to start a union. It was true that they had little money, no property, and no promise of work. Nevertheless, it was Helen's hometown. Two of her sisters lived in Delano, and two brothers were nearby. It was also the town in which Chavez's brother Richard had made his home. There was no better place than Delano, they agreed, to chase a dream. After filling the tank of the battered Mercury, they headed north.

STARTING A UNION

Soft-spoken, with heavy eyes and an occasional wry grin, Chavez was thirty-five years old when he arrived in Delano with his family in the spring of 1962. With a shock of coal black hair sweeping across his broad face, he seemed almost boyish, his peaceful demeanor and quiet voice masking a fiery spirit. He had a natural sense of community, gathering around him many loyal friends who trusted him, sensed his roots and purpose. However unlikely it seemed, Cesar Chavez was ready to make a difference.

A town of 12,000 in 1962, Delano was in the center of the nation's table grape industry. Harboring no illusions, Chavez knew that rounding up supporters for a full-scale union would be difficult and slow. Most labor leaders privately believed that Chavez's goal of creating the first successful union of farm workers in U.S. history was close to impossible. Farm laborers presented a union organizer with a number of seemingly overwhelming hurdles. The workers were largely illiterate, extremely poor, and divided culturally from mainstream America. They did not usually remain very long in one locality, making stability and communication highly dubious. They had, up to this point, little economic power. If they refused to work, growers could replace them with cheaper bracero labor.

Using the family's life savings of about $1,200, as well as small gifts and loans from some friends and relatives and the wages that Helen was able to earn by returning to work in the fields, Chavez began the painstaking groundwork of building an association of farm workers. As he began to make the rounds of Delano and nearby fruit-growing areas, he avoided using the term "union" because, to most of the workers, that meant "strikes," through which some of them had already suffered. From one labor camp to another, he worked the San Joaquin Valley. He talked about the potential strengths of a social movement or "movimiento," the idea that to gain real power the workers must consolidate and use whatever nonviolent muscle they had.

One of the men later said, "Here was Cesar burning with a patient fire, poor like us, dark like us...moving people to talk about their problems, attacking the little problems first, and suggesting, always suggesting, ever more solutions that seemed attainable. We didn't know it until we met him, but he was the leader we had been waiting for."[7]

By the fall of 1962, Chavez had not only lined up workers who were interested in joining the union, but he also had drawn to his side other loyal and talented lieutenants. In 1959 Dolores Huerta was involved in an effort by the AFL-CIO (Congress of Industrial Organizations) to organize a farm workers' union. The infant group was called the Agricultural Workers Organizing Committee (AWOC), and it made enough progress to attempt a few strikes against growers in the Imperial Valley in the early 1960s. Huerta later said, "When Cesar told me, 'I'm going to start my own union,' I was just appalled, the thought was so overwhelming. But when the initial shock wore off, I thought it was exciting."[8]

On September 30, 1962, a Sunday, approximately two hundred workers gathered to show their solidarity in an abandoned theater in Fresno, California. They called the new organization The National Farm Workers Association (NFWA). They adopted a union motto: "Viva la causa!" or "Long live the cause!" They also waved a new flag bearing the organizational symbol— an black Aztec eagle, emblematic of pride and dignity, in a white circle on a field of red. The white circle in the flag signified the hopes and aspirations of the farm laborers; the black represented the plight of the workers; and the red field stood for the hard work and sacrifice that the union members would have to give.

In his new plan of action, delivered at the organizational meeting, Chavez talked about lobbying the governor's office for a minimum wage of $1.50 an hour and for the right to unemployment insurance for farm workers. He talked about the possibility of collective bargaining in which the association would approach the growers as a group to negotiate working conditions and pay, now an unheard-of proposition in California's migrant farm labor industry. He also talked about plans for an association-run credit union and a hiring hall to help workers locate jobs. In short, this was going to be a union. Other organized supporters rallied to *La Causa*, such as the California Migrant Ministry, a group of Protestant ministers dedicated to helping the farm workers. Chavez was emotionally moved by the relationship of these ministers to the farm laborers. He often used the example of the California Migrant Ministry to persuade other religious organizations, including the Catholic Church, to send more representatives to the fields and barrios.

At a constitutional convention held in Fresno on January 21, 1963, Chavez became president of the new organization; Dolores Huerta, Julio Hernandez, and Gilbert Padilla became vice presidents. The preamble to the constitution that Chavez had drafted at a table in his garage made clear the abuses against which the movement would march:

> We the Farm Workers of America, have tilled the soil, sown the seeds and harvested the crops. We have provided food in abundance for the people in the cities, and the nation and world but have not had sufficient food to feed our own children. While industrial workers, living and working in one place, have joined together and grown strong, we have been isolated, scattered and hindered from uniting our forces.[9]

SMALL STEPS IN ASSERTING UNION POWER

In the formative months and years of the NFWA, the union leaders fanned out across the farm areas of California, slowly gaining recruits. Progress was painstakingly slow. Workers would agree to join and then change their minds. Many were not in the area long enough to be of help to the union. Chavez would often be on the road in the middle of the night heading for work sites. Chavez's own children, as well as his nephews and nieces, all pitched in to help as the registration drive mounted. On some occasions he would squeeze his eight children into his battered station wagon and try to make the trips a family outing.

By 1964, the NFWA had signed up more than 1,000 families. For the first time, Chavez could go on a salary from union dues. The organization had launched a credit union, run by Helen, as well as other community service programs such immigration counseling and assistance with voter registration. The organization was also able to begin publishing its farm work newspaper called *El Malcriado* (the ill-bred or unruly one). Through its pages, workers could follow the cartoon figure Don Sotaco as he surveyed the area scene regarding jobs, calls for higher wages, and issues involving worker conditions.

Although the NFWA had made substantial progress by 1965, Chavez was not yet planning a major strike. The power of the growers and affiliated companies represented a formidable adversary. Chavez figured it would take at least another couple of years for the union to have the money, the number of members, and the experience necessary to take on that kind of power. Nevertheless, in the spring of 1965, Chavez suddenly found himself in the middle of a small strike that broke out among eighty-five workers at a McFarland, California, rose farm called Mount Arbor. Aware of the growing influence of the NFWA, the flower workers approached Chavez for help in gaining a wage increase. Both Chavez and Huerta, without deeply involving their association, worked for several days helping prepare the workers for the strike. Their efforts were successful, at least in the short run. The growers agreed to a wage increase but not to any long-term guarantees. Nevertheless, on the front page of *El Malcriado* the union proclaimed victory in the "War of the Roses."

THE DELANO GRAPE STRIKE

At the end of the summer, the grapes in the fields of Chavez' home base of Delano ripened. Grape pickers were expected to work in the vineyards for $.90 an hour plus $.10 a basket. Working conditions in the camps and fields were miserable. Emboldened by the talk of strikes and the small successes they had seen in California earlier in the year, workers demanded a pay raise to $1.25 cents an hour. The growers refused. The stage was set for a drama that Chavez himself could not have anticipated.

Chavez had sent out word through local disk jockeys on Spanish radio and in the union's paper that something big was in the works. On September 16, 1965, the membership of the NFWA gathered at Our Lady of Guadalupe Church in Delano. More than five hundred excited workers and their families wedged themselves into the pews and balconies.

Eight days earlier, Filipino grape workers, led by Larry Itliong of the AWOC, went on strike against the Delano growers demanding higher wages, better living conditions, and fair hiring practices. The leaders had come to Chavez asking that his union, the NFWA, join the strike. Although apprehensive about the readiness of his union to undertake a strike, Chavez recognized a growing restlessness and spirit for confrontation among the workers. He realized that to turn his back on a strike so close to home and so close to the workers he represented would be emotionally demoralizing. He decided to ask the membership to vote on whether to join the Filipinos and turn this small, infant protest into a big-time fight against the growers. He knew what their answer would be.

The NFWA voted unanimously to go forward with the strike that night at the church. The cry was now "Viva la huelga!" (Long live the strike!). Personally, Chavez remained cautious. The union had $100 in its bank account. But Chavez, by his decision to move forward, had put himself and his union in the forefront of an unprecedented effort to improve the lives of agricultural field workers.

DOGGED, DETERMINED, AND NONVIOLENT

From the first days of the strike, Chavez preached to his troops the message of nonviolent confrontation. It was working in the civil rights movement for black Americans; it would work, he believed, in the fields of California. Although some of his fellow strike leaders urged Chavez not to recruit extensively from outside the Delano area, he followed his own instinct to bring in the widest group of supporters he could, even though his enemies charged the movement with communist infiltration. They were, however, not communists, as FBI investigations would clearly discover over the years. They were students, civil rights workers, priests, ministers, rabbis, social workers, union leaders, and others who saw a chance to help a just cause.

Covering an area of more than 400 square miles, the strike force soon involved thousands of workers. For most of them, this was a first-time, unique experience. Nevertheless, they learned quickly. Although they could not set up picket lines at all of the ranches at the same time, the strikers selectively shut down work at a number of the larger ranches and set in motion the inevitable next phase: the retaliation of the growers.

Led by Di Giorgio Fruit Corporation, Schenley Industries, and other major companies, the growers began to bring in scab labor to replace the union workers. Soon the new workers, many of whom had no idea they had been brought in to replace striking workers, were being persuaded by the picketers to put down their hoes and join the strike. Carrying signs flying the union black eagle and calling for "Huelga," the strikers were remarkably effective.

Attempts to break the strike became progressively uglier. Local police arrested workers attempting to enter some of the ranches. Ranch foremen, racing their pickup trucks up and down the strike lines, choked the picketers with dust. Some sprayed them with sulphur and other chemicals and brandished shotguns. They brought in dogs. They fired buckshot through picket signs. The determination of the strikers seemed to increase with the ferocity of methods used to put them down.

Even though Chavez and his lieutenants did not at first have a strike fund, the national publicity garnered through the print and television media soon after the strike began started to pay off. College students from California universities and even from out of state began to show up at the work sites. Checks began arriving from individuals across the country appalled at the treatment of the strikers. Large unions like the United Auto Workers also began to lend financial support.

Several times a week "Huelga priests" held masses for the workers. People began to talk about Mexican history and the relationship of this strike to other battles of the poor and dispossessed. Slogans appeared on the sides of buildings and fences. Strikers waved banners of the Virgin of Guadalupe, the patron saint of Mexico, and carried both the Mexican and United States flags.

By late October, the counterstrike forces began to arrest picketers on the charge of disturbing the peace. With newspaper and television camera crews at work and press writers taking down notes, forty-four picketers including Helen Chavez were arrested and escorted to the Bakersfield jail. With bail set at $276 for each person, the men and women of the unlawful assembly prepared to spend three days in jail. For Chavez, the incident was a political godsend. The union leader, in several speeches, told of the egregious assault against free speech. Money and telegrams arrived by the score in Delano. Soon, a contingent of 350 protestors gathered in front of the county courthouse, singing protest songs. Helen was freed along with the others.

After absorbing the first round of volleys from the growers, Chavez decided to raise the level of the protest. In early December 1965, he decided to call for a boycott of Schenley Industries. Recruiting additional volunteers from churches, community organizations, labor organizations, and universities, the union set up boycott centers in a number of cities. Signs appeared urging the public to "Help Farmworkers—Do Not Buy Grapes." The protest had thus moved from the fields to the urban areas.

It quickly became clear that Chavez was no ordinary leader and this was no ordinary strike. This was more than a typical fight for wages and working conditions; Chavez had focused the movement on the ethnic identity of Latinos and a quest for justice rooted in Catholic social teaching.

Through the winter months into 1966, Chavez gathered supporters to explore ways to maintain the fervor and commitment of the strikers. In February, at a meeting near Santa Barbara, the union leader and his advisors decided to adopt another tactic that had been successful in the civil rights movement: a long march. It would cover a route from Delano to the state capital of Sacramento, through such towns as Madera, Fresno, Modesto, and Stockton. For Chavez, the march would emphasize the religious spirit behind the union movement. Union organizer Marshall Ganz recorded in his diary: "… then Chávez asked, why should it be a 'march' at all? It will be Lent soon, a time for reflection, for penance, for asking forgiveness. Perhaps ours should be a pilgrimage, a 'peregrinacion,' which could arrive at Sacramento on Easter Sunday."[10]

MARCHING TO SACRAMENTO

On the morning of March 17, 1966, Chavez and about one hundred individuals gathered in Delano to begin the march. Somewhat disorganized but enthusiastic, they set off through the town and onto Highway 99, followed by members of the press, several FBI agents, and other onlookers. Soon, they began to pass some of the vineyards in which they had worked and against which they had organized pickets six months earlier. They carried banners, portraits of the Virgin of Guadalupe, and union flags. Some carried large crosses; some wore Veterans of Foreign Wars hats. As Catholic and Episcopal bishops voiced support for the strike and as rabbis appeared along the route, it was clear that Chavez, now limping badly on his swollen feet and using a cane, had succeeded in framing the march in religious as well as cultural terms. He had also succeeded in casting the strike, not as a labor action or a left-wing political maneuver, but as a fight for justice.

On Sunday, April 3, a week before the marchers were due to reach Sacramento, Chavez received a call from a representative of Schenley Industries. Damaged by the publicity garnered by Chavez and hurt economically by the strike and boycott, the company had decided to formally recognize Chave's union. This was the first time in U.S. history that a grassroots, farm labor union had achieved recognition by a corporation. Schenley also agreed to a substantial increase of wages and to an improvement of working conditions.

On Saturday afternoon, the day before their arrival in Sacramento, the marchers rested on the grounds of Our Lady of Grace School on a hill looking across the Sacramento River to the capital city; they held a rally that evening. The next morning, Easter of 1966, the marchers, led by several supporters on horseback carrying the union flag and many others wearing sombreros, crossed the bridge, paraded down the mall, and ascended the capitol building steps to thunderous cheers.

USING BOYCOTT AS A WEAPON

In the spring of 1966, Chavez's union stayed on the attack, launching a boycott against Di Giorgio Fruit Corporation. Since its founding, Di Giorgio had gained a reputation for taking ruthless action to keep union organizers far from its workers. The company decided to turn to the giant International Brotherhood of Teamsters union, whose leadership was anxious to incorporate the farm workers under its own enormous control. To gain a foothold in this new labor area, the Teamsters would offer much more favorable contract terms than the fledgling but spirited Chavez union. Di Giorgio invited the Teamsters to organize its workers with no job security, seniority rights or hiring hall. The Teamsters agreed.

In the summer, the company held an election in which the farm workers apparently chose to be represented by the Teamsters. After reports of numerous cases of voter irregularity, an investigation by the California state government proved that the election had been rigged. The company agreed to a new election to be held on August 30, 1967. A few weeks before the second election, Chavez employed a counter-strategy. He agreed to merge the NFWA with the AWOC, with whom he worked in the Delano strike. Together, they would form the United Farm Workers Organizing Committee (UFWOC) and affiliate with the AFL-CIO, the national labor federation. On August 22, 1967, the two organizations officially united. Chavez and his union, the United Farm Workers of America, would now receive organizing funds from the AFL-CIO.

In the second election, the workers at Di Giorgio overwhelmingly voted to support the new United Farm Workers. Soon afterward, the company agreed to sign a three-year contract.

By 1967, the farm workers union numbered about 8,000 members. Chavez, as unlikely and unusual a union leader as the nation had ever seen, remained cautious yet exuberant in his early successes. The membership of the union had spread outside the boundaries of California and so had its influence.

Chavez now turned his sights on the Giumarra Vineyards Corporation, the largest producer of table grapes in the United States. This strike, Chavez believed, would represent much more than merely labor conditions in the fields of California. As it gained momentum, Latinos would rally to *La Causa* because for them it symbolized their own cultural and racial struggle in American society. Richard Chavez later wrote, "What Cesar wanted to reform was the way he was treated as a man."[11]

Chavez did it from his the tiny two-bedroom house in Delano where, for a number of years, his wife and eight children found a way to share the small amount of space. The family was living on $10 a week from the union and on food from a communal kitchen in the nearby union headquarters. As the union began completely to dominate his time and energy, he had almost given up even casual socializing. He no longer smoked or drank alcohol. He liked Chinese food, and he enjoyed matzos along with traditional Mexican food and low-calorie sodas—a diet long in ethnic diversity if short in nutritional quality.

Soon, across the nation, thousands of demonstrators picketed and marched, asking the public not to purchase table grapes from California vineyards. Supermarket chains from the east coast to the west reacted in various ways. Some began purchasing grapes from Israel or Africa and refused to buy California grapes. Others decided to leave the choice to the purchaser and carried California grapes.

The personal pressures on the strikers, many of whom were nearly impoverished and were the targets of increasing harassment and physical abuse, were enormous. They found it increasingly difficult to stand by their pledge to Chavez to remain nonviolent. By early February 1968, Chavez's concern about increasing attitudes of violence in the ranks of his own protestors reached, for him, a critical point. For this student of Gandhi, the great Indian independence hero, of whom a large portrait hung in Chavez's office, the union leader's reaction to these unfolding events was not totally surprising. He decided to fast. It was what Gandhi had taught; it was what Gandhi himself had practiced. On February 14, Chavez stopped eating. At first, he told only a few of his closest friends. After a few days, the word spread quickly.

In many ways the fast was a logical extension of his fight for social change. It emphasized perfectly the approach of his movement—nonviolent, spiritual, speaking of a willingness to sacrifice for the greater good. Most of his fellow lieutenants, although very worried about the health of their leader, saw the extreme sacrificial gesture, religious in nature, as a way to rededicate the cause to nonviolence.

Chavez had no plan to refuse food for any specific length of time. Increasingly worried about his ebbing strength, Helen frequently argued that everything that they were working for would be imperiled if he lost his health or his life. It was no small irony, members of Chavez's team began to realize, that the fast had turned out to be one of the most dramatic organizing tools the new union had ever employed. Across the country, people from various backgrounds began to voice support for the union and its strike. The press flocked to Delano. Money arrived. All of this occurred when its leader was completely immobilized.

Senator Robert Kennedy, who would announce his candidacy for the U.S. presidency the following month, sent a telegram to Chavez, asking him to consider the consequences to the movement if he should not survive. Senator Kennedy was a strong supporter of both the civil rights movement and of the farm labor strike.

For twenty-one days Chavez fasted. His doctor began to fear for his life when he had lost thirty-five pounds and had grown progressively weaker. On March 10, 1968, Chavez gave in to the entreaties and ended the fast. He did it with a celebration. A crowd of several thousand watched as Chavez, seated with his wife and mother, broke bread with Senator Kennedy, who had flown in for the event from a political dinner in Des Moines, Iowa. At an open-air mass, several priests and nuns distributed bread to the crowd. Chavez later remembered one particularly humorous moment during all the swirl of activity. Addressing the crowd, Senator Kennedy said, "The world must know that the migrant farm worker, the Mexican American, is coming into his own right." The victory would be theirs, Kennedy said, but they must do it with nonviolent means.[12]

LOST BROTHERS—KING AND KENNEDY

Less than three weeks after Chavez ended his fast, on the evening of April 3, 1968, civil rights leader Martin Luther King, Jr., was in Memphis, Tennessee. Early the next morning, April 4, King prepared to leave the Lorraine Motel to meet with march organizers. As he stepped out from his room on the second floor, he had only an instant more to live. When an assassin's rifle bullet ended his life that day in Memphis, he was thirty-nine years old.

Chavez was stunned and profoundly saddened by King's assassination. The civil rights leader was not only a heroic figure to many Americans; he was also in Chavez's mind a great teacher. Chavez said, "Dr. King's dedication to the rights of the workers who are so often exploited by the forces of greed has profoundly touched my life and guided my struggle."[13]

In the wake of King's assassination, the work of Chavez and *La Causa* continued apace. For two months, Chavez's union troops eagerly honored their pledge to help Senator Kennedy in his bid for the White House. Throughout Chicano barrios in the major cities and in the harvesting areas of California, volunteers answered Chavez's call to help the Kennedy campaign. They canvassed door-to-door, encouraging residents to register and vote. They helped bring out a large number of Mexican-American votes for the Senator on California's primary election day, June 4, 1968.

At the Ambassador Hotel in Los Angeles, Chavez, Dolores Huerta, and other friends of the farm workers union celebrated Kennedy's victory along with thousands of supporters in the hotel ballroom. Huerta was among many of Kennedy's friends and supporters on stage. Chavez waited in a private room of the hotel with a mariachi band that eagerly waited to play in the Senator's honor.

After Kennedy completed his victory speech to a tumultuous ovation, he stayed for a time, thanking personally many of those who had helped in his campaign, including Huerta. Along with several associates, Kennedy then walked off the stage, heading from the ballroom through the kitchen. They walked into pandemonium. A lone gunman named Sirhan Sirhan fired several shots, hitting Kennedy, who was gravely wounded, and several others. Kennedy died the following day.

Chavez and the farm workers' union had lost two towering and inspirational supporters. Devastated by the two assassinations within the space of two months, they would, nevertheless, carry on the fight.

AN EXPANDING BOYCOTT

Throughout 1969, shipments of California table groups were stopped by strikes in Boston, New York, Philadelphia, Chicago, Detroit, Montreal, and Toronto. In some British ports, dockworkers refused to unload grapes. In September, Chavez had recovered sufficiently from his fast and his chronically painful back to embark on a seven-week, nationwide tour. In November he testified before a Senate committee that the union had evidence that growers were poisoning workers with pesticides. Chavez would increasingly fight the growers over the pesticide issue as *La Causa* moved forward in its various campaigns.

On July 29, 1970, with the grape growers realizing that the boycott was having a definite deleterious impact both financially and in the eyes of the public, more than twenty growers, led by John Giamarra, Jr., signed an historic pact with Chavez's United Farm Workers Organizing Committee. It had been five years since the union strike hit the vineyards of the San Joaquin Valley. Hundreds of farm workers and union leaders mingled with representatives of the growers at the union's headquarters in Delano. This was a day for which Chavez had labored for so long, a day for the *campesinos*, the workers of the field, their backs bent and pained by years of labor, their hands roughened and skin weathered like leather.

The contract called for a wage of $1.80 plus $.20 for each box picked. Before the strike, the workers made approximately $1.10 an hour. In addition, growers would begin to contribute to a health plan, and the agreement included stringent safety requirements with regard to the use of pesticides. For the workers, this was not merely a victory for wages and better working conditions; for them, the battle was for dignity and for affirmation. On this day, as they jubilantly sang the songs of *La Causa,* as they sang "Nosotros venceremos," the civil rights song of "We Shall Overcome," as they shouted "Viva la huelga," they were asserting newly won respect.

THE LETTUCE STRIKE AND BOYCOTT

On July 29, 1970, with the jubilant singing of farm workers celebrating their new labor contracts still reverberating around Delano's union headquarters, Cesar Chavez retired to his office. He had immediate work to do in preparing for the next battle.

In California's Salinas Valley, Chavez had recently learned, lettuce growers were attempting to avoid the same fate that befell the grape growers. A narrow, fertile pocket of about 100 miles, Salinas Valley produces a lion's portion of the nation's vegetables—iceberg lettuce, broccoli, artichokes, celery, carrots, and other produce that appears on kitchen tables across America.

And now, in 1970, almost every lettuce grower in the area had begun signing union contracts with the Teamsters Union, agreements far more favorable to the growers than any contracts they could possibly work out with Chavez's farm workers' union. Once again the Teamsters were attempting to add to their already considerable power by destroying Chavez's union.

With its identification with the civil rights movement and with Democratic politicians, the Chavez union was a special irritant to most Republican party leaders. Its success was especially irritating to Governor Ronald Reagan, the former movie actor who had won the California governorship a few years earlier and who enjoyed the strong support of the state's agribusiness establishment. The Reagan administration conducted a mean-spirited attack on Chavez and his union, a campaign tinted with ethnic resentment and personal mockery of Chavez himself. During the grape boycott, Reagan frequently found it convenient to have himself photographed popping a grape into his mouth or offering grapes to reporters and other visitors.

Chavez had not planned to take on the lettuce growers so quickly after the grape boycott, but the collusion between the Teamsters and the companies forced his hand. He called a strike against the lettuce ranches in Salinas. On the third day, an estimated 10,000 workers had already walked out of the fields and the fight was on. Soon, for more than 100 miles in each direction, from Monterey County to Santa Cruz, the red flags waved. "It looked like a revolution," said Jerry Cohen, General Counsel for the strikers. "And some of these right-wing growers thought it was."[14]

The growers hired guards armed with shotguns to protect their ranches. As the chaos escalated, police were now also quick to brandish guns to prevent further violence. On December 4, 1970, Chavez went to jail, charged with contempt of court after he refused to call off the nationwide boycott of lettuce. By the time of his release on Christmas Eve, Chavez had reenergized the farm workers' struggle. Once again, in attempting to thwart the farm workers' movement, Chavez's enemies had given him greater visibility on the national scene and an increasingly sympathetic ear from large segments of the American population.

In 1971, Chavez and his family and some of the union's administrators moved from Delano to Keene, California, located southwest of Bakersfield in the foothills of the Tehachapi Mountains. The credit union, clinic, and hiring hall remained in Delano. Chavez called the new headquarters "La Paz," a shortened version of Nuestra Senora de la Paz, or Our Lady of Peace.

Especially in the large cities such as Los Angeles and Chicago, young Latinos now followed closely the drama being played out in the fields of California. A new generation of young people looked to reclaim the pride and heritage of their culture. They began to use the name "Chicano," a term once used as a racial slur by non–Mexican Americans. They took the name as a gesture of political defiance and ethnic pride. One of their heroes was Cesar Chavez.

OVERCOMING THE TEAMSTERS

In 1973, when the farm workers' three-year contracts were up for re-negotiation, most of the grape growers quickly signed contracts with the Teamsters. Chavez responded with another strike. Beginning with farms in the Coachella and San Joaquin valleys, approximately 10,000 farm workers walked out of the fields.

This time the strikers faced increasing strong-arm tactics. Many of the striking farm workers were arrested or beaten. It was not the attackers, however, that went to jail. Throughout the summer local judges, with close personal and political ties to the growers, issued injunctions limiting legitimate strike activity.

By the end of the summer of 1973 the Chavez union, despite its heroic efforts, seemed destined to fail under the onslaught of its opponents. Against the strong-armed, aggressive force of the Teamsters, backed by their political friends in power, Chavez's union now had only a token number of contracts with the growers. The membership of the organization had shrunk from a high of 40,000 to less than 10,000. It seemed to most outside observers that the halcyon days of the United Farm Workers were over.

On September 1, Chavez, despairing over the loss of life and the injuries to his union members, decided to call off the strike. He did not, however, call off the war. Instead, he decided to resume the nationwide boycott. In a letter that was distributed across the country, Chavez pleaded for consumers to back the union in this critical time. "You are the crucial element they cannot control ... please boycott *all* grapes and Gallo wines and don't buy or eat iceberg (head) lettuce unless you are sure it bears our label.... Please join with us in our struggle for self-determination and dignity."[15]

Chavez now faced his greatest challenge. His union was nearly broke. It faced formidable enemies and a growing belief that he could not win the war. It was this sense of vulnerability and decline in his ranks that Chavez braced himself to attack. He decided to do it with a method that was successful nearly a decade earlier. He decided to gather his forces for another march.

ON THE LEGISLATIVE FRONT

On February 22, 1975, several hundred members of the United Farm Workers of America began a 110-mile march from San Francisco to Modesto, headquarters of the Ernest & Julio Gallo winery. Other contingents of the march headed out from Stockton and Fresno. The Gallo winery would thus be approached from the north, south, and west, a kind of siege on the winemaker. In addition, Chavez thought, the march could also have a very important political purpose. A new Democratic governor, Jerry Brown, was now in charge in Sacramento and was far more sympathetic to the plight of the farm workers than his predecessor.

On March 1, well over 10,000 members and supporters of the United Farm Workers converged in Modesto, a line of marchers more than a mile long carrying the union flag and chanting "Chavez si, Teamsters no; Gallo wine has got to go!" Chavez, who joined the marchers in Modesto, was ebullient over the large turnout and declared, "This should make it clear to Gallo that we're not going away."[16]

Shortly after the march, Chavez and his lieutenants met with Brown about the possibility of introducing farm workers legislation in the

California legislature in the next few months. After a succession of meetings, proposals, and counterproposals, Brown's assistants, with the advice of representatives of the United Farm Workers, shaped the outlines of a bill that had the makings of a significant legislative leap forward in establishing legal bargaining rights for migrant laborers in California. Finally, when the union leaders decided they had reached a point in the negotiations that represented the minimum they could accept, Brown and his advisors had the outline of a compromise to offer to the state legislators and to the growers. The outline of the bill essentially, for the first time in California history, granted migrant and farm labor workers the right to vote in secret ballot elections for union representation.

On Sunday, May 4, 1975, Brown and his advisors summoned growers and their representatives for a meeting on the legislation. When the negotiations were completed, Brown called Chavez at his headquarters near Bakersfield. The union leader was joyous.

For farm workers the passage of California's Agricultural Labor Relations Act was a legislative triumph of profound consequences, not necessarily for the economic gains it immediately afforded the workers, but for the power it conferred to them. It was no less than the first bill of rights for farm workers in the continental United States, protecting the rights of farm workers to unionize and boycott and guaranteeing secret ballots in farm workers' union elections.

After a number of secret negotiations, Chavez's union and the Teamsters finally reached an agreement. The Teamsters granted the United Farm Workers exclusive rights to represent the field workers covered by the Agricultural Labor Relations Act. The United Farm Workers agreed that the Teamsters would have labor jurisdiction in industries surrounding agricultural production, such as canneries, packing sheds, and frozen food operations. Covering not only California but also eleven other western states, the agreement was set for five years. This was clearly a victory for Chavez; indeed, on March 21, 1977, *Newsweek* ran a story entitled "Cesar's Triumph."

THE GREAT LETTUCE STRIKE OF 1979

In January 1979, Chavez decided to call for strikes against eleven lettuce growers in the Salinas and Imperial Valleys because their offers of wage hikes were well below what the farm workers demanded. At the time of the negotiations, lettuce pickers were making a base wage of $3.70 an hour. At first, Chavez believed that they could win their demands with a relatively short walkout. He did not anticipate the virulent opposition that the strike would set off.

At first, the solidarity among the workers raised Chavez's spirit to great heights. It was a demonstration of the enormous lengths to which the organization had traveled in establishing a disciplined union. Field workers up and down the Imperial Valley acted as one united team, with strikers bolstering each other's determination. To Chavez and other union leaders, the performance of the union members in the strike was a coming of age of the organization as a professional union.

On February 10, the strike turned deadly. Rufino Contreras, a twenty-eight-year-old lettuce worker, was shot dead by ranch guards. The union held a large funeral march. The procession was led by Cesar and Helen Chavez and attended by Governor Brown. The violence continued in the fields. Police lobbed tear-gas canisters into bands of strikers on a number of occasions. When some of the strikers lobbed the canisters back at the police, they were hauled off to the police station. A number of fights broke out. When asked to comment on the violence, Chavez pointed out that all of the blood shed in the confrontations appeared to come only from the union members.

In late summer of 1979, Chavez called for a march on Salinas. It lasted twelve days with two groups parading from San Francisco, over 100 miles to the north, and from San Ardo, 70 miles to the south. More than 25,000 individuals took part in the march. Union leaders welcomed the sight of workers in the fields who threw down their tools and joined the march when it passed. When the marchers from San Francisco reached Salinas, Chavez, who had fasted for part of the journey, looked pale. Nevertheless, when the marchers reached the center of town, merged with the other farm workers and filled the center of town, Chavez smiled broadly.

VIVA LA CAUSA

Chavez's movement, with its energy and appeal to the religious and cultural heritage of Mexican Americans, had lit a spark in the harvest fields that consumed old notions that life could not improve, that the system holding down the workers was too intractable and too powerful for it to be changed. Through grit and stubbornness, Chavez and his lieutenants had weeded out the stereotypes and the defeatism, convincing large numbers of people that they could fight back.

Nevertheless, given the tensions and constant financial strains on the organization, dissension within the ranks had grown in the early 1980s. Many of his lieutenants had grown frustrated with Chavez's strong control of union policy. A number of Chavez's closest supporters over the years drifted off to other jobs. Chavez, they insisted, was an enormously successful crusader for justice but a less-than-adequate administrator. Many pointed to the enormous backlog in the union's medical plan, where claims were being processed at a glacier's pace.

A REPUBLICAN IN SACRAMENTO

In November 1982, Republican George Deukmejian became governor of California. He did not disappoint the growers. He packed the Agricultural Labor Relations Board with representatives who supported the interests of the growers. Under the new leadership of the board, enforcement of the farm labor election law became gnarled in delay and inaction. Chavez's union thus had no state authority to which it could issue complaints of grower labor violations and expect action. Growers soon realized that if they simply ignored the farm workers law, they would not be prosecuted. Even on some of the farms that had held elections and had chosen the United Farm Workers as their union, the process came to a grinding halt with the Republicans in control in Sacramento.

In 1984, Chavez called for another grape boycott. In a fiery speech in Fresno, Chavez told supporters that Deukmejian's efforts to undermine the Agricultural Relations Act and to bury the United Farm Workers was a new call to action. He declared, "Let us take off where we left off in 1975 with the most effective weapon which served us so well—the consumer boy- cott—and see how they like it."[17] When he looked two or three decades down the road, he said, he saw communities such as Modesto, Salinas, and Bakersfield, as well as the great cities of California, dominated by the eco- nomic power and the votes of the children of farm workers, not the children of the big growers. The new grape strike he announced would drive home to Americans the continuing need to reform the harvest fields of California and the farm labor areas in the rest of the United States.

CRUSADING AGAINST PESTICIDE POISONING

In 1985, in the middle of the grape boycott, Chavez decided to increase the pressures on the growers in another controversial area—the use of pesti- cides. He announced that, as part of the boycott, the union would launch a campaign titled "Wrath of Grapes." The union had used the title for a short documentary film it had produced a few years earlier demonstrating evi- dence of birth defects and high cancer rates among the children of farm workers caused by the use of pesticides in the southern San Joaquin Valley. Now was the time, Chavez felt, for a full-scale war on pesticide poisoning.

The pesticides, some of which were applied by airplanes, routinely drifted away from targeted fields and landed on workers and their families and eas- ily reached their living quarters. Even when the spray accurately hit the tar- geted area, small amounts of the chemicals remained on the plants. When workers who thinned and harvested crops returned to the fields after the spraying, they breathed the chemicals and touched them and rubbed them into their eyes. Studies had begun to suggest that farm workers and their children were vulnerable to a long list of illnesses potentially related to pesticides, which included, in addition to cancer and birth defects, liver disease, childhood leukemia, and infertility.

Chavez talked about the cumulative effect that pesticides, herbicides, soil fumigants, and fertilizers had produced in the soil and water. Thousands of acres in California alone, he claimed, had been irrevocably contaminated by the unrestrained, wanton use of these chemicals. Many thousands more, he said, would be lost unless growers were prevented from dumping an ever-increasing amount. The boycott focused on five pesticides that had been listed as possibly hazardous by the Environmental Protection Agency. As with any claims of cause and effect on health by chemicals, the two sides produced their own studies and their own scientists to prove entirely opposite conclusions. Chavez took his crusade against unsafe pesticide use around the United States, visiting various cities to give speeches and conduct meetings.

In the summer of 1988, back in his headquarters at Delano, he began a fast. He was now sixty-one years old. Helen Chavez, other family members and friends, as well as Chavez's doctors, were very concerned that he would again jeopardize his health. As Chavez's fast extended over a month, his health deteriorated to the extent that doctors began to fear for his life. Finally, after thirty-six days, he agreed to end the fast. On August 21, 1988, two of Chavez's sons carried the union leader into a large tent. Flanked by Helen and his ninety-six-year-old mother Juana, Chavez, sitting in a rocking chair, accepted a piece of bread from Ethel Kennedy. Months after he had regained his strength after the fast, Chavez was back on the campaign.

Chavez continued to campaign against pesticides into the 1990s. He fought in the courts as growers tried to use such legal loopholes as switching ownership rights to void previous contracts with the union. He went from town to town trying to convince consumers not to eat grapes until grapes were pesticide-free.

In the spring of 1993, Chavez was in the tiny southwest Arizona town of San Luis, near Yuma, where a half century earlier the Chavez family had been forced out of their small farm and had begun their lives as migrant farm workers. He was there to help United Farm Worker's attorneys defend the union against a lawsuit brought by Bruce Church, Inc., a giant lettuce and vegetable producer based in Salinas, California.

In preparing for his court appearance in the trial, Chavez began a short fast to regain moral strength. After two days on the witness stand, the union leader was exhausted but confident. He broke his fast and was taken on a drive around Yuma by long-time friend David Martinez. They toured the barrios of the south side, seeing the playground where Chavez had played stickball with his brother Richard and the school where his teachers had admonished him for speaking Spanish. That evening, saying he was very tired, he took a book about Native American art with him to bed. The next morning, April 23, 1993, David Martinez found Chavez's lifeless body.

On April 29, 1993, more than 40,000 mourners honored Chavez at the United Farm Workers headquarters in Delano. In caravans, the people came: entertainers, politicians, church leaders, social service directors, and union leaders and fellow associates in the United Farm Workers. But mostly the farm workers lined up. At an all-night vigil inside a large tent they filed past his plain pine coffin. The workers brought children of all ages. Fathers and mothers carrying infants said that they just wanted to be able to tell their children someday that they had been in the presence of a great man.

In August 1994, Chavez was posthumously awarded the Presidential Medal of Freedom, the highest honor for nonmilitary personnel in the United States. His wife Helen accepted the award at the White House.

Herlinda Gonzalez stitched together her own United Farm Workers flag forty years ago. It is now a bit faded, with the once flaming red now somewhat pink and the black Aztec eagle turning gray. Nevertheless, she flies the flag today as she did then. She remembers the day in 1966 when the members of the farm workers union and their supporters marched along Highway 33 on their way to Sacramento.

Chavez had helped them make progress. Although the numbers of workers covered by contracts with the United Farm Workers are substantially lower than in the heyday of the movement, there have been improvements in the fields. Farm laborers are covered by workers' compensation laws. They are working for at least the minimum wage as set by the state legislature.

When Chavez Delgado, one of Cesar's many grandchildren, walks the streets of San Jose, his grandfather is never far from his mind. "This area has so many ties to my grandfather and his work," Delgado said. "This is where he began organizing." The site of the Mexican Heritage Plaza used to be a Safeway, which itself was the site of one of the first boycotts here in San Jose against lettuce and grapes. "I look at these kids and think, perhaps we have the next Cesar Chavez right now, walking around here in San Jose."[18]

A reporter once asked Chavez, "What accounts for all the affection and respect so many farm workers show you in public?" Chavez looked down and smiled. He said, "The feeling is mutual."[19]

NOTES

1. Kim Benita Furumoto, "Viva La Causa! Cesar Chavez Remembered," *Diatribe*, May 1993, http://www.sfsu.edu/cecipp/cesar_chavez/remembered.htm.

2. Susan Ferriss and Ricardo Sandoval, *The Fight in the Fields: Cesar Chavez and the Farmworkers Movement* (Orlando, Florida: Paradigm Productions, 1997), 33.

3. Furumoto.

4. Cletus Daniel, "Cesar Chavez and the Unionization of California Farm Workers," http://www.lib.berkeley.edu/ljones/UFW/documents/cletus.html.

5. Jacques Levy, *Cesar Chavez: Autobiograhy of La Causa,* http://chavez.cde.ca. gov/ModelCurriculum/Teachers/Lessons/Resources/Documents/Chavez_Biography_by_Levy.pdf.

6. Ferriss and Sandoval, 62.

7. Dick Meister, "'La Huelga' Becomes 'La Causa'," *New York Times Magazine,* November 17, 1968, 52.

8. Carol Larson Jones, "Dolores Huerta: Cesar Chavez' Partner in Founding the United Farm Workers Union in California," http://www.csupomona.edu/jis/1997/Mullikin.pdf.

9. Jones.

10. "Chavez Banner," *History Detectives,* http://pbs.org/opb/historydetectives/df/208_banner.df.

11. "The Little Strike That Grew to *La Causa,*" *Time,* July 4, 1969, 17.

12. "Head of Farm Workers Union Ends 25 Day Fast in California, *NewYork Times,* March 11, 1968, 22.

13. Cesar Chavez, "Lessons of Dr. Martin Luther King, Jr.," January 12, 1990, http://aztlan.net/cesarMLK.htm.

14. Ferriss and Sandoval, 170.

15. Cesar Chavez, "A Letter from Cesar Chavez," *New York Review of Books,* October 31, 1974, http://www.nybooks.com/articles/9359.

16. "10,000 in Protest at Gallo Winery," *New York Times,* March 2, 1975, p. 44.

17. "Cesar Chavez Tries New Directions for United Farm Workers," *New York Times,* September 19, 1983, 38.

18. Maria Alicia Gaura, "Celebrated with Holiday," *San Francisco Chronicle,* March 30, 2001, 3.

19. Marc Grossman, "By Giving Our Lives, We Find Life," http://www.soup4world.com/ssli/cesarchavez.html.

FURTHER READING

Bruns, Roger. *Cesar Chavez: A Biography.* Westport, CT: Greenwood Press, 2005.

"Cesar's Triumph," *Newsweek*, March 21, 1977, 70.

"Cesar's War," *Time*, March 22, 1968, 23.

Ferriss, Susan, and Ricardo Sandoval. *The Fight in the Fields: Cesar Chavez and the Farm Workers Movement.* New York: Harcourt Brace, 1997.

Griswold del Castillo, Richard, and Richard A. Garcia. *Cesar Chavez: A Triumph of Spirit.* Norman: University of Oklahoma Press, 1995.

Levy, Jacques E. *Cesar Chavez: Autobiography of La Causa.* New York: W. W. Norton & Company, 1975, http://chavez.cde.ca.gov/ModelCurriculum/Teachers/Lessons/Resources/Documents/Chavez_Biograhy_by_Levy.pdf.

Matthiessen, Peter. *Sal Si Puedes: Cesar Chavez and the New American Revolution.* New York: Dell Publishing Company, 1969.

Meister, Dick, and Anne Loftis. *A Long Time Coming: The Struggle to Unionize America's Farm Workers.* New York: Macmillan, 1977.

Quintanilla, Antita. "Remembering a Modest Cesar," http://www.azteca.net/aztec/modest_cesar.html.

Ross, Fred. *Conquering Goliath: Cesar Chavez at the Beginning.* Keene, CA: El Taller Grafico Press/United Farm Workers, 1989.

Chiles, Tortillas, and the Mexican Food Explosion

In the 1950s, most Americans outside the Southwest and California knew almost nothing about Mexican food. They could not identify tortillas, tamales, quesadillas, or, for that matter, refried beans. They rarely used fresh chiles in their cooking and had no idea of the origins of the chile itself. A taco was a mystery. There were no fast food chains selling nachos and burritos.

Today, metropolitan areas are dotted with hundreds of Mexican restaurants along with many other establishments featuring foods from various Latin American countries. The range is extraordinary, from the one-dollar tacos at any of the locations of the Taco Bell restaurant chain to new, innovative restaurant locations offering the latest in "nueva Latino" fare. At an upscale restaurant one can try lamb taquitos, two soft corn tortillas filled with shredded lamb, or Brazilian-style chicken pasteles, deep-fried and well-drained, or mushroom quesadillas shaped like half-moons with a whiff of truffle oil in the stuffing and a dollop of fresh guacamole on top.

But the influence of Latin-American cuisine as it has melded into the culture of the United States has taken on other forms. The chili, the tortilla, and other Mexican foods have taken on iconic status.

Several pepper species, because of their unique shapes and bright fruit colors, have been widely used as ornaments. Colorful lights made in the form of chiles, for example, adorn Christmas trees every year from San Diego to Boston, from Miami Beach to Seattle.

A major rock band is named the Red Hot Chili Peppers. Visual artists have used dried tortillas as canvases for their work. One artist, after creating an image of a famous Latino figure on a tortilla, quipped that he had put an icon on an icon. Other forms of the arts have used the foods as cultural reference points. The play *Tortilla Heaven*, written in 2004, focused on several generations of a Tejano family living along the border. The message is that the characters absorb and weave together the various elements of several cultures; they shape and mold them as they do tortillas.

For many Latinos, then, chiles, tortillas, and other Mexican and Mexican-American foods are a connection to family, friends, and the lives of their ancestors. For the larger American society, the chile and the tortilla stories mean something different: They have become an exchange of culture and tradition at the most basic level of life.

A SHORT HISTORY OF THE CHILE

Zarela Martinez was born in Agua Prieta, a town in the state of Sonora, Mexico, and she grew up on a cattle ranch in Chihuahua, Mexico. Her earliest memory of food was the smell and taste of tortillas on the wood-burning stove. From those early beginnings, Martinez became a renowned chef, writer, and memoirist. Her restaurant in New York City became known as one of the finest Mexican restaurants in the world.

The Nacho Story

Another so-called Mexican food that seemed to be everywhere as the nation moved into the twenty-first century was nachos. One could buy them at gas stations and truck stops, in mall food courts, in movie houses, at ball games—almost anywhere, it seemed, fast food was sold. All that the seller needed were some corn chips, some chili cheese sauce, and some chili peppers.

Although historians have not definitively proclaimed an official inventor of the nacho, there was a gentleman who seized credit. His name was Ignacio (Nacho) Anaya. His nickname evolved from a shortening of his first name. His story began in 1941 at the Victory Club in Piedras Negras, Mexico, on the Rio Grande River just across the border from Eagle Pass, Texas. Anaya, a waiter at the club, was serving four ladies, his story goes, who were drinking chicos, a cocktail made with tequila and blackberry liqueur.

The four tourists to the city asked for some fried tortillas to go along with their drinks. At the time, Anaya recalled, the cook had stepped out and there was no one in the kitchen. Undaunted, he went into action. "I sliced a tortilla in four pieces, put some cheese and slices of jalapeno on top, and stuck it in the oven for a few minutes." Fascinated by the taste, the women wanted to know what they were called. Anaya quickly replied, "Just call them "Nacho's Especial."[1]

An early nacho promoter of distinction was Victor J. Bergeron, founder of a restaurant in Oakland, California, called Hinky Dinks, the forerunner of Trader Vic's. Although Trader Vic's establishments were not Mexican in orientation (they were Polynesian), Bergeron was determined to go beyond the fare that was served up by the mostly Chinese cooks that he had hired. He began to feature nachos in a string of new restaurants. His nachos spread around the country along with his restaurants.

If Bergeron was a national promoter of nachos, the legendary sportscaster Howard Cosell gets even higher credit. In Arlington Stadium, home of Dallas Cowboys football, the concession stands began to sell nachos in 1977. When Cosell and his broadcasting team arrived for a game in Dallas, Cosell tried nachos. He loved them. That night, Cosell mentioned on national television how much he liked the product. Perhaps more than any single individual, Cosell, through unintended mass advertising, contributed to the strength of a growing national craze for nachos. They had come a long way from the day when Ignacio Anaya allegedly made the first one.

[1] Robb Walsh. *The Tex-Mex Cookbook* (New York: Broadway Books, 2004), 193.

When talking about the chile pepper, Martinez quoted sixteenth-century religious figure Fray Bartolome de las Casas, "Sin el chile los mexicanos no creen que estan comiendo" (Without the chile, Mexicans do not believe they are eating). Martinez said that chile is not only the culinary backbone of

Mexican cuisine, it is "a common denominator that defines what is Mexican."[1]

The chile, said Martinez, outlasted histories, religions, and government. Growing wild in the various Latin-American countries, for centuries it has been one of the three major dietary components, along with corn and beans. Corn and beans are the staples, but chiles provide the critical vitamins A and C and the spice that makes possible the various dishes. "The combination of the three," said Martinez, "makes a nutritionally balanced meal. It's magic."[2]

Although no one knows the exact origin of the chile pepper, it is believed that the plant originated in the Andes mountains and that the seeds over the years migrated north by bird droppings, making their way into Central America and Mexico. Archaeologists think the chile pepper was used in the diets of Latin-American peoples as far back as 7500 B.C.

Through the centuries, cooks have used well over one hundred varieties of cultivated chili peppers. They have been diced, sliced, dried, and cooked in various ways. So popular was the plant that it was honored by Southwest Indians in pottery, tapestries, and other art forms. For a time, it even functioned as a form of currency.

In recent excavations, plant remains found in two caves in southern Mexico and analyzed by scientists indicated that, as much as 1,500 years ago, inhabitants of the region enjoyed a spicy fare similar to Mexican cuisine today. The two caves yielded ten different varieties of chili peppers. The remains of these domesticated chili peppers were often found with corn, forming part of a major, ancient food complex that predates pottery in some regions.

One archeologist stated that ancient peoples there "would have used fresh peppers in salsas or in immediate preparation, and they would have used the dried peppers to toss into stews or to grind up into sauces like moles."[3]

"It is hard to imagine modern Latino cuisine without chili peppers," stated another archeologist on the project: "We demonstrate that prehistoric people from the Bahamas to Peru were using chilies in a variety of foods a long time ago. The peppers would have enhanced the flavor of early cultivars such as maize and manioc and may have contributed to their rapid spread after they were domesticated."[4] Centuries later, Christopher Columbus took the chili back to the Old World. W. Hardy Eshbaugh, a renowned botanist, studied the evolution of peppers. He has written, "Few could have imagined the impact of Columbus' discovery of a spice so pungent that it rivaled the better known black pepper from the East Indies. Nonetheless, some 500 years later, on the quincentennial anniversary of the discovery of the New World, chili peppers (*Capsicum*) have come to dominate the world hot spice trade and are grown everywhere in the tropics as well as in many temperate regions of the globe. Not only have hot peppers come to command the world's spice trade but a genetic recessive non-pungent form has become an important 'green' vegetable crop on a global scale especially in temperate regions."[5]

By the early 1500s peppers were carried by the Spanish and Portuguese explorers to their territories in Asia and Africa as well as their native Spain. According to anthropologists, the Turks likely introduced the chile pepper to Hungary in the mid 1500s, and, like Latin America, made the plant an important ingredient in its own cuisine.

For many centuries, chiles have also served medicinal purposes. Chiles were used as a cough remedy, as an antiseptic, and as a laxative. In Europe, scientists began to study the possible medicines that could be produced using the plant. Entire books and other publications talked about the chile plant's restorative powers.

Throughout Europe and Asia, the spread of the chile in its many forms progressed. In Turkey, ground chili peppers became known as paprika. In the south of France, the red chili became known as *rouiulle* (rust); in regions of Italy, chefs began to use peppers with olive oil to serve with fish; across northern Africa, fiery dishes were spiced with chiles mixed into so-called "vindaloo" dishes.

Yet, despite its travels to new lands and its cultivations by different cultures, the chile pepper, in its many forms, is still primarily noted for its uses in Latin America. And, as people in the United States have increasingly tried new dishes from south of the border, the chile has become a significant mark of Latino culture.

A SHORT HISTORY OF THE TORTILLA

In most Spanish language dictionaries, the first definition for tortilla describes an egg dish cooked with potatoes, seafood, and other ingredients and served in pie wedge slices. The familiar thin, flat, round bread tortilla of the Americas is the cousin of this pie-like food of Spain.

For centuries, one of the dietary essentials of the natives of South America was a product made from maize or corn. The kernels were cooked with lime to remove the husks and ground with a stone roller on a slab called a *metate*. The product was a dough called *masa* that was then rolled into balls, flattened into round cakes less than one-eighth of an inch thick, and tossed on a hot griddle or *comal* for half a minute on each side. These were tortillas.

In northern Mexico and across much of the United States, a "tortilla" over the years came to mean a flour version. Flour tortillas became the foundation of Mexican border cooking, their popularity driven by the low cost of flour provided to border markets. But the history of tortillas began with maize. Geological excavations in the valley of "Valle de Tehuacán", in the state of Puebla, uncovered evidence that for more than 7,000 years people had used as a food staple a wild cob with roots and fruit. Around 3000 B.C., people of the Sierra Madre Mountains in Mexico hybridized wild grasses to produce large, nutritious kernels now known as corn. The development of corn came with the rise of Mesoamerican civilizations such as the Mayans and the Aztecs. In addition to their development of corn, those civilizations were advanced in art, architecture, math, and astronomy. The significance of corn was not lost on indigenous cultures that viewed it as a foundation of humanity." As one anthropologist put it, "It is revered as the seed of life. According to legend, human beings were made of corn by the gods."[6]

When the Spanish explorer Hernán Cortés arrived with his group of conquistadores in 1519, they discovered that the inhabitants made flat corn breads. The native Nahuatl name for these was *tlaxcalli*. The Spanish gave them the name *tortilla*.

In a letter to King Charles V of Spain, Cortés described public markets where inhabitants sold maize or corn:

> This city has many public squares, in which are situated the markets and other places for buying and selling ... where are daily assembled more than sixty thousand souls, engaged in buying and selling; and where are found all kinds of merchandise that the world affords, embracing the necessaries of life, as for instance articles of food ... maize or Indian corn, in the grain and in the form of bread, preferred in the grain for its flavor to that of the other islands and terra-firma.[7]

Within the next decade a Franciscan friar named Bernardino de Sahagun had compiled a manuscript he titled *General History of the Things of New Spain (Historia general de las cosas de Nueva Espana)*. Sahagun's accounts described an Aztec diet centered on corn and tortillas with chiles of many varieties.

In 1540, Francisco Vasquez de Coronado led a Spanish expedition into regions occupied by the Pueblo Indians. He described their diets as including corn, deer, rabbits, and tortillas. The Pueblo Indians, one man from the expedition reported, made "the best tortillas that I have ever seen anywhere, and this is what everybody ordinarily eats. They have the very best arrangement and method for grinding that was ever seen."[8]

Many centuries later, in the 1700s, as native peoples moved into areas that became Texas, Arizona, and California, they brought with them the tortilla. In succeeding years western cowboys used tortillas as an inexpensive and easily carried foot staple. By the time of the famous 1849 Gold Rush into California, isolated miners carried tortillas along. A staple of working people from its earliest beginnings, the tortilla, in both its corn and wheat flour varieties, and used with beans and rice, became widely used in the American Southwest.

By the middle of the nineteenth century, the word tortilla was common in areas north of the Rio Grande River. Shortly after the Civil War, in the

Superstition Mountains north of what is now Phoenix, Arizona, about 120 miles north of the Rio Grande, arose a very small town called Tortilla Flat, named because of a large section of the mountain rock that is shaped like a tortilla. The small town was later a freight camp along the road during the construction of the Roosevelt Dam at the turn of the century.

In 1935, the renowned American novelist John Steinbeck wrote *Tortilla Flat*. It had nothing to do with the little town in Arizona. Much of the novel was based on Steinbeck's own youth living near the town of Monterey on the California coast during World War I. Revolving around the lives of a colorful gang of ne'er-do-wells who routinely lived outside the normal conventions of society, Steinbeck likens their adventures to the exploits of King Arthur's knights. The group is made up mostly of so-called "paisanos," descendent from the Spanish, Indians, and Mexicans and a half dozen Caucasian heritages. The area had long been called Tortilla Flat, and all of the characters in the book as well as John Steinbeck himself had certainly eaten many tortillas in their lifetimes.

By the 1960s, especially in California, New Mexico, and Arizona, Americans used small-scale tortilla machines that could turn out the steaming-hot products every few seconds.

By the year 2006, tortillas had become the second most popular bread type in the United States after white bread. Tortillas and their related products, such as tortilla chips and taco shells, generated more than $6 billion in sales in 2004. Beginning in the new century, tortillas became now more popular in the United States than all other ethnic breads, including bagels, English muffins, and pita bread.[9]

The simple, flat, round tortilla has been a staple of the Mexican diet since pre-Columbian days. It has also been a cultural symbol for millions of people across all social classes. For many of Latin America's poor it has stood for survival itself. And now, in the twenty-first century, it has become so familiar in the United States that U.S. astronauts carry them as part of their diet into space.

MEXICAN FOOD IN THE UNITED STATES

Mariano Galvan Rivera's *Diccionario de Cocina*, published in 1845, was the first comprehensive Mexican cookbook. A mammoth gathering of more than a thousand pages of recipes and commentary, the compendium contained many dishes and ingredients that have since become common in the United States, including chili peppers, tortillas, tamales, quesadillas, and enchiladas. Not surprisingly, the book did not mention other items that have also become popular in the United States including tacos, chili con carne, burritos, corn chips, or nachos.

A visitor in San Antonio, Texas, around the time of the Civil War described a main plaza where "one could get Mexican luxuries of tamales, chili con carne, and enchiladas, can find them here cooked in the open air in the rear of the tables and served by lineal descendants of the ancient Aztecs."[10] The first chili sauces appeared in cookbooks prior to the Civil War. Also, chili sauce became the first Mexican product commercially distributed under such names as Tabasco Pepper Sauce and Durkee's Essence of Chili. By the 1880s, Mexican dishes were incorporated occasionally into regional cookbooks, mostly in the Southwest. An 1881 cookbook published in Los Angeles included recipes for Spanish Hash, Stuffed Chilies, and other dishes and featured a section of the book entitled "Spanish Department."

Tamales are one of the oldest foods in Latin America. When newly arrived Spaniards stepped off their ships, they saw natives preparing the corn husk staple mixed with seafood and dipped in chili pepper sauce. Later, with the arrival of Old World livestock, the most popular tamale became those filled with pork.

Tamales became increasingly available in Texas after the Civil War. Although men of Mexican heritage fought on both sides in the war, a much larger percentage joined the Anglos of Texas when the state joined the Confederacy in 1861. Some historians attribute the popularity of tamales following the war to the experience of one particular Confederate unit: the 33rd Texas Cavalry, commanded by Colonel Santo Benavides, fought border battles against Union-supported Mexican forces.

The 33rd Cavalry was ill-equipped and had to forage for food. And so, as the mix of Anglos and Mexicans in the unit roamed through the border areas, it is likely, some historians conclude, that the Anglos in the unit ate tamales for the first time. And as their taste buds responded, so did the demand for tamales throughout the state after the war. Soon, tamale vendors became the most common purveyors of street food in Texas and in much of the South.

Although tamales were considered by most a delicious concoction sure to become increasingly popular in the American diet, this was not the opinion of one Kate Sanborn, a resident of San Diego. In 1893, Sanborn advised anyone who visited the city to stay clear of the tamales. "Whatever other folly you may be led into," she said, "let me implore you to wholly abstain from that deadly concoction, the Mexican tamale." Sanborn went on to describe the tamale as a combination of "chicken hash, meat, olives, red pepper and I know not what, enclosed in a corn-husk, stewed until furiously hot, and then offered for sale by Mexicans in such a sweet, appealing way that few can resist the novelty." She warned that the effects of eating tamales were "serious."[11]

By the end of the nineteenth century, a few national cookbooks and cookery magazines began to introduce Mexican recipes. *Mrs. Rorer's New Cook Book*, published in 1902, featured "A Group of Spanish Recipes," which included tamales, enchiladas, and frijoles. In the late 1930s, the Federal Writers Project, one of the programs of the Works Progress Administration, sent interviewers into various parts of the United States to record what life was like for many in the rural areas of the country. One resident of Anthony, New Mexico, a small town about twenty miles from El Paso, Texas, recalled his own introduction to Mexican food shortly after the turn of the century. The following is an excerpt from the interviewer's notes:

> 'Did you like the food the natives cooked?' 'Not at first,' he said, with a twisted smile, 'but it didn't take me long to learn, and in a short time I was takin' my frijoles, tortillas and chili straight.' Frijoles are beans, but not white beans. The Mexicans buy the mottled pinto beans. Tortillas are the wafer-thin corn cakes made from hand-ground corn flour. The Mexican housewife scorns the tortilla flour sold by grocers. When making chili, they use the large, dark red, chili pods. First they steam, or roast the pods, then peel them, and use the thick rich pulp to make chili sauce.[12]

In 1936, President Franklin D. Roosevelt visited his son Elliot who lived in Fort Worth, Texas. The younger Roosevelt suggested one day that they visit a restaurant that served up Mexican food. It was called the Original Mexican Restaurant, one of several in Texas that had followed the first Original that had opened in San Antonio in 1900. The historic dining moment in Fort Worth was celebrated at the restaurant for generations after the event. They called the plate of food that Roosevelt consumed in 1936 "The Roosevelt Special," and it consisted of one beef taco, one bean chalupa, and an enchilada with a fried egg on top.

The Original Mexican Restaurant in Fort Worth was opened by Otis Farnsworth, an Anglo who, on a visit to Forth Worth, had dined with some friends in a tiny eatery in the Mexican section of the city. Farnsworth decided to build an establishment more accessible and attractive to fellow Anglos. It has been noted that Farnsworth's Original Mexican Restaurant "was a bold new concept in marketing, a Mexican restaurant created by an Anglo for an audience of fellow Anglos. The Original Mexican Restaurant approached Texas biculturalism from the American side of the equation. It was a restaurant that made it easier for Anglos to feel as if they were experiencing Mexican culture."[13]

One of the most important figures to introduce native and Hispanic cooking to the United States was Fabiola Cabeza de Baca. Born to a wealthy and prominent family that traced its roots back to Spain, Cabeza de Baca became a teacher in small schools among the poor of New Mexico. For over thirty years she worked as an agricultural extension agent for the federal government, teaching and assisting poor families trying to make a life on the frontier. As she roamed the mountains and valleys helping poor native families, she began to collect Latino folklore, especially recipes. Later, she became a respected writer whose works included the first definitive description of Indian-Hispanic cooking techniques in the upper Rio Grande.

In the mid-1930s, Cabeza de Baca published two pamphlets that became the groundwork for a two-volume book called *Historic Cookery*. Featuring an array of recipes gathered from men and women that she had come in contact with on the frontier as well as food preparations handed down from her own family, the book was a groundbreaking examination of the cultural impact of food on newly merging peoples.

Published in 1939 in pamphlet form by the New Mexico State University Extension Service and reissued in 1956, the work was as much about cultural icons, such as the chili, as it was a cookbook. Cabeza de Baca wrote about the cultural evolution of cuisine in the southwest—why women on the frontier are so skilled at preparing tortillas; why hamburger is never used in making chili; that certain ancient methods of food preparation such as drying corn and chili remain the preferred methods even in modern society; and that many aspects of native diets have proven to be rich in nutritional value.

Many historians and sociologists credited *Historic Cookery* as being a major influence in introducing Latino food preparation to a wider Anglo audience. Here, published for the first time, were the keys to the magical properties of various chili and corn dishes, passed down through the generations. Published for wide distribution in 1956, the book sold more than 100,000 copies in the first years after its publication. In 1983, *Historic Cookery* appeared in a hardcover edition from the Museum of New Mexico Press. It again became a bestseller.

The popularity of Mexican restaurants has been seen to coincide with the arrival of large numbers of Mexican immigrants after 1950. Those restaurants for the most part followed the style of what was called "Tex-Mex" food, a combination of Northern Mexican peasant food and Texas farm and cowboy fare. From about 1950, the term was taken up by restaurants beyond Texas throughout the Southwest, especially New Mexico, Arizona, and California. Combinations of enchiladas, tacos, tortillas, and refried beans became the standard platters of Tex-Mex menus. As cooks in the United States began incorporating and experimenting with the basic foods from south of the border, new dishes became standard fare. Some were simply old dishes given new names or modified; others were entirely new spin-offs from the old standards.

In 1972, a major, authoritative, Mexican cookbook called *Cuisines of Mexico* was authored by Diana Kennedy, the wife of Paul Kennedy, a *New York Times* correspondent who had been stationed for a time in Mexico City. As Cabeza de Baca had done, the book took seriously the ethnic origins and culture of Mexican food. She pointed out clearly that this was the food of the poor. She took offense at the types of food that were beginning to be recognized as authentic Mexican food. Although she did not use the term Tex-Mex, she was undoubtedly referring to what she saw as a wretched lowering of the standard of what had been a unique ethnic cuisine.

As increasing numbers of restaurants sprung up across the Southwest, most did not specifically call themselves Tex-Mex; they simply called themselves "Mexican food" restaurants. After Diana Kennedy's book began to make the rounds of food critics, restaurant owners, cooks, and the eating public, there began something of a movement to encourage in the restaurant business "authentic Mexican cooking."

At a restaurant in Houston called Fonda San Miguel, Kennedy herself was asked to consult on the menu. "We started out to be really purist," said owner Tom Gilliland. "We wanted everything to be just like in Mexico. But we ended up being realists. We had to make some concessions. Diana made us commit to not serving chips and salsa, not only because it's not done in Mexico, but because the chips fill you up, and the hot sauce dulls your palate."[14]

The experiment failed. The clients rebelled, insisting that the owners put before them the chips and salsa they had always expected before a meal at Fonda San Miguel. Gilliland bowed to the wishes of his customers. He did not call Diana Kennedy to tell her the news. Gilliland noticed as other Mexican restaurants sprang up in Houston, they began to add items to their own menus that had little to do with so-called "authentic Mexican cooking." Even though many of the chefs were new immigrants from Mexico, many of the dishes were definitely not from south of the border. "They didn't care what Diana Kennedy said," Gilliland noted. "They'd never heard of her."

And so, not only in Fort Worth but across the country, the integration of chiles, tortillas, and other foods from Latin America produced a variety of dishes and delights that became generally known as Mexican food. Some of them had little to do with Mexico or any other Latin American locale. Like the entire subject of Tex-Mex and Mexican food, myths and tall stories surround the origins of many of the dishes. For example, Diana Kennedy clarified the term "refried beans." "During all my years of living in Mexico and teaching Mexican cooking in New York," she said, she thought of frijoles refritos as refried beans. "Several people have asked me why, when the beans are fried, they are called refried. Nobody I asked in Mexico seemed to know until quite suddenly it dawned on me. The Mexicans have a habit of qualifying a word to emphasize the meaning by adding the prefix *re-*. They will get the oil very hot (requemar), or something will be very good (retebien). Thus refrito means well fried, which they certainly are, since they are fried until they are almost dry."[15]

Chimichanga

A chimichanga is a tortilla wrapped around meat or cheese or other ingredients and then deep-fried. The popular theory behind the origin of the chimichanga is that a cook, either accidentally or as an experiment, dropped a burrito into a deep fryer to see what would happen. Most of the stories about the emergence of the chimichanga place the historic event in a particular restaurant in Tucson, Arizona. The establishment was El Charro, a Mexican restaurant opened in 1922 by Monica Flin, well before Mexican food achieved general popularity. El Charro claims to be the oldest, continuously family owned and operated Mexican restaurant in the United States. When El Charro first opened in a small building on South Fourth Avenue, the restaurant had just three tables and a menu of tortillas, tamales, and chili. A legend arose over the years that it was a cook at El Charro who had dropped that first burrito into the frying pan, thus creating a chimichanga. That legend has come under scrutiny in succeeding years, however, and El Charro itself makes no such historical claims.

Fajitas

The origin of fajitas is equally murky. A fajita is grilled steak served in a wheat tortilla. The word is from the Spanish *faja*, meaning strip. The creators of the fajita dish itself were probably Hispanic ranch hands who, when given unwanted beef cuts for dinner, grilled the meat and ate them with tortillas and salsa.

The first fajitas sold in eating establishments may have been produced by Sonny Falcon, who introduced grilled fajita tacos in an outdoor festival held in Kyle, Texas, in 1969. A local newspaper dubbed Sonny the "Fajita King." In 1973 Ninfa Laurenza featured fajitas, which she called "tacos al carbon," at her new restaurant in Houston. Some writers claimed that her restaurant was the first to sell fajitas in a regular restaurant.

Tacos

As old-time Mexican dishes and cuisine merged into American society, it was the taco that gained perhaps more prominence than any other. From diners to rest stops along freeways, from school lunchrooms to restaurants of all kinds and sizes, there is the taco.

In Mexico, the word *taco* was a general term that meant *sandwich*. Tacos in Mexico were any food rolled, folded, or fried into tortillas and eaten by hand. Fillings included pork, chicken, sausage, beans, and other ingredients. Tacos were eaten either as an entree or as a snack. Mexican tacos were usually soft-shelled, unlike the crisp, U-shaped tortillas served increasingly in the United States.

The earliest mention of what the world came to know as tacos appeared in the famous chronicle by Bernal Diaz del Castillo, a Spanish soldier who accompanied Hernán Cortés to the New World. He wrote *A True History of the Conquest of New Spain*. Among his writings are descriptions of lavish feasts and banquets held for the captains of the conquering force. The Spanish soldiers ate pork folded in tortillas.

The first-known English-language taco recipes appeared in a 1914 California cookbook authored by Bertha Haffner-Ginger. She instructed her readers to put chopped, cooked beef and chili sauce in a tortilla made of meal and flour, add an egg to seal the edges, then fry in deep fat and serve with chili sauce over it.

From Bertha Haffner-Ginger it was a long taco road to Glen Bell. Born in 1923, Bell returned home to San Bernardino, California, after serving in the Marine Corps. He opened a hot dog stand called Bell's Drive-In, an establishment similar to many roadside drive-up restaurants that opened in California in the 1950s, including McDonald's. For the next ten years Bell experimented with several of his own small drive-ins and with a number of menus. Finally, he hit upon tacos. What if patrons could get tacos at a fast-food outlet instead of the usual burgers and fries?

It worked. By 1956, Bell had three Taco Tia restaurants in San Bernardino, Barstow, and Redlands, California. These establishments generated $50,000 per year, and Bell decided to franchise his operation. The result was Taco Bell, yet another story of a relatively penniless entrepreneur with an idea that made it big.

How big? Taco Bell, with its symbol of a sleeping Mexican sitting under a sombrero, quickly expanded around Los Angeles. In 1978, there were an amazing 868 locations. Soon, Bell sold out to the Pepsi Cola Corporation. The sitting Mexican under a sombrero became a mission bell and, by 1980, Taco Bell had 1,333 outlets in forty-five states and Guam and Glen Bell was a rich man. As of 2005 the number of Taco Bell establishments had reached nearly 6,000.

Taco Bell had turned Mexican food purist Diana Kennedy's dream of authentic Mexican restaurants into something of a nightmare. Many patrons of Mexican descent who first walked into or drove up to the window of a Taco Bell ordered food that bore only the most scant connection to the tortillas and chili dishes created and enjoyed by their forbears. Nevertheless, throughout the latter half of the twentieth century, the story of the Mexican food explosion in the United States was not just about the degradation of Mexican-American and Mexican cuisine. Many chefs, restaurateurs, and business executives saw the growing demand for dishes that bore close resemblance to the cuisine handed down through the generations, and in the success of a continuously growing number of such establishments is a genuine cultural exchange.

SOME ICONS HAD TO GO: THE FRITO BANDITO WAR

In 1932 a young businessman named Elmer Doolin walked into a small San Antonio snack shop and purchased a bag of corn chips called friotes. Already the operator of an ice cream store, Doolin was looking to expand his business. Later, when he found that the manufacturer of the corn chips, a man who had come to the United States from Mexico, was anxious to sell his small business and return to Mexico, Doolin purchased his recipe and his nineteen accounts.

With the help of his mother and brother, Doolin began to make corn chips in his mother's kitchen. They hand-rolled the dough, thinned it with water, cooked the chips, packaged them in small bags, and delivered them in his Model T Ford to his accounts, the small restaurants carrying the product.

Soon, the operation moved to the garage and then to a house next door. Within a year, Doolin hired employees and found many new restaurants and grocery stores anxious to sell the product. The business expanded with new distributors in Houston and Dallas. They named the product Fritos and called the business The Frito Company.

Doolin's extraordinary success in founding the Frito Company was nearly the same as the experience of a man named Herman W. Lay. Like Doolin, Lay began a small business in his own home and delivered his first products in an old Ford. His food was potato chips and his company became known as the H. W. Lay Company.

In the mid 1940s, the two companies began a merger process that would result in the creation of the Frito-Lay Company, one of the most powerful snack-producing companies in the world. And its main product was those friotes, those Fritos, that Elmer Doolin had tasted in a San Antonio snack shop back in 1932. As Fritos became increasingly popular around the United States, the company began a number of advertising blitzes to make them even more popular. The most successful, and infamous, was the creation in 1967 of a cartoon figure that the business executives at Frito-Lay assumed would carry the torch for Fritos for many years. The cartoon figure was the Frito Bandito. He would become an icon in the most negative sense.

The Frito Bandito was what the name implied: a Mexican bandit. Unshaven, scowling, with guns and holsters on each side of his squat body, bearded and mustached with a gold tooth, and wearing an oversized sombrero, he went around stealing the Fritos corn chips of Anglos at gunpoint. The business executives thought that the Bandito was a huge success. Profits rose. New commercials appeared with the Bandito holding up even more Anglos and stealing their corn chips. One of the advertisements was a wanted poster that read: "Wanted for Theft of Fritos Corn Chips, The Frito Bandito, Caution—He Loves Crunchy Fritos Corn Chips so Much He'll Stop at Nothing to Get Yours. What's More, He's Cunning, Clever and Sneaky. Citizens, Protect Yourselves![16]

In the 1970s, the Frito Bandito faced an adversary that, unlike his Fritos victims, fought back. Latino civil rights groups and Mexican-American organizations offended by the caricature and its gross stereotypes took aim at the Bandito in organized petition drives and boycott actions.

Frito-Lay backpedaled. At first, the company did not remove the character from commercials but cleaned him up. Gone were the scowl, the menacing drawn weapon, the mustache, and the gold tooth. Here was a new Frito Bandito, smiling and clean-shaven, his guns in their holsters.

The protestors were undeterred by the make-over. Chicano groups turned their fire to broadcasters and some of them responded. And then the protests moved into the legal arena. In 1971, a $610 million suit was filed against Frito-Lay in federal court "for the malicious defamation of the character of 6.1 million Mexican Americans in the United States."[17] Soon, members of Congress added their voices to the cause. The press picked up the story around the country. Reluctantly, Frito-Lay finally backed down. The Frito Bandito was dispatched to cartoon oblivion.

CHILI CON CARNE—WAS IT AN AMERICAN INVENTION?

As early as the ancient Aztec and Mayan empires, a form of chili was a food staple, a dish comprising beans served in a spicy tomato sauce. The argument among food historians is whether the chili dish prepared with meat originated in Latin America or whether it was a concoction first introduced in the United States. Food historians Waverly Root and Richard De Rochemont wrote in 1976:

> Chili con carne sounds authentically Spanish, which it could hardly be, for the Spaniards had never seen a chili before they reached America; it was an element of Indian, not of Spanish, cooking. The Spanish name could have been explained by a Mexican origin, but the only persons who deny that provenance more vehemently than the Texans, who claim credit for it, are the Mexicans, who deny paternity with something like indignation.[18]

There was no fight over who invented chili con carne, the authors stressed, just over the historical facts. Mexican chili lovers thought the dish was a second-rate spin-off of the real thing. As a matter of fact, one Mexican dictionary referred to chili as a detestable dish sold across the United States and erroneously called Mexican. Root and De Rochemont finally surmised that the claims that the dish had been invented in the city of San Antonio might have merit. Frank X. Tolbert, perhaps the leading historian on the subject of chili, backed them up, asserting in his book *A Bowl of Red*, published in 1994 by the Texas A&M University Press, that the dish had, indeed, originated in San Antonio.

A number of travel accounts in the first half of the nineteenth century did discuss a form of what could be called chili con carne. When a man named J. C. Clopper visited San Antonio in 1828, he commented on how poor people would cut the little meat they could afford "into a kind of hash with nearly as many peppers as there are pieces of meat—this is all stewed together." In a book by S. Compton Smith published in 1857, the term itself was mentioned. In fact, it was on the cover: *Chile Con Carne, or The Camp and the Field.*[19]

Some historians point to the immigration of a number of families from the Canary Islands, a Spanish possession off the coast of Africa, as the beginning of what Texas chili became in the late 19th century. The secret ingredient that the people from the Canary Islands gave to chili was cumin. Although cumin was already available in the New World, the Islanders had a strong preference for the spice and added it to various dishes.

A San Antonio city official later wrote about the chili stands that appeared in the 1880s in the city, especially in a municipal market called El Mercado: "The chili stand and chili queens are peculiarities ... of the Alamo City." He talked about the rickety chili stands with jovial women dishing out chili, along with bread and water, to soldiers and citizens alike. "They started away back there when the Spanish army camped on the plaza."[20]

Chile rapidly made its way out of the American Southwest. At the Columbian Exposition held in Chicago in 1893, someone from Texas set up a "San Antonio Chili Stand" on the grounds. Soon, street vendors began selling chili con carne in Chicago, along with hot chicken tamales. And in other cities across the Midwest, chili stands and restaurants appeared. In one particular city, chili makers created a version of the dish that a century later still retained its name: Cincinnati chili.

TORTILLAS AND CHILES AS ART AND ICONS

At the San Jose Museum of Art a new exhibit opened in March 2006. Titled "Tortillas, Chiles, and Other Border Things," the exhibit was sponsored by the Movimiento de Arte y Cultura Latino Americana, a local arts group in San Jose. The exhibit, which demonstrated vividly how extensively food continues to play a vital part in merging cultures, was created by noted artist Consuelo Jimenez Underwood. Daughter of a migrant agricultural worker, Underwood sought in the exhibit to illustrate the struggle of indigenous Latino peoples in confronting the challenges of survival and recognition. She had learned that in 2004 the sale of tortillas in the United States had rivaled that of bread. Tortillas, she recognized, served as a notable cultural and social icon, representing the forging of Latino and Anglo life.

As visitors entered the gallery, it was as if they were entering a cultural food fantasy world. There were large-scale chilis of all sizes and shapes, great *molcajetes* or grinding stones, and tortillas. There were seven colorful tablecloth paintings and weavings that served as a backdrop to large jalapeno and serrano peppers hanging from the ceiling. The paintings and weavings were done on brightly colored oilcloth that brought to mind the tabletops in Latino eateries. In the center of the gallery was a large tortilla basket loosely woven of reed. Nestled in the basket were five 48-inch diameter tortillas woven of silk and dyed corn husks. Framing the gallery was a ten-foot high "Tortilla Wall," lightly colored and made of silk. The wall represented a visual contrast with the actual wall of steel planks that was, at the time of the exhibit, being constructed along the border between the United States and Mexico. For Underwood, the exhibit was a statement of cultural blending and a visual protest against cultural division.

Shortly after Underwood's exhibit opened in San Jose, Joe Bravo, another artist using food as a cultural icon, began to display his work. Bravo's exhibition opened at the Mexican Cultural Institute in the historic Olvera Street section of Los Angeles. Bravo's canvases were tortillas. He described himself as a tortilla artist. He used the medium, he said, because the tortilla represented an integral part of Latino culture and his own heritage. The imagery on the tortillas, he said, speaks to the hopes, beliefs, and history of Latinos everywhere.

When he was a boy in the border town of Calexico, Bravo's family could not afford store-bought toys. So he made mud figures and carved wooden swords and slingshots. Later, as a struggling art student, he found it almost impossible to afford canvas or any other substance suitable for a work of art. From a position of financial necessity, he decided to use stale tortillas. First, he tried making a mobile out of a few tortillas. When that project literally broke apart, he decided to paint on them. The paint seemed to adhere to the surface of the tortillas well enough. With acrylic paint and a final varnishing, they seemed to be permanent and stable.

In 1973, Bravo graduated from college with a bachelor's degree in graphic design. For a time, he painted murals and worked for ad agencies and magazines. But his Mexican heritage and influence of the Chicano movement began to influence his work. In the neighborhoods where he grew up, he saw the murals painted by Chicano artists on the sides of buildings. They were cultural and political icons, he thought, speaking to Latino heritage.

In 1976, with a number of other artists, Bravo designed and painted the Wilhall anti-gang violence mural at the Wilmighton Recreation Center, a mural that, for nearly thirty years had stood as a symbol of peace in the neighborhood. In 1996 Bravo was asked by a community-based organization and local government officials to restore the mural. At a rededication ceremony, he met several youths who had tattoos of some of the images he had painted on their bodies. And then a friend reminded him of the days in art school when he had used tortillas as a medium. He decided to approach the idea with more seriousness.

Bravo was not the first tortilla artist. Since the civil rights protest demonstrations of Chicano activists in the 1970s, a number of artists had used tortillas in representational art. San Francisco's Jose Montoya used a soldering gun to sear images onto tortillas. Los Angeles artist Alfredo de Batuc painted images of Los Angeles City Hall on snack-sized flour tortillas.

Bravo worked with a company called the Tortilleria San Marcos, a family-owned business in Los Angeles, to produce the tortillas. The recipe is the same for standard tortillas, but Bravo's work called for special treatment because of their size—28 inches in diameter. Bravo finished the artistic process by exposing the tortillas to an open flame, which produced a black-speckled texture. After covering the finished tortillas in varnish, he covered the backs with burlap to protect them further.

The exhibit drew thousands of people and many buyers. Flea, the bass player for the rock band the Red Hot Chili Peppers, was so intrigued by the concept of tortillas as canvases that he ordered a framed, 2-foot rendering of the Virgin de Guadalupe for his Malibu, California, home.

Abelardo de la Pena, Jr., board member of the Mexican Cultural Institute, said that the exhibition had left a mark by exposing a slice of Latino culture. He said, "It's been the one exhibit in all the time I've been here that really captures the new Los Angeles, by using tradition in a contemporary way. People see that an everyday part of life is now a work of art, and that brings out wonderment."[21]

Bravo commented, "I think I am following folk tradition and working with my environment, and what I choose to put out there is a social and political statement. Using a tortilla is a statement in itself, and the themes can make it political. Being involved in the Chicano movement, I put the culture first; it's not just limited to politics."[22]

TORTILLA HEAVEN

Jade Estrada, born in 1975 at Lackland Air Force Base in San Antonio, Texas, became a successful Latino comedian, actor, pop singer, and human rights activist promoting AIDS awareness. He won a scholarship to the American Musical and Dramatic Academy in New York and studied dance, alongside Jennifer Lopez and Slam, the lead dancer from Madonna's Blonde Ambition Tour.

Estrada also worked with Tony award–winning actress Zoe Caldwell in New York. For a time, Estrada was choreographer for Latino television personality Charo. In 1998 he gained international attention for his pop single, "Reggae Twist." Estrada appeared regularly on Comedy Central and HBO Latino.

In 2004, Celeste Angela Estrada, Jade Estrada's sister, won the 2004 Gertrude Stein Literary Award for best play. Her work was called *Tortilla Heaven*, and it revolved around the lives of three generations of Mexicans living in San Antonio. In 2007, Jade Estrada decided to produce *Tortilla Heaven* as a one-actor play, and he would play all of the parts. With the help of his sister and his brother, David Miguel Estrada, also a successful playwright who acted as director, Estrada went to work. Like the stories of all families, there are the warm times and the cold, the likes and dislikes, but also the understanding that there is connection. In the case of the Ruiz family portrayed in *Tortilla Heaven*, the generational differences were both sources of comedy and tension. When the oldest generation of Spanish-only speakers attempts to communicate with their grandchildren who speak no Spanish at all, numerous possibilities for misunderstanding and farce abound.

One reviewer wrote, "the monologue at the end, done by the character Charles, is one of the best and most poignant realities that many within the Mexican community face, that of finding those who have taken care of them all their lives, supported their dreams, accepted their differences and loved through them. Charles' monologue tells the story that is so prevalent within the Mexican community, one of being left behind by a mother, raised by a grandmother, yet proving to be successful because of the wonderful love they truly received at home."[23]

One powerful connection of that family love through the generations was food, the tortillas. As Jade Estrada said, "You smell them cooking before you wake up. If you're hungry before bed, they're a great snack. Tortillas are more than a food, they are a ritual in our culture that goes all the way back to the Mayans. And, of course, you can put anything on them. Tortillas are the basis of everything."[24]

NOTES

1. Zarela Martinez, *Food from my Heart* (New York: Macmillan, 1992), 217.

2. Martinez, 218.

3. "Ancient Americans Liked It Hot: Mexican Cuisine Traced to 1,500 Years Ago," *Science Daily*, July 11, 2007, http://www.sciencedaily.com/releases/2007/07/070709171645.htm.

4. "Americans Cultivated and Traded Chili Peppers 6,000 Years Ago," *Science Daily*, February 16, 2007, http://www.sciencedaily.com/releases/2007/02/070215144334.htm.

5. W. Hardy Eshbaugh, "Peppers: History and Exploitation of a Serendipitous New Crop Discovery," available at *Uncle Steve's Hot Stuff: Anything and Everything about Hot Peppers*, 1993, http://www.ushotstuff.com/history.htm.

6. Linda Stradley, "History of Tortillas and Tacos," http://whatscookingamerica.net/History/Tortilla_Taco_history.htm.

7. Stradley.

8. Andrew Smith, "Tacos, Enchiladas and Refried Beans: The Invention of Mexican-American Cookery." Presented at the Symposium at Oregon State University, http://food.oregonstate.edu/ref/culture/mexico_smith.html.

9. Stefan Lovgren, "New Texas Wheat May Wrap Up Tortilla Market," *National Geographic News*, March 9, 2006, http://news.nationalgeographic.com/news/2006/03/0309_060309_tortillas_2.html.

10. Smith.

11. Smith.

12. Interview with Marie Carter, "American Life Histories: Manuscripts from the Federal Writer's Project, 1936–1940," Library of Congress.

13. Robb Walsh, *The Tex-Mex Cookbook* (New York: Broadway Books, 2004), 65.

14. Walsh, 121.

15. Diana Kennedy, *The Cuisines of Mexico*, (New York: Harper & Row, 1972), 282.

16. "Uncle Ben, CEO? *Slate,* http://www.slate.com/id/2164062/slideshow/2164626/fs/0//entry/2164636/.

17. Walsh, 197.

18. Waverly Root and Richard De Rochemont (New York: William Morrow, 1976), 277–278.

19. John Mariani, *Encyclopedia of American Food and Drink* (New York: Lebhar-Friedman, 1999), 76.

20. Walsh, 44.

21. Augustin Gurza, "Tortilla Art Proves a Treat," *Los Angeles Times*, March 31, 2007, http://www.azcentral.com/ent/pop/articles/0331tortillaart0331.html.

22. Marissa Rodriguez, "Joe Bravo, Tortilla Artist," *Hispanic Heritage*, http://hol.hispaniconline.com/HispanicMag/2007_9/Feature-Heritage.html.

23. W. Brian Moore, "Estrada Rocks 'Tortilla Heaven,'" *QBliss Magazine,* April 2007, http://www.getjaded.com/media-rev42.htm.

24. Judith Newmark, "Family and Culture Make Up 'Tortilla Heaven,'" *St. Louis Dispatch*, May 2, 2005, http://jadeestebanestrada.com/media-int29.htm.

FURTHER READING

"Ancient Americans Liked It Hot: Mexican Cuisine Traced To 1,500 Years Ago," *Science Daily,* July 11, 2007, http://www.sciencedaily.com/releases/2007/07/070709171645.htm.

"Food Timeline: Mexican & Tex Mex Foods," http://www.foodtimeline.org/foodmexican.html#salsa.

Gurza, Agustin. "Tortilla Art Proves a Treat," *Los Angeles Times*, March 31, 2007, http://www.azcentral.com/ent/pop/articles/0331tortillaart0331.html.

Kennedy, Diana. *The Cuisines of Mexico.* New York: Harper & Row, 1972.

Newmark, Judith. "Family and Culture Make Up 'Tortilla Heaven,'" *St. Louis Dispatch*, May 2, 2005, http://jadeestebanestrada.com/media-int29.htm.

Rodriguez, Marissa. "Joe Bravo, Tortilla Artist," *Hispanic Heritage*, http://hol.hispaniconline.com/HispanicMag/2007_9/Feature-Heritage.html.

Root, Waverly, and Richard De Rochemont. *Eating in America: A History.* New York: William Morrow, 1976.

Smith, Andrew. "Tacos, Enchiladas and Refried Beans: The Invention of Mexican-American Cookery." Presented at the Symposium at Oregon State University, http://food.oregonstate.edu/ref/culture/mexico_smith.html.

"Tortillas, Chiles, and Other Border Things: New Work by Consuelo Jiménez Underwood, March 10 to April 29, 2006, MACLA, http://www.maclaarte.org/TortillasChilesandOtherBorderThings1.htm.

Walsh, Robb. *The Tex-Mex Cookbook.* New York: Broadway Books, 2004.

AP Photo/Dana Tynan

Sandra Cisneros

In 1983 a young Latina writer named Sandra Cisneros excited the literary world with a novel entitled *The House on Mango Street*. An intensely personal and human narrative about coming of age in a Chicago barrio that was beset by racism, sexism, and poverty, the book gave voice, as few had ever done, to young Latinas making their way through a web of challenges. So real and honest was the account that the book became standard reading in high schools and colleges around the country. It was for many Anglo readers the first insights they had ever gained into the neighborhoods across town. For Latinos it was a world they knew that was now laid bare to scrutiny and understanding.

With her subsequent works, including *Woman Hollering Creek and Other Stories* (1991), her poetry collections *My Wicked, Wicked Ways* and *Loose Woman,* and a bold novel of a Mexican-American family entitled *Caramelo,* Cisneros not only gained distinction in literary fields, but her works became treasured sources of inspiration to working-class Latinos. Her novels, short stories, poetry, and essays helped bridge cultural divides.

SOLITARY CHILDHOOD

Sandra Cisneros was born on December 20, 1954, in a Latino barrio in the South Side neighborhood of Chicago. Mostly populated by residents from Puerto Rico, many of them second-generation, the neighborhood was crowded with small apartment buildings.

Her father, Alfredo Cisneros Del Moral, was a Spanish-speaking Mexican immigrant; her mother was a Mexican-American. Alfredo came from several generations of relatively wealthy Mexican citizens whose money had finally been drained away by the unchecked gambling practices of his great-grandfather. Although he had briefly attended college in Mexico, Alfredo Cisneros was more interested in parties than in studies and began failing his courses. Rather than face the reactions of his father, a strong-willed man, impatient with such frivolities, Alfredo left home and illegally crossed the border from Mexico into the United States.

In one of her short stories called "Never Marry a Mexican," Cisneros wrote of her father: "But he was an economic refugee, no immigrant fleeing a war. My father ran away from home because he was afraid of facing his father after his first-year grades at the university proved he'd spent more time fooling around than studying."[1]

After crossing the border into the United States, Alfredo Cisneros was soon apprehended. He was given the choice to be sent back to Mexico or to join the United States military in World War II service. He chose the military. After the war, Cisneros returned to the United States, finally landing in Chicago. There, at a dance, he met twenty-one-year old Elvira Cordero Anguiano.

Elvira's father had made his way to Chicago from the Mexican state of Guanajuato to work on the railroads. After settling in Chicago and earning some money, he sent for his family to join him. Elvira grew up in Chicago on the Near West Side. Ashamed of her clothing, and she dropped out of St. Pius High School because she began to work in factories. Although she would never graduate from high school, she loved to read, a trait she would hand down with much eagerness to her daughter, Sandra.

After Alfredo married Elvira, he became a skilled upholsterer and started a business called A. Cisneros & Sons. The establishment existed for decades. Although the business was relatively successful, the family continuously lived on the margins of poverty.

Sandra was the only girl in a family of seven children. She often talked later of being something of an outsider in the family because she was a girl. Her father, she insisted, would have been happier to have had seven boys. Often, she remembered, when friends would ask about the family he would indicate that all of his children were boys. Sandra spent much of her childhood relatively isolated. She remembered the bleakness of the surroundings in the neighborhood, the oppressive feeling of people struggling and suffering just to exist. The cramped conditions, the bitter winters, and the drab atmosphere, she believed, were stifling.

Sandra was "la consentida," the little princess, of the family, she said later. With her brothers as well as her father all attempting to control her life, she said it was like having seven fathers. Shy and lonely, she endured the poverty of the family by losing herself in books such as Virginia Lee Burton's *The Little House* and Lewis Carroll's *Alice's Adventures in Wonderland*. She also loved reading fairy tales, especially one written by Hans Christian Andersen called "Six Swans." It involved a girl with many brothers and how she coped.

Her mother suggested all kinds of literature. She saw that her daughter had an opportunity to move toward much greater intellectual heights than she had been able to reach herself. Cisneros would later realize that her mother had been bound by a culture that discouraged women from intellectual discourse and achievement. Her mother had deeply resented this oppression and hoped better for her daughter. "Because of my mother," Cisneros wrote, "I spent my childhood afternoons in my room reading instead of in the kitchen.... I never had to change my little brothers' diapers, I never had to cook a meal alone, nor was I ever sent to do the laundry. Certainly I had my share of housework to do as we all did, but I don't recall it interfering with my homework or my reading habits."[2]

"She fed her spirit," Cisneros said later of her mother, "and she did this by doing very creative things all the time." "She would paint the apartment in these run-down neighborhoods in very fabulous colors. She would make puppets with us or make stuffed animals of all the characters we liked in books. She would sing arias along with the opera recordings. And every weekend, we went to the library and a cultural event."[3]

Although her mother was especially eager that Sandra begin to appreciate good literature, her father also encouraged her to excel in whatever she attempted. He was determined that hard study could allow all of his children to avoid the kind of hard days on the job that both he and his wife had experienced just to pay the bills. Cisneros later talked about her father's hands, which were thick and hard from a lifetime of hammering and twisting twine.

But Cisneros' childhood was also often disrupted by her father in a very unusual and dispiriting way. Homesick and uneasy in the United States, he felt a constant need to return to his paternal grandparents' house in Mexico City. Cisneros blamed much of her father's obsessive need to return to Mexico on her grandmother, who made constant demands for his attention. "She was a hysterical woman," Cisneros said, "over-sentimental, spoiled. (Come to think of it, she was not unlike myself.) She had favorites. Her best baby was my father whom she held tight to." Cisneros would later portray the figure of her grandmother in a very unfavorable light in one of her novels.[4]

And so, almost yearly, her father kept the family on the roads between Chicago and Mexico City, visiting his native country. In her major novel *Caramelo*, Cisneros' main character recounts those cramped journeys, with the car filled and hot and the many days on the road wandering like nomads from their apartment in Chicago. Past a giant Turtle Wax sign, and onto the roads leading south, they began: "Saint Louis, Missouri, which Father calls by its Spanish name, San Luis. San Luis to Tulsa, Oklahoma. Tulsa, Oklahoma, to Dallas. Dallas to San Antonio to Laredo on 81 till we are on the other side. Monterey, Saltillo, Matehuala. San Luis Potosi. Queretaro."[5] And then, finally, at the big X marked on their road map, they reached Mexico City. A few months later, the family would return to Chicago by the reverse route under the same laborious conditions and resume their lives in a different apartment.

Shuttled to a number of Catholic schools during their early years, the children thus lost track of whatever friends they had made before their latest trip. Cisneros later remembered the constant moving and relocation as a powerfully negative impact on her spirit, driving her to be more and more detached from other children and having very few lasting friendships. "The moving back and forth, the new schools, were very upsetting to me as a child," she wrote. "They caused me to be very introverted and shy. I do not remember making friends easily, and I was terribly self-conscious due to the cruelty of the nuns, who were majestic at making one feel little. Because we moved so much, and always in neighborhoods that appeared like France after World War II—empty lots and burned-out buildings—I retreated inside myself."[6]

Cisneros' feelings of isolation extended beyond those she had for her family. Her teachers, she remembered, were of little encouragement. Instead of attempting to excel in a school atmosphere in which she felt threatened and lonely, she reserved her most creative work for the nights at home alone in her room. She began to write in secret, pouring out her emotions in bursts of small poems, penned in spiral notebooks.

In 1966, when Cisneros was eleven years old, the family borrowed enough money for a down payment on a house. For the first time, she and her family would not be wedged into a tiny apartment. Although excited by the prospect of moving into an actual house, the first sight of it was discouraging. It was not like houses she had envisioned, the ones she had read about in books or seen on television. It was small, not a great deal larger than some of the apartments. Located in a Latino area called Humboldt Park, on Chicago's North Side, the house and the neighborhood would provide the backdrop for early teenage years and for the characters that would come alive later in her first book, *The House of Mango Street*.

In 1968, she entered Josephinum High School. There, she began to release some of the pent-up frustrations that had marked her pre-teen years. She began reading some of her poems in English classes. One of the teachers in her sophomore year, a poet herself, recognized immediately the breadth of feeling and the passion that spilled out in Cisneros' crude but promising writing. Finally, Cisneros felt the air of encouragement at her back and wrote now with the knowledge that someone was interested in what she had to say and the ways in which she expressed herself.

By the time of her senior year in high school, she became an editor of the school's creative writing journal. Often, she would read some of her poems aloud at school occasions. But Cisneros longed for the time when she could leave the confinement of the neighborhood behind, along with the constant fears of the rats that had always infested the building, as well as the seeming indifference of some in the family to her oftentimes distressed emotional state. As Esperanza, the main character in *The House on Mango Street*, said, "One day I will pack my bags of books and paper. One day I will say goodbye to Mango. I am too strong for her to keep me here forever. One day I will go away. Friends and neighbors will say, 'What happened to that Esperanza? Where did she go with all those books and paper?'"[7]

COLLEGE AND DREAMS OF BEING A WRITER

To the question, "What happened to Sandra Cisneros with all those books and papers?"—she took them to college. Although a college education might have seemed improbable for a young Latina from a poor Chicago neighborhood, her poetry and other literary successes in high school made the difference. She was offered a scholarship to Loyola University, a Jesuit-run institution in Chicago. She became one of the few Latinas on campus. Cisneros' father supported his daughter's decision to attend Loyola, although not from any expectation that her writing would result in a profession or unusual accomplishment. "In retrospect," she wrote, "I'm lucky my father believed daughters were meant for husbands. It meant it didn't matter if I majored in something like English. After all, I'd find a nice professional eventually, right? This allowed me the liberty to putter about embroidering my little poems and stories...."[8]

Although the young college student did not particularly distinguish herself in her first two years of college, her literary skills and ambition stirred in a creative writing workshop she took in 1974, her junior year. It was during this workshop that she looked much more closely at her own work, comparing and contrasting it with other poets.

It was also there that she became aware of a program at the University of Iowa dedicated to the study and practice of creative writing. Founded in 1936, the program was called the Iowa Writers' Workshop. It was the first creative writing program in the country and became the model for more than three hundred writing programs in other colleges and universities. Such luminaries as Robert Penn Warren, Dylan Thomas, and Robert Lowell were products of the workshop, and for many years it was one of the most selective graduate programs of any kind, admitting less than five percent of its applicants. One of the poets whose work Cisneros had come to admire during her writing seminar as a college junior was Donald Justice. A winner of a major poetry prize given by the Academy of American Poets in 1961 and later winner of the Pulitzer Prize for Poetry, Justice was a teacher at the Iowa Writers' Workshop.

Strongly impressed with Cisneros' writings, one of her instructors at Loyola suggested that she apply to enter the Iowa program. Although she regarded her chances as slim, Cisneros decided during her senior year to submit an application, dazzled by the prospect of being tutored by Donald Justice. To the judges reviewing the writings of the newest prospective members of the workshop, Cisneros' work was as impressive as it had been to the faculty members at Loyola. Much to her surprise and shock, she learned that her home for the next year would be Iowa City, Iowa.

The distance between Chicago and Iowa City in miles was relatively short, only 200 miles. But the distance in atmosphere was profound. She was now on her way from one of the world's most cosmopolitan and culturally mixed cities to a small town on the American plains and its mostly homogenous Anglo population, surrounded by hundreds of miles of flat farmland. As she entered her first classes at the University of Iowa, Cisneros felt the old pangs of ioslation again. To make matters worse, after only a few months she learned that Professor Justice had left the university to work on his own writing. She would not, after all, benefit from his tutelage.

At Loyola, Cisneros had become so identified with her writing and poetry that many of her classmates had regarded her as a kind of "Poet in Residence." At the Writers' Workshop, she was one of many students who were also gifted academically and singled out for their literary promise. In addition, most had come from upper middle class or upper class backgrounds. For the most part, they were Anglos. Cisneros, a Latina from an economically poor, inner-city neighborhood, felt immediately an enormous pressure to succeed. Once again, there was the cloud of inadequacy to overcome.

She later recalled a particular discussion in one of her seminars called "Memory and the Imagination." The students were arguing the themes and meanings behind a book called *The Poetics of Space*, written by a French literary theorist named Gaston Bachelard. As the students debated, Cisneros later recalled, her differences and alienation from others in the class became magnified. They were talking about attics and stairways and large yards that were part of the homes in which they grew up; she had known nothing similar. Most of her classmates had gone to the finest private schools in the country; she had spent her youth shuttling from one school to another interspersed with long trips to and from Mexico City.

But as she thought about her situation now at Iowa in relation to the lives of the others around her, something else became evident. Although the other students had careful breeding, she had experience. "It was not until this moment," she said, "when I separated myself, when I considered myself truly distinct, that my writing acquired a voice. I knew I was a Mexican woman, but I didn't think it had anything to do with why I felt so much imbalance in my life, whereas it had everything to do with it! My race, my gender, my class! That's when I decided I would write about something my classmates couldn't write about."[9]

She came to realize that she had had a remarkably distinctive early life from which she could draw inspiration. She knew poverty. She knew the real-life limitations that had held down Latinos, especially women. She knew about third-floor rats and neighbors who threw objects through windows when on a drunken rage and about street violence and domestic quarrels that spilled out onto the sidewalks of the barrio.

Indeed, she had seen and met unique individuals among her own friends as well as those with whom her family had come into contact. She remembered herself as "a yellow weed among the city's cracks." But the weed had seen and heard things to which she as a writer could give voice. "This is how *The House on Mango Street* was born," she said, "the child-voice that was to speak all my poems for many years."[10]

In 1978, Cisneros completed the Iowa Writers' Workshop and earned a graduate degree. She returned to Chicago and took a job as a school counselor at the Latino Youth Alternative High School. Here were students who were now facing some of the obstacles of poverty and isolation that she had faced. But many of their stories were far grimmer than her own. Some of their lives had been directly touched by death and violence and family abuse. Here were kids already on a road toward alcohol or drug addiction. Many of them had parents, relatives, and friends behind bars; many expected their own lives would follow a similar path. Cisneros worked hard, giving as

The Emergence of Spanglish

"Spanglish" is a blend of Spanish and English words and phrases used mostly in conversation among individuals along the border between the United States and Mexico. In the last few decades, "Spanglish" has been the theme of a movie and the subject of scholarly research, and it has assumed an increasingly prominent place in the larger culture of the United States.

Ilan Stavans, professor of Latin American and Latino Culture at Amherst College, has written a book on Spanglish and has noted that the phenomenon is changing so fast that it is difficult to follow. His own book includes a Spanglish dictionary. *Backupear*, for example, means to back up your car, and *pregneada* means pregnant.

But Spanglish is not only individual words that have melded from a combination of English and Spanish; it is also the practice of using Spanish phrases in the midst of generally English sentences. Although some scholars argue that Spanglish is something of a corruption of language, Stavans argues differently. "There are many people out there that speak English, Spanish, and Spanglish," he said. "It is a language that, to this day, academics [distrust], that politicians only recently have begun to take into more consideration. But poets, novelists, and essayists have realized that it is the key to the soul of a large portion of the population." For many individuals, Stavans said, "Spanglish is a creative way of saying, 'I am an American and I have my own style, my own taste, my own tongue.'"[1]

Sandra Cisneros' work is heavily infused with Spanish passages and words that suddenly appear in the middle of her English language prose and poetry. In *Caramelo*, Cisneros gives the reader an adventure in language, moving from English to Spanish phrases effortlessly. Even a reader totally lacking any familiarity with Spanish can in most cases understand what the phrases or words mean or suggest by the context in which they are placed. She writes in Caramelo,

> "Please. Quit the theatrics. That's what comes from being raised in the United States. *Sin memoria y sin verguenza.*"[2]

Very few individuals who are not literate in Spanish would know the meaning of the phrase "Sin memoria y sin verguenza." A general translation would be "Without memory and without shame," but set in the context of the narrative, the reader gets a general understanding of the feeling and sense of the meaning.

According to Stavans, Spanglish is making its way into mainstream America. "It's hot," he said. "This Spanglish thing is very cool, even if you don't speak it. It makes you attractive to younger people, to a particular audience that's out there and that corporations want to address."[3]

[1]"Spanglish, A New American Language," http://www.npr.org/templates/story/story.php?storyId=1438900.

[2]Sandra Cisneros, *Caramelo* (New York: Alfred A Knopf, 2002), p. 205.

[3]Teresa Wiltz, "Spanglish: Pop Culture's Lingua Franca," *The Washington Post*, January 26, 2003, G01.

Lalo Alcaraz's comic strip, "La Cucaracha," used Spanglish to poke political fun at both Anglos and Chicanos. The characters on the PBS series "American Family," starring Edward James Olmos, often use forms of Spanglish. Even pre-schoolers have gotten a continuing dose of Spanglish on Nickelodeon's bilin-gual "Dora the Explorer."

Josefina Lopez, a Latina playwright and creator of the celebrated play and television series *Real Women Have Curves,* said, "There's a rhythm to Spanish, especially if it's Mexican or Puerto Rican. I hear it a lot on TV when they do it.... As long as they get the rhythm right, I'm happy that they're doing that. It shows a respect for our language and our culture."[4]

_____
[4]Wiltz.

much insight and encouragement as she possibly could to these youngsters, especially helping them learn to put their thoughts and emotions down on paper. She tried to calm their frustration and anger through writing.

While teaching high school students back in the barrio, Cisneros now had increasing confidence in taking her own work to a broader public. She had survived the competition at Iowa. She had a growing realization of the kinds of personal themes and images that would mark her future writing efforts. She began to give public readings, and many in the community began to look forward to her presentations.

When the Chicago Transit Authority sponsored a poetry project in collab-oration with the Poetry Society of America, Cisneros was one of the writers asked to participate. The Transit Authority collected poems to post inside their subway cars and buses. Chicago's bus and subway riders thus read the words of Cisneros along with the words of other writers, such as the noted poet and Abraham Lincoln biographer, Carl Sandburg.

Other noted poets became aware of Cisneros' talent. Mexican-American writer Gary Soto, the youngest American poet to be included in the Norton Anthology of Modern Poetry, had grown up in a poor Chicano community in the San Joaquin Valley of California. He recognized the vitality and truth that filled verse after verse of Cisneros' work and helped her publish her first book through a small publishing group called Mango Press in San Jose, California. She called the collection of poems *Bad Boys.* Although the print run for the book was limited to 1,000 copies, many of the poems in this an-thology would later be published in Cisneros' later books.

She was now a published author. As she accepted invitations to read at schools and coffeehouses in Chicago, she was both flattered and overcome by her sudden prominence. In 1980, Cisneros decided to give herself more time for her special craft, more time to reach out with her thoughts and visions to a wider reading public. She left the Alternative High School and returned to Loyola University, where she had earned her bachelor's degree a few years earlier. She took a job in school administration as an assistant enrollment recruiter of high school students. She was especially effective when visiting parents and schools in the Chicago barrios.

Now twenty-six years old, Cisneros was striking in appearance—dark, with long black hair, a prominent nose, and a kind of quiet elegance with which she carried herself. She dated often but never considered marriage. Many women, she realized, had sacrificed their gifts and talents to a life at home with children; this was a vision that never settled easily into her mind when she thought of her own life. For Cisneros, the relative isolation of her childhood that she deeply resented became for her as an adult a more grounded way of life. For most authors, solitude and quiet are desirable. Cisneros later joked that her relatives had long since given up asking why she seemed to make no progress toward getting married. They grudgingly accepted her decision, she said, although they never understood it.

In 1982, the National Endowment for the Arts provided a grant to Cisneros that allowed her to give up work temporarily and concentrate on her writing. She spent some time in Greece, France, Yugoslavia, and other European countries, making a number of close friends with whom she could share the joys of writing. She also spent time in Provincetown, Massachusetts, to be near a friend named Dennis Mathis, a fiction writer. Cisneros could now see the outlines of her first book; they were in the individual stories of men and women whose lives crossed her path in her formative years. Mathis, whom she had met while in the Iowa Writers' Workshop, offered to help her work on the book, and she accepted the offer. Provincetown, for generations a haven of American writers, would be a welcome change of atmosphere, a special place to give literary birth.

With the manuscript completed and awaiting publication, Cisneros spent the spring of 1983 in Venice, Italy, working as an artist-in-residence at the Michael Korolyi Foundation. She taught a few hours every week and continued her writing. She returned to the United States in 1984 on the eve of the publication of her first book.

THE HOUSE ON MANGO STREET (1984)

At a time when mainstream presses mostly ignored the works of Latino writers, Nick Kanellos, son of a Puerto Rican mother and Greek father, and a young scholar of Hispanic culture founded a journal in which to publish such writings. The journal soon grew into a small press called Arte Publico Press. Housed on the campus of the University of Houston, the press launched the careers of a number of notable writers who gained attention not only in the Latino community but in the mainstream press as well. Cisneros became one of those writers.

In 1984, Cisneros' *The House on Mango Street* appeared from Arte Publico Press. The book is a series of short vignettes, stories told by a young Latina narrator named Esperanza Cordero about her life and observations. Unquestionably drawn from many first-hand experiences of Cisneros in her youth both in the United States and Mexico, the vivid, compact narratives are poignant and blunt, filled with unique glances at a world unseen by most adolescents. Through the eyes of Esperanza we see the neighborhood of the Latina teenager riding her bicycle "fast and faster. Past my house, sad and red and crumbly in places, past Mr. Bennky's grocery on the corner, and down the avenue which is dangerous."[11] We see the occupants of houses in the neighborhood trying to adjust, to get by, and merely to break even. We see a cousin handcuffed and placed in the back seat of a police car. They all waved as the police car drove away. We see an old woman with too many children, a girl terrified of mice, the death of a grandparent, and the strange ways of a woman known as "Elenita, the Witch Woman." All of this we see from the perspective of a world opening up to this young Latina girl who is wide-eyed, scared, lonely, puzzled, and learning the oddities of life and culture.

On first glance, the vignettes in *The House on Mango Street* seem almost too simple. The language, from the voice of Esperanza, is spare, often illiterate, a smattering of Spanish mixed with the English. In some ways the stories seem awkward. Nevertheless, the portraits are astonishingly honest, and the observations direct and unadorned. Esperanza talks about Sally, a pretty girl who often comes to school bruised and battered. She says that her mother rubs lard on the places that hurt. One day, Sally's father catches her talking to a boy. The next day Sally did not come to school at all. And she did not come to school the next day either. Esperanza talks about the four skinny trees that manage to stay alive amidst the concrete of the barrio. She admires them and their effort to stay alive and to exist. They are heroic.

By the end of the book, Esperanza gains the maturity and confidence to leave the house on Mango Street. But as she prepares to say goodbye, one of the characters reminds her never to forget where she came from and the people and culture that was in her blood. You cannot erase that, the character says. You cannot leave behind your past and forget who you are. Sandra Cisneros never did.

Most reviewers praised the work, finding it alive, complex, and revealing. One writer said, "Yet, as with the clearest water, beneath the surface, Cisneros's work is alive with complexity and depth of meaning. Cisneros's voice is the sound of many voices speaking—over the kitchen table, out on the street, across the borderlands, and through the years."[12]

The House on Mango Street won several prestigious awards, such as the 1985 Columbus Foundation's American Book Award. Within a few years, teachers and educators across the world would begin the use the book in their classes, from junior high school through graduate studies. They would assign students to read the book in such varying fields as Chicano studies and psychology. At Stanford University, it was adopted as part of the institutions "new curriculum." Eventually, the book would sell more than two million copies.

From the memories of her own isolation and uncertainty in the Chicago barrio, a young Latino writer had produced a first novel that would prove to be a durable contribution to American literature. The praise and notice of the work, however, would not sustain a career. She needed a job. In 1984, she began work as the arts administrator at the Guadalupe Arts Center in San Antonio, Texas.

SETTLING IN SAN ANTONIO

The city of San Antonio seemed right for Sandra Cisneros. Away from the congested barrios of Chicago and its big-city atmosphere, San Antonio was almost like a definition of Cisneros' own personality—a cross-cultural mix of Latino and Anglo, a town where the history of Mexico and Texas seemed still to breathe. It was a constant reminder of her childhood wanderings from the big city up north to the big city further south across the border.

The community in San Antonio was more than half Latino, including recent immigrants, second- and third-generation Americans, and many who spoke both Spanish and English fluently. The place made Cisneros feel at home, comfortable in a way that her childhood apartments in Chicago never did. Nevertheless, after living in San Antonio for a time she began to feel a growing anger toward many of the whites with whom she tried to establish close ties. As an arts administrator, she made a number of efforts to introduce programs that might attract the interest of all members of the communities. On such occasions, she was disappointed that almost all of the visitors to exhibits or presentations were people from the barrios.

In 1985, Cisneros received the Dobie Paisano Fellowship, an award established after the death of folklorist J. Frank Dobie to provide a retreat for young writers. Along with a grant of money, the award included a six-month stay at the small ranch house in the Texas hill country outside Austin where Dobie himself used to work. With this gift of solitude and time to return to her first love, writing, Cisneros once again found a peace and contentment she rarely felt in her life. She began to see the area of San Antonio as home.

As she prepared a group of poems for publication, Cisneros again faced the constant dilemma of a writer—how to make a living? As her identity and talent became more widely known in the community, she advertised in the local papers to teach creative writing classes. She handed out fliers in local laundromats and supermarkets. Few people answered the advertisements. She began to search more widely for employment that would be satisfying and economically sufficient yet, at the same time, still allow her time for writing.

Finally, she realized that she would have to leave San Antonio to find work. She brooded, sank into depression, and feared for her future. She found it difficult to imagine how she could make a life and career, and her spirits darkened. And so, with much regret, she was on the move again, this time to the California State University in Chico. Here she would hold a temporary position teaching creative writing and acting as a visiting lecturer. The fees would allow her enough money to live on and would give her time to continue writing at a faster pace. Nevertheless, the depression followed her to California. "I thought I couldn't teach," she said. "I found myself becoming suicidal.... I was drowning, beyond help.... It was frightening because it was such a calm depression."[13]

Her spirits were lifted somewhat in 1987 when a small publisher called Third Woman Press published a collection of poems on which Cisneros had been working for several years. The book, *My Wicked, Wicked Ways*, received several positive reviews and would later be released in hardcover in 1992 by Turtle Bay Books. In the series of poems, Cisneros pursued the tensions of her upbringing in the Catholic tradition and issues of power and sexuality. On the cover of the small volume is a photograph of Cisneros playfully dressed in a rather low-cut dress with cowboy boots, and red earrings. Nearby is a glass of red wine and she is holding a cigarette.

Cisneros received a second fellowship in fiction from the National Endowment for the Arts. The fellowship allowed her to spend less time in the part-time work with the students and gave her greater opportunity to plunge more deeply into her own work.

For some time Cisneros had been carrying around the telephone number of an experienced and well-respected literary agent named Susan Bergholz, who had admired *The House on Mango Street* and saw the potential in Cisneros as a nationally important talent. Cisneros finally contacted Bergholz and soon sent a small collection of additional poems she had completed. Within a few months, Random House, one of the major publishing houses in the world, decided to offer Cisneros a contract for a book that would be called *Woman Hollering Creek*. The amount of the advance payment the company offered was for Cisneros staggering: $100,000. It was the largest advance given up to that time to a Mexican-American writer.

From the deep recesses of doubt had come to Cisneros an enormous, liberating vote of confidence. She would now have time freely to work on her writing. She had renewed confidence that serious readers thought highly of her work. She could return to San Antonio, the place she now felt was home.

WOMAN HOLLERING CREEK (1991)

In 1991, Random House published *Woman Hollering Creek*. In many ways, the book was an extension of the kind of vignettes of various individuals and situations that had marked *The House on Mango Street*. But this book expanded the horizon of voices and added new layers of society in the stories. Filled with vivid images, the book introduced an astonishing array of subjects from the actor who played the "Marlboro Man" on television commercials to the rosaries, statues, and icons that directed the lives of the religious.

The world Cisneros charted in *Woman Hollering Creek* was now beyond the alleys of the barrios; it probed experiences of the educated Latino artist and academic. As she worked on the book, Cisneros was conscious of getting the tone and feeling of each character in their own voices. It produced anxiety and responsibility, she said, a fear that she would misrepresent individuals and their stories. In many ways, she said, the book was a kind of transcription of things she had seen and heard. She saw herself as something like a ventriloquist.

Some critics described the book as mostly poetic prose; others thought it was mostly poetry. Cisneros later said that what she sought in the book was to create a deluge of many voices that spoke in a language embodying the two cultures of which her life had been a part. In this book we begin to see a unique merging of language. A character may use Spanish idioms and English in unusual and fascinating combinations. The characters were a blend of two cultures; so was their use of language. The book also had much to say about the rebellion of women against the conditions into which they had fallen because of society's constraints or because of their own timidity. It was a call to action, to stand up against the abuse.

The title story of *Woman Hollering Creek* is based on Mexican myth and tells the story of a young woman named Cleofilas, mired in a life in a small town with a Mexican-American husband who constantly beat her. Through the help of a number of women, she is able to overcome her dreadful condition. As a woman named Felice, driving a pickup truck, escorts Cleofilas away from her abusive relationship to safety, she lets loose with a yelp and holler that sounded something like that of the cartoon and movie character Tarzan. "Then Felice began laughing again," wrote Cisneros, "but it wasn't Felice laughing. It was gurgling out of her own throat, a long ribbon of laughter like water."[14]

Cisneros said that of all the stories in *Woman Hollering Creek* "the one that everyone—man, woman, white, brown, old, young—tells me, 'oh, that happened to me'" is called "Eleven."[15] In the story "Eleven," the birthday of a young girl named Rachel is ruined by her teacher who forces her to claim responsibility for an ugly, stretched-out sweater abandoned in the coatroom. Despite Rachel's protests that it is not hers, the angry teacher forces her to wear it. Although the incident seemed trivial to the teacher, it was traumatic for the girl who saw, yet again in her life, her own lack of power. Rachel laments, "I'm eleven and it's my birthday today and I'm crying like I'm three in front of everybody. I put my head down on the desk and bury my face in my stupid clown-sweater arms. My face all hot and spit coming out of my mouth because I can't stop the little animal noises coming out of me...."[16]

With this book, Cisneros won a major award from PEN USA, an organization that works to forge a literary community among diverse writers living in the United States. She also won the prestigious Lannan Literary Award for Fiction, given annually for exceptional books. The award was not just an honor; it came with a prize of $50,000. *Woman Hollering Creek* also garnered the Anisfield-Wolf Book Award, given annually for works dealing with racism and ethnicity, was selected as a noteworthy book of the year by *The New York Times* and *The American Library Journal*, and was nominated Best Book of Fiction for 1991 by *The Los Angeles Times*.

In addition to these numerous awards, Cisneros landed advances for two more books: a poetry collection to be called *Loose Women* and a novel that would eventually be called *Caramelo*. The publication of *Woman Hollering Creek* marked Sandra Cisneros' transition from relative obscurity into the limelight of American literary culture and international notice.

HOUSE WITH THE PURPLE PAINT

In 1992, enjoying her literary success, Cisneros was much more in control of her life financially. She could return to the city that for her held so much emotional pull—San Antonio. She loved its colorful architecture. She was comfortable being in a place where Spanish was spoken extensively. She once described the city as the place where Latin America begins.

Cisneros purchased a 1903 metal-roofed, Victorian house in King William, one of the oldest neighborhoods in Texas, a national historic district south of downtown. Settled by wealthy German merchants in the late 1800s, San Antonio's first suburb was filled with a diverse collection of stately mansions as well as a few bungalows. The beautiful landscaping, marked by ancient cypress trees and a quiet atmosphere, was the perfect setting, Cisneros decided, to continue her literary endeavors.

Cisneros fulfilled other desires that she had held for a long time. She bought a bright red pickup truck and decorated it in a typical colorful Mexican style, complete with a colored fringe hanging around the windshield. The neighbors soon realized that a special character was now in their midst.

Cisneros had now settled into a position of being a full-time writer, a very unusual accomplishment in the world of publishing. Most authors never gain the luxury of being able to live off the financial earnings of their work. She was also now in a position to speak to students and community organizations about vital issues. She encouraged Latinos to broaden their dreams and to come together in solidarity. She encouraged businesses and organizations and also publishers to be more inclusive in hiring Latinos and other minorities.

When the national retail clothing company The Gap asked Cisneros to appear in several commercials in 1992 that would be photographed by the internationally celebrated photographer Annie Leibowitz, Cisneros turned down the offer. The Gap, she said, had not used other Latinos in their commercials and had not demonstrated a commitment to the Latino community. If she had accepted the lucrative offer, she explained, it would have felt to her as something of a betrayal to Latinos rather than a breakthrough.

In 1994, Cisneros' second collection of poetry appeared in print. *Loose Women* examined the powerful forms love took in the lives of women, especially for independent women of Mexican heritage. In 1995, Random House issued *La Casa en Mango Street,* a Spanish-language translation of the author's first acclaimed work. Cisneros also published a children's book called *Hairs/Pelitos,* exploring the issues surrounding family and cultural diversity. Also in 1995, Cisneros received one of the nation's most prestigious awards: a MacArthur Foundation fellowship. Known widely as "genius grants," the fellowships are annually awarded to accomplished, creative, and promising scholars, scientists, and others in diverse fields. The grant was for $250,000.

As Cisneros worked on the manuscript of what would be her major novel, she began to give public readings of some of the parts. This unusual step for a writer increased the anticipation among her fans and the literary community about the forthcoming work.

In February 1996, her life was jolted by the unexpected death of her father. After years of much resentment about her childhood, Cisneros had grown much closer to her father in recent years. He had rejoiced at her talent and success, and his pride in her fulfilled one of the longings she had held throughout her life. His death blanketed her life for a time in grief, and she had a difficult time returning to her work. The novel, on which she was making great progress, suddenly seemed disjointed. She began painstakingly revising and reconsidering. Her work slowed.

In May 1997, still in the grip of depression, she decided to brighten her surroundings. She decided to paint her house. Normally a decision to paint one's house would not create a major stir, even among neighbors living close by. Certainly such a decision would not make national news. But this was Sandra Cisneros.

In honor of her cultural background and in line with the bright colors such as red, orange, pink, green, and purple that predominate in neighborhoods south of the border, Cisneros painted her house a vivid purple with shades of violet and lilac. This was land formerly owned by Mexico, she reasoned, and she wanted to celebrate the rich history of San Antonio that united Mexicans and Anglos.

But this was also land that was part of the King William Historic District. There were now rules and regulations enacted by the residents of the community regarding the maintenance of the area, codes that required certain palettes of paint that would conform to the natural and historic look of the community. Any deviations from these rules and codes would have to be approved by a governing body made up of the area's residents. Those residents mostly did not like the fresh coat of paint they saw on Cisneros' house. She had not consulted them about her plans and had not gained the required approval. Soon, the leaders of the King William Historic District were demanding that Cisneros change the color of the house. Some of the neighbors, however, sided with the literary celebrity in their community and began referring to themselves as "Sandranistas."

Cisneros took on the assault with characteristic energy and passion. She submitted a paper tracing the development of the district and pointing out that her particular home stood at the district's edge where poor immigrants had once lived. There were no historical records indicating the color palette of those homes. She reasoned that a number of them probably featured the same hues that now shone from her own house.

None of her arguments won approving nods. The demands that she relent stood. Lawsuits were threatened. Cisneros remained firm. The battle of the purple house in San Antonio continued. At one point, Cisneros called in the national media and staged a press conference on her lawn. She had prepared a petition, on purple paper, of course, to be signed by those who agreed with her on the issue. Soon, some neighbors began to display purple ribbons on their own gates to show support.

For Cisneros, the fight was about a number of issues, all of which she was not about to abandon. It had to do with Latino culture. It also had to do with individuality, the right to free expression, and, perhaps most of all, the right just to be herself.

Her persona around San Antonio delighted some neighbors who took pride in her accomplishments. Her ways shocked and alienated others. But much of her life had been a statement. On her small red pickup truck was a bumper sticker that said, "Wild Women Don't Get the Blues." She shared her two-bedroom house on Guenther Street with five cats, three dogs, and two parrots. Her appearance shouted out rebellion. Wearing Mexican shawls and cowboy boots, with her hair cut short and black lipstick, she was not an ordinary neighbor.

"Of course her house is purple," said Jan Jarboe, another writer living in San Antonio and a big fan of Cisneros. "I'm surprised it isn't dripping with rhinestones."[17] In fact, rhinestones did decorate the horseshoe beside Cisneros' front door. Also, her dog Violetta, a small mutt who often accompanied her to readings, sported a rhinestone collar.

The city of San Antonio finally threatened Cisneros with fines that could have amounted to $1,000 a day if she did not paint the house. Aware of her strategic disadvantage in the struggle, she agreed to paint the house pink, an action that temporarily froze the controversy in place. Then she waited.

The threats and demands continued for more than two years. Then, after the strong Texas sunshine had done its work, Cisneros peeled off a slice of the paint from her house, took it to the city commission, and demonstrated that it was no longer purple. The commission members conceded that it had turned to violet. The color now matched the palette. The battle of the purple house was history.

CARAMELO (2002)

Cisneros continued to speak out on behalf of causes close to her heart, especially those that encouraged young Latinos to seek challenging goals and careers and to develop self-esteem. She returned to Chicago, for example, to help the Chicago YMCA dedicate the new Chernin Center for the Arts that served three Chicago Housing Authority neighborhoods.

Her activism ranged from speaking out against capital punishment to challenging the old but persistent stereotypes and discrimination that severely limited Latinos and buried many in desperation and isolation. She said, "I try to speak because we've been silent as women for so long, especially Latinas, to the point of self-destruction. I speak because to not speak is to be complicit in this pain. I was silent as a child, and silenced as a young woman; I am taking my lumps and bumps for being a big mouth, now, but usually from those whose opinion I don't respect."[18]

But there were a great many people for whom she had great admiration throughout her life. She especially pointed to "women who gave their lives for community rights or who donated their life earning's to a college. They are nameless women. Women who loved flowers, raised children ... there are plenty of examples of women around me whom I admire fiercely; women who work very hard in the community as educators, or artists, or community activists. They are my friends."[19]

In 2002 Alfred A. Knopf publishers issued *Caramelo*. For Cisneros it represented nine long years of work, much of it interrupted by other writings, speaking engagements, and personal concerns. It is was by far her longest work, more than 440 pages, a kind of cultural epic tracing the lives of three brothers whose roots and memories were formed from both sides of the United States border.

The rich story, filled with Mexican lore, tradition, and cultural celebrations, is told from the perspective of one of the grandchildren, Lala Reyes. It is a book not only of family history but also of Mexican history. "I didn't think I was going to be writing a history book," she said, "I thought I was writing a story about my father, based on my father's life. But in telling my father's story, I had to place him in time and history, and then I had to go back and look at how he became who he was. So I had to invent my grandmother's story and how she became who she was, so next thing I knew, there were a lot of tributaries from my main story...."[20]

The title of the book comes from a traditional, striped Mexican shawl called a *rebozo*. A *caramelo* is a caramel-colored *rebozo*. A product of both Spanish and Native-American roots, over the centuries the *rebozo* has been used as an apron, scarf, tablecloth, and even a baby sling. In parts of Mexico, women wore the cloth to signal their status as married or single. Cisneros often saw the *rebozo* as representative of culture, the stitching together of patches of life and values into a whole. She saw her own work, especially on this book, as a weaving of stories.

A fictionalized autobiography, *Caramelo* is not driven by plot but is a general sweep of time and culture. It begins with a photograph taken in Acapulco during a tumultuous family vacation. The Reyes family stands in the photo: Inocencio, his wife Zoila, and his six sons, along with Inocencio's mother, called "the Awful Grandmother" by the narrator of the book, five-year old Lala. The only one missing from the photo is Lala herself. It was, she says, as if the family had forgotten about her. The scene, indeed the book, reflects the lifetime of hurt in Cisneros about her childhood. But the book also demonstrated just how far Cisneros had come emotionally, especially when thinking about the life of her father. *Caramelo* is dedicated *Pari ti, Papa* (For you, Father).

Cisneros said that originally she had set out to explain the life of her father. To do that, however, she had to explain her "Awful Grandmother," as the character is named in the book. Her father's mother, Cisneros said, was a bossy and melodramatic woman who constantly nurtured a sense of guilt in her father who now lived so far away. At one point in the book, in one of the frequent comic interludes, the character of "Awful Grandmother" breaks into the prose to complain how she is being portrayed by the author.

> why are you so cruel with me? You love to make me suffer. You enjoy mortifying me, isn't that so? Is that why you insist on showing everyone this …dirt, but refuse me one little love scene?
>
> For crying out loud, Grandmother. If you can't let me do my job and tell this story without your constant interruptions.…
>
> All I wanted was a little understanding, but I see I was asking for too much.[21]

But then, to explain "Awful Grandmother," Cisneros found that she had to go back further into the roots of the family. The book became increasingly long and complex. Nevertheless, in that complexity, Cisneros uncovered a richness and vitality rarely produced in a novel.

Filled with references to popular music, comic books, food, traditions, fables, and other bits and pieces of information and speculation, the book is a cultural ride rich in memory and feeling. Like works of history, the book even sports footnotes and chronologies, explaining historical references and terms. Historical characters are interspersed, figures such as dancer Josephine Baker, events from the Mexican Revolution of 1910, and memories of famous Mexican film stars.

Essentially, it is, like *The House on Mango Street*, the story of Cisneros' own family and their treks to Mexico. But it is also multigenerational, partly tracing the great Latino immigration to the United States. "I was making something completely new," Cisneros said, "I wasn't writing the *House on Mango Street*. If I was writing that I could have gotten that done in a couple of years. I didn't want to do something I had done before. I really wanted to expand and push myself and do something that I didn't have a model for. I didn't even know how to make what I wanted. I just knew that I could see it in my mind's eye for a flash of a second and then I was in the dark. So I was mainly in the dark, experimenting with this book."[22] This towering literary achievement did not come easily to Cisneros. She compared it to those agonizing automobile trips from Chicago to deep into Mexico. "Writing this book," she said, "has been like making a walking pilgrimage to Tepeyac from Chicago. On my knees."[23]

Cisneros was especially gratified about the reception given to the book and to her lectures about her work by people of varying backgrounds. "If you are Mexican, they feel like crying because they feel no one has written about this and they are emotionally overwhelmed. I get a lot of weepers. If you are of another culture, say Persian or Chinese or African-American, you will come up surprised and say, 'Well, I'm Persian but this could have been my family.' People from very different cultures than mine see themselves in this book. Even the most gringo *gringo* will, when I see them in the audience, will be laughing at the appropriate moment."[24]

Literary scholar Ilan Stavans said of *Caramelo*, "Cisneros' talent for succinct, impressionistic imagery is well recognized. The stories in the collection *Woman Hollering Creek*, as well as those in *The House on Mango Street*, which is barely 100 pages long, are all brief. They are also intense, compression being one of her hallmarks. To read a 440-page volume by Cisneros, then, is a shocker. Somehow, in the sweeping chronicle that covers more than a century of history, she manages to remain concise. *Caramelo* is composed of chapters so condensed, so meteoric, they feel like snapshots arranged in a family album."[25]

Caramelo was selected as notable book of the year by several publications, including *The New York Times*, the *Los Angeles Times*, the *San Francisco Chronicle*, the *Chicago Tribune*, and *The Seattle Times*. It also received several international awards and nominations.

THE HONOR OF WRITING

When Cisneros looked at her career, she stressed her commitment to help all races in America understand the lives of Mexican Americans, especially women. "I feel very honored to give them a form in my writings," she said, "and to be able to have this material to write about is a blessing."[26]

As she matured both personally and professionally, Cisneros took an increasing role as an activist. From the days of the isolated and shy youngster from the Chicago barrio she became a highly visible spokesperson, defending the rights and interests of Latinos across a range of programs and issues. A number of Latino organizations have praised not only her creativity and writing accomplishments but also her active participation in civic and cultural programs.

Cisneros established the Macondo Foundation, a unique writers' workshop with a Latino focus and a commitment to community service. Also, in the name of her father, she set up in 2002 the Alfredo Cisneros Del Moral Foundation, an institution that provides grants to Texas writers. "My father lived his life as an example of generosity and honest labor," Cisneros has written. "Even as he warned us to save our centavitos, he was always giving away his own. A meticulous craftsman, he would sooner rip the seams of a cushion apart and do it over than put his name on an item that wasn't up to his high standards. I especially wanted to honor his memory with an award showcasing writers who are equally proud of their own craft."[27]

Cisneros has been a shining influence to many aspiring writers. "I knew Sandra before she was Sandra Cisneros," joked Dagoberto Gilb, a 51-year-old writer from Austin, Texas, author of *Woodcuts of Women* and contributor to *The New Yorker* magazine. Like Cisneros, Gilb received a Dobie Paisano Award and spent time at the ranch house working on his own writings. "She's like my sister," he said. "We came up together. But her rise—her rise went much higher than mine. Talking about Sandra Cisneros these days is like talking about Frida Kahlo."[28]

Being compared with Frida Kahlo, one of the most influential Mexican painters of the twentieth century, places Cisneros in an unusually lofty company of famous women. But the still growing importance of her literary works and the increasing influence she exerts on behalf of Latino culture never overwhelmed her sense of proportion. She balanced her serious work with an infectious enjoyment of life. "I live with many creatures little and large," she said, "... six dogs (Beto, Dante, Lolita, Chamaco, Valentina P-nut Butter, and Barney Fife), four cats (Gato Perón, Pánfilo, Apolonia, and Lulu), and a parrot named Agustina. I am nobody's mother, nobody's wife, am happily single and live in San Antonio, Texas, with the love of my life. I'm currently at work on several projects, including a collection of fiction titled *Infinito*."[29]

But the activist instinct in Cisneros, the searching for hope that she could make a difference, continued to grow. In the fall of 2007, she spoke at Cornell University in Ithaca, New York. She urged her audience to work for peace. She had come to the university from a retreat for Buddhist people of color, she said, a "Buddhist boot camp" with the Zen monk and peace activist Thich Nhat Hanh. She suggested writing to first lady Laura Bush, as she has done, to protest the war in Iraq. "We all have our personal terrorists who make our twin towers shake when we see them," Cisneros said. "I'm embarrassed and ashamed that I still have some left."[30]

Cisneros said that a large part of her motivation in writing *Caramelo* was for the work to "be a healing medicine for the current climate of violence and fear." It was the best way, she said, she could "respond to people's fear that was being promulgated in media, by our politicians, in the letters to the editor. I could be a one-person peace demonstration. I could work nonviolently for communities to come together and understand each other." She believes that good stories and a stronger grasp of the past and the culture ties people together. Reading such stories, she said, is healing.

Cisneros believed good stories change their readers. 'It creeps up on you like a Trojan horse," she said. "You take it home, you think about it, and you suddenly realize that you look at the world in a different way. It's much more persuasive than bonking someone over the head with a big peace sign."[31]

For Cisneros, one of the great satisfactions in her work was the reaction of children. Throughout her career, she made a point of traveling to various cities to make appearances at schools, libraries, and other organizations that brought together young people, not only to interest them in literary matters but to inspire them, as much as she could, to make the most of their energies.

In the spring of 1994, Cisneros appeared at a branch library in Brooklyn, New York, to read excerpts of some of her writings to children. During the appearance, she held up a report card. It was from a Chicago parochial school and it showed scores of mostly C's and D's. It was her own report card, from many years earlier. The message: The woes of school can and must be temporary. They need not ruin your future.

At New York's Lexington School for the Deaf, Cisneros made an appearance using a sign-language interpreter. Liz Wolter, a teacher at Lexington School said, "She read the new introduction to *Mango Street*, which answered a lot of questions which the students have, then she read the story from *Mango Street* called 'My Name,' and we watched the interpreter sign it. She was extraordinary, really inspiring."[32]

In many respects, Cisneros viewed herself as an ambassador between the Anglo and Latino worlds. "I'm very conscious that I want to write about us so that there is communication between the cultures," she said. "That's political work: Making communication happen between the cultures."[33]

In the public school system in Denver, Colorado, Latino children make up nearly 60 percent of the students. Cisneros appeared at North High School to promote the city's book program called "One Book, One Denver." *Caramelo* was selected as one of the books most valuable to encourage students to appreciate literature and to engage in writing. It was also selected as a book that allows Latino children to see that their lives have great value, even if their culture is not the predominant one shown in magazines and television. In the audience to hear Cisneros that day was seventeen-year-old Carmen Martinez. She said that the sounds and images seemed real to her.

"I've really connected to it," she said. "I can see my family here. The women in the book are powerful." For Cisneros, no words more satisfying could have been said by a young Latina.[34]

NOTES

1. Sandra Cisneros, *Women Hollering Creek and Other Stories,* (New York: Random House, 1991), 70.

2. Robin Ganz, "Sandra Cisneros: Border Crossings and Beyond," *Melus*, Spring, 1994, 19.

3. Patricia Trebe, "Elvira Vera Cisneros: 1929–2007; Mother was an artist, muse; 'Independent thinker' was the inspiration for her daughter's book," *Chicago Tribune,* November 7, 2007, 9.

4. Ganz.

5. Sandra Cisneros, *Caramelo.* (New York: Alfred A. Knopf, 2002), 5.

6. Jim Sagel, "Sandra Cisnerros: Conveying the Riches of the Latin American Culture is the Author's Literary Goal," *Publishers Weekly*, March 29, 1991, 74.

7. Sandra Cisneros, *The House on Mango Street,* (New York: Vintage Contemporaries, 1984), 110.

8. Himilce Novas, *The Hispanic 100* (New York: Citadel Press, 1995), 260.

9. Sagel.

10. Ganz.

11. *House on Mango Street*, 16.

12. Ganz.

13. Sagel.

14. *Woman Hollering Creek*, 56.

15. "Major Writers for Children and Young Adults," http://www.princeton.edu/ howarth/557/house_bio.html.

16. *Woman Hollering Creek*, 9.

17. Sara Rimer, "Novelist's Purple Palette Is Not to Everyone's Taste," *New York Times,* July 13, 1998, A14.

18. Maria-Antónia Oliver-Rotger, "An Interview with Sandra Cisneros," http:// voices.cla.umn.edu/vg/interviews/vg_interviews/cisneros_sandra.html.

19. Oliver-Rotger.

20. "Conversation: Cisneros," Online NewsHour, October 15, 2002, http://www. pbs.org/newshour/conversation/july-dec02/cisneros_10-15.html.

21. *Caremelo*, 172.

22. "Sandra Cisneros: Author of *Caramelo* talks with Robert Birnbaum," December 4, 2002, http://www.identitytheory.com/interviews/index.html.

23. *Caramelo*, 443.

24. "Sandra Cisneros: Author of *Caramelo* ..."

25. Ilan Stavans, "Familiar Faces," *The Nation*, February 10, 2003, 30.

26. Gale: Free Resources: Hispanic Heritage, http://www.galegroup.com/free_resources/chh/bio/cisneros_s.htm.

27. Alfred Cisneros Del Moral Foundation, http://www.sandracisneros.com/ foundation.php.

28. Jerome Weeks, "The weaver: the country's leading Latina author makes a sweet return with *Caramelo*, her first novel in nearly twenty years," *Book*, September/October 2002, 54.

29. "About Sandra Cisneros," http://www.sandracisneros.com/bio.php.

30. George Lowery, "Cisneros Tries to Make Peace with the Creative Process," *Chronicle Online*, September 17, 2007, http://www.news.cornell.edu/stories/Sept07/Cisneros.cover.gl.html.

31. Robin Vidimos, "Antidote for a climate of fear; Complicated 'Caramelo' has some challenging ideas," *Denver Post*, March 27, 2005, F09.

32. David Mehegan, "Sandra Cisneros still writes from border country; Even with success, she sees herself as an outsider," *Boston Globe*, May 17, 1994, 73.

33. "One Writer's Bicultural Blend," *Christian Science Monitor*, March 12, 1993, 12.

34. Cindy Rodriguez, "*Caramelo* helps unite cultures," *Denver Post*, April 7, 2005, F1.

FURTHER READING

Cahill, Susan, ed. "Sandra Cisneros." In *Writing Women's Lives: An Anthology of Autobiographical Narratives by Twentieth-Century American Women Writers*. New York: Harper Perennial, 1994, 459–468.

Cisneros, Sandra. *Caramelo*. New York: Alfred A. Knopf, 2002.

Cisneros, Sandra. *The House on Mango Street*. New York: Vintage Contemporaries, 1984.

Cisneros, Sandra. *Woman Hollering Creek and Other Stories*. New York: Random House, 1991.

"Conversation Cisneros," Online NewsHour, October 15, 2002, http://www.pbs.org/newshour/conversation/july-dec02/cisneros_10-15.html.

Lowery, George. "Cisneros tries to make peace with the creative process," *Chronicle Online*, September 17, 2007, http://www.news.cornell.edu/stories/Sept07/Cisneros.cover.gl.html

Oliver-Rotger, Maria-Antonia, "An interview with Sandra Cisneros," http://voices.cla.umn.edu/vg/interviews/vg_interviews/cisneros_sandra.html.

Sagel, Jim. "Sandra Cisnerros: Conveying the riches of the Latin American culture is the author's literary goal." *Publishers Weekly*, March 29, 1991, 74.

"Sandra Cisneros: Author of *Caramelo* talks with Robert Birnbaum," December 4, 2002, http://www.identitytheory.com/interviews/index.html.

Stavans, Ilan. "Familiar Faces." *The Nation*, February 10, 2003, 30.

Roberto Clemente

Since the earliest days of professional baseball in the United States, the game has been dominated by the ethnic minorities in the ascendancy at the time—Germans and Irish after the Civil War, followed by Italians, and, today, Latinos. The Dominican Republic is now the per-capita leader in producing major league players, higher than any of the major baseball-producing states such as California and Texas. Latin-American baseball players have expanded the boundaries of the "American pastime," asserting their ethnic and national identities, and are accepted as representatives of a sport most closely aligned with a white United States identity. At a time of accelerating tensions with regard to immigration issues, Latino players help act as a counterweight to racism and xenophobia. The legacy of the first Latin-American player to be named to the Baseball Hall of Fame still towers over the sport. He was Roberto Clemente from Puerto Rico.

A KID FROM PUERTO RICO

Born on August 18, 1934, in the small barrio of San Anton in Carolina, Puerto Rico, Roberto Clemente was the youngest of seven children of Melchor and Luisa Clemente. Melchor was a foreman at a sugar cane mill and ran a small grocery store from one of the rooms of the house; Luisa did laundry for the owner of the mill. Strongly religious, with a raw strain of humanitarianism running through her daily activities, she often fed poor laborers and their children who dropped by the house. The two oldest children, Luis and Rosa, were from Luisa's first marriage, which had ended with the death of her first husband. Melchor and Luisa had five children from their own marriage: Osvaldo, Justino (Matino), Andres, Anairis, and Roberto.

Respect, dignity, hard work, and tolerance—these are the values that were preached to the young boy at an early age, but they were also demonstrated to him by his parents. He never heard hate in his house, Clemente often said. There were never harsh words between his parents.

Although the Clemente family was not poor compared with the many farm worker families around it, the small house, with orange fields in front and sugar cane fields behind, strained to accommodate the numbers. Some of the children slept in the living room.

His sister Rosa gave the young boy the nickname of "Momen" when he was very young and the name stuck. It had no special meaning, just a garbled word from the mouth of a child. Nevertheless, to his family, many of his friends, and even, later, to his wife, he would be Momen.

When Roberto was still an infant, the family suffered a grievous loss. The youngest daughter, Anairis, accidentally ignited an outdoor cooking stove and suffered fatal burns. Although he had been too young to know his sister, her death, so tragic and senseless, would haunt the young boy throughout his life. He would often hear his mother crying in private, knowing in his mind that it was still the grief of the accident that caused her such agony.

Years later, with a growing sense of the mystical that became characteristic of him, Clemente would claim that he still felt Anairis by his side.

The family tragedies would not end with the death of Anairis. Two brothers would die young of cancer, and Roberto's half-sister, Rosa, later died in childbirth. Given the trauma of the family, it was not unusual that Clemente throughout his life was extremely conscious of his medical well-being; many people remarked on the hypochondria that plagued him his entire life.

His family and friends saw early on the determination and effort that young Clemente could summon. For three years, beginning at the age of nine, he got up daily at six o'clock to deliver milk for a penny a day to save money for a bicycle.

The boy's athleticism was evident from his very early years. Fast, agile, and strong, he was a physical marvel. When he was in high school he was such a fine javelin thrower that there was some talk that he might be on Puerto Rico's 1942 Olympic Team. But track and field always took a distant back seat to his obsession—baseball. "When I was a little kid," he said later, "the only thing I used to do was play ball all the time ... with a rubber ball, with a tennis ball."[1] He and his friends would hit tin cans and bottle caps with broomsticks. Neighbors remember Roberto spending hours throwing rubber balls against walls and the sides of the house.

The boy's love of baseball was not unusual in Puerto Rico, where it was widely popular. Introduced to the island by immigrants from Cuba in the last half of the nineteenth century, baseball became increasingly popular when United States Marines landed in 1898. Although his father had never been interested in the sport, his older brother, Matino, became a very skillful amateur player and encouraged his younger brother at every stage.

As a young teenager, Clemente would catch a bus from Carolina and travel to San Juan to see games in the Puerto Rican Winter League for a quarter. His hero, Monte Irvin, a star for the New York Giants, played for the San Juan Senedores in the Winter League. For black major league players in the 1950s, winter ball was exhilarating, an escape from the winters in the northern big cities and a refreshing break from the persistent racial hostilities they faced in the states. Monte Irvin became conscious of the rapt attention that the youngster from Carolina paid to his every move in every game, from warm-ups to the final pitch. The two became close, Irvin often asking Clemente to carry his bag into the stadium in return for a free ticket.

While playing ball with his friends, young Roberto caught the eye of Roberto Marin, who was putting together a softball team for the Stello Rojo Rice Company. Marin asked the boy to try out for the team. Although he had not hit softballs before, the youngster swatted the new objects as well as he had hit stuffed socks, tin cans, and bottle caps. A freshman in high school, Clemente joined the team and played part-time for two years. He first played shortstop but Marin, aware of his speed and fielding instincts, tried him in the outfield. He began to impress the softball crowds with his range, glove, and, especially, his strong throwing arm.

Later, Clemente joined a baseball team called the Ferdinand Juncos, one of the top amateur teams in Carolina, and he starred against many players who were much older. During that winter, he caught the eye of a scout for the Santurce Cangrejeros, the principal rival of the San Juan Senedores, the team with Clemente's idol, Monte Irvin.

In 1952, Clemente joined Santurce. The team offered $40 a week. The wide-eyed Clemente, eighteen years old and still in high school, readily signed up. The youngster would play against such legends as Roy Campanella, Junior Gilliam, and other major leaguers, including Monte Irvin, his hero. He would be on the same team with the great Willie Mays.

Even at an early age, he had the tools to be great: the strong arm, the impressive hand–eye coordination, the quick bat that over the years would rocket line drives in every park he played, and the hustle and effort on the bases, arms flaying, legs churning. At the age of eighteen, Clemente hit .356 for Santurce in the winter of 1952–1953.

The major league scouts took notice. Al Campanis, a scout for the Brooklyn Dodgers, held a tryout for a number of Puerto Rican players. By the end of the tryout, he was left looking at just one, Clemente. Campanis later said that Clemente was the most impressive free agent athlete he had ever seen.

For slightly more than a year, the youngster continued to play in the winters for the Santurce Cangrejeros while he finished high school at the Institute Comerical de Puerto Rico, a technical school near his home and the San Juan stadium. Awaiting him were contract offers from major league teams and the career that he, and all who saw him play, anticipated with much eagerness.

1954 AND MONTREAL

Spurred by Al Campanis' scouting report, the Brooklyn Dodgers offered Clemente a minor league contract. Although several other teams also offered to sign the youngster, Clemente decided that he wanted to make the roster of a team in New York, where he would find the greatest proportion of Puerto Ricans. Under the conditions of the contract, the youngster would be assigned to the Dodgers minor league roster with no chance to be promoted to the major leagues within the first year. The Dodgers, after all, one of the top teams in major league baseball, were already stocked with a number of great outfielders including Duke Snider and Carl Furillo. Under baseball rules, Clemente could be drafted by another major league team at the end of the 1954 season.

In February 1954, Melchor Clemente signed a contract on behalf of his son. The Dodgers agreed to pay the young Puerto Rican prospect a bonus of $10,000 and a first-year salary of $5,000. White players with Clemente's prospects were typically offered more money; nevertheless, Clemente was now on the road to fulfill a dream. He headed for his first assignment—spring training in Florida with the Montreal Royals of the Triple-A International League. The Royals were the team for which Jackie Robinson had played eight years earlier on his way to break the color barrier in the major leagues. His older brothers, Andres and Matino, drove Roberto to the airport in San Juan for the first leg in his baseball odyssey.

When he arrived at the baseball compound in Vero Beach known as Dodgertown, Clemente was the youngest player on the Montreal team and the only Puerto Rican. Only one of the other players spoke Spanish, Chico Fernandez, a shortstop from Havana, Cuba. For the first time in his life, Clemente began to feel the isolation that any young player feels away from home, but he also felt the not-so-subtle stabs of racism through which blacks and Latinos had to fight every day.

By the time Clemente reached Vero Beach in 1954, baseball had been struggling with the integration process started by the Dodgers in 1947 when Jackie Robinson was brought from the Negro Leagues by the Dodgers through Montreal and then on to the National League parent team itself. After Robinson joined the Dodgers, the introduction of new black players had been slow and wrenching. The Cleveland Indians had quickly followed the Dodgers' lead and signed Larry Doby as the first African-American player to appear in the American League. Both men had suffered abuse and ridicule as they made their way through spring training and through the major league seasons.

Although several Latino players had very brief stints in the major leagues, the first highly successful Latino player was also given his shot by the Cleveland Indians. Minnie Minoso, who had starred in the Cuban League, came to the Indians in 1949. Minoso, an exciting and durable player, would be the premier Latino player in the majors for most of the 1950s.

When Clemente arrived at Vero Beach, many of the facilities in Florida were still segregated. For the first time in his life, Clemente, whose complexion was very dark, came face to face with the humiliating and senseless rules against blacks, with the signs that told him where he could eat and drink and where he could not. He could see in Florida the sections marked out in the bleachers for blacks. He noticed that in the Dodgertown compound the black service workers were boarded onto buses and taken out of the area before sundown. He could feel early on the terrible constraints of language. Although he would eventually manage to speak a limited amount of English with a thick accent, his relationships with whites would often suffer. Few of the whites with whom he came into contact could speak even a small amount of Spanish. In those early days at Dodgertown he missed his family, friends, and the warm sense of home in Puerto Rico.

When the Montreal Royals opened their 1954 season, Roberto Clemente, number 5, was in centerfield, batting fifth in the lineup. During the first few games, International League fans could see what scout Buzzie Bavasi had seen in the tryouts, what other scouts, players, and fans had seen in Puerto Rico—a budding superstar.

After the first four games, Clemente was hitting .500, leading the team in hitting, and making impressive, acrobatic plays in the field. Nevertheless, after the first week, Clemente began to see only sporadic playing time. Outfielder Sandy Amoros, who started the season with the Dodgers, was soon shipped back to the minors and became an instant fixture in the outfield. Even with his growing "can't miss" reputation, Clemente was suddenly invisible.

There were two likely reasons. Many thought it was the Dodgers' front office, worried about too great an influx of black players on their major league squad, who balked at developing Clemente quickly. Others claimed that the Dodgers were simply hiding Clemente for the year, hoping that other teams would not be interested when he became eligible for the draft in 1955 because of the nature of the contract he signed. In any case, Clemente did not have a breakout professional debut at Montreal simply because he did not have an opportunity.

He roomed with Chico Fernandez, the Cuban infielder, in a house a few blocks from the stadium. Neither of them could speak much English. For Clemente, all of it was new and challenging—ordering breakfast at a diner, meeting new people, understanding street signs, reading newspapers. But mostly it was the frustration of not playing regularly so that, even in the ballpark, he did not feel welcome. He told Fernandez that he might quit. He gradually adapted enough to stay on, but the anger and disappointment were never far from the surface.

In the later part of the season, Branch Rickey, head of the struggling Pittsburgh Pirates, sent scouts to Montreal to follow Clemente for a time. During the 1940s Rickey had run the Dodgers; he still had many contacts in the organization and was aware of the promise of the young outfielder who had not seen much playing time. With their woeful win-loss record, the Pirates would have the first pick in the following year's draft. One of the scouts dispatched by Rickey talked privately with Clemente during his visit and made it clear that the youngster could very well be playing in the outfield next year with the Pirates. Clemente finished the season knowing that in the span of only a few months his disappointing minor league experience in Montreal would probably be only a memory.

On December 30, 1954, Clemente, along with his brothers, Andres and Matino, drove from Ponce, Puerto Rico, where Roberto had played in a Winter League game, back to the San Juan area. They were on their way to visit their oldest brother, Luis, who was gravely ill with a brain tumor. On the road at night, with Clemente at the wheel of a 1954 Pontiac he had purchased with his bonus money, another car flew recklessly into the intersection and smashed into their side. Although Clemente and his brothers said they were not seriously injured, Clemente had severely wrenched his neck. It was an injury that would plague him throughout his career.

The next day, the three were at the side of their brother, who passed away at noon.

PITTSBURGH AND THE MAJORS

The Pittsburgh Pirates of the early 1950s were a pathetic lot. The team, whose origins predated the turn of the century, had a long history of success and failure but this was failure on a grand scale. In 1952, the Pirates' record was 42 wins and 112 losses, a winning percentage of .273. The next two seasons were not much better. In 1953 and 1954 they lost 104 and 101 games, respectively. In 1952, only slugger Ralph Kiner, who would hit a home run every fourth game or so, gave the team any point of respectability. When Kiner got embroiled in a salary dispute with Branch Rickey in the following year, the slugger was shipped off to Chicago with a memorable parting shot from Rickey that the team could finish last with or without him.

On April 17, 1955, in the old Forbes Field stadium, now almost half a century old, Clemente made his major league debut for the Pirates, batting third and playing right field, against the Dodgers. On the roster he was listed by the team as "Bob" because Roberto sounded too foreign.

On the mound for the Dodgers was lefthander Johnny Podres, who would later in 1955 lead the Dodgers to a victory in the World Series against the New York Yankees. In this first trip to the plate, Clemente ripped a Podres pitch into the hole between short and third. Although shortstop Pee Wee Reese was able to knock the ball down, he did not have time to make a throw. Clemente stood at first base with the first hit of his major-league career.

To the fans and others who witnessed the event, it was nothing special. The Pirates lost this game as they did the first eight games of the season. They were off to another miserable year. No one could have dreamed that this hit, by this young Puerto Rican newcomer, playing for this lowly team, would be only the first in a phenomenal career that would yield another 2,999.

Although a slim, gazelle-like man of modest build, 5 ft. 11 in., and 175 pounds, he nevertheless wielded an improbably large 36-ounce bat. Many of his fellow players could not understand how the trim Clemente could generate such robust bat speed. When they looked at his very large hands and wrists, however, their question was answered. His batting stroke was unlike that of most of the other great players of his time. In baseball terms he hit from the inside out. Standing far back from the plate, his hands close to his chest, he waited late on the pitch. Then, generating great torque and bat speed, he lashed with an even stroke, whipping the ball just before it reached the catcher's glove. Throughout his career, Clemente hit line drive after line drive.

He once told a reporter that if a pitcher threw him outside pitches he would hit .400; pitch him inside, he said, and you might lose the ball. Future Hall of Fame pitcher Sandy Koufax agreed with Clemente's assessment of his own hitting strengths. Koufax's advice: Roll the ball to him. With unparalleled arm strength and accuracy, Clemente led National League outfielders in assists five times; an extraordinary achievement considering that, after a few years, runners only sporadically tested him. He often asked a coach to hit fly balls off the Forbes Field wall so he could throw them toward baskets at the various bases. He routinely hit them on the fly with a rifle-like trajectory from the fence.

He once threw out Lee May of the Cincinnati Reds trying to score from third on a single to right. So aggressive was his play that Clemente once fielded a bunt while playing right field. With runners on first and second, the hitter bunted the ball toward the shortstop position. When the shortstop vacated the position to cover third, Clemente rushed in from right field, scooped up the ball as it slowly dribbled toward the outfield, and threw out the runner who tried to reach third base from first.

Pittsburgh was a typical steel town, blue-collar, mostly white, not used to hearing anyone with a Spanish accent. Except for the few players on the Pirates, Clemente saw few people on the streets or in the restaurants that were Latino or, indeed, black. Often offended by remarks he did not understand or questions that seemed far too intrusive, Clemente took on a defensive posture. Tony Bartirome, the Pittsburgh Pirates trainer, said, "He was very leery of the media. He was misquoted a lot of times and they made fun of the way he spoke. They made him sound like one of those Indians in the movies. This was a proud man, and this really got to him. He had fierce pride. He was proud of being Puerto Rican."[2]

The press had difficulty communicating with Latinos long after the initial influx of players from the Caribbean. Many of the players simply were not interviewed—such standouts as Tony Oliva of Minnesota and Tony Perez of Cincinnati—because they resented the phonetic spelling that writers seemed to delight in putting in their columns. If a player said with an accent "bay-zebol," that is how it would often appear in newspapers and magazines. Only a handful of baseball writers knew any Spanish at all.

On many occasions in the press, the young Puerto Rican was called "dusky" and "chocolate-colored" and other such adjectives. "Lots of time I have the feeling people want to take advantage of me, especially writers," Clemente once said. "They talk to me, but maybe they don't like me, so they write about me the way they want to write ... they thought Latins were inferior to the American people. Now they know they can't be sarcastic about Latins. Which is something I have fought all my life."[3] But the city and those around baseball gradually came around. Pirates broadcaster Bob Prince began greeting Clemente's plate appearances with "*Arriba! Arriba!*" (Go! Go!) With Prince, the language reference was not biting or sarcastic, and Clemente delighted in it.

Clemente often remarked about the lack of product endorsements that came his way from U.S. companies. "You have to be American," he said, "or you can't be 'my sweetheart next door.' If they don't like my face, they can send me to get plastic surgery."[4] After complaining for a number of years about the lack of endorsements, a snub he regarded as a lack of respect, he later would say that he did not need them. He got them from Latino companies, he said, and gave the money to charity.

He was also constantly annoyed that the expectation was that he fit into the places designated for him, that somehow he must subordinate his individuality to the predominant culture. Even in the black community where he lived, he did not fit in; there were just too many language and cultural collisions. The slights and perceived slights that seem to bombard him took a toll on his spirit. When the Topps baseball card company issued their first card on Clemente, they Americanized his name, just as the team had done on its roster. He was "Bob" Clemente; he did not want to be "Bob." Even though Clemente made the company aware of his feelings, for years afterward the cards continued to be issued in the same way.

His closest friend in Pittsburgh was a postal worker named Phil Dorsey, with whom Clemente had become acquainted through one of the Pirate pitchers. Dorsey would drive Clemente to and from the park, and the two would share evenings together shooting pool, playing cards, and watching movies. The films, Clemente said, helped him learn some English.

Later, Dorsey introduced him to his friends Stanley and Mamie Garland, who had an extra room at their house in a middle-class black area of Pittsburgh called Schenley Heights. So close did the relationship grow between the young player and the older couple that Clemente began referring to them as his parents in the United States.

Pirate pitcher Steve Blass once said that Clemente had the ability to make old-time veteran players, guys who had been around for a long time and had seen all of the great ones, act like fans when they watched him play. Casey Stengel, for example, who, some joked, had been around since the advent of the game itself, said that he had never seen a better right fielder than Clemente.

Despite his unquestioned skills and promise, the first few years of Clemente's career were not of all-star caliber. In his first five seasons, he hit over .300 in only one year, 1956. The team itself gradually rose from the depths of futility. In 1958, the Pirates posted a very respectable season of eighty-four wins and seventy losses; a year later, the team lost some steam, winning seventy-eight games. Nevertheless, the Pirates had turned a corner.

Looking back over his first few years, Clemente claimed that his less-than-stellar record was principally due to his physical maladies. Most significant was the chronic condition of his back, which resulted from the car crash. Each time he stepped into the batter's box, he would roll his shoulders and twist his neck, as if tying to align his spine. The motion became a kind of ritual.

Although he did not miss an unusual number of games because of injury or illness, he frequently complained of backaches, headaches, and pulled and strained muscles. When reporters dismissed much of Clemente's complaints as his usual hypochondria, the young superstar would rail at the deference the press took toward other hitters who suffered physical ailments, such as Mickey Mantle. The treatment, he insisted, was just another example of the prejudice meted out against a Latino. His various ailments led to feuds with his manager Danny Murtaugh, who had no use for such complaints. Even the Pirates' team doctor grew especially annoyed when Clemente flew back to Puerto Rico on a number of occasions to visit a personal healer.

Despite the early trials of the young Puerto Rican—from the emotional challenges of coping in a culturally foreign atmosphere to the physical demands of performing at a level at which he believed himself capable but which thus far had eluded him—Clemente was making progress. Joe Brown, who became the Pirates' general manager in 1956, later said that he never saw Clemente make a mental mistake. He always threw to the right base and, when running, always took the extra base. He was, Brown said, simply the most intelligent Pirate player he had ever seen.

As an overflow April crowd gathered in Forbes Field for the first game of the 1960 season, there were reasons for optimism. Clemente had had a solid spring training and felt relatively healthy. The team itself seemed to have a nucleus of players, youngsters and veterans, who could, with a few breaks and some surprises, be a contender for the first time in many years. With a starting pitching staff led by Vernon Law, Bob Friend, and Harvey Haddix, a top-flight bullpen ace in Elroy Face, and a solid starting lineup anchored by Dick Groat, Bill Mazeroski, Bill Virdon, and Clemente, the Pirates were a far superior club to the one that Clemente had joined five years earlier.

Facing the Cincinnati Reds on opening day, all the expectations of the hometown crowd were fulfilled and more. The Pirates cruised to a 13-0 shellacking of the Reds, behind the shutout pitching of Law and a super day at the plate from Clemente, who lashed out three hits and drove in five runs. After the game, Hal Smith, the team's reserve catcher, walked over to Clemente and said, "If you play in 140 games, we'll win the pennant."[6]

Hal Smith was a prophet. This was Clemente's year; this was the Pirates year. Sleek and graceful, Clemente patrolled right field as if he owned the grass, the foul line, and the wall. From nonchalant basket catches on routine fly balls to acrobatic, lunging catches in all manner of contorted positions, he dazzled crowds.

In one of the games that summer, at a crucial point in the seventh inning with the Pirates leading the Giants 1-0, Clemente got a spectacular jump on a line drive drilled by Willie Mays heading toward the concrete wall in right. His attention focused like a laser on the ball, Clemente spread out his body full-length, speared the ball in his glove, and smashed head first into the wall. Now, an eerie quiet enveloped the stadium, the crowd waiting for Clemente to move. When he held up his glove to show the ball, a great roar followed. Blood gushed from his chin.

On the bases and in the field he routinely ran out from under his cap, flying about at great accelerations and with an unusual fury. And, finally, in 1960, the bat awoke. For the first of what would be eight consecutive years, Clemente hit over .300. He was named to the National League All Star team. Most important for Clemente, fans in Pittsburgh had warmed up to their right fielder; in a ballot taken by the local media, Clemente was voted the favorite Pirate and given a small trophy.

For the Pirates, 1960 was like a great awakening from a long slumber. The year 1927 was the last time that a Pirates team had made it to the World Series and that was not a good year to do it. The '27 Yankees, with the murderer's row of Babe Ruth, Lou Gehrig, Bob Meusel, and Tony Lazzeri, rocketed ball after ball into the outfield seats in the series. Mercifully, the Pirates only had to play them four times and it was over quickly.

And now in 1960 the Pirates were back, and again the Yankees awaited them. This time there was no Ruth or Gehrig, but there were Mickey Mantle, Yogi Berra, and Roger Maris. It was a remarkable roller-coaster ride of a series. The Yankees would win a game with an awesome display of power reminiscent of the '27 Yanks. And then the Pirates would come back to nip the Yankees in tight games. Within the first six, the Bronx Bombers won by scores of 16-3, 10-0, and 12-0; the Pirates won by scores of 6-4, 3-2, and 5-2.

In the eighth inning of the seventh game, the Yankees led 7-6. When Pirate catcher Hal Smith belted a three-run homer to give Pittsburgh a 9-7 lead, the Forbes Field crowd anticipated an improbable World Series win. But the Yankees did not quit. In the top of the ninth, they scored two runs to tie the score. And then, in the bottom of the ninth, second baseman Bill Mazeroski, not known as a long ball hitter, clobbered a Ralph Terry fastball over the head of leftfielder Yogi Berra and into the seats. Bedlam ensued. Waving his cap in exuberance, Mazeroski ran frantically around the bases into the arms of his teammates at home plate. The celebration was on. Baseball Commissioner Ford Frick, who had attended the game, said it was "the most dramatic finish to a World Series I've ever seen."[7]

Clemente, who had batted .310 in the series against the Yankees, hitting safely at least once in every game, skipped the team party. He still felt very uncomfortable in these kinds of situations, with the media pressing him with questions, and he decided to leave early. With a friend, he left the locker room and exited the stadium. When recognized by a large crowd that had gathered outside Forbes Field, Clemente was surrounded. For an hour, he signed autographs, shook hands, and exchanged good wishes. The uncertain, defensive look on his face turned to a wide grin.

MARRIAGE TO VERA

In January 1964, Vera Zabala was walking to a drugstore in the central plaza of Carolina. Twenty-two years old, classically beautiful with long, black hair, she had recently graduated with a business degree from the University of Puerto Rico and had taken a job with the government bank. As she neared the drugstore, she saw a young man in a white Cadillac drive slowly by and look at her. By the time she walked in, he was already there, sitting near the counter reading a newspaper. It was an awkward, fearful moment, she recalled later. She had seen him before around town but he had never introduced himself. Normally reserved and shy, Clemente asked her name and if she was from Carolina. The conversation lasted seconds before she was out the door.

With the help of the druggist and another friend, Clemente arranged to see her. She accompanied a number of friends and Clemente to one of his games in the winter league. It was rained out; the courtship was not. "On our first real date," Vera says, "he told me he was going to marry me. On our second date he brought pictures of houses."[8]

They were married on November 14, 1964, before a crowd of 1,500 at the San Fernando Chapel. He was thirty years old and had now dashed the hopes of a number of other women he had met over the years in Pittsburgh and other cities in which he played. She had undoubtedly dashed the hopes of other men, also. One of Clemente's friends said that the marriage was between the hero of the island and the most beautiful woman of the island. On August. 17, 1965, Roberto Clemente, Jr. (Robertito), was born. A year later Vera gave birth to Luis Roberto (Luisito), and three years after that to Roberto Enrique (Ricky).

Vera said later that she knew immediately that there was something very special about Clemente—not his fame or athleticism, she said, but his wide interests and passion for justice. They traveled extensively in the off-season. No longer would Clemente play winter ball as much as he did prior to the marriage. They went to Europe and South America. And anywhere they went, she said, he left the tourist havens to talk to the people on the streets.

He became a staunch, outspoken supporter of Martin Luther King and the cause of civil rights. He started making speeches about the need to help those less fortunate. Vera remembered how he saved letters from sick children from various cities in the United States in which he played and tried to arrange unpublicized visits whenever the Pirates were in those towns. "I go out to different towns, different neighborhoods ... I get kids together and talk about the importance of sports, the importance of being a good citizen, the importance of respecting their mother and father."[9]

Clemente took a strong stand on behalf of players' rights against the prevailing rules of baseball. In 1969, when Curt Flood challenged baseball's reserve clause, Clemente spoke eloquently to the player's association about supporting Flood's case. Ultimately Flood's challenge ended the mentality that ball players could be treated like property and opened the way for free agency.

He often took younger Latin players under his wing. All of them faced, in varying degrees, the same racial taunts, language barriers, and loneliness that he had. "When you go to Pittsburgh, you always go to see Clemente. When the Pirates come to town, you always go to his hotel. And we just talk baseball all night," said Hall of Famer Orlando Cepeda.[10]

Players often talked later about Clemente's courageous, if risky, stance against segregation in Florida during spring training. The team bus once stopped at a restaurant that the blacks knew was off limits. The normal practice was for the white players to bring food out to the bus after they had eaten. Clemente stepped in front of the aisle and said to his teammates, "If any of you touches one bite of food from this place, you'll have to fight me." When one of the players said, "I'm starving," Clemente shot back, "Then, we starve."[11]

"Clemente is a great hero for all Latin players," said Juan Gonzalez, a later Puerto Rican superstar. "He wanted to make sure you had a place to live, that you were getting food to eat," said Cepeda. "Some guys, they only learned enough English to order one thing. He wanted to make sure you had money. If you didn't have money for something, he would give it to you."[12]

In 1966, Clemente was finally accorded the honor and recognition for which he had yearned; he won the National League's Most Valuable Player award. In the eyes of Pittsburgh fans it was a long overdue acknowledgment. For Clemente, it meant that the baseball experts had at last looked past his ethnic and racial lines and instead looked to his performances within the lines on the field.

For the first time in his career, Clemente played in all 154 games. Although his batting average at .317 was not the best of his career, he hit a career-high twenty-nine home runs and batted in 119 runs. His fielding prowess was as distinguished as ever. In addition, Clemente was an excellent influence on younger Pirates hitters, passing along important suggestions as they matured in the league.

Although Clemente's remarkable abilities were apparent to all of baseball, the nagging injuries took an increasing toll and sapped his confidence. He talked to Vera about quitting after the 1968 season. "I hit only .291 and my back hurt all year," he said. "But my wife, she always knows how much I love this game, and she talked to me and say, 'Never quit when you are down. You have to give it another try. If you want to quit after another year, I won't say another word.'"[13]

1971 WORLD SERIES

By October 1971, Clemente and the Pirates had battled their way into the World Series again by defeating the San Francisco Giants in the National

League Championship Series. Eleven years earlier, when they had faced the New York Yankees in the World Series, the Pirates had been a prohibitive underdog. Few scribes had predicted the Pirates victory.

Now, in 1971, the Pirates were again facing long odds, this time against the Baltimore Orioles, who had topped the 100-victory mark for the third straight year and were riding a fourteen-game winning streak, including a sweep of the Oakland Athletics in the American League Championship Series. If the Pirates had to face a murderer's row of Yankee sluggers in 1960, including Mickey Mantle and Roger Maris, this year they faced one of the greatest starting pitching rotations in Major League history: Jim Palmer, Dave McNally, Mike Cuellar, and Pat Dobson, all of whom had won more than twenty games. The Orioles also featured a formidable lineup that featured Frank Robinson and Brooks Robinson.

As he prepared for his second World Series, Clemente had won four batting titles. He had won his eleventh consecutive Gold Glove, and he had played in eleven All-Star Games. He was thirty-seven years old, still playing superbly, and yet, once again, the press attention was on other players, other stories. The columnists talked about the arms of the Orioles, the magnificent fielding of Brooks Robinson, the experience of the Orioles, and their high-flying winning streak. They talked about the Pirates, certainly, but most of the talk was about slugger Willie Stargell, who was fresh off a season of forty-eight home runs and 125 runs batted in. Brooks Robinson himself expressed some worry about Pirate hitter Bob Robertson. If Clemente needed additional fire for the series, this lack of attention by the media stoked it. Anger building, he quietly readied himself to take on those legendary arms of the Orioles.

In the first two games in Baltimore, Clemente was fabulous, picking up two hits in each. In game two, Clemente made a play of which legends are born. With Merv Rettunmund on second base, Frank Robinson hit a ball into a swirling wind deep in the right field corner. Anticipating that Clemente would catch the ball, Rettunmund trotted back to second base to tag up and advance to third on what he, and everyone else in the park, believed would be a routine play. Clemente speared the ball in his glove, twisted his body around toward third base in the same motion, and, as he fell in the opposite direction from his target, fired a bullet into third that arrived at the same time as a shocked Rettunmund. Although the umpire called him safe, and although the play had no consequence in deciding the game, many fans in Baltimore's Memorial Stadium Park that day thought it was the best throw they had ever seen. The problem was the rest of the team, and, as they headed back to Pittsburgh, the Orioles were up two games to none. In the Pirate clubhouse after game two, a quiet gloom reigned. Clemente took it upon himself to speak in front of the team, trying to restore some confidence. They were going back to their own ballpark, he said, and all would be well.

At home in Three Rivers Stadium, the new Pirates facility that had replaced Forbes Field a few years earlier, the team rebounded just as

Clemente had predicted. They won the next three games. Suddenly the upstart Pirates, led by their veteran star, were poised to win it all. As if clearing fog from their view, some of the reporters now began to hail Clemente as perhaps the greatest player in all of baseball. Certainly, they said, he was dominating the Baltimore Orioles in this series as no single player had done in some time.

In game six, Clemente and the Pirates faced strong-armed Jim Palmer. When Palmer busted a fastball inside to Clemente in the first inning, the ball screamed off the bat down the third base line to the fence. Clemente streaked around the bases for a triple. In the fourth inning, Palmer again tried to retire the red-hot Clemente. This time the ball flared in the opposite direction. Right fielder Frank Robinson futilely chased it at the wall and watched it disappear. With the Pirates nursing a 2-0 lead, the Orioles came back to tie the game in the ninth and then win it in extra innings. The trend of the first six games had held; no team had yet won on the road.

In the locker room before the deciding seventh game of the series, Clemente again cheered his teammates on. He went around the room, telling each of them that it was going to be all right. Trust him. The Pirates would win. The reticent loner of years ago was now a clubhouse leader, his broken English no longer a barrier to a team made up of many more Latino players, and his excellence on the field acting as a sterling example of professionalism.

It was Steve Blass pitching for the Pirates, and Mike Cuellar for the Orioles. The crowd that packed Memorial Stadium looked for the home team to win another game and to take the series. In the early innings both pitchers were in command. Cuellar retired the first eleven hitters in a row. In the top of the fourth, however, Clemente turned on an inside fast fall and planted it over the 390-foot sign in left field. The Pirate bench erupted.

In the top of the eighth, the Pirates picked up another run. They led 2-0 going into the bottom of the inning. Steve Blass was pitching the game of his life. When the Orioles picked up a run in the eighth and threatened to tie the game or go ahead, manager Murtaugh had a critical decision. Should he leave Blass in or go to the bullpen? He stayed with Blass. The Pirates got out of that inning and also the ninth. Blass jumped into the arms of Pirate catcher, Manny Sanguillen. Clemente raced in from right field to a clubhouse of World Series champions.

Within minutes of the end of the game, Clemente was named by sportswriters as the 1971 World Series Most Valuable Player. He was the clear star of the series, with an eye-popping .414 batting average, typically spectacular defense, and a crucial solo home run in the deciding 2-1 Game 7 victory. As he had done in the 1960 classic, Clemente had hit safely in each game.

When announcer Bob Prince turned to him in the locker room for his reaction, Clemente said. "Thank you, Bob... And before I say anything in English, I'd like to say something in Spanish to my mother and father in

Puerto Rico...." For millions of fans listening to the game in the Spanish-speaking world, this was a gesture they would always remember. This was the moment that Clemente could tell the world what he believed his career had been all about—respect and recognition. "En el dia mas grande de mi vida, para los nenes la benediction mia u que mi spades me echen la benediction. (In the most important day of my life, I give blessings to my boys and ask that my parents give their blessing.)"[14] And then, in English, Clemente said that he wanted everybody to know that this was the way he played all the time, every season. He gave his all, he said. His performance should not have been a surprise to anyone. He did not play just for himself, but for the team.

Years later, Julio Pabon, the head of the Latino Sports Clubhouse in the Bronx, New York, began exhibiting Clemente memorabilia every Christmas. Pabon became intrigued by Clemente when he saw him, after the 1971 World Series, ask for his parents' blessing in Spanish. Pabon says,

> To a generation of young people who had endured years of watching a character on a television sitcom say 'My name Jose Jeemenez' in faux Spanglish, it was a revelation. I had never heard anything in Spanish on TV. To hear it that day was like an out of body experience. That always stayed in my mind.[15]

Steve Blass later remembered the aftermath of the final game. "I was talking to the reporters, and so was he," Blass said. "Even after we got dressed, he and Vera went on one bus to the airport, and my wife, Karen, and I ended up on the other. On the plane we sat in the back while they sat up front. After the plane was in the air, Roberto walked back to where we were sitting ... I'm sorry, I'm getting the chills remembering... and he leans over and says, 'Come out here, Blass. Let me embrace you.'"[16]

At a banquet in New York hosted by *Sport* magazine to honor his achievements in the World Series, Clemente, accompanied by Vera, was asked to give some remarks, something that over the years had been very difficult for him. He talked about baseball and about the World Series and what the victory had meant to him. But, more importantly, he talked about the poor kids of Puerto Rico and the need for those who had the means to give them a head start and to treat them with dignity.

For several years, Clemente had talked about his dream of building a sports complex, a sports city, in Puerto Rico where kids could learn about games but also how to live and play together. With tears welling in his eyes, he continued to describe his plan at length. Most of the writers there that day had little idea of this dimension of Clemente's life. As Vera said many times, Clemente was much more than a baseball star.

In 1972, the relaxed and talented World Champion Pirates cruised through the season to a playoff series with the Cincinnati Reds. Beset with a number of nagging injuries that kept him out of many games, Clemente, nevertheless, had a fine season in which he reached a milestone in the final game. In baseball history, going back to the last half of the nineteenth century, only ten players in the major leagues had ever collected 3,000 hits. On September 29, on an overcast, chilly day before a relatively small crowd at Three Rivers Stadium, Clemente and the Pirates faced the New York Mets and pitcher Jon Matlack. Clemente now had 2,999 hits. Anticipating the rare achievement from Clemente were a number of visitors from Puerto Rico, including a team of broadcasters who aired the game back to the island, and several Puerto Rican press representatives and photographers. In the first inning, Matlack struck out Clemente. In the fourth inning, Clemente slashed a ringing double against the wall. With a wildly cheering crowd celebrating the moment, Clemente was handed the game ball.

The memory of that day remained very pronounced over the years to many of his Pirate teammates. Pitcher Nelson Briles remembered: "I saw him get his three thousandth hit. It was at a time when he had become the consummate major-league professional ballplayer. He had no more to prove—he'd won his batting titles and MVPs, and now he could play for the love of the game. After the hit all he did was stand on second base and tip his hat. It was a very regal moment."[17]

When Steve Blass, his friend and teammate, was asked a number of years later about the greatest memory he had of Clemente, Blass said, "He is standing on second base … he has one foot on the bag, and his hands are on his hips. The fans are cheering wildly, but he is just standing there, like a statue, the essence of dignity and pride and grace. That is my freeze-frame of him, how I picture him to this day."[18]

TRAGEDY

On December 23, 1972, a powerful earthquake struck the Central American country of Nicaragua. Devastation and death were widespread—more than 10,000 dead and more than 200,000 left homeless. To Roberto and Vera Clemente, this was not simply a story about a distant land unrelated to their lives. They had visited Nicaragua and made many friends there. Just three weeks earlier, Clemente had been in Nicaragua coaching a Puerto Rican amateur baseball team playing in a tournament.

When the pleas for relief issued forth from the Nicaraguan government, the Red Cross, and other humanitarian relief organizations, Clemente did not hesitate. The Christmas presents under the tree at home would have to wait.

Soon, Clemente was on television urging fellow Puerto Rican citizens to donate to a relief committee. He set up a collection station in the parking area of the baseball stadium and soon organized two planeloads of supplies to be sent to the ravaged country. As he prepared to send a third plane, rumor reached him that some of the supplies he had sent on the first two planes had not reached the victims, that perhaps corruption was involved. He decided on a fateful mission; he would personally accompany the third plane to see that the relief supplies reached their intended targets.

Although Vera, other family members, and friends advised Clemente against making the trip, he was undeterred. One of Clemente's close friends, Luis Mayoral, said, "One of my lasting memories of Roberto is also my last. Four days before he flew off to Nicaragua with relief supplies for the earthquake victims there, he was at Hiram Bithorn Stadium in San Juan, moving bags of goods, cartons of clothes. He could have just lent his name to the relief effort or done a public-service announcement. But there was Roberto, pardon the expression, working his ass off, and he had this look of determination." It was the same look, Mayoral said, that the intense Clemente always wore on the field.[19]

On December 31, 1972, New Year's Eve, along with four other men, he boarded a plane they had reserved on quick notice and loaded it with additional supplies. He had no idea of the condition of the plane. Purchased for $25,000 from a graveyard of surplus cargo planes known in Miami aviation circles as "Cockroach Corner," the prop-driven DC-7 had been flown to San Juan International Airport in September, where it underwent some cosmetic repairs. Then, during a test run in December, a pilot had driven the plane into an airport drainage ditch. Despite the problems, mechanics deemed the plane ready for service.

With a bad maintenance record and its recent near crash, the plane was, in fact, a mechanical death trap. In addition, the pilot recently had had his license suspended, the flight engineer was an unqualified mechanic, and the cargo was well over the recommended weight limit. The Federal Aviation Administration had cited the cargo company sixty-six times for transport violations.

Although the flight was due to take off in the middle of the afternoon, it was delayed twice because of mechanical questions. Not until well after dark did it taxi down the runway and attempt to get airborne. Many witnesses saw the plane struggle in its ascent and saw licks of flame suddenly spurt from the left side of the engine as it banked to the left, sputtering. It managed to stay in the air only a few minutes and then plunged into the sea about a mile and half offshore.

In the aftermath of the accident, thousands of Puerto Ricans stood on the beach and stared at the ships and helicopters involved in the search and rescue. Among the searchers was Clemente's teammate, Manny Sanguillen, who, in a quiet act of desperation and human agony, put on a swimsuit and joined several divers who checked out several areas on the ocean floor where they might find the wreckage. All they found of Roberto after several days of searching was one of his socks and his briefcase. Twelve days later they called it off.

On January 13, thousands filled the stadium in San Juan to say goodbye to their hero. Vera and her sons looked on in shock and grief. A helicopter dropped flowers into the ocean where the plane disappeared.

Many times in his life Clemente had talked darkly about his fate. Many times Vera would try to ease his deep-seated, near-desperate thoughts about mortality, his gnawing preoccupation with sickness and injury. And now, tragically, it had all come to this. To citizens of Puerto Rico and to millions of others in the United States and around the world, this had been a New Year's Eve tempered by great solemnity.

THE LEGACY

In 1973, five players were inducted in the National Baseball Hall of Fame in Cooperstown, New York, including Warren Spahn, long-time ace of the Boston Braves and Milwaukee Braves; Charles Kelly, New York Giant first baseman in the 1920s; Mickey Welch, nineteenth-century New York Giants pitcher; and Monte Irvin, star of the Negro Leagues and of the New York Giants, boyhood hero of Roberto Clemente. One other player was inducted in the Hall of Fame that year. The Baseball's Writers Association of America waived the customary five-year waiting period and voted Roberto Clemente a Hall of Famer. He was the first Latino player in history to make it into Cooperstown.

From the hard statistics alone, he deserved to be in the Hall of Fame. Clemente was a four-time National League batting champion, finishing in the top ten in batting average thirteen times. He finished his career with exactly 3,000 hits, the eleventh player in history to reach this number. His lifetime batting average was .317, and he batted .300 or better thirteen times, with 240 home runs and 1,305 runs batted in. He also hit 166 triples during his career, finishing in the top five of the league eleven times. He won four batting championships and twelve consecutive Gold Gloves for fielding excellence, and he was named the league's Most Valuable Player in 1966. He led the Pirates back to the World Series championship in 1971.

But as many writers, public figures, and people on the street said after his death, he was deserving of the highest award in baseball for other reasons— his humanitarianism in a number of areas and his work for the recognition and well-being of fellow Latinos. At his induction ceremony in Cooperstown on August 6, 1973, Vera Clemente said, "This is Roberto's last triumph. If he were here now, he would dedicate this honor to the people of Puerto Rico, to the people of Pittsburgh, and to the people all over the United States.... I have difficulty expressing myself the way I really feel. It's not just for me and my children. It's a goal for all Latin American children, too."[20]

ROBERTO CLEMENTE'S LIFETIME BATTING STATISTICS

Year	Team	Lg	Age	Org.	Level	Pos	G	AB	R	H	2B	3B	HR	RBI	SB	CS	BB	SO	HBP	IBB	SH	SF	DP	AVG	OBP	SLG
1954	Montreal	IL	20	Brk	AAA		87	148	27	38	5	3	2	12										.257	—	.372
1955	Pittsburgh	MLB	21	Pit	MLB	of	124	474	48	121	23	11	5	47	2	5	18	60	2	3	4	3	14	.255	.284	.382
1956	Pittsburgh	MLB	22	Pit	MLB	of	147	543	66	169	30	7	7	60	6	6	13	58	4	2	8	4	14	.311	.330	.431
1957	Pittsburgh	MLB	23	Pit	MLB	of	111	451	42	114	17	7	4	30	0	4	23	45	0	1	0	1	13	.253	.288	.348
1958	Pittsburgh	MLB	24	Pit	MLB	of	140	519	69	150	24	10	6	50	8	2	31	41	0	1	3	3	15	.289	.327	.408
1959	Pittsburgh	MLB	25	Pit	MLB	of	105	432	60	128	17	7	4	50	2	3	15	51	3	2	3	3	10	.296	.322	.396
1960	Pittsburgh	MLB	26	Pit	MLB	of	144	570	89	179	22	6	16	94	4	5	39	72	2	4	4	5	21	.314	.357	.458
1961	Pittsburgh	MLB	27	Pit	MLB	of	146	572	100	201	30	10	23	89	4	1	35	59	3	10	1	3	18	.351	.390	.559
1962	Pittsburgh	MLB	28	Pit	MLB	of	144	538	95	168	28	9	10	74	6	4	35	73	3	9	1	6	18	.312	.352	.454
1963	Pittsburgh	MLB	29	Pit	MLB	of	152	600	77	192	23	8	17	76	12	2	31	64	4	6	4	3	24	.320	.356	.470
1964	Pittsburgh	MLB	30	Pit	MLB	of	155	622	95	211	40	7	12	87	5	2	51	87	2	16	3	5	9	.339	.388	.484
1965	Pittsburgh	MLB	31	Pit	MLB	of	152	589	91	194	21	14	10	65	8	0	43	78	5	14	2	3	17	.329	.378	.463
1966	Pittsburgh	MLB	32	Pit	MLB	of	154	638	105	202	31	11	29	119	7	5	46	109	0	13	1	5	14	.317	.360	.536
1967	Pittsburgh	MLB	33	Pit	MLB	of	147	585	103	209	26	10	23	110	9	1	41	103	3	17	0	3	15	.357	.400	.554
1968	Pittsburgh	MLB	34	Pit	MLB	of	132	502	74	146	18	12	18	57	2	3	51	77	1	27	0	3	13	.291	.355	.482
1969	Pittsburgh	MLB	35	Pit	MLB	of	138	507	87	175	20	12	19	91	4	1	56	73	3	16	0	4	19	.345	.411	.544
1970	Pittsburgh	MLB	36	Pit	MLB	of	108	412	65	145	22	10	14	60	3	0	38	66	2	14	1	2	7	.352	.407	.556
1971	Pittsburgh	MLB	37	Pit	MLB	of	132	522	82	178	29	8	13	86	1	2	26	65	0	5	1	4	19	.341	.370	.502
1972	Pittsburgh	MLB	38	Pit	MLB	of	102	378	68	118	19	7	10	60	0	0	29	49	0	7	0	6	15	.312	.356	.479
Major League Totals - 18 Season(s)							2433	9454	1416	3000	440	166	240	1305	83	46	621	1230	35	167	36	66	275	.317	.359	.475
Minor League Totals - 1 Season(s)							87	148	27	38	5	3	2	12										.257	—	.372

Accompanying Vera to New York were Roberto's mother, Louisa, now eighty-four years old, and Roberto's three young sons. Also at the ceremony were several of Clemente's teammates, as well as Eleanor Gehrig, the wife of Lou Gehrig, the baseball legend who had also died in his thirties and who had been inducted into the Hall of Fame without the waiting period. Eleanor Gehrig told a reporter that she had never met Vera Clemente "… but I thought of her often…, very often."[21]

Clemente was also awarded the Congressional Gold Medal in 1973 and was the first baseball player so honored. In addition, Major League Baseball renamed its annual sportsmanship/humanitarian award "The Roberto Clemente Award."

Roberto had long dreamed about developing a youth complex in his native Puerto Rico. After his death, Vera Clemente took the lead. Although funding was uncertain and the project unsteady, Ciudad Deportiva Roberto Clemente nevertheless rose on 304 acres of marshland donated by the Puerto Rican government. Over the years, it has grown into the kind of institution envisioned by its namesake. Its baseball academy has developed a number of major league stars, including Juan Gonzalez, Roberto Alomar, and Ivan Rodriguez. In addition to its athletic facilities, it also features programs in drama, dance, music, folklore, and crafts.

Over the years, the story of Clemente has increasingly taken on a sense of the mythic. His legendary baseball feats, his death in the service to others, his aggressive drive to instill hope and pride to Latinos, especially children— all of it has inspired myriad acts and occasions to honor his memory. At the 1994 All-Star Game in Pittsburgh, a bronze statue honoring Clemente was unveiled at Three Rivers Stadium. Among the players who raised funds for the statue was the Pirates' right fielder, Orlando Merced, who had grown up across the street from the Clemente family in Puerto Rico.

State parks, streets, bridges, and schools now bear Clemente's name as well as athletic clubs. Over the years an increasing number of Latinos have followed Clemente to baseball greatness. More than a quarter of the players on Major League rosters in 2006 were men from the Dominican Republic, Venezuela, Puerto Rico, and other Latin American countries.

In Puerto Rico, the United States, and countries around the world where baseball is played, youngsters wear the number 21. When they put on that number, they are told or they already know about the man who wore it. They know that to wear that number calls for a respect for the game and an obligation to give it everything you have.

NOTES

1. David Maraniss, *Clemente: The Passion and Grace of Baseball's Last Hero* (New York: Simon & Schuster, 2006), 21–22.

2. "Baseball and The Multi Cultural Experience, Latin America—Document-Based Questions, http://www.projectview.org/BBHOFEFT.LatinAmerica.htm.

3. C.R. Ways, "'Nobody Does Anything Better than Me in Baseball,' Says Roberto Clemente ... Well, He's Right," *The New York Times Magazine*, April 9, 1972, 42–4.

4. "Belting Buccaneer," *New York Times*, October 18, 1971, 51.

6. Maraniss, 94.

7. "World Series," *Time,* October 24, 1960, 84.

8. Steve Wulf, "Arriba Roberto!" *Sports Illustrated*, December 28, 1992, 114.

9. Jay Feldman, "Roberto Clemente Went to Bat for All Latino Ballplayers," *Smithsonian*, September 1993, 136.

10. T.J. Guinn, The late Roberto Clemente remains symbol of Latin baseball. *New York Daily News*, Sept 21, 2005, http://web5.infotrac.galenet.com/itw/infomark/710/240/96335716w5/purl=rc1.

11. Guinn.

12. Guinn.

13. "Belting Buccaneer"

14. Maraniss, 264.

15. David Gonzalez, "Reliving the Heroics of a Baseball Great, *The New York Times*, December 28, 2004 pB1.

16. Wulf, 114.

17. "Cold War at the Pool, Shaking a Leg, in Pantyhose," *Newsweek*, October 25, 1999, 63.

18. Wulf, 114.

19. Wulf.

20. "Hall of Fame," http://www.baseballhalloffame.org/whats_new/press_releases/2000/pr2000_09_19.htm.

21. "Baseball Inducts Five With Joy, One Sadly, *New York Times,* August 6, 1973, 42.

FURTHER READING

Feldman, Jay. "Roberto Clemente Went to Bat for All Latino Ballplayers." *Smithsonian*, 1993, 128–142.

Maraniss, David. *Clemente: The Passion and Grace of Baseball's Last Hero*. New York: Simon & Schuster, 2006.

Markusen, Bruce. *Roberto Clemente: The Great One*. Champaign, IL: Sports Publishing, 1998.

Musick, Phil. *Who Was Roberto? A Biography of Roberto Clemente*. Garden City, NY: Doubleday, 1974.

Regalado, Samuel O. *Viva Baseball! Latin Major Leaguers and Their Special Hunger*. Chicago: University of Illinois Press, 1998

Wagenheim, Kal. *Clemente!* New York: Praeger Publishers, 1973.

Walker, Paul Robert. *Pride of Puerto Rico: The Life of Roberto Clemente*. New York: Harcourt Brace Jovanovich, 1988.

Courtesy of Library of Congress

Celia Cruz

When Celia Cruz died in 2003, Ruben Blades, noted musician, actor, social activist, and friend of Cruz, said she was a cultural icon who "became a symbol of quality and strength, and... a symbol of Afro-Cuban music." Known as the Queen of Salsa and the Diva of Latin song, Cruz "could take any song and make it unforgettable. She transcended the material," Blades said. "With Celia, even the most simple of songs became injected with her personality and her vigor."[1]

In 1950, Cruz became the lead singer of one of the most celebrated Cuban orchestras, La Sonora Matancera. When she left Cuba in 1960, she exploded onto the New York scene, recording classic albums with Willie Colon and other big names in the genre. She joined with the legendary band leader Tito Puente in a collaboration that helped spread Latin music around the world. With great energy, flamboyant style, and extraordinary talent, she radiated Latino spirit.

CUBA HOMELAND

Celia Cruz was born to Simon and Catalina Cruz on October 21, 1925, in Havana, Cuba. She was the second of four children. The family was of Afro-Cuban heritage, descendants of African slaves who were forcibly brought to the island nation to work in the sugar fields. Her father worked with the railroad, and her mother took care of an extended family of fourteen nieces, nephews, and cousins in a small house in a working-class neighborhood called Santos Suarez. As the second eldest child, Cruz often helped put the younger ones to bed and would invariably sing them to sleep. Her parents realized from those early years that Celia had a musical gift.

Cruz later remembered an incident when she was going to grade school in Santos Suarez's Public School No. 6 that seemed to point to her future. When she returned home one afternoon, friends of her parents had gathered and Celia's mother asked her to sing. The couple was so pleased that the next time they visited they gave the child a pair of white, patent leather shoes. She loved those shoes—so much, she remembered later, that this might have been the incident that sparked her lifelong fascination with clothes and fashion.

As a teenager, Cruz was aware that her parents hoped for her to attend college and perhaps become a teacher. She was also aware, however, of the central place that music had in her heart. She later remembered secretly going to a local carnival with some friends, even though her parents were concerned about her safety and the raucous atmosphere surrounding such events.

"Although I really enjoyed it," she said, "I still remember the odd combination of fear and joy—the fear of getting caught and the joy I felt in my heart. I knew I wasn't supposed to be there, but the colors, the music, the sense of energy, and living life to its fullest potential were very intoxicating."

As she walked home with her friends, she was euphoric. "We had to walk," she said, "because we didn't have enough money for the bus ride back. It was the longest and best walk of my life."[2]

An aunt constantly encouraged Cruz to sing and often took her to cabarets to hear local musicians. As she attended to her secondary studies at Havana's Academy of the Oblate Nuns, Cruz and several of her cousins also ventured off to hear local musical performers. Nevertheless, acceding to the wishes of her parents that she begin preparing for a career in teaching, she enrolled in Havana's Teachers College.

Within a few months, a cousin named Serafin took an unusual step that propelled Cruz on a different career path. Without her knowledge, he signed her up for an amateur talent show called *La Hora del Te* (Tea Time), which was broadcast on the radio from a music studio near her home. Still shy, Cruz was both quite nervous but also overjoyed at the opportunity. She knew she was talented; everyone who had heard her sing had told her so again and again. Here was a challenge both to her self-confidence and to her barely hidden aspirations to be a singer.

She rode to the competition with Serafin. Performing a tango called "Nostalgia," accompanying herself with a pair of claves, she won the contest and was invited to return the following month for another competition. As she rode home with her cousin on the bus, she carried on her lap the cake that was the prize in the contest. At home, she and Serafin and other members of the family celebrated. Many years later, Cruz said, she could still imagine the taste of the cake. Her success had been exhilarating.

At subsequent contests, she won more cakes. She also won boxes of chocolates, milk, soap, bread, and other necessities and, on some occasions, money. "And when I won," she said, "I wanted to go to all the amateur shows in Cuba.... At the beginning, I'd go alone, and later with a cousin named Nenita, who still lives in Cuba. I was very skinny and tiny. And since the tram cost five cents each way and we didn't have enough money, I'd sit on Nenita's lap, because she was bigger. The drivers knew us and, sometimes, they'd let me sit on the seat beside her, if it was empty. One time, we had no money to return and we walked back. We arrived at 2 A.M."[3]

With each new victory in the talent shows, she began to see herself as a future performer and not as a teacher. As she made her wishes more clear, her father became increasingly distant. He had seen the inside of many of the cabarets in Havana and had assumed that most of the women performers there were of loose morals. He did not want his daughter to be associated with people and places that would degrade her and the family. Despite continuing arguments with other members of his family, Simon Cruz remained opposed to his daughter's increasing involvement in music. Cruz stayed in school and entered only those singing contests that did not interfere with her classes. She was able to buy most of the books she needed for college with her winnings in the contests.

In the late 1940s, Cruz began performing with a local band called El Boton de Oro (The Golden Button). Although the group did not pay her for her performances, the opportunity to perform before audiences was worth every bit of time invested. She became well known at several local radio stations. She performed at school events. Government officials began asking her to perform in Cuban patriotic ceremonies.

In 1949, she sang at the Teachers College commencement activities on graduation day. When she finished her performance, one of the professors took her aside to offer some advice. "Celia, God gave you a wonderful gift," said Marta Rainieri. "With the voice you have, you can make a good living. If you pursue a singing career, you'll be able to make in one day what it takes me one month to make. Don't waste your time trying to become a teacher. You were put on earth to make people happy—by using your gift."[4]

It was at that moment, Cruz later remembered, that she knew what lay ahead for her; that she would take her God-given talent and follow what she now clearly saw as her future in music. She was now determined to meet the objections of her father head-on and take personal responsibility to ensure that her talent would be used for the most good that she could manage. She would use it to honor her family and in no way disgrace it. She would, in the end, make her father respect her decision.

"My mother was always on my side, but at first my father did not like to tell his friends I was a singer," Cruz said. "People thought that singers and nightclub artists were not good women. But when my father saw I was a very good girl, his mind changed."[5] Cruz moved quickly to make herself the most accomplished singer possible. She began to study music and learn piano at the Havana Music Academy. She took private lessons with a music teacher hired by her aunt. She studied piano with the highly respected composer Oscar Boufartique.

Cruz became a freelance entertainer at CMQ Radio Studios, taking music time slots whenever they were available. As she became acquainted with many of the recording artists, musicians, and radio personalities, she steadily gained confidence. Some of her acquaintances at the station began to call the tiny, thin, dark-skinned Cruz such affectionate nicknames as El Cisne Negro (the Black Swan) and La Munequite de Chocolate (The Little Chocolate Doll).

Cruz met choreographer and producer Roderico Neyra (Rodney), who hired her for the famed musical "Sun Sun Ba Baé." She joined the female dance group Las Mulatas del Fuego as their singer and traveled throughout Latin America. In 1949, she toured in Venezuela with the all-female Anacaona Orchestra. Formed in 1932, the group was named in honor of a legendary Cuban Indian princess of the Siboney tribe. Cruz traveled to Mexico City with another group and performed in such venues as the Folies Bergeres Theater and a nightclub called The Zombie. While performing in Mexico City, she met the famed radio star Don Vallejo and later became the godmother to his son.

Cruz quickly became a skilled performer, noted for pregón singing (a vocal style which evolved from the calls, chants, and cries of street vendors). With such songs as "Manicero" and "El Pregón del Pescador," she soon gained a name in Cuban music circles. She studied music arduously. Whenever she traveled to performances, she was accompanied by a female relative who acted as a chaperone. All over Cuba, she appeared at radio stations and theaters. She sang with a dancing troupe, and entertained the audience while the dancers changed costumes.

Finally, in 1950, she capitalized on an opportunity that would vault her into greater prominence and essentially launch her musical career.

LAUNCHING A MAJOR CAREER

In August 1950, Cuba's most famed Afro-Cuban orchestra, La Sonora Matancera, was looking for a replacement for its lead singer, the popular Puerto Rican soloist Myrta Silva. They asked Celia Cruz to be that singer.

Formed in 1924 in the Cuban province of Matanzas, the La Sonora Matancera, a classic Cuban conjunto with trumpets, guitar, piano, bass, and percussion, had gained international success. Led by director Rogelio Martinez, the band had hosted over sixty different singers throughout its history, including many such as Myrta Silva who had come from other Latin American countries. The band performed in several clubs, did live radio programs, and made numerous concert appearances at a time when live dance music was an integral part of Cuban daily life.

Cruz debuted with Sonora Matancera on August 3, 1950, to an audience that included most of her family members sitting in the first row. With the Sonora Matancera, Cruz performed many popular genres of Cuban dance music from boleros to cha-chas. With blaring trumpets, the conjunto sound was a mix of percussion, Cuban guitar, double bass, voices, and piano. This highly rhythmic dance music was rooted in the traditional, Africa-based styles of music revived decades later by the Buena Vista Social Club.

Early in her career with Sonora, some old-time fans of Myrta Silva groused about her replacement. Cruz's powerful voice was not quite made for this particular orchestra, many said at first. Some began to send letters to Cruz, suggesting that she move on. Unfazed and confident, Cruz stepped into the role as if it had been meant for her all along. Soon, the angry letters became letters of praise. Suddenly music fans wanted to know more about this exciting, electric personality with the prodigious voice.

Cruz's first recording with the orchestra was in late 1950. It was a guaracha song, one of the pieces that came from the bars and dives of Havana. An early form of peasant street music with much satire, guarachas also had their share of down-and-dirty references. It was through such artists as Sonora and Cruz that some of this music made its way out of the dark streets into the mainstream venues and popular recording studios. She would record a new album with Sonora on a regular basis—almost every three months—for many years.

One of the musicians Cruz met when she joined Sonora was a trumpet player named Pedro Knight, who had been with the band for six years. A powerful and well-trained musician, Knight was particularly helpful to Cruz in her early days with the orchestra. The two would gradually form a strong bond that would last their lifetimes. On tours throughout Latin America, Cruz and Sonora played to sold-out venues. It was like having nine brothers, she said later. They looked after her and protected her. Her stature in the music world grew with each performance. With these musicians, she said, she was gaining a full-fledged education in Cuban musical technique and history.

She also gained notice from commercial radio and television advertisers. On stations throughout Cuba, listeners now heard the singing voice of Celia Cruz on jingles selling Barcardi rum, Coca-Cola, and assorted coffees, cigars, soft drinks, beers, and colognes. Her contralto voice somehow seemed right on the mark for the advertisers, and they called on her in droves. She even modeled for Allyn's, a hair care company whose ads appeared in most of Cuba's magazines. "It's amazing how things happen!" she wrote. "In two years I went from being criticized by segments of the public because I wasn't Myrta Silva to doing jingles on television, which was then the most exciting medium around."[6]

Sonora was an Afro-Cuban band whose members were, for the most part, dark-skinned. Their musical style merged elements from traditional Spanish music with the African rhythms that came from the island's former slave population. In the Cuban music scene of the 1950s, most black musicians and performers were denied access to some of the glamorous clubs that catered to American tourists. Because of their extraordinary popularity, this particular band and Cruz were able to leap over that unwritten restriction.

They began to play regularly at Havana's famed Tropicana nightclub and casino. Looking back, historians and others have termed this period in Cuban music as "The Golden Era," a time in Havana of booming nightlife filled with theaters, nightclubs, and elaborate gambling emporiums. Havana's entertainment area was the Las Vegas of Cuba, and the Tropicana was at its center.

Glitzy and swinging, the Tropicana was emblematic of the spectacle of the Cuban entertainment mecca in the 1950s. Buxom dancers in outrageous costumes swirled on stage, with bird feathers of all hues and colors in their headdresses. Elaborate musical revues produced by world-renowned choreographers thrilled the well-dressed clientele. The whole posh scene reeked of money and a bit of hedonism.

But the Tropicana also became a place offering serious music with extraordinary musicians and performers. For those on the stage, performing at the Tropicana meant that you had arrived, had climbed the ladder to the greatest showcase of talent in the country.

In addition to her performances with Sonora, Cruz also was invited to the Tropicana to participate in a number of great musicals. With her booming vocals and voluptuous, rhythmic moves, Cruz gave as much to the Tropicana as it gave to her.

In 1955, Cruz appeared in her first motion picture, along with the members of Sonora, in a Cuban film called *Gallega en La Habana* (A Spanish Woman in Havana), starring the well-known Argentine comedic actress Nini Marshall. Cruz and the band would appear in several other films in that decade, including an American movie filmed in Cuba called *Affair in Havana*, starring John Cassavetes and Raymond Burr.

In 1957, Cruz traveled to New York City for the first time to receive an award for one of her recordings. The concert at the Saint Nicholas Arena in the Bronx featured, along with Cruz, the legendary Latin-jazz band Machito. To a completely filled arena and with many fans outside crowding the building, the concert began. The raucous musical event suddenly turned ominous. The overcrowding led to pushing and shoving, which in turn led to something of a panic and then a near riot. People were injured in the chaos. No one died in the melee, but Cruz said later that she had never been more frightened. A Spanish-language newspaper the next day ran a headline reporting that the concert had sparked anarchy. This was Celia Cruz's introduction to New York, and she was devastated.

At the same time as Cruz's career increased in brilliance, the political turmoil in Cuba rocked the foundations of government. General Fulgencio Batista's military government that gained power in 1952 faced a growing insurgency of rebels led by a young lawyer named Fidel Castro. Son of a Creole sugar plantation owner, Castro attended a Jesuit boarding school and later became a lawyer in Havana. His experiences as a lawyer made him increasingly critical of the great inequalities of wealth and power that existed in Cuba. He especially resented American businessmen and organized crime figures who dominated many of Havana's entertainment palaces such as the Tropicana and other nightspots where Celia Cruz would gain national acclaim.

In 1953, with an armed group of 123 men and women, Castro led an attack on a Cuban army barracks. The disastrous and pathetic assault led to the deaths of eight of the attackers. Another eighty were murdered by the army after their capture. Castro was fortunate that the lieutenant who arrested him ignored orders for his execution and placed him instead in a local civilian prison. He lived to fight on. Put on trial for organizing an armed uprising, Castro used the opportunity to make a speech about Cuban inequalities, a speech that would later become the centerpiece of a book titled *History Will Absolve Me*. He was sentenced to fifteen years in prison, but his trial and book made Castro a national celebrity with a growing following.

Faced with considerable pressure from the Cuban population, Batista decided to release Castro after only two years of confinement. The young rebel left for Mexico to plan for another attempt at revolution. Surrounding himself with a group of other young adventurers such as Che Guevara and Juan Almeida, Castro returned to Cuba in 1956. Planning to set up base in the Sierra Maestra Mountains, they were attacked by government troops. By the time they reached the mountains, they had only sixteen men left with twelve weapons between them. But, from this mountain base, they began a long, patient effort to build up a force strong enough to challenge the government. Using guerilla attacks, they raided isolated army garrisons and built up a stock of weapons. When they took control of a territory, they redistributed the land among peasants and thus gained new recruits. They were joined by students, priests, and others who took on a revolutionary fervor.

By New Year's Day, 1959, this unlikeliest of revolutions had won out. Batista resigned and fled the country. Castro became the Prime Minister of Cuba in February 1959 and soon named himself president for life. And Celia Cruz's life was about to change drastically.

In its first hundred days in power, Castro's government began to confiscate property and redistribute land. It nationalized the telephone company. It also began to take action against the entertainment center in Havana. Attacking alcohol, drugs, gambling, and prostitution as immoral, Castro and his government began to close down many of the nightclubs and casinos and to force American businessmen and organized crime figures to leave the country.

This political cataclysm had a profound effect on the life and career of Cruz. In addition to shutting down many cabarets and music halls, the government began confiscating radio and television stations. The programming on those stations changed dramatically, limiting severely any opportunities for Cruz to make appearances or to sing the music she loved. Castro had in mind a use for Cruz; he would order her to sing political anthems supporting the revolution instead of the decadent music of the cabarets.

Cruz showed little respect for Castro. On more than one occasion when Castro attended concerts at which Cruz performed, most musicians went out of their way to pay their respects. Cruz tried to ignore him. "I realized that by way of his arrogance and despotism," she said, "he was destroying all free expression and artistic expression in Cuba. He had turned what once was beautiful into a weapon to prove how he could control others."[7]

FLEEING CUBA

In 1960, both Cruz and Sonora were offered contracts to perform in Mexico City. When the members of the band took off from the Havana airport on July 15, six months after Castro had seized the reins of government, most of them knew in their hearts that they would not return to Cuba. Cruz knew that also.

Saying goodbye to her parents, both of whom were ailing, her aunt, and other friends was an anguish that she would never forget. All of them realized, however, that under the Castro regime Cruz's professional music career would be totally stifled. The chance to perform in Mexico was a way out of Castro's Cuba and they took it.

After only a month in Mexico, Cruz received word that her father had passed away. Under great stress and emotional upheaval, she put everything she had into her work. Mexican audiences loved her performances. Soon, along with Sonora, she hired on for a five-month engagement at Mexico City's Los Globos nightclub. On several occasions, they performed with the famed Luis Trapaga Ballet, a company known throughout Latin America.

Throughout her first year in Mexico, she welcomed a number of other Cuban entertainers who had also fled Castro's government. She was an enormous success in Mexico, and, as in Cuba, she became well known in several forms of media. She performed in her first Mexican film, *Amorcito Corazón*, which was followed by other films. She made many appearances on Mexican television and recorded albums with several Mexican orchestras and musicians, including the renowned composer Pedro Vargas. Looking back on those days, she said later that the times were both exciting and extremely sad.

The sadness grew as she received word in early 1962 that her mother did not have long to live. She was determined to return to Cuba to see her one last time and even booked a flight for April 17, 1961. When she arrived at the airport to board her flight to Cuba, she was told that the political situation in Cuba was so tense that no flights were landing on the island. Her efforts to return briefly to Cuba had coincided with a bumbling effort by the United States government to overthrow the Castro regime. On April 14, three days before Cruz tried to board her plane in Mexico, the U.S. administration of President John F. Kennedy had sent a small force of Central Intelligence Agency–trained soldiers to bomb Cuban airfields and land approximately 1,400 Cuban exiles at the Bay of Pigs. The attack was a total failure: two ships were sunk, two of the planes attempting to give air cover to the ground forces were shot down, and within seventy-two hours all the invading troops had been killed, wounded, or had surrendered.

Cruz was not able to visit her mother before her death. She swore never to set foot in Cuba again as long as Castro remained in power. "When my mother was sick," she said later in the United States, "I wanted to go there, but people who had left were not allowed to go back. When my father died, I could not go there. My parents and my country were the important things, but if I die now, I want to be buried here...."[8]

Cruz and Sonora toured all across Mexico in a caravan of performers. They performed in large venues and in small towns. She loved the direct contact with people who ordinarily would not be able to see big-time entertainment figures. Nearly every inch of Mexican roads, she later claimed, had been traversed by the caravan by the time they had finished touring.

In July 1961, Cruz traveled to the United States to perform at the Los Angeles Palladium. While in California, her travel documents to Mexico expired. She then made another critical decision. Because the process of becoming a naturalized Mexican citizen was long and complicated and because she was tiring of singing the same kind of music every day, she decided not to return to Mexico.

A NEW HOME IN THE UNITED STATES

In the United States, Cruz reasoned, the opportunities to experiment with new music and to work with a variety of performers were much greater than in Mexico. Following her appearances in Los Angeles, Cruz traveled to New York in November 1961 for a series of gigs.

By early 1962, Castro's government had become closely allied with the Soviet Union, the primary Cold-War adversary of the United States. When the U.S. government began to freely admit Cuban exiles, Cruz took advantage. After a waiting period, any Cuban could apply for permanent residency status. Cruz became one of those exiles, and she remained in the United States and became a naturalized citizen.

Fidel Castro was reportedly irate upon learning that Cruz and the Sonora had ended up in the United States. One of his country's most popular singers and one its most celebrated bands had by their actions made a public statement against his government. He vowed that none of them would ever be granted entry into Cuba again. His vow never wavered.

In 1962, her personal life, despite the loss of her mother, had a joyous development. Pedro Knight, La Sonora Matancera's trumpet player who had been such a close friend for many years, asked Cruz to marry him. The dashing, accomplished trumpeter had been at her side for several years. It was not love at first sight, he said later. At one point, when he suggested that the relationship be more than friendship, she had balked. "She said musicians had too many women and she didn't want to suffer," Knight said. "And, well, it was true. I had a lot of women. But I told her that if she would have me, she could leave that problem to me."[9]

By 1962, Cruz and Knight had forged a strong relationship, and she decided to accept his proposal. They married on July 14, 1962, in a judge's chambers in Greenwich, Connecticut. She had known him for more than fourteen years. The two became inseparable. Eventually, Knight decided to give up his own music career and become Cruz's personal manager. He would serve as her protector, manager, and musical director and give her constant, enthusiastic support.

As Knight got older, his rich, black hair turned white, and Cruz affectionately called him "Cabescita de Algodon" (Cotton Head). Louis Ramirez, a song arranger for Cruz, once described the important role Knight played in her career. "When discord arises on how best to sing or play a part," he said, "everyone turns to Pedro. Pedro presides quietly in a corner, with his arms crossed. After he hears us argue back and forth, he says 'si' or 'no.'"[10]

In the same year that Cruz began the one and only marriage of her life, she also had the opportunity to meet and perform with another man who would make an enormous difference in her life, the renowned musician and bandleader Tito Puente. At New York's famed Carnegie Hall, Cruz, performing with Puente and the Count Basie Orchestra, became the first Latino woman to appear on that stage. When she walked out to begin the performance, she said later, she felt as if she were walking on a cloud hearing the voice of her mother pouring out her love and pride.

But even with such honors as playing Carnegie Hall and the notice that such an event draws, Cruz's career did not take off in the United States as it had in Cuba, Mexico, and other Latin American countries. Although she spoke English, she refused to record in the language, insisting that she would do justice neither to the music nor to the language.

Also, young Latinos now were more drawn to the newest sounds of rock and roll than to the music loved by their parents and grandparents. For much of her early time in the United States, she remained relatively unknown outside of the Cuban exile community. She had to work hard in her adopted country to generate the excitement that had come so naturally in Latin America.

She pressed ahead, continuing to make appearances in the New York area and to meet fellow performers, making an increasing number of contacts with producers and promoters. In 1964, Cruz had the opportunity to perform at the Apollo Theater in Harlem, one of the great stages for black music in the world.

In 1965, her career once again took off in a sizzling new direction. Tito Puente called Cruz with a simple offer: Would Cruz want to collaborate with him on a steady basis? She told him that she would be honored.

JOINING TITO PUENTE

Tito Puente was Puerto Rican and his roots were in Spanish Harlem. At an early age Puente wanted to be a dancer but that ambition was lost because of a leg injury. Instead, he began working in a Latin band, studied orchestration and piano at Juilliard and the New York School of Music, and became a sensational percussionist musician, revolutionizing both the playing and use of the timbales (kettledrums). In most Latin bands the instrument was in the background, but in Puente's dynamic hands it moved to the forefront.

In 1947, he formed the nine-piece Piccadilly Boys and then expanded it to a full orchestra. His recordings helped fuel the mambo craze that gave him the unofficial—and ultimately lifelong—title "King of the Mambo," or just "El Rey." Puente also helped popularize the cha-cha during the 1950s, and he was the only non-Cuban who was invited to a government-sponsored "50 Years of Cuban Music" celebration in Cuba in 1952.

At New York's Palladium in the 1950s and 1960s, Puente led Cuban musicians through a period of great excitement and popularity. As Cuban music became less of a rage in the 1960s, Puente was the principal force in keeping it alive, in experimenting with new sounds and collaborating with musicians of other musical genres. And now he was allied with one of the most powerful Afro-Cuban singers ever to grace a stage. Puente recalled, "I was listening to the radio in Cuba the first time I heard Celia's voice. I couldn't believe the voice. It was so powerful and energetic. I swore it was a man, I'd never heard a woman sing like that."[11]

By the time Cruz began to work with Puente, she had recorded nineteen albums. She would record several additional albums with Puente, including *Cuba y Puerto Rico Son* in 1966. But it was her fiery stage presence that made her such a unique and compelling figure in Latin music. Her husky voice held its own against the rhythm section, and she was a tireless dancer and storyteller. She once explained that she told stories not only to amuse and entertain the audience but also to allow the horn players to rest their mouths.

As her career moved on, she began to wear ever more glitzy stage clothes, often comprising pounds of fabric and sporting sequins, feathers, and lace. Her high heels and large wigs added to her spitfire image. As she strode onto the stage and during her acts, she would often shout "*Azucar!* (Sugar!)" It became her trademark. She once explained where the exclamation came from: "I was having dinner at a restaurant in Miami, and when the waiter offered me coffee, he asked me if I took it with or without sugar. I said, 'Chico, you're Cuban. How can you even ask that? With sugar!'"[12]

Latino journalist Myriam Marquez said, "When she yelled her trademark Azucar during a song, she had that crisp "drop-your-s's-and-your-r's" Havana accent. No sense properly pronouncing *azucar*. That would have been to put on airs, and sweet Celia never was full of herself. She was full of life, bigger than life."[13]

After a Cruz-Puente performance in Madison Square Garden in New York, music critic Jon Pareles of the *New York* Times wrote that Cruz brought the house to its feet just by stepping onstage. "Miss Cruz is the kind of singer who electrifies not just audiences, but musicians," said Pareles. "With her rough-and-ready contralto voice, she rips into the rhythmic exhortations of salsa tunes far more boisterously than most male salsa singers. She rolls her r's with a percussive vengeance, and sometimes lets loose a raspy holler. When she sang a ballad, there was so much power in her voice that it threatened to burst right through the melody. Mr. Puente's band responded with its usual drive and then some. Mr. Puente answered Miss

Cruz with intricate salvos of timbales and cowbell, twirling his drumsticks with elaborate flourishes, and his horn section shouted out its parts."[14]

Cruz and Puente recorded eight albums together and made hundreds of appearances. They performed together in many countries, especially Japan, where Puente already had a large following. The two became close friends. Puente often spoke of Cruz's enormous energy, a statement that meant something special from someone who was known around the musical world as a man who spent prodigious time perfecting his musical compositions. He said that Cruz kept all the musicians on their toes. If they were huffing and exhausted, she was still ready to go on to the next piece. She was, he said, always on a roll.

SALSA AND FANIA RECORDS

It was not until the early 1970s that Cruz gained notice and a fan base among young Latinos. She played in the opera *Hommy* at Carnegie Hall. Inspired by the rock opera *Tommy*, it was composed by Larry Harlow and Puerto Rican musician, dancer, and composer Henny Alvarez. As a pianist, composer, and orchestra leader, Harlow recognized the potential of Cruz's powerful voice and presence and signed her to play the role and be the voice of Gracia Divina (Divine Grace). The opera was an enormous success and both the show and Cruz, with her remarkable voice and boundless energy, received rave reviews. Cruz's performance in *Hommy* opened up her career to a long-term association with Fania Records, the home to some of the greatest Latin-inspired musicians in the history of twentieth century music, including Harlow, Johnny Pacheco, Willie Colón, Héctor Lavoe, and Ruben Blades.

Fania Records got its start in 1964, founded by the Dominican-born composer and bandleader Pacheco and Italian-American lawyer Jerry Masucci. It was their dream to create a label that would be a birthplace for a new style of Latin music, one that would meld the sounds coming from Spanish Harlem and the Bronx with other genres of Latin music such as boogaloo, Latin rhythm and blues, and Afro-Cuban jazz. Fania got its name from an old Cuban song. The fusion of sounds that so attracted the younger Latino audiences became known as salsa, and Fania Records was the company that began to record salsa for the world. The word "salsa" was something of a catchall, a marketing term meant to convey the rich mix of Latin music with which various composers and performers were experimenting. Fundamentally, salsa had its roots in eighteenth century Cuba, where African slaves were brought to work the island's sugar plantations and their music fused with the dominant Spanish culture. Featuring piano, brass, percussion such as the congas or the timbales, horns, and a vocalist, salsa rhythm maintained a steady beat that rendered most listeners unable to stay calm; it was meant for dance. A salsa song often ran on for half an hour.

So You Want to Start a Salsa Band?: The Ingredients

Although salsa bands vary widely in size, talent, and direction, most have common instruments and characteristics. The musical instruments used in salsa are basically the same as those in a typical jazz band, with the addition of Latin percussion instruments derived from African cultural roots. The instruments usually include alto, tenor, and baritone saxophones, several trombones, several trumpets, piano, and an upright or electric bass. The percussion instruments that turn a jazz band into a salsa band are conga drums, bongos, cowbells, and timbales.

The congas (sometimes called conga drums) are known as *tumbadoras* in Cuba. Their origin is obvious from their name; they were derived from the Congo or former Zaire. Most often, two drums make up the conga set, one set at a higher pitch than the other. They are always played only with the hands.

The timbales are similar to a small drum set without a bass drum, including two sizes of shallow frame drums, a cowbell, and a woodblock. The *timbalero* (timbales player) stands when playing. Unlike the conga drum player, the timbales are always played with drumsticks.

The bongos (bongo drums) are a set of two, single-head drums tied together. During a typical salsa piece, the bongos are played only during the verse part of the composition. When the improvisation section begins, the bongo player switches from bongos to cowbell (*cencerro*). Made of metal, the cowbells are struck with a stick; the tone is modulated by striking different parts of the bell and by damping the sound with the hand holding the bell.

The claves consist of a pair of short, thick dowels. Traditionally they were made of wood but now are also made of fiberglass or plastics. When struck they produce a bright clicking noise. They are often used to play a repeating rhythmic pace throughout a piece.

These five instruments constitute the percussive rhythmic section of a typical salsa ensemble. This use of heavy percussion, with each instrument playing a specific rhythm, has strong roots in African culture. Many salsa bands do not use claves, but every salsa musician knows and feels the clave beat.

Typical salsa bands have a lead singer (*guia* or guide) and a small chorus (*coro*). The choruses can be aligned in many configurations and interact with the soloist in a number of different combinations.

Salsa music also uses short repeated patterns or *ostinatos* (called "riffs" in jazz) played by musical instruments. Often the patterns accompany the lead singer, but they may accompany individual instrumental soloists as well.

One of the most famous salsa bandleaders in the world, Tito Puente, kept his distance from the term "salsa." Whatever the terms and definitions, these are the musical pieces needed for a salsa band. The key to a salsa band's success, however, is simple. Take those instruments and those singing positions and put them in the hands of such talents as Tito Puente and Celia Cruz.

Incorporating elements of jazz, traditional Afro-Caribbean rhythms, and other forms, salsa was an ideal medium for showcasing Cruz's vocals, for she was both an exciting improviser, known for her vocal imitations of instruments in the manner known as "scat" singing in the jazz world, and a singer with the power to stand up to an intense orchestral sound.

Even though no one can really claim to have invented the term "salsa," Cruz said she remembered hearing the term in Venezuela as early as 1967. A local radio broadcaster invited Cruz to sing on a show called "La Hora de la Salsa" (The Salsa Hour). The music the disk jockey played was the same music performed by La Senora Matancera and other Cuban groups. "Today we call it salsa," she said, "but before we used to call the music what it was, rumba, guaracha, guaguanco, mambo, cha-cha-cha, guajira, and bolero. These are the folkloric rhythms of my country. These are the different rhythms that exist in Cuba." Tito Puente, who was Puerto Rican, never liked the term "salsa," which he passed off as something you eat. He always referred to his music as Afro-Cuban.[15]

Whatever the origins of the term, young people both in Latin America and especially in the United States soon became attracted to it, and Cruz, along with other performers who recorded for Fania, were at the center. They soon became known as "The Fania All-Stars" and included such artists as singer Bobby Cruz, drummer Ray Baretto, singer Ismael Quintana, and others. Because she was the only well-known female soloist singing the music, Cruz soon became known as "The Salsa Queen."

With her powerful voice that moved through high and low pitches with ease and with her style of improvising rhymed lyrics, she added a distinctive flavor to salsa. A commanding figure on stage, she had masterful control over audiences as they engaged in the call-and-response patterns from Afro-Cuban musical roots. Onstage, she would leap and dance about, flaunting, flirting, and teasing the audience with outrageous gyrations. And then she would get lost in a song about a love affair doomed to end, and then, eyes moist, she would break out with a quick comment that the guy was a jerk anyway.

In a single performance she could range from moments of raw sexiness to true passion, from the comedic to the sublime. No one, including the band, knew when she would break into an improvisation or a joke. She was known to keep up her explosive pace on some occasions for more than three hours. Sitting close to Cruz as she lit up the stage was, on the one hand, to invite ear pain, but, on the other, to experience one of the most exhilarating and all-consuming musical treats.

And those flamboyant costumes, those tight sequined dresses, became so famous that one of them was later acquired by the Smithsonian Institution. One of the costumes featured a five-foot train of more than 400 multicolored lace handkerchiefs. "Sometimes my gowns were longer or wider than the stage," she explained. "Duets were the worst; my partners either couldn't stand close enough to me, like you should when doing a romantic duet, or they'd get feathers in their faces."[16]

Cuban-American writer and Pulitzer Prize–winning author, Oscar Hijuelos marveled at Cruz's stage presence. He wrote:

> It is hard to describe the dazzling energy and warmth she was able to convey to an audience. That she could create a rush to the dance floor, and yet do so while maintaining an air of intimacy and connection with her listeners, is a testament to her great personality and charisma as a performer. Without belaboring her virtues as a natural musician (one who was classically trained in piano and voice at the music conservatory in Havana), I think it would be fair to say that Celia Cruz was one of the greatest talents ever to grace a musical stage.[17]

In 1973, Cruz recorded an album with Johnny Pacheco entitled *Celia y Johnny*. The album contained one of the signature songs of the salsa genre, "Quimbara," a piece about a set of drums talking to each other. This production achieved a gold record as Latinos throughout the United States snatched copies from their local record stores. Soon, other collaborative albums met with similar success, especially a 1974 album she made with conga player Ray Barretto.

Cruz performed to sold-out crowds with the Fania All-Stars each year in the largest venues in New York, Madison Square Garden, and, in 1976, at Yankee Stadium, a concert that was recorded and released as an album. Living in the New York City area, Cruz became a star among the Latino population much as she had in Cuba and other Latin American countries. She was also especially loved in Miami, with its large Cuban exile community, and she performed there often. Like Cruz, most of the Cuban-Americans in Miami had fled the Castro regime, gained a new livelihood in the United States, and vowed never to return to Cuba until the hated dictator had vanished. Cruz usually included in her repertoire "Canto a la Habana" (Song to Havana), which featured the line, "Cuba que lindos son tus paisajes" (Cuba, what beautiful vistas you have). Invariably, the line would incite an emotional eruption from the Cuban-American audiences.

Cruz worked with a number of established stars over the years that helped her cross over from strictly a Latin market to a larger audience, even though she never sang in anything but her native Spanish language. She teamed with rhythm and blues star Patti LaBelle, operatic tenor Luciano Pavarotti, and David Byrne, the main head of the Talking Heads. Cruz says:

> The people I surround myself with are talented, people who are musically astute, who have a precise feel for rhythm, for what sounds good. I'll sing a song one way, and someone will say, 'Celia, try it this way,' and I will, and often

it'll be exactly what I was looking for but couldn't pinpoint. You don't work that way because you're nice, you do it because you're professional. On the other hand, if I disagree, if I feel a suggestion will hurt a sound, I'll refuse. I can't be bullied.[18]

Cruz was named the best female vocalist in 1977 and 1979 by the *New York Daily News*, and *Billboard* magazine did the same in 1978. Latino publications gave her similar honors.

In 1982 Cruz reunited with La Sonora Matancera for an album. A Madison Square Garden tribute concert for Celia Cruz sold out. By 1987 she released her fifty-third album and won an Obie, an off-Broadway theater award presented by the *Village Voice* newspaper to New York artists, and her fourth Grammy nomination.

Throughout the 1980s, Cruz kept up a schedule of appearances and recording dates that resembled her frenzied stage presence. In 1985, with various groups, she sang music based on Yoruba religious chants that once praised West-African deities. Thousands of members of the Yoruba tribes of Africa were seized in the early 1800s and brought to Cuba to provide workers for the infant sugar industry. In Cuba, Yoruba speakers became known by the collective term *Lucumí* after the Yoruba phrase *oloku mi,* meaning "my friend." In the 1950s there was an increased infusion of *Lucumí* ritual styles and subject matter into the Cuban popular music mainstream. Celia Cruz was an important figure in singing in that native language. In 1985 she brought those lyrics and that music to the larger American audiences.

When young people began to flock to Cruz's performances, she was overjoyed. "They come by themselves," said Cruz. "Rock is a strong influence on them, but they still want to know about their roots. The Cuban rhythms are so contagious that they end up making room for both kinds of music in their lives."[19] Much of Celia Cruz's career was about the celebration of culture. First across Latin America and then in the United States and around the world, Cruz experimented with the various sounds from Latin cultures, especially as they reflected the influences of the music brought by slaves from Africa. In October 1989, at the Abyssinian Baptist Church in Harlem, Cruz hosted a show honoring that music. Backed by a large orchestra and the percussion sounds of Tito Puente, Cruz brought the large crowd to its feet.

Peter Watrous, a *New York Times* reporter at the event, said that the music "underscored the connections between the various outposts of the African diaspora in the New World." The show included the work of Marco Rizo, the musical director of the *I Love Lucy* television show, one of the first examples through which United States citizens received a favorable image of Cuban culture. Watrous marveled at Cruz's performance, calling her "one of the world's great singers." The event, he said, "made clear that music and culture are inseparable."[20]

THE QUEEN OF SALSA KEEPS ON PERFORMING

In 1992, Cruz helped bring a story of Afro-Cuban music to the big screen. Directed by Arne Glimcher, the film tried to capture the essence of Oscar Hijuelos's Pulitzer Prize–winning novel, *The Mambo Kings Play Songs of Love*. Although the book spanned three decades, the film focused on the years 1952 through 1955, when two Cuban musicians—Cesar Castillo (Armand Assante) and his younger brother Nestor (Antonio Banderas)—try to make it in New York as mambo musicians. For Cruz, the outlines of the story were familiar enough. To achieve the most authentic sounds for the film, the director asked both Tito Puente and Cruz to participate.

For the first time, Cruz performed in English, not only in a singing part but as a character, Evangelina Montoya, the owner of a nightclub called Club Babalu. Although Cruz's English was never fluent, she managed to pull off the part of the movie as she had done with other great challenges—with grit and determination. *Rolling Stone* said of the film, "*Mambo Kings* celebrates the mysterious power of a music that can make you feel like dancing and bring you to your knees."[21]

As she reached her seventieth birthday, Cruz remained a vital force in celebrating that mysterious power of that music. With seventy albums and forty years of performing behind her, she could still bring magic to a stage, gyrating in her sequined gowns, and belting out innumerable pieces of music honed to perfection. When she would break into a refrain of one of songs close to her heart, such as "Canto a la Habana," crowds would still go wild. Her life was singing, Cruz told a reporter in 2002, when asked how long she intended to perform. She had no plans for retirement. She planned to die on stage while shouting "*Azucar!*"

Cruz participated in numerous charitable enterprises over the years. In 2002, she, along with her husband Pedro Knight and her manager Omar Portillo, established the Celia Cruz Foundation. The Foundation's mission is two-fold: to provide financial aid to low-income students who want to study music, and to assist cancer victims. She participated in numerous fundraising events to fight AIDS. She worked to help orphans in Honduras and the handicapped in Costa Rica. She was very concerned about public education and appeared a number of times on the PBS series "Sesame Street." One of her fondest memories was singing to Big Bird.

In the early years of the new century, Cruz herself became a victim of cancer. In December 2002, she underwent surgery to remove a brain tumor. Despite her very serious condition, she recorded a final album in 2003 called "Regalo de Alma" (Gift from the Soul). She spent her final months at her home in Fort Lee, New Jersey. She died on July 16, 2003, with Pedro at her side. They had just celebrated their forty-first wedding anniversary.

As she had requested, her funeral included two public viewings—one in New York and the other in Miami, where she was buried. Thousands turned out for each. In Miami, Cruz's casket stood inside a building known as the Freedom Tower, once an immigration-processing center that was the first stop in the United States for some half a million Cuban exiles in the 1960s and 1970s. The long lines at each location included not only her beloved Cubans but fans who carried flags of Puerto Rico, Mexico, Venezuela, Ecuador, and Jamaica, a tribute to Cruz's enormous popularity and respect throughout the Latin and Caribbean world.

"To lose her, said María Vázquez, fifty-three years old, a businesswoman who left Cuba when she was eight years old, is to finally recognize that an era has passed. "I call her and people like her, the last of the true Cubans," Vázquez said. "She was part of the Cuba of our parents, a Cuba we didn't really know and that doesn't exist anymore. It's the Cuba of our imagination, a virtual Cuba, if you will."[22]

William Argüello, twenty-six years old, after placing a red rose near the coffin, told a reporter that Cruz was the one artist who made him feel closer to his roots and connected to his family. "My grandmother, my parents, my aunt, they have all danced to her," Argüello said. "And I do, too."[23]

AMBASSADOR OF LATIN CULTURE

The story of Celia Cruz's musical journey is far more than a simple rags-to-riches tale, although that element is part of it. It is also a story of the extent to which a singer of Afro-Cuban music was able to influence popular culture across countries and continents. She was not the typical "crossover" artist; indeed, she sang her music almost exclusively in her native Spanish. But by the end of her career, she and others with whom she collaborated had fused music from various tribes and societies in a way that touched people across the world and across generations.

The awards she received in her lifetime told only a small part of the story; nevertheless, they are indicative. She received numerous music awards, civic awards, humanitarian awards, and awards from various countries and leaders, from the National Endowment for the Arts Medal presented by President Bill Clinton to an annual scholarship given in her name by the University of Panama. Not only did she have a star in her honor on the famed streets of Hollywood, but she also was honored with a star on the Walk of Fame in Caracas, Venezuela. She received three honorary doctorates, from Yale University in 1989, Florida International University in 1992, and the University of Miami in 1999. She was a White House guest of five presidents. One of the most satisfying aspects of her career, however, was the enormous influence she had on young Latino singers. As a model of guts, determination, hard work, and courage, Cruz had few equals.

Her appeal came from many superb qualities—a glorious voice, an infectious enthusiasm, an eagerness to accept new musical challenges, and a vivacious personality that seemed, at least for those moments on stage, to shake out all feelings of anger and distrust, a personality that called on everyone to share in the joy of music. "When people hear me sing," she said, "I want them to be happy, happy, happy. I don't want them thinking about when there's not any money, or when there's fighting at home. My message is always *felicidad*—happiness."[24]

Upon her death, singer Gloria Estefan, born in Havana, Cuba, wrote, "I don't want to say that we've lost Celia because her music, her spirit and her '*azucar*' (sugar) will always be with us. Cubans and Latinos alike can feel proud that with her voice and her wonderful qualities, she showed the world the best of our culture. Although I will miss her very much, my heart will always hold all the beautiful things that, through her example, she showed me."[25]

Ricardo Bustos, a percussionist with Los Alfa Ocho, a Latin orchestra that plays tropical and salsa music, was among many musicians who paid tribute. One of his group's albums included the song "Celia, Colombia te Canta," (Celia Sings for You). "We were lucky to share the stage with her in 1995 in Medellin, and after the concert I spoke to her and her husband," Bustos said. "She was very kind and offered me these words of advice: 'Always be very professional about your music and your career, but above all love the music you play,'" Bustos said. "I think that all of Latin America is grieving right now."[26]

The Latin Academy of Recording Arts and Sciences said of Cruz, "One of Latin music's most respected and most revered vocalists, Celia Cruz was an icon of salsa, tropical and Latin jazz music. The legendary Queen of Salsa brought the world to its dancing feet with her visceral vocals, infectious energy, and vibrant smile."[27]

Latino journalist Myriam Marquez, who worked for many years with the *Orlando Sentinal*, felt almost a personal loss with the passing of Celia Cruz. "She died without going back to her native Cuba, without putting flowers on her parents' graves, without seeing her Havana house again—her little bedroom kept spotless by her Cuban cousins, who adorned it with signed pictures she sent from her tours," Marquez wrote. "It seems like yesterday when my college friend Ana and I dragged our salsa-impaired boyfriends to see Celia and Tito jam at an outdoor Washington concert almost twenty years ago. The guys couldn't get over her get-up, all glittery and tight. Oh, but that booming voice. Soon enough our guys were up and shaking their booty with the rest of us. Nor will I forget the pride I felt when I pointed out Celia to my little sons watching Sesame Street. She's like me, I told them, born in Cuba. One of us."[28]

Author Oscar Hijuelos said that Celia Cruz transcended the notion of nationality. "Of course she will always be loved by Cubans, as a living symbol of pre-Castro Cuba. But to Latinos of other nationalities, from Puerto Rico to Peru, she will always be remembered, and cherished for the absolute love she felt—and conveyed—for all Hispanics."[29]

SELECTED RECORDED MUSIC

Cruz, Celia. *100% Azucar!: The Best of Celia Cruz con la Sonora Matancera.* 1997. CD.
Cruz, Celia. *Roots of Rhythm.* 2000. CD.
Cruz, Celia. *Celia Cruz and the Fania All-Stars in Africa.* 2002. DVD.
Cruz, Celia. *Éxitos Eternos.* 2003. CD.
Cruz, Celia. *Feliz Navidad: Christmas in Cuba.* 2003. CD.
Cruz, Celia. *Regalo del Alma.* 2003. CD.
Cruz, Celia. *Siempre Celia Cruz Boleros Eternos.* 2003. CD.
Cruz, Celia. *Celia Cruz—Azucar!* 2004. DVD.
Cruz, Celia. *Celia Cruz & Friends: A Night of Salsa.* 2004. DVD.
Cruz, Celia. *A Night of Salsa by Celia Cruz & Friends.* 2004. DVD.
Cruz, Celia. *Sesame Street—Fiesta!* 2004. DVD.
Cruz, Celia. *Very Best of Celia Cruz.* 2004. CD.
Cruz, Celia. *Celia & Johnny.* 2006. CD.
Cruz, Celia. *Cuba y Puerto Rico Son by Celia Cruz & Tito Puente.* 2006. CD.
Cruz, Celia. *Azucar! A Lady and Her Music by Celia Cruz.* 2007. CD.
Cruz, Celia. *Celia & Willie.* 2007. CD.
Cruz, Celia. *Very Best of Tito Puente & Celia Cruz.* 2007. CD.

NOTES

1. "Afro-Cuban Music Icon Dazzled with her Personality," *Honolulu Star-Bulletin,* July 17, 2003, http://starbulletin.com/2003/07/17/news/story15.html.
2. Celia Cruz, *Celia: My Life* (New York: Rayo/HarperCollins, 2004), p. 21.
3. Leila Cobo, "The Billboard Interviews Celia Cruz," Billboard, October 28, 2000, 50.
4. Cruz, 38.
5. Jon Pareles, "Celia Cruz: At the Top of Salsa," *New York Times,* November 19, 1985, C17.
6. Cruz, 66.
7. Cruz, 82.
8. Pareles.
9. "Celia Cruz' Widower Knight dies at 85," *USA Today,* http://www.usatoday.com/life/people/2007-02-04-pedro-knight-obit_x.htm.
10. Gale Research. "Celia Cruz." In *Dictionary of Hispanic Biography.* Reproduced in Biography Resource Center. Farmington Hills, MI: Thomson Gale. 2007. http://galenet.galegroup.com/servlet/BioRC.
11. Gale Research.
12. Ulrich Bose, "¡Azucar!," Smithsonian, July 2005, 40.
13. "Myriam Marquez, Celia was one of us and always will be," *Knight Ridder/ Tribune News Service,* July 22, 2003, K2164.
14. Pareles.
15. Nestor Louis, *Siempre Vivir: An Interview With Celia Cruz,* http://www.salsaweb.com/music/articles/interview%20celia%20cruz.htm.

16. Elixabeth Llorente, "Celia Cruz: Salsa Star, Expatriate, Whirlwind," *New York Times,* August 30, 1987, http://query.nytimes.com/gst/fullpage.html?res=9B0DE4D91539F933A0575BC0A961948260&sec=&spon=&pagewanted=1.

17. Oscar Hijuelos, "A Song of Love for Celia," *New York Times,* July 23, 2003, http://query.nytimes.com/gst/fullpage.html?res=9E01E3D6173FF930A15754C0A9659C8B63&n=Top%2fReference%2fTimes%20Topics%2fPeople%2fC%2fCruz%2c%20Celia.

18. Llorente.

19. Michael Walsh, "Shake Your Body; the "Black-Bean Invasion" Arrives: From Salsa to Hip-Hop, Latino Sounds Go Pop," *Time* (July 11, 1988), p. 50.

20. Peter Watrous, "Celia Cruz Takes Cuba to Harlem," *New York Times,* October 29, 1989, http://query.nytimes.com/gst/fullpage.html?res=950DEEDC173BF93AA15753C1A96F948260&n=Top%2fReference%2fTimes%20Topics%2fPeople%2fC%2fCruz%2c%20Celia.

21. "The Mambo Kings," *Rolling Stone,* March 19, 1992, http://www.rollingstone.com/reviews/movie/5949013/review/5949014/the_mambo_kings.

22. Mirta Ojito, "For Cuban Exiles, the End of an Era," *New York Times,* July 20, 2003, http://query.nytimes.com/gst/fullpage.html?res=9B01E2D71E3CF933A15754C0A9659C8B63&n=Top%2fReference%2fTimes%20Topics%2fPeople%2fC%2fCruz%2c%20Celia.

23. Ojito.

24. Bose.

25. "Gloria and Emilio Estefan Say Goodbye to Celia Cruz" (July 21, 2003), http://ca.music.yahoo.com/read/news/12043381.

26. Madeline Baro Diaz, Jennifer Valdes, and Jean-Paul Renaud, "Cruz's Star Still Shines for Hispanic Americans," *Knight Ridder/Tribune News Service,* July 16, 2003, K7750.

27. Gil Kaufman, "'Queen of Salsa' Celia Cruz Dead," MTV, July 17, 2003, http://www.mtv.com/news/articles/1474090/20030717/cruz_celia.jhtml.

28. Marquez.

29. Hijuelos.

FURTHER READING

"Azucar! The Life and Music of Celia Cruz," http://americanhistory.si.edu/celiacruz/printable/index.asp?sectionID=QGw434505957KZJBQ&lang=NMx5264041148jbtG&ContentID=Ote2764187881E3453N9393n1133711661116613453u8961b1263312309127411133712741110905Vbs.

Cobo, Leila. "The Billboard Interviews Celia Cruz," *Billboard,* October 28, 2000, 50.

Cruz, Celia. *Celia: My Life.* New York: Rayo/HarperCollins, 2004.

"Gale: Free Resources: Hispanic Heritage: Biographies: Celia Cruz," *Contemporary Hispanic Biography,* vol. 1, reproduced in Biography Resource Center, Farmington Hills, MI: Thomson Gale, 2007. http://gale.cengage.com/free_resources/chh/bio/cruz_c.htm.

Llorente, Elizabeth. "Celia Cruz: Salsa Star, Expatriate, Whirlwind," *New York Times,* August 30, 1987, http://query.nytimes.com/gst/fullpage.html?res=9B0DE4D91539F933A0575BC0A96194860&sec=&spon=&pagewanted=1.

Walsh, Michael, "Shake Your Body; the "Black-Bean Invasion" Arrives: From Salsa to Hip-Hop, Latino Sounds Go Pop," *Time* July 11, 1988, 50.

Courtesy of Photofest

Placido Domingo

In the world of opera, each generation or so there emerges an extraordinary talent, an individual of gifted voice and star presence who excites the musical world. Placido Domingo has been one such opera star since the 1960s.

Born for the stage, Domingo was the son of Spanish parents who were both singers in zarzuela, a form of Spanish drama with music. Living in Mexico, barely out of his teens, his mind and voice impeccably suited for a musical career, Domingo joined the Hebrew National Opera, singing as many as twelve performances a month. He is a tenor who became one of the more celebrated of the second half of the twentieth century and on into the twenty first. He has reached the summit of the musical world, both on the stage as a singer, before the orchestra as a conductor, and behind the scenes as an opera administrator. He became General Director of both the Washington National Opera and the Los Angeles Opera. Domingo is a humanitarian, awarded Mexico's highest civilian honor, the Order of the Aztec Eagle for his heroic work during the 1985 Mexico City earthquake. He has been a teacher of young singers, especially Latinos struggling to find their own voice and place in the world of music.

BORN INTO A WORLD OF MUSIC

Placido Domingo was born in the Barrio de Salamanca section of Madrid on January 21, 1941. His mother's family was Basque, and his father's family was half Catalan and half Aragonese.

His mother, Pepita Embil, was celebrated as "The Queen of Zarzuela." Composers wrote musical pieces especially for her. She had made her debut at the Teatro Liceo in Barcelona, the most lavish opera house in Spain. A form of light opera, zarzuela mixed musical numbers with spoken dialogue. Often, its plot was related to current national affairs, either as comedy or drama, and it usually involved scenes from everyday life. Domingo's father, Placido Domingo, Sr., had played the violin in opera and zarzuela orchestras and had been a baritone singer in zarzuela productions. His promising stage career was cut short by an illness that affected his vocal chords.

It was at a zarzuela performance that Placido Domingo, Sr., met Pepita Embil. They married in 1940. He was thirty-three; she was twenty-two. Placido, Jr., was born a year later, and his sister Mari Pepa was born in 1942.

For Domingo, who has remained throughout his life emotionally attached to his family, his one great regret from his childhood was that he never had the opportunity to know any of his grandparents. Three of them had died before he was born and the last when he was an infant.

In 1946, his parents joined a zarzuela company that eventually traveled to Cuba, Puerto Rico, and Mexico. They fell in love with Mexico and its marvelous scenery and culture, Domingo later recalled, and they decided to stay for a couple of additional weeks. Those weeks, it turned out, would last for several decades.

Two years after his parents had become established in Mexico and had formed their own zarzuela company in Mexico City, they sent for their son, his sister, and their maternal aunt, Agustina, who had been left to care for the children and whom Domingo often referred to as his second mother. In 1948 they sailed from Spain, headed for Mexico.

"Zarzuela was the first music I ever heard," Domingo once said, "As a small child, I knew the big numbers, the arias. And I knew the making of it, because my parents had their own zarzuela company. They would travel with their own decors—in those days, paper from boxes, very simple. I have never seen harder work than what my parents did in that company. My parents used to do two different zarzuela works every day, and on Sundays three!"[1]

At the age of eight, Domingo began a serious effort to study the piano. "My parents wanted me to be a pianist," he said. "They didn't want me to go on the stage. They saw the world in terms of zarzuela and how difficult it was, and they wanted to spare me that."[2] His parents realized early on the potential for greatness in their son. By age nine, he had won song-and-dance contests. His mother later recalled that he had extraordinary musical intuition, apart from the things that they and his tutor were teaching him. And, he also had considerable charm. Even if she had twenty people in the house, she said, her son would move from one to the other exchanging kisses to the cheek.

For a time, Domingo, along with his sister, studied piano with an expert teacher named Manuel Barajas. When Domingo was fourteen years old, Barajas passed away. As Domingo later looked back on his life, he saw the death of Barajas as a crucial turning point, a moment of destiny. He had been heading for a career as a concert pianist, but with his piano teacher's death, Domingo's life took a new direction.

From 1955 to 1957, Domingo was enrolled at the National Conservatory of Music in Mexico City under the tutelage of Carlo Morelli, a former Metropolitan Opera singer. Under Morelli's direction, Domingo switched from developing a baritone voice to that of tenor. Domingo later said of his tutor, "Morelli had very spiritual thinking. He believed that the most important thing for success was will power. He was a baritone, but one day he sang me an aria from *Andrea Chenier* and he went all the way up to a B. And he was over 60 [years old]. So I said to myself, 'My God, if he can do it, I just have to do it.' So I did."[3]

Domingo attended the Instituto Mexico high school, where he played soccer and baseball. He was such a soccer fan that throughout his life he would often find time in his hectic schedule to attend matches. Domingo also enjoyed bullfighting, and he performed as an amateur matador at private fiestas and even, at one point, expressed an interest in becoming a professional bullfighter, a notion that drew disapproving looks from the family. During one incident in a training ring, he later remembered, when he was flung to the ground by a young bull not much bigger than a large dog, he gave up the idea altogether.

Even though his father had discouraged a stage career, Domingo was asked by his parents to join them on a number of occasions in the chorus of their zarzuela troupe in 1957. He and his sister often attended stage rehearsals, watched the costume and set makers at work, and placed music on the stands of the musicians. He loved the stage. "I was lucky to grow up in the theater," he said later. "When I was very young I saw my parents do three performances of zarzuela on Sundays and often two on a weekday—and then rehearse the next day's show after the performance. With this kind of example, I naturally learned about stamina."[4]

Domingo also said that watching his parents work as a team both in performing and managing was a model for his own career. "Just seeing all the things they were doing, I was fascinated. There were hard times, too. Sometimes people didn't come to the theater in very great numbers in some places, and they were so honest, and so honorable, that they never stopped paying their people, or tried to pay them anything less than they should. This was sometimes a sacrifice. I have a big admiration for them. Their example has stayed with me."[5] Domingo later remembered that at one point the group gave 185 consecutive performances, never missing a single curtain call. Domingo also sang in their productions of Lehar's *The Merry Widow* as either Camille or Danilo.

But at the age of sixteen, the naturally impulsive Domingo suddenly left home and moved in with a girl two years his senior. She was a fellow piano student at the conservatory. Looking back, he said it was one of those first-time infatuations in which both of them believed they were part of a great love story. In June 1958, when Domingo was seventeen years old, the two had a son they named Jose.

Domingo now was in the position that he needed to support his own family. Hectic times followed. He worked at any kind of job he could find in the music business. He sang in musicals, he arranged songs, and even worked in an adult nightclub. In *My Fair Lady* he sang the role of the drunkard. He provided backup vocals for Los Black Jeans, a rock-and-roll band led by Cesar Roel, a seventeen-year-old Mexican guitarist who later changed his name to Cesar Costa. The band sang Spanish versions of American hit singles and recorded its first album in 1959 with Peerless Records. For Domingo, the hectic days also brought an end to his marriage. The hasty union ended almost as quickly as it had begun.

In 1959, however, at the age of eighteen, with his commanding voice and considerable stage command, Domingo achieved a breakthrough that would lead to a remarkable career.

DEBUT AS A TENOR

Domingo auditioned for the National Opera of Mexico in 1959 by singing several baritone arias. During the audition, he was asked also to sing as a tenor. On the strength of the audition, he received a contract as a tenor *comprimario* (singer of secondary roles) and as a coach for other singers. Domingo's first role, in September 1959, at the age of nineteen, was in Giuseppe Verdi's *Rigoletto*. Domingo played the small part of Borsa, a man in the service of the Duke of Mantua.

It was as a tenor that he would make his mark but he had to work for it. "Many tenors," he said, "just open their mouths and bang—out come the high notes, just like nothing. Not me. I still have to work tremendously hard to get to the high tessitura (pitch range)."[6]

To supplement his income, Domingo also landed a job playing piano for a ballet company that produced musical productions for Mexico's new cultural television network. The industrious and multi-talented Domingo had no difficulty playing everything from the zarzuelas, the music with which he had been familiar from his earliest childhood, to operettas and musical comedies. He also played a few dramatic roles in plays by such artists as Russian dramatist Anton Chekhov.

In 1961, Domingo sang the lead role of Alfredo Germond in Verdi's *La Traviata* in Monterey, Mexico. So impressive was his first major operatic performance that the Dallas Civic Opera signed him to sing with one of the great divas of the opera world, Joan Sutherland. The two performed side by side in Gaetano Donizetti's *Lucia di Lammermoor*. It was Domingo's first performance on a stage in the United States. A year later, Domingo sang the central role of Edgardo in the Fort Worth production of Donizetti's *Lucia di Lammermoor* alongside another great diva, Lily Pons, singing the title role in her farewell to the stage.

It was during these years that Domingo met a young musical sensation named Marta Ornelas. Much like Domingo, she came from a family that was deeply involved in the artistic and musical worlda. Her family had encouraged her by the time she was eight years old to study the piano as well as art and painting. She entered the Conservatory of Mexico, studying voice and learning many soprano roles. She later joined the Opera Bellas Artes in Mexico City. In 1961, Ornelas received the highest award as the best singer of Mozart for her performances of Susanna in *Le Nozze di Figaro* (*The Marriage of Figaro*).

Domingo and Ornelas formed a strong attachment. Together they established a chamber opera company that toured Mexico. Then, on August 1, 1962, the two were married. They would have two sons, Placido in 1965 and Alvaro in 1968.

IN ISRAEL

In 1962 Domingo and his young wife traveled to Tel Aviv, along with their friend Franco Iglesias, a baritone, where Domingo joined the Israel National

Opera Company as a lead tenor. Although he intended to stay in Israel for six months in order to enlarge his repertoire in several languages, he remained there for two and a half years. He sang eleven separate roles in 280 performances.

With a group of singers from various countries and nationalities, the company produced multi-lingual presentations. A rendering of *La Traviata* might include a baritone singing in Hungarian, a tenor in Italian, a soprano in German, and the chorus in Hebrew. Looking back, Domingo credited this cosmopolitan group for improving his abilities in several languages. When he arrived in Tel Aviv, Domingo spoke only Spanish and understood a small amount of Italian. In Israel, he began to learn French and Hebrew.

Because of the extraordinary number of appearances in which he appeared in Israel, he also credits those two and a half years with his growing realization that he needed to avoid abusing his voice. He said, "When I went to Israel, as a young beginner, with my wife, Marta, we both used to sing an average of ten, twelve performances a month. So when my international career began, I was really prepared for pacing myself, knowing what and how much I could do without harming me. But in all that I did, I was always thinking about my voice, about the technique for using that voice."[7]

RAVE REVIEWS IN NEW YORK

In 1965, Domingo completed his stay in Israel and returned to the United States. He auditioned successfully for the New York City Opera and performed both in Georges Bizet's *Carmen* and Giacomo Puccini's *Madame Butterfly*.

At the beginning of the 1966 opera season, Domingo opened the North American premiere of *Don Rodrigo*, an opera composed by Argentinian Alberto Ginastera. When it first premiered in Buenos Aires in 1964, the work had not played to rave reviews. Nevertheless, two years later, with the young Domingo in the lead as the Visigoth king of eighth-century Spain, the critics lauded the work and the performance. It became so popular that extra performances had to be added and the work repeated again the same year. It also later played to equally generous praise in Los Angeles. Domingo, now just twenty-five years old, had made a solid mark in the United States.

Soon, he began to perform in the most celebrated opera houses around the world. He made his debut at the Vienna State Opera in 1967, at the Lyric Opera of Chicago in 1968, at both La Scala in Milan and the San Francisco Opera in 1969, and at London's Covent Garden in 1971.

One day in 1967, Domingo sat at a canteen table at the Vienna State Opera and met the man who would be his operatic rival, friend, and collaborator and the man with whom he would often be compared by music critics and public for the rest of the twentieth century. They would be at the center of a growing competition of sorts, a fight for tenor supremacy, the title of "World's Greatest Tenor." There was, of course, no such real contest, no games or votes or final statistics to determine the winner—just the perceptions and loyalties of the public, the press, and millions of fans.

The man was Luciano Pavarotti, the leading Italian opera tenor. Six years older than Domingo, Pavarotti was born in 1935 near Moderna, Italy, to a family of quite modest means. His father was a baker who had a fine tenor voice but was plagued throughout his life by the fear of appearing on stage. His mother worked in a cigar factory. For a time during World War II the family lived in a single room. At around the age of nine Pavarotti began singing with his father in a small local church choir. Friends and relatives took notice of his talent. But like Domingo in his youth, Pavarotti loved soccer and hoped to pursue a career as a professional player. His mother, however, convinced him to work to become a schoolteacher, which he did for two years, working in an elementary school.

It was not until the age of nineteen that Pavarotti began his serious study of music under the tutelage of Arrigo Pola, a professional tenor in Moderna who offered to teach him without compensation. Pola's generosity in 1954 became the world's gift. Pavarotti had perfect pitch and an exquisite voice. He later trained with another professional teacher while working as a teacher and then as an insurance salesman.

By 1961 Pavarotti had won a major music prize, and by 1963 he had debuted at London's famous Covent Garden venue. In 1965 Pavarotti made his American debut in Miami performing as Edgardo in Donizetti's *Lucia di Lammermoor.* In December 1969, Domingo, then twenty-eight, made his debut in the title role of Verdi's *Ernani* at La Scala in Milan, the oldest of the world's greatest opera houses. Domingo would have many triumphs on that revered stage. By the time the two singers met that day in Vienna, they both were at the beginning of remarkable singing careers.

It is notable that both Domingo and Pavarotti made their operatic debuts at the famed New York Metropolitan Opera Company in the same year, 1968. Domingo was scheduled to make his official debut with the Met on October 2, 1968, as Maurizio in Francesco Cilea's opera *Adrienne Lecouvreur,* about a famous French singer of the same name who died under mysterious circumstances.

At the time, Domingo lived in a house in Teaneck, New Jersey, just across the Hudson River from Manhattan. On September 28, 1968, with thirty-five minutes remaining before curtain time, tenor Franco Corelli, who was to perform Maurizio that evening at the Met, canceled, and Domingo was summoned to replace him. Domingo later remembered jumping into his station wagon at his home in New Jersey to drive to the Met for the performance. "It was a balmy evening," he recalls, "and the windows of the car were open. Since it was so close to curtain time, I was vocalizing in the car. At a red light, I noticed that some people in the next car were laughing. I leaned out the window. "Where are you going?" I asked them. "To the Met," they said. "Well, don't laugh," I shot back. "You'll be hearing me in a few minutes!"[8]

New York Times critic Allen Hughes favorably reviewed Domingo's performance. It was the first of many appearances that Domingo would make on that historic stage. Indeed, after his debut he performed in every season at the Met, logging more than three hundred performances in twenty-eight different roles. He would also sing opening night at the Metropolitan Opera more times than the celebrated tenor Enrico Caruso. Many thought that Caruso's record would never be broken.

In February of the following year, Domingo sang the title role in the North American premiere of Alberto Ginastera's *Don Rodrigo*, an event that also marked the opening of the New York City Opera's new home at Lincoln Center.

Domingo was building an international reputation. In 1971 he sang Cavaradossi in a Covent Garden revival of Giacomo Puccini's *Tosca*. Major debuts followed: *La Boheme* in San Francisco and *Turandot* in Verona in 1969, *La Gioconda* in Madrid in 1970; *La Boheme* at the Bavarian State Opera in 1972; and *Don Carlo* at the Paris Opera in 1973. Critics began to marvel not only at his resonant voice but also at his dramatic presentations, often a weakness for conservatory-trained singers but a talent that Domingo had developed from his earliest stage days in Mexico.

At six foot two, with a powerful build and barrel chest, Domingo struck an impressive physical appearance in most of the roles. In the long flowing robes and other costume accessories that were part of many of the operatic roles in which he performed, he had an impressive athletic build and stature to go along with his immensely gifted voice. But the magical essence of Domingo's performances was not just the power of his voice but the carefully measured dramatic effects that fit the time and place. For all of his potential power, which he unleashed at precisely the appropriate times, he also had a velvety and smooth touch that most listeners regarded as astonishing.

Antonio Pappano, the fine pianist and music director of London's famed Royal Opera House at Covent Garden, remembered performing with Domingo in Oslo, Norway. "I got to Oslo very late. I felt a right idiot, because Placido had got there first," said Pappano. "So just before the performance I went into Placido's dressing room, and Placido was at the piano. And so we rehearsed very quickly and the wrong way round. Placido played, and I sang, and we had five minutes and we were done. But I'll never forget hearing his voice that first time in the theatre—this is not to flatter him, because it's just true—but when he started the aria in the first act, my God, the whole sound of the orchestra just changed immediately to the sound of that voice. It was quite something."[9]

Although Domingo had established a reputation as a remarkably versatile performer, he was perhaps best known for his performances in Verdi's *Otello*. Here, in this role where dramatic inflection and power are so vital,

Domingo excelled. He first sang *Otello* at a performance in Hamburg on September 28, 1975. He called the date one of the most important in his life. *Otello*, Verdi's second to last opera, was one of the masterpieces of the theater and one of the great challenges for tenors. The second act of *Otello*, Domingo often said, is in itself as demanding for a tenor as most entire operas—and when you have finished the second act, you will still face three additional acts to go. The renowned stage and screen actor Laurence Olivier, who had played the part of Shakespeare's Othello, once saw Domingo perform in *Otello* and told a friend, "You realize that Domingo plays Othello as well as I do, and he has that voice!"[10]

Journalist Daniel Snowman wrote of seeing the transformation of Domingo as he prepared to mount the stage for a production of *Otello*. "He stands erect, carries his flowing robes with immense dignity, and with his olive skin darkened and his wavy black hair now flecked with grey and gently crinkled, he becomes an imposing figure of unassailable authority."[11]

It was at an opening night at La Scala in 1976 that Domingo performed *Otello* in the first live telecast of opera in Italy. Conductor Richard Chailly remembered the performance with a sense of awe. "That was the greatest performance I saw in my life," recalled Chailly. "If I were given the chance of witnessing just one performance of opera before I died, it would have to be that Scala *Otello*."[12]

Domingo began to accept invitations from around the world and took on a grueling schedule that would continue throughout his career. When asked about his endurance, he often remarked that it was all in the genes. His parents, after all, had given two or three appearances in a single day. By the mid-1970s, Domingo was considered one of the top tenors in the world.

As his career progressed, Domingo's range of roles increased with remarkable swiftness. He learned them by heart, with all their nuances and peculiarities. He studied the parts as if taking college examinations, going over the music any place that he could—on planes, in taxicabs, wherever he had time to spare. In one instance he was seen studying a piece of music while on a plane to San Francisco to substitute for another singer who had taken ill. He changed into his costume on the way to the opera house as the curtain was about to be raised.

Music critic Edward Greenfield said in 1970, when Domingo was still in his twenties, that Domingo was "... almost too good to be true, the possessor not only of a superlative voice, but of a kindly, modest temperament that stands correction without fuss."[13] A number of critics have pointed out that Domingo, unlike most other singers, seemed to understand the mechanics of his own voice and the delicate balancing act between the resonances achieved both from the chest and the head. He seemed to grasp the mechanics both intellectually and instinctively from his earliest days on the stage. He knew how his voice worked, how to get the most from it, and how to preserve its energy and stamina.

In addition to his seemingly indefatigable appearances in various tenor roles throughout the United States and Europe, Domingo began actively to pursue conducting opportunities. He would once again appear in front of audiences—this time with his back to the fans and a baton raised in his hand. The love of conducting for him was a natural move. Even as a young man working with his parents in Mexico, he had occasionally conducted performances for the zarzuela company. He had also studied conducting in Mexico.

Domingo took on various conductor roles throughout his career. In 1972 he conducted the Philharmonic Orchestra of London, and a year later, in October 1973, he conducted a New York City Opera production of *La Traviata*. In 1984 Domingo made his debut as a conductor at New York's Metropolitan Opera, leading the orchestra and cast in *La Boheme*, an opera that he had often sung. He conducted leading opera performances in the most celebrated opera houses across the world. Although some music fans and critics believed that Domingo's new interest in conducting had something to do with building a place for himself once his singing abilities had waned, Domingo, however, had no intention of reducing his efforts as a performer.

Domingo's move into a new realm was yet another example of his eagerness to take on new challenges. "Conducting an opera is like being the charioteer in *Ben-Hur*," Domingo once said. "It's like holding ten horses in one hand, and ten more in the other. You can never predict what is going to happen."[14]

By the time he starred in the Metropolitan Opera's 1979 season with a production of *Otello*, Domingo had sung in an estimated eighty operas, fifty of which had been released in recordings. Concentrating largely on the nineteenth-century Italian and French operas, he had also performed Mozart, Wagner, and had even appeared in some modern works. Not yet forty years old, he had performed on stage nearly 1,400 times.

MORE THAN OPERA

As Domingo's career advanced, he often expressed a desire to make opera more accessible to those who had never experienced it. In addition, with his ascent into the range of an international star, he now had the name and visibility to try new communication mediums. Not only would he promote the musical form he cherished, it would also be lucrative.

For Domingo, the opportunities were varied. There were television appearances, filmed and televised opera performances, popular music venues, and other possibilities. For those who thought it unusual for an internationally recognized performer of so-called high-brow music to venture forth into other areas, they needed only to look at the success of such towering opera performers of the past such as Enrico Caruso and John McCormack.

Caruso was likely the highest-paid performer in the world during his heyday from 1903 to his death in 1921. In 1914, when the average weekly salary in the United States was about twelve dollars, Caruso was paid about $2,500 for an appearance at New York's Metropolitan Opera. In Latin America, he received as much as $15,000 for a single appearance, a staggering sum considering the economic conditions in those countries. And so, when Caruso decided to appear in two silent movies in 1919, *My Cousin* and *A Splendid Romance*, each of those roles earned him $100,000.

McCormack, an Irish-born naturalized American, was so popular that he went by the title of Count John McCormack, an honor that was conferred to him in 1928 by Pope Pius XI. At a recital in London's Albert Hall in 1938 he was encouraged to run as a candidate for the Irish presidency. Like Caruso, McCormack made vast sums of money appearing in new artistic mediums. He sang Irish ballads extensively and with great power and beauty. Both he and Caruso were pioneer opera voices in a new industry at the turn of the century—recorded music.

By 1980, a new niche opened for Domingo. Televised and filmed opera became increasingly popular and Domingo was at the forefront. He appeared in fully staged operas and recitals on the Public Broadcasting Service programs "Live from Lincoln Center" and "Live from the Met." He also produced several opera films that were very well received. In 1983, he won praise for portraying Alfredo in Franco Zeffirelli's film version of *La Traviata,* and in 1984 he garnered rave reviews for his passionate Don Juan in Francesco Rosi's spectacular screen version of *Carmen*. Domingo also starred in Zeffirelli's film productions of Mascagni's *Cavalleria Rusticana* and Leoncavallo's *Pagliacci*.

In 1981, Domingo branched out further. He recorded a duet with the greatly popular singer John Denver. The pop hit was called "Perhaps Love," and it made its way into the national top twenty list of records. Later, he recorded a duet with pop singer Jennifer Rush called "Till I Loved You," which made it into the Top 30 in the United Kingdom.

When critics and even friends began sniping about the master tenor taking off in this direction, he dismissed the criticisms. "I just love to sing anything that is good music," he said. "The best zarzuela songs or those of Lennon and McCartney or Sammy Cahn or John Denver are the *lieder* [songs] of today and I want to sing these just as much as the greatest operas."[15] Besides, he said, by making his own name and the art he performed increasingly public through various mediums he could perhaps lead listeners to opera. "You should see the letters I get from people saying they're coming to the opera because they heard me sing 'Perhaps Love' or saw me launch one of my pop albums on TV," he said.[16]

Domingo also recorded tangos and songs from Viennese operettas. In 1984 he costarred with Carol Burnett in a variety special in which he sang

"Be a Clown" and "*Vesti la giubba*" from *Pagliacci* and accompanied Burnett in Cole Porter's "Night and Day." In his own 1985 television special, *Steppin' Out with the Ladies*, he shared the stage singing Broadway musical numbers with such pop singers as Maureen McGovern, Marilyn McCoo, Leslie Uggams, and Patti LaBelle. Domingo collected his family's native zarzuela pieces and performed them himself in recordings titled *Zarzuela Arias* and *Zarzuela Arias and Duets*. He also began to give zarzuela performances all over the world. Throughout his career, Domingo constantly amazed critics with his versatility and stamina. Opera critic Peter G. Davis once said that Domingo was a phenomenon who seemed to have a compulsive nature of overachieving. During the 1986 season alone, Domingo, among other things, performed more than six times as Cavaradossi in *Tosca*, performed in a Lincoln Center concert honoring the Statue of Liberty's centennial, conducted *Romeo* at the Met, and on November 15, 1986, sang the title role in Menotti's *Goya*, an opera the tenor had commissioned, at its premiere in Washington, D.C. Domingo then played the part of Verdi's tragic Moor in Zeffirelli's film version of *Otello*. At the same time, Angel Records released Domingo's official debut on compact disc (CD) as a conductor, an all-star version of *Die Fledermaus*.

AN INTERNATIONAL FIGURE

On September 19, 1985, a powerful earthquake struck Mexico City. With a magnitude of 8.1 on the Richter scale, the quake was one of strongest ever to hit the area. The effects of the quake were particularly devastating because the city sits on a plateau surrounded by mountains and volcanoes, and the combination of dirt and sand underpinning the city is much less stable than bedrock.

Several old hotels crumbled, including the Regis, the Versailles, and the Romano. Hundreds of students attending early morning classes at the National College of Professional Education were crushed or trapped as the building collapsed. Many factories in the city, built with shoddy materials, also could not withstand the quake. Further, the tremors caused gas mains to break, causing fires and explosions throughout the city. When the damage was finally assessed, three thousand buildings in Mexico City had been destroyed, and another 100,000 suffered serious damage.

At the Nuevo León apartment block in the Tlatelolco housing complex, many were killed or injured. Many of Domingo's family members and friends lived in that complex. Domingo lost an aunt, an uncle, his nephew, and his nephew's young son. As soon as it was possible, Domingo and Marta flew to Mexico City to help rescue victims from the rubble. He canceled many operatic events to do what he could to help in the ensuing months. During the following year, he performed benefit concerts for the victims and released an album of one of the events. Later, he was honored by the president of Mexico with its highest honor, the Order of the Aztec Eagle, for his humanitarian work.

Profoundly shaken by the tragedy, Domingo became increasingly committed to using his celebrity profile and Latino heritage to help forge closer ties between Mexico and communities in the United States. Not only because of his towering professional accomplishments but also because of his charity and concern, he became an inspiration to many young Latinos as they developed their own musical gifts.

Domingo raised millions of dollars for SOS Children's Villages in Mexico, an organization that provides a stable environment for children who have lost their parents or have been abused, for Frankfurt's Albert Griesinger School for disabled children, for victims of the devastating mudslides in Acapulco in 1997, as well as many other charities.

In 1987, Domingo had the honor of singing at the centennial anniversary performance of Giuseppe Verdi's *Otello*. It was on February 5, 1887, that the opera was first performed on the stage of the world's oldest opera house, La Scala in Milan. It was at La Scala where Caruso first made his name and where the legendary Maria Callas gave many of her finest performances. And now, it was Placido Domingo on that same stage in the lead role, the role that always seemed made for his voice, his theatrical talent, and his physical presence. It was an honor for Domingo to pay tribute both to Verdi and La Scala.

On June 30, 1991, at the Vienna State Opera, Domingo and the cast of a production of *Otello* basked in one of the longest ovations for a performance on the operatic stage. One of the participants, along with Domingo, was baritone Sherrill Milnes. That night, Milnes said, could be described by the German word *Sternstunde* (great moment). At the end of the performance, he said, the audience erupted and the curtain calls began. By the time the performers left the stage for the last time, he said, the number of curtain calls had reached about one hundred. Domingo recalled the event vividly, "You don't know anymore what to do, you know? You go out, and the public is still there. And you say, 'Well, what are we doing?' And you come out again, and you take a little longer to come next time. And you say, 'I hope they go.' No, they continue. But it was a great, great experience, very thrilling."[17]

In 1993 Domingo celebrated his twenty-fifth anniversary of performing at the Met in New York. He shared the stage that night with Luciano Pavarotti, who had also debuted at the Met twenty-five years earlier.

In 1995, Domingo completed a recording of some of the Latino world's most memorable melodies on an album called *De Mi Alma Latina*. Joining him were such popular stars as the Mexican vocal trio Pandora and singers Ana Gabriel, Daniela Romo, and Patricia Sosa. When the recording was released, Domingo said that it showed his heartfelt passion for the popular music that included everything from Argentine tangos to Mexican boleros.

It was a tribute to Latino culture, compositions that he said "sing and exalt man's deepest feelings, songs of love and weeping, of languishing nostalgia and playful rhythm, of cane sugar and sea salt, songs of yesterday and today, unhurried and timeless songs."[18]

And in 1999, EMI Latin released a Domingo compilation called *100 Years of Mariachi*. With his wondrous voice, Domingo marvelously executed the romantic ballads that he had come to know from his earliest years in Mexico. It was an emotional exploration of his roots. Domingo would also later record an album of love songs by the Mexican composer Agustin Lara.

THE THREE TENORS

In 1990, at the World Cup soccer finals held in Rome, Italy, a phenomenon known as "The Three Tenors" was born. It was the brainchild of Italian concert manager Mario Dradi. The idea was not only to celebrate the soccer championship; it was also to celebrate the recovery from leukemia of another world-class tenor: José Carreras.

Born in 1946 in Barcelona, Spain, Carreras first sang in public at the age of eight, performing "La Donna e Mobile" on Spanish Public Radio. At age eleven he sang at the famous Grande Teatre del Liceu in Barcelona. In 1970 he started his professional career on that same stage and followed with debuts at the world's most prestigious opera houses including La Scala, the New York Metropolitan Opera House, and the Vienna Staatsoper. Carreras became one of the most prominent singers of his generation, particularly in performing operas of Verdi and Puccini. His career encompassed more than sixty roles on stage and in the recording studio.

In the late 1980s Carreras was diagnosed with leukemia and given only a one in ten chance of survival. Nevertheless, through a grueling treatment regimen in the Fred Hutchinson Cancer Research Center in Seattle, Washington, including a bone marrow transplant, he gradually recovered and was able once again to begin appearing in concerts. In 1988 he embarked on a tour of recitals. He had returned not only to an active life but to the stage. His brush with death inspired Carreras to establish in 1988 the José Carreras International Leukemia Foundation. Like his fellow tenors, Carreras was an avid fan of soccer. The World Cup, which is held every four years, seemed to promoter Mario Dradi an ideal chance to welcome back Carreras. The proceeds for the concert in Rome would be directed toward the Carreras foundation.

At the ancient site of the Baths of Caracalla, public baths built in Rome between 212 and 216 AD, the first Three Tenors concert, held before an audience of 8,000 spectators, caught the public imagination around the world. On July 7, 1990, with Zubin Mehta conducting the Orchestra del Maggio Musicale Fiorenino and the Orchestra del Teatro dell'Opera de Roma, the three performers sang a variety of selections, together and individually.

Three Latin American Tenors

Audiences worldwide thrilled to the "The Three Tenors," the collaboration of Placido Domingo, Luciano Pavarotti, and José Carreras. The following three tenors of a new generation are making a dramatic mark on the field of opera. They are from Latin America.

José Cura

José Cura was born in Rosario, Argentina, on December 5, 1962. When he was twenty years old, he enrolled at the School of Arts at the National University of Rosario. A year later, he became assistant conductor for the university choir. After winning a grant, he moved to the School of Arts of Teatro Colón in Buenos Aires where he studied composition and conducting. In 1988 he began working with the esteemed voice teacher Horacio Amauri. Later, he worked with Italian tenor Vittorio Terranova who helped him to master Italian operatic style.

In March 1993, in Trieste, Italy, he sang the role of Jan in Bibalo's *Miss Julie.* Since then his career has flourished, not only in Italy and other parts of Europe but also in the United States.

In July 2000, he sang in the extremely successful performance of *La Traviata* from Paris, which was televised and broadcast in more than 100 countries. Also in 2000, he was knighted "Chevalier de l'Ordre du Cedre" by the Lebanese government—equivalent to the British title of "lord."

Like Placido Domingo, Cura is a highly successful opera singer as well as a conductor. He has also exhibited extraordinary innovation in bringing so-called high-brow music to a much larger listening audience. For example, Cura directed and starred in a combination musical and theatrical event based on Ruggero Leoncavallo's masterpiece *Pagliacci.* Called "Lacommediaefinita," the program is an unusual excursion into the fairy tale world of clowns and puppets that is visually stimulating as well as musically inspiring.

Juan Diego Flórez

The son of popular Peruvian folk singer Ruben Flórez, Juan Diego Flórez was born in Lima, Peru, on January 13, 1973. At age seventeen, he began his classical training at the Conservatorio Nacional de Música in Lima. He also trained at the Curtis Institute in Philadelphia and received instruction from the American opera singer Marilyn Horne at the Music Academy of the West in Santa Barbara, California.

While a student in Philadelphia, Flórez was given the opportunity to audition for the Rossini Festival in Pesaro, Italy, and was given a small role. After completing his studies, he returned to Italy to rehearse for another small role but then, while filling in for another singer, had the opportunity to perform

(continued)

the lead tenor in the opera *Matilde di Shabran*. The performance was a major success, and Flórez was suddenly in the eye of opera aficionados.

In 1998, Flórez made his debut at Covent Garden, London, stepping in for an ailing Giuseppe Sabbatini in the first modern performance of Donizetti's *Elizabetta*. By 1999, he had sung *Barbiere* at the Wien Staatsoper in Austria, and the New York Metropolitan Opera welcomed him for the first time in February 2002.

In April 2000, he was awarded two prestigious music awards in Italy. In the following two years he won Germany's Echo award for the Best Operatic Male Recital album, and in 2003 he won a Cannes Classical Music Award. Like Placido Domingo, Flórez has successfully ventured into the popular music arena.

Rolando Villazón

Born in 1972 in Mexico City, Rolando Villazón, by the age of eleven, began studying music, acting, contemporary dance, and ballet. In 1990, he met baritone Arturo Nieto, who became his voice teacher and directed him toward the world of opera.

Villazón soon joined the National Conservatory of Music. After winning two national contests in Mexico City and Guanajuato, Villazón became a student of baritone Gabriel Mijares, with whom he continued his studies before launching an international career.

In 1998, Villazón traveled to the United States to become a member of the Pittsburgh Opera's Young Artists Program, where he appeared in productions of *I Capuleti Ed I Montecchi, Lucia di Lammermoor,* and Samuel Barber's *Vanessa.* In 1999, Villazón won second prize in Placido Domingo's 1999 Operalia competition, as well as first prize in Zarzuela.

After making his European debut at the Teatro Carlo Felice in Genoa, Italy, Villazón appeared as Rodolfo for the Opéra de Lyon in December of 1999. He then made his debut at the Teatro Verdi in Trieste in the opera *La Traviata.* These performances brought the artist international attention.

Villazón's meteoric career vaulted him into the ranks of the leading lyric tenors in the world, acclaimed for performance in the great opera houses including New York's Metropolitan Opera, Opera National de Paris, Royal Opera House in Covent Garden, the Berlin State Opera, and many others.

Villazón signed an exclusive contract with Deutsche Grammophon, which released his production of *La Traviata* in both CD and DVD, one of the most commercially successful opera recordings in recent times.

The concept was grand, the willingness of the three world-class performers to work together was a coup, and its success astonished even the promoters who expected an outpouring of support. About 800 million people worldwide saw the television broadcasts. The recorded music turned into the best-selling classical album of all time with total sales of around ten million copies, and the figure climbs every year. Only a few albums in the history of recorded music ever outsold the Three Tenors concert in Rome.

The program's most popular aria, Puccini's "Nessun dorma," became a fight song not only for the World Cup competition but also for record buyers everywhere—"All' alba vincero" (At dawn I shall win).

Domingo immediately recognized the potential, telling a friend that The Three Tenors could sing six or eight concerts a month all over the world. The three, each with enormous egos, of course, generally enjoyed the camaraderie and personal connections that brought them together, although the normal tensions between the three occasionally flared. They were not casual fans of soccer but dedicated ones. Domingo, in fact, refused engagements during the World Games tournament during the times the Spanish team competed.

In 1994, once again at a World Cup championship, The Three Tenors performed. This time the venue was the baseball stadium in Chavez Ravine, home of the Los Angeles Dodgers. Nothing like the classical architecture that still existed in Rome, the baseball stadium was transformed for the occasion from a baseball field into a theater with a neoclassical stage flanked by graceful columns that had been shipped in from Hungary. Thirty truckloads of greenery flanked a waterfall four stories high.

The Los Angeles concert was aired live on the Public Broadcasting Service. Unlike the first concert, the three performers were guaranteed a phenomenal financial reward for appearing together: $1 million each. The vast promotion campaign started months before the event, attempting to reach far beyond opera buffs. Promoters negotiated with the Federal Aviation Agency to divert air traffic from the stadium during the concert. Merrill Lynch provided 56,000 binoculars to those lucky enough to get a ticket for the event. Companies rolled out the usual paraphernalia of coffee mugs, baseball caps, and T-shirts. Commercials ran during the soccer matches of the preliminary rounds of the World Cup tournament. The sports channel ESPN kept up a constant hype. A music video was shot showing the singers kicking around a soccer ball and singing. Although the hype and hoopla seemed far beyond restraint for many opera lovers, promoters pointed out that Caruso himself once merrily stepped through a routine on a vaudeville stage with Al Jolson.

Setting aside their vanities and generally having a good time, the three once again put on a magnificent show with a variety of classical numbers and show tunes, all divided so that the three great talents could toss the melodies back and forth. The concert came off as a brilliant collaboration. The men seemed to enjoy the fellowship. Carreras said, "The audience loves most the things that seem to happen spontaneously, and we are all Latins who like improvisation."[19]

The 1994 concert in Dodger Stadium was viewed on television by 1.3 billion people and sold more than 10 million CDs and videos. It was recognized as the most-seen and most-heard serious music event of all time. "It has been beautiful for the people, as well as very rewarding for us," said Domingo. "Some critics may pick apart these events, but I know many, many people who are now interested in opera because of a Three Tenors concert."[20] It was at the concert at Dodger Stadium that Pavarotti suggested to the other two men what Domingo had thought about earlier: What about a formal tour that could take the group around the world? By June of that year, it had come together.

Originally, promoters worked out a schedule of five stops, including one in another sports venue, Giants Stadium in New Jersey, just outside New York City. The other planned stops were London, Tokyo, Munich, and Melbourne in Australia. Soon, the list was enhanced to include Vienna, Goteborg in Sweden, Dusseldorf in Germany, and two stops in Canada— Toronto and Vancouver.

The Three Tenors was a phenomenon that refused to lose its sense of appeal. It introduced millions in a gentle way to forms of music that they had before never experienced; it gave to others a more immediate connection to three of the most talented musical performers in the world. The trio continued their four-year performances at the World Cup events; their participation seemed now a part of the overall production of the games. In Paris in 1998, and in Yokohama, Japan in 2002, they filled stadiums and thrilled audiences.

In August 2003, more than a decade after their first performance together, The Three Tenors performed in the town of Bath, England. Located in the valley of the River Avon in the southwestern part of England, the Romans once built baths there from the natural hot springs. Two centuries after the Romans, the town celebrated the rejuvenation of the thermal spas after they had been shut down thirty years earlier. The Royal Philharmonic Orchestra and the Bath Abbey and Camerator choirs filled a huge stage. Thousands gathered in the crowd along with music critic John Maguire. The sound of the voices and music were awe-inspiring, he said. Of Domingo, Maguire wrote, "His performance was magnificent. Looking around, people watched with mouths open and eyes filled with awe.[21]

In September 2007, Pavarotti died in Modena, Italy. Domingo said, "One of the most gratifying aspects of my life is that Luciano and I became friends in spite of what many important people in the entertainment industry had planned for us. They thought that feuding would not only be good for promoting our then still young careers but also for the music business in general. What really happened was that our careers encouraged each other. ... Eventually we both fooled everybody by becoming real friends who respected each other for their individual strengths and weaknesses."[22] There would be no more collaboration of The Three Tenors. The recordings and films, however, live on.

UNPARALLELED CREATIVE ENERGY

In the 1990s and in the early part of the twenty-first century, Placido Domingo's career as a singer, conductor, administrator, philanthropist, and promoter of young artists took him to levels that no single figure in music had ever attained in the course of one career. As a singer, his accomplishments were extraordinary. As a conductor, he performed at the highest levels. As an administrator, he made enormous contributions. And as a philanthropist and promoter of talent, his efforts have resulted in enormous change.

As one of the most gifted, creative, and inspiring tenors, he has been on a level with the best ever. Perhaps no opera singer in history has commanded a wider repertoire or been more ambitious to stretch it further at such a high level of perfection. His roles stretched from lyric Verdi tenor parts to roles of Wagner that required incredible stamina. And as his career moved forward, he constantly looked for new directions and ways to expand. In 1998, Domingo told a reporter, "I am happy with my voice—the way that I am handling the aging. One of the reasons that I think my voice has lasted so long is because I teach myself the parts alone at the piano, rather than singing for a coach after rehearsals and on off days. Only with German roles and now Russian do I go to a coach. This Russian is giving me a lot of headaches; in your mind you think you know it, but when it comes to actually singing it, you don't. So, not a day goes by without study. But I am constantly seeking something fresh. That is my credo: to always find new repertoire, new challenges."[23]

As he looked back over his career, Domingo emphasized over and over again that watching his parents work as both performers and managers gave him a model for his own multi-faceted career: "Their example has stayed with me," he said. "When I started singing in opera, I was already starting to think about company work." Even that early in his career he was talking about "being able to take care of young singers in the future. This was when I was thirty."[24]

As a conductor Domingo led operatic performances in all the important theaters from New York's Metropolitan Opera to London's Covent Garden to the Vienna State Opera. Often he conducted purely symphonic concerts and did it with the most renowned orchestras in the world, from the Vienna Philharmonic to the London Symphony.

One day in 2003, at the famed Covent Garden opera house in London, Domingo was both singer and conductor. The event was unprecedented. In the afternoon, the tenor sang a Pagliacci matinee. Then, a few hours later, after putting aside his costume, he was back in the opera house and on the podium to conduct. British opera critic Martin Kettle, who called Domingo "the greatest operatic artist of modern times," said,

> Even by Domingo's standards this is a groundbreaking career move. He has conducted operas before, of course, including *Die Fledermaus* and *La Traviata* at Covent Garden. But never before has Domingo alternated singing and conducting the same opera. Nor has anyone else in modern times. No one I have asked has been able to come up with anything like it at this level.[25]

In 1996, Domingo was named the artistic director of the Washington National Opera in the U.S. capital. Four years later, he was appointed to the same position with the Los Angeles Opera. He held both jobs simultaneously and was so successful with each that his contracts were extended. He will continue his work as the general director of two opera companies, the Washington National Opera and the Los Angeles Opera, through the 2010–2011 season.

The positions have afforded Domingo the unique opportunity to shape the course and direction of the field of opera in the United States in two major venues, one on each coast. He has used the opportunity in each case to promote a range of music that went beyond the previous bounds of the two opera institutions. Although in both places he has expanded the scope and breadth of the programs to include music from around the world, he has especially emphasized the music and new talented performers from Latin America. He increasingly saw for himself an opportunity to highlight the contributions of Latinos.

In his autobiography, *Placido Domingo: My First Forty Years*, published in 1983, Domingo talked about a desire very close to his heart—to help reclaim for the Hispanic population in the United States some of the cultural roots that have been shamefully ignored or forgotten. "Many of these people," he said, "feel justifiably offended by what is presented to them and to the outside world as their cultural heritage: long-running television soap operas; brash, rhythmical music from the Caribbean, and not much else."[26]

Domingo followed through on his desire. After taking the position in the nation's capital, Domingo introduced the zarzuela plays *El Gato Montes* and *Doña Francisquita*. This was music that hearkened back to his youth, to the days and months with his family on the road with their zarzuela company. Speaking in 1997 of opera in Latin and South America, Domingo said, "Teatro Colon, in Buenos Aires, has a great tradition. They can afford to do unknown works. There are some good composers, and I want to encourage them to write. In a future season here I will be doing a world premiere of a work by a Spanish composer and will call for a new work for the turn of the century."[27]

When he accepted his role in Los Angeles, he said, "I would like to include the music of some Hispanic composers: zarzuela and newly commissioned works. I would like very much to help bring to the Hispanic people in America some culture of their own beyond what they have on TV. And I would like to make it easy for students to be exposed to opera, inviting them to rehearsals and having special performances for them as we do in Washington."[28]

In 1993, Domingo founded The Operalia contest, an annual showcase for promising new opera talent. Many cite the rising number of new singers and musicians in the opera field as evidence of the powerful impact that Domingo has had in nurturing this new talent. His continued interest in promoting new talent led to the inauguration of the Domingo-Cafritz Young Artist

Program of the Washington National Opera and the Domingo-Thornton Young Artists Program of the Los Angeles Opera. He also launched The Plácido Domingo Intern-Apprentice Program to prepare the next generation of opera professionals, from those who work in technical capacities behind the scenes to those work in administration.

Domingo's increasingly active conducting schedule in the opera house, concert hall, and studio not only reflected his consummate musicianship but also led to frequent personal counsel he gave to young singers. Conducting London's Philharmonic, he guided Jose Cura's 1997 debut disc of Puccini arias—a worldwide hit that helped herald the Argentinean as one of the bright young tenor stars.

In 2004, Domingo received an award in Hollywood from the Imagen Foundation. The award was established in 1985 to encourage and recognize the positive portrayal of Latinos in all media and to increase Latino representation at all levels of the entertainment industry.

Over sixty years old, with a storied career already behind him, Domingo decided in 2007 to make another career move. No longer would he sing tenor, he said. After more than forty years exploring the tenor repertoire, he would now venture forth into another area—he would become a baritone.

In 2009, on the stage at Berlin's Staatsoper, Domingo plans to take on one of Verdi's most demanding baritone roles, as Simon Boccanegra, the Doge of Genoa, in the opera of the same name. He also plans to appear at La Scala and Covent Garden.

As Domingo has continued performing well into the new century, he has sung in approximately 125 different operatic roles, more than any other tenor in history. His repertoire spanned Mozart to Verdi to Wagner. He has sung in every important opera house in the world and has made an unparalleled number of recordings, of which more than 100 were full-length operas. He has earned nine Grammy awards and two Grammy awards in the newly established Latin Division. He made more than fifty videos and three theatrically released films. His telecast of *Tosca* from the authentic setting in Rome was seen by more than one billion people in 117 different countries. He opened the season at New York's Metropolitan Opera a record twenty-one times.

An abbreviated listing of some of the numerous honors and awards that Domingo accepted over the years from around the world is indicative of his remarkable achievements. He received the Prince of Asturias Award given in Spain in 1991, the Kennedy Center Honors Award in 2000, the Presidential Medal of Freedom in 2002, the Society of Singers Ella Award in 2002, the Order of the British Empire in 2002, Commander of the French Ordre national de la Légion d'honneur in 2002, and two Classical Brit Awards. He has received an Honorary Doctorate from England's Oxford University, one of many honorary doctorates presented to him. He was given President Gorbachev's World Award for Humanitarian Causes and was selected as the first winner for the inauguration of Opera News Magazine's Annual Awards.

As he headed into the 2007–2008 season, Domingo showed no signs of slowing down. Indeed, the schedule was daunting. Two new roles would be added to his repertoire and would be sung at the Met and at the Teatro Real in Madrid. He also scheduled singing engagements at La Scala, Covent Garden, and in Barcelona. In his work as a conductor he scheduled stops at the Met, the Washington National Opera, the Los Angeles Opera, and Théâtre du Chatelet in Paris.

In September 2007, the Washington National Opera showed a free, live broadcast from the Kennedy Center of a production of Puccini's *La Bohème* on a screen at the Washington Monument on the National Mall. The production was simultaneously broadcast to thirty-two schools across the country. Prior to the simulcast, the Washington National Opera distributed educational materials to the schools. In addition, Washington National Opera's *Generation O* program began targeting young audiences aged 18–35, providing affordable ticket prices and devising programs specifically for the new generation of opera-goers. Domingo continued his strong, determined efforts to influence the next generation of opera lovers and performers.

British music critic Martin Kettle, who assiduously followed Domingo's career, wrote, "For a man who has nothing left to prove to the operatic world, Placido Domingo remains a restless spirit." His creative energy, said Kettle, "marked Domingo out from every other singer of his time."[29]

Perhaps the highest compliment to Placido Domingo was given by José Carreras. In describing the attributes of a great performer, he said that "one must have vast musical intelligence, a good physical appearance and, hopefully, a charismatic stage presence. Above all, one must be an expressive singer and actor. When all these qualities are wedded to a great voice, then one is in the presence of a great artist. And for me, Placido Domingo represents this ideal."[30]

SELECTED RECORDED MUSIC

Domingo, Placido. *Domingo Favourites*. Deutsche Grammaphon, 1995. CD.

Domingo, Placido. *100 Years of Mariachi*. EMI Latin, 1999. CD.

Domingo, Placido, Aprile Millo, Dolora Zajick, and Sherrill Milnes. *Verdi's Aida*. Directed by Brian Large. Deutsche Grammaphon, 2000. DVD.

Domingo, Placido. *Wagner's Parsifal (The Story of the Opera)*. Kultur Video, 2001. DVD.

Domingo, Placido, Kiri Te Kanawa, Thomas Allen III, Forbes Robinson, and Robin Leggate. *Puccini's Manon Lescaut*. Directed by Brian Large. 2003. DVD.

Domingo, Placido. *Very Best of Placido Domingo*. EMI Classics, 2003. CD.

Domingo, Placido, Bo Skovhus, Ingvar Wixell, and John Adams. *The Essential Placido Domingo*. Sony, 2004. CD.

Domingo, Placido, Fiorenza Cossotto, Raina Kabaivanska, and Jose van Dam. *Verdi's Il Trovatore*. Directed by Günther Schneider-Siemssen. TdK DVD Video, 2004. DVD.

Domingo, Placido, Renée Fleming, James Morris, IX, and Jane Bunnell. *Verdi's Otello*. Directed by Brian Large. Deutsche Grammaphon, 2004. DVD.

Domingo, Placido, Jessye Norman, Ofra Harnoy. *Symphony for the Spire*. Kultur Video, 2006. DVD.

Domingo, Placido, Anna Netrebko, Rolando Villazon, and Marco Armiliato. *The Berlin Concert: Live from Waldbuhne*. Deutsche Grammaphon, 2007. DVD.

NOTES

1. Paul Driscoll, "The sun never sets: now in the fifth decade of his professional life, Placido Domingo shows no sign of slowing the pace of his multi-dimensional career. Quite the opposite: the shaky state of the music business seems to have filled him with a new urgency," *Opera News*, March 2005, 14.

2. Annallyn Swan and Abigail Kuflik, "Bravissimo, Domingo!" *Newsweek* March 8, 1982, 59.

3. Swan and Kuflik, 62.

4. Rudolph Rauch, "Three-Cornered Hat: Placido Domingo after 30 Years at the Metropolitan Opera (Interview), *Opera News*, September 1998, 24.

5. Driscoll.

6. Swan and Kuflik, 60.

7. Rauch.

8. Rauch.

9. Martin Kettle, "Placido's Pit Stop: While his partners from the Three Tenors are starting to put their feet up, Placido Domingo has set himself an extraordinary challenge: to sing the lead and conduct in the same opera," *The Guardian* July 4, 2003, 2.

10. "Biography of Placido Domingo," The Kennedy Center, http://www.kennedy-center.org/calendar/index.cfm?fuseaction=showIndividual&entitY_id=3525&source_type=A.

11. Daniel Snowman, *The World of Placido Domingo* (Santa Barbara, California and Oxford, England: Landmark Books, 1985). 32–33.

12. Snowman, 177.

13. "Placido Domingo." Contemporary Musicians, Volume 20. Gale Research, 1997. Reproduced in Biography Resource Center. Farmington Hills, Mich.: Thomson Gale. 2008. http://galenet.galegroup.com/servlet/BioRC.

14. Kettle.

15. Snowman, 74.

16. Snowman, 75.

17. "Placido Domingo: Tenor of Our Times," *CBS News*, December 5, 2000, http://www.cbsnews.com/stories/2000/12/05/entertainment/main254768.shtml.

18. "Music," *Hispanic* January/February 1995, http://web.ebscohost.com/ehost/detail?vid=3&hid=3&sid=360975c6-aef8-4b3f-88ce-591539d0fda4%40sessionmgr8.

19. Martha Duffy and Michael Walsh, "They're Baaack!" *Time*, July 18, 1994, 52.

20. Bradley Bambarger, "Domingo Reflects Back, Eyes Future," *Billboard* (December 26, 1998), 1.

21. "John Maguire, "Three Tenors Delight Crowds," *BBC News*, August 8, 2003, http://news.bbc.co.uk/1/hi/england/somerset/3134663.stm.

22. Tim Page, "Opera World Loses a Leading Ambassador," *Washington Post*, September 6, 2007, http://www.washingtonpost.com/wp-dyn/content/article/2007/09/06/AR2007090600137_pf.html.

23. Bambarger.

24. Driscoll.

25. Kettle.

26. Placido Domingo, *Placido Domingo: My First Forty Years*, New York: Alfred A Knopf, 1983, 201.

27. Sorab Modi, "Placido Domingo: Master of the Whole Score." *Americas*, September-October 1997, 22.

28. Bambarger.

29. Martin Kettle, "Placido Plays His Trump," *The Guardian*, March 22, 1999, 13.

30. Domingo.

FURTHER READING

Bambarger, Bradley. "Domingo reflects back, eyes future." *Billboard*, December 26, 1998, 1.

"Domingo, Placido." *Discovering Biography*. Online ed. Detroit: Gale, 2003. http://find.galegroup.com/srcx/infomark.do?&contentSet=GSRC&type=retrieve&tabID=T001&prodId=SRC-1&docId=EJ2102100509&source=gale&srcprod=SRCG&userGroupName=chan86036&version=1.0.

Domingo, Placido. *My First Forty Years*. New York: Penguin, 1984.

Kettle, Martin. "Placido's pit stop: While his partners from the Three Tenors are starting to put their feet up, Placido Domingo has set himself an extraordinary challenge: To sing the lead and conduct in the same opera." *The Guardian*, July 4, 2003, 2.

"Placido Domingo." *Contemporary Musicians*, vol. 20, Gale Research, 1997. Reproduced in Biography Resource Center, Farmington Hills, MI: Thomson Gale, 2008, http://galenet.galegroup.com/servlet/BioRC.

Rauch, Rudolph. "Three-cornered hat: Placido Domingo after 30 years at the Metropolitan Opera (Interview)." *Opera News*, September 1998, 24.

Snowman, Daniel. *The World of Placido Domingo*. Santa Barbara, CA, and Oxford, England: Landmark Books, 1985.

Swan, Annallyn, and Abigail Kuflik. "Bravissimo, Domingo!" *Newsweek*, March 8, 1982, 59.

Walsh, Michael. "Orchestrating a revival: Can supertenor Placido Domingo and conductor Leonard Slatkin turn Washington into the nation's capital of culture?" *Time*, January 27, 1997, 64.

AP Photo

Jaime Escalante

In February 2006, in a packed hall at Capistrano Valley High School in Mission Viejo, California, students gathered to see a legend, a hero. They had seen the movie that told his story; had discussed with parents, teachers, and fellow classmates how his life and mission related to their own; and eagerly looked forward to seeing and meeting in person the famous individual about whom they had heard so much. When he walked into the auditorium to give a speech, they chanted the nickname they had heard in the movie. He warmly waved his approval.

This was not an athlete, a movie star, a singer, or a politician. This was a teacher, Jaime Escalante. His life's work, portrayed in the 1988 film *Stand and Deliver*, had been about motivating Latino youngsters who faced the challenges of culture, language, and low expectations. Now seventy-five years old, he had demonstrated, as no one before, how they could take on those challenges and prevail.

Escalante's essential message was "You have to work hard—you have to have *ganas*," referring to the word he translated as "desire." The term, which he learned as a young boy playing sports, served throughout his life as a motto: to succeed you must have an intense desire and will. It served as a rallying call to his students in the movie: "If you don't have *ganas*, no big deal, I'll give you *ganas*."[1]

Speaking in both English and Spanish, Escalante delivered simple advice: Choose your own destiny; don't fear and shrink from mistakes but learn from them; and, most of all, realize that nobody, even though from better economic conditions and from the dominant culture in which he or she lived, is better than you.

When he finished the speech, the crowd gathered around for autographs and to chat. One girl wore a sweatshirt with his image embossed on it. Another student remarked that Escalante was an idol. In the classes taught by their teacher, Fernanda Villalba, the movie *Stand and Deliver* is required viewing. Villalba's parents showed the film to her and her sister about eighty times, in her estimation. A drawing of Escalante hangs in her classroom.

Now semi-retired and living in his native Bolivia, Escalante had moved to the United States early in his career as a math teacher. At Garfield High School in Los Angeles, beginning in 1981, he taught calculus to inner city youths. So proficient did many of his students become that they took the advanced placement calculus examination, a test so difficult that only two percent of students across the United States even attempt it. Their preparation and their success against all odds defined the work of Escalante and what he taught them. From this teacher, they not only learned calculus; most of all, they learned self-respect.

In Mission Viejo in 2006, the students, with their words and emotions, paid tribute. "He knows your background," said Cindy Alvarez, a sophomore who was inspired to take advanced placement history this year after seeing *Stand and Deliver*. "The stuff that goes on today with us as

Mexicans," she said, "with people not believing in us. Other teachers maybe say it, but he really believes in us."[2]

BOLIVIAN YOUTH

Escalante was born in La Paz, Bolivia, on December 31, 1930. Both of his parents, Zenobio and Sara Escalante, were teachers who worked in a small, isolated Indian village called Achacachi, high on a plateau in the Andes Mountains. The Aymara and Quechua Indians who lived in the village traced their ancestors back to the days of the Inca Empire. In the early years of his life, Escalante's parents and grandparents gave him his first lessons in reading and counting. His mother and his maternal grandfather, Jose Gutierrez, a retired teacher, were especially diligent in feeding his young, racing mind with riddles and games, many of which were mathematically oriented. Escalante later said of his mother:

> When I was a kid she asked me to take a basket of oranges; she had me carry that basket to school. I didn't want to carry it. My mom started to explain with the oranges. She said, 'This is a sphere,' and she peeled it, and she said, 'This is the circumference.' And she took a knife and cut, and said, 'This is symmetry.' That impressed me. Later on, when I was in the classroom, and the teacher was talking about that, I pictured it.[3]

His father, oppressed with bouts of alcoholism and depression, was a harsh disciplinarian.

When he was nine years old, Escalante's life was severely disrupted when his parents separated. Sara, along with Jaime, his two sisters Olimpia and Bertha, and his brother Jose, left the mountains and moved to La Paz. Sara took up a teaching job to support the family. The new environment in a large city was difficult at first. After speaking the Aymara language for the first years of his life, the boy now had to learn Spanish. For the first time, he had to adjust to a classroom setting, which seemed confining and stressful. But he quickly adjusted, learning Spanish and also showing a keen intelligence. From early on, he loved practical jokes, some of them more than a little dangerous—he once gave an electrical shock to his sister Bertha using a small generator.

Escalante loved sports—handball, soccer, and basketball. With very little money to afford handballs or other things during his young teenage years, he took a number of odd jobs around La Paz. He worked for both a shoemaker and a tailor.

Escalante's behavior and grades were less than satisfactory, mostly because, as Escalante said later, he could not sit quietly in the classroom. Much of the instruction he found laborious and unchallenging. One of his teachers, Umberto Bilbao, discovered the motivational key that stirred

Escalante's mind—mathematics. As Escalante's grandfather and mother had done years earlier, Bilbao devised activities and games around mathematical equations and principles for the young student, and suddenly the boy's enthusiasm for learning exploded. Escalante remembered the influence of Bilbao:

> I was so active, I couldn't stay still for more than two minutes. I was hyperactive, and my teachers used to complain about that. And I had a teacher that told me, 'I'm going to teach you something that you will remember all your life—fractions.' And he taught me fractions. Those are the ones that motivated me.[4]

Realizing that her son was exceptionally bright, Sara Escalante managed to scrape enough money together to enable him to attend one of the best secondary schools in Bolivia. In 1945, at the age of fourteen, Escalante entered San Calixto High School, founded and run by Jesuit priests. At San Calixto, Escalante's educational road opened up, his mind devouring new concepts not only in mathematics but in chemistry and physics. One of his physics teachers, a French Jesuit named Father Descottes, seemed to Escalante like a magician. His tools were an electric motor, a compass, and a pendulum. So fascinated did the boy become with the physics class that he volunteered to clean the laboratory just to be able to handle the equipment.

Soon, Escalante was borrowing books from his instructors to read after school. His mind was now in full gear; nevertheless, his antics continued, many of them requiring keen intelligence, if less than appropriate behavior. Sometimes the pranks and mischief affected the operation of the school. Escalante once greased the school's main clock located in the tower so that the school bells would ring fifteen minutes early, ending some of the class days for subjects that did not hold his imagination, such as history and religion. When the school principal discovered the culprit of the plot, Escalante was suspended for a week.

On another occasion, Escalante damaged a school desk while fighting with another student. When a teacher informed him that he had to pay a twenty-peso fine to repair the desk, Escalante said that the fine should be divided by three. He would pay one part; the boy he fought would pay another part; and a third boy on his way to help the second boy would pay the last part. The teacher's response: "I don't think we can do that." Escalante responded, "You can't divide by three, sir? I can help you." His exasperated mother and his teachers lived through many such incidents.[5]

After high school, Escalante, at age nineteen, was obligated to serve in the Bolivian army. With Bolivia frequently in a state of political agitation, this could be a dangerous assignment for a young man. Although he did see some limited military action, he fulfilled his obligation safely and returned to La Paz ready to focus on a career.

He decided to become a teacher, following the path of those he most respected. His parents had been teachers. The mentor who had most affected his early educational development, Umberto Bilbao, had been a teacher. When Escalante enrolled at the teacher training college called Escuela/Instituto Normal Superior in La Paz, Bilbao was there to greet him. As Escalante had moved through high school and the military, Bilbao had also been on the move. He was now a professor at Normal Superior and would once again exert his uncommon educational influence on Escalante.

In Escalante's second year at Normal Superior, Bilbao asked the young student to assist him with some of the workshops. Later, he asked Escalante to help with some science classes at another college, the Instituto Americano. For a second-year college student, this kind of assignment was a testament to his unusual talents and promise.

Escalante's work with Bilbao soon paid off in another assignment. The Bolivian government had recently built a new high school for boys and it needed teachers. Although Escalante was only in his second year of college and had not had formal training in teaching techniques, he accepted an offer to become a teacher. He was twenty-one years old.

Villarroel School had a building and three teachers but as yet no students. Because attendance in secondary schools in Bolivia was not required, students and their parents had to be convinced to sign up. Before Escalante could teach, he had to recruit. When the task bogged down, Escalante, whose mind was never far from mathematics or sports, turned to soccer for help. Along with the physical education teacher, he bought several soccer balls and approached children jokingly saying that at this new school all they did was play soccer and the only grades they gave were A's. Could there be anyone interested in such a school?

In the first year, the school attracted sixty students. The boys and their parents were poor, the school had no textbooks, and teachers wrestled with ways to motivate and inspire learning. Escalante remembered the tricks and hands-on methods that he had learned from his parents and Bilbao and began to use them with great effect. The boys did play a lot of *futbol*, but they also began to learn math. And in learning math, they became, under Escalante, a team.

Escalante later said of his early teaching experience: "In 1952, while still an undergraduate in La Paz, Bolivia, I began teaching mathematics and physics.... I found early in my career that children learn faster when learning is fun, when it is a game and a challenge." He cast teacher in the role of the coach, he said, and the students in the role of a team, and he made sure they worked together. "In La Paz, in the fifties and early sixties, our 'opponent' was the annual secondary school mathematics competition. Our goal: to reign as the champion over all the local schools."[6]

Throughout his later career, Escalante would hone and refine his teaching methods; nevertheless, the main approach would not be significantly

A Jaime Escalante Math Trick

In the movie *Stand and Deliver*, actor Edward James Olmos, playing math teacher Jaime Escalante, says to Chuco, a student who is a gang member:

Escalante: Oh! You know the times tables?

Chuco: I know the ones ... twos ... three. (On "three" Chuco makes an obscene gesture to Escalante.)

Escalante: Finger Man. I heard about you. Are you The Finger Man? I'm the Finger Man, too. Do you know what I can do? I know how to multiply by 9! 9 times 3. What you got? 27. 6 times 9. 1, 2, 3, 4, 5, 6. What you got? 54. You wanna hard one? How about 8 times 9? 1, 2, 3, 4, 5, 6, 7, 8. What do you got? 72."

While Escalante was sounding off multiples of nine, he was holding both hands up with his palms facing Chuco. He was demonstrating a way of multiplying by nine by simply counting fingers. As you hold both hands in front of you, each of your fingers from left to right represent the numbers 1 through 10. The finger on the far left represents number 1; the figure on the far right represents the number 10.

When Escalante told Chuco that 9 times 3 equals 27, he demonstrated how to arrive at that figure on his fingers. If you want to multiply 9 by 3, you simply bend the third figure down. The other nine fingers that are not bent will give you the answer. On the left of the bent finger are two fingers. On the right of the bent finger are seven fingers. The answer is 2 and 7 or 27.

When Escalante told Chuco that 9 times 6 equals 54, he bent down his sixth finger from the left. What he had left were five fingers to the left of the bent finger and four fingers to the right of the bent finger. The answer was 5 and 4 or 54.

Sidney Kolpas, "Finger multiplication," *Mathematics Teacher*, April 2002, http://www.pen.k12.va.us/Div/Winchester/jhhs/math/puzzles/finger.html.

different from the approach he took at Villarroel. While teaching at Villarroel, Escalante took on another assignment: He taught a few classes at Bolivar High School. For a young man who was still making his way through college, he was gaining extraordinary teaching experience in Bolivian schools.

In 1954, Escalante earned his college degree. In that same year, he married Fabiola Tapia, a fellow student at Normal Superior. She was the daughter of a family of evangelical Protestants, a distinct religious minority in the largely Catholic Bolivia. Escalante and the dark, attractive Fabiola shared laughs, interests, and a strong and growing bond. In September 1955, they had a son they called Jaime, Jr. (Jaimito).

Escalante's first major teaching assignment was a homecoming: San Calixto, the private school where he first began to display his enormous genius in higher mathematics and science. In the school where he had also displayed a never-ending supply of pranks and practical jokes, he was now a science teacher.

Escalante had reached a comfortable position. He and Fabiola had a house, a son, and a DeSoto sedan. He had developed teaching strategies that clearly motivated his students. But Fabiola, who had relatives in California, often urged Escalante to consider trying his educational techniques in the United States. Not only would a move be worthwhile for his own career, she argued, but it would remove him from the considerable political unrest that continually plagued Bolivia. She feared that Escalante, although not directly involved in the intrigues of party conflict, was increasingly endangered, if merely because of his own success and notoriety. Fabiola was also worried and frustrated about Escalante's social life. Always the first to be invited to a party, he increasingly began to drink too much. She feared for his health. For a time, Escalante did not seriously consider his wife's entreaties to leave Bolivia for the United States. Nevertheless, she refused to let the matter drop.

Escalante put together teams of science students at San Calixto that consistently won city-wide contests against other schools. His teams were also successful in the annual national San Andreas science and mathematics contest, a competition that brought together high school teams from across the country. In 1959, he organized the first national symposium of physics and mathematics instruction for the country's high school teachers.

His energy was extraordinary. With a full teaching schedule, he spent evenings tutoring students and teaching classes at the police academy. After eight years, he seized an opportunity made available by the U.S. government through a program called Alliance for Progress started under the presidency of John F. Kennedy. In 1962, Escalante accepted a Department of State scholarship for Latin American teachers to spend a year in San Juan, Puerto Rico, a U.S. territory.

When he returned to Bolivia, Escalante seemed exhilarated by the experience, interacting with other notable teachers and sharing ideas of education. In addition, in the following year he and the other teachers toured some cities in the United States. He attended an international conference in Pittsburgh, Pennsylvania, toured a physics laboratory in a Tennessee high school, and traveled to Washington, D.C. where he, along with the other teachers, shook the hand of President Kennedy. Perhaps Fabiola was right. Perhaps leaving Bolivia to take on a new challenge was the right step. Perhaps, in this case, he should demonstrate his *ganas*.

In 1963, he told Fabiola that he was ready to take on a new part of his life. Later, he recalled thinking, "I cannot progress here. Fabiola is right. My friends always call me up, have me out for a drink. I'm drinking too much. I am going to succeed. I am going down there to America and I'm going to start from zero."[7]

When the time came for his departure, Escalante could not bear to say goodbye to his mother in person. Instead, he left a note on a half-sheet of paper written in green ink. She would keep it under her pillow for the rest of her life. "God grant that I may return home someday to live in peace," he said. "It is my destiny to elevate the name of my family and I am optimistic that I will succeed. Dear Sarita, don't worry about your son Jaime, who always has you in his thoughts."[8]

NEWLY ARRIVED IN THE UNITED STATES

In late December, 1963, Escalante arrived at the Los Angeles International Airport. Leaving behind Fabiola and his son until he could settle down and find a job, he began life in the United States at the residence of his brother-in-law, Sam Tapia in Pasadena, California. Before his departure, the Escalantes sold their house and most other belongs. Fabiola and Jaimito would stay with family members in Bolivia until Escalante felt ready to ask them to join him in the United States.

Most of the money he brought with him from Bolivia went immediately for a green 1964 Volkswagen Beetle. In Los Angeles, one needed a car to get around and Escalante had always wanted a Volkswagen.

Escalante faced numerous challenges. He could not begin to teach immediately because his degree in Bolivia did not meet the qualifications for a teaching certificate in the United States. Also, he could not speak English. At age thirty-three, learning a new language could be daunting, especially for someone eager to enroll in a university to fulfill the requirements for a teaching position. He took classes at Pasadena City College and hired tutors. When he took the two-hour math placement test, including calculus and trigonmetry, he handed in the paper in thirty minutes. He answered every question correctly.

In the meantime, he took on a variety of jobs to support himself. He worked as a janitor, handyman, busboy, and then cook at Van de Kamp's coffee shop, across from the college. Later, at the Burrough's Corporation's manufacturing plant, he worked in the parts department and then as an electronics technician. His keen abilities in mechanics and computer electronics and his ability to solve puzzling production problems impressed his superiors so much that they continued to give him increasingly responsible positions. They sent him to Guadalajara, Mexico, to teach engineering seminars and to Europe to make technical presentations. They also paid his night-school tuition.

In 1969, Fabiola gave birth to a second son, Fernando. Jaimito, now in his teens, had arrived in the United States with his mother in May 1964. He excelled in school and was especially fascinated by electronics. Father and son would often talk about physics and calculus over the years, and the father's influence proved lasting. Jaimito would enter the California State Polytechnic University in Pomona to prepare for a career in electrical engineering.

Meanwhile, after working for five years at the coffee shop and eight years at Burroughs, Escalante continued to work toward earning the necessary college requirements to teach in the United States. After taking courses for several years at Pasadena City College, he enrolled at California State University, Los Angeles, to complete a degree in mathematics. He studied calculus under the noted matethematics professor Louis Leithold.

Even after earning the degree in mathematics, however, Escalante still needed additional preparation to teach in California's public schools. In 1973, Escalante received a National Science Foundation scholarship that enabled him to complete the degree at California State and thus fulfill the necessary requirements for the teaching credential.

A year later, after ten years of struggling to learn the English language, of working full-time at a variety of jobs, and, finally, earning a degree and teaching certificate, Escalante was ready to begin what he regarded as his life's mission. He was again ready to teach, this time in the United States.

TEACHING AT GARFIELD HIGH

Escalante received several offers from the Los Angeles Unified School District officials in 1974. Because of his Latino background, they asked him to pick from high schools in different areas of the city, all of which had large Latino student populations. He chose Garfield High School in East Los Angeles. He was asked to teach computer science, a prospect that excited Escalante. It would combine his teaching skills, his mathematics genius, and a great deal of mechanical knowledge gained during his years of work at Burroughs.

Garfield's educational problems were emblematic of those facing other urban schools in working-class immigrant communities. It was overcrowded. It had too many unqualified teachers, too few textbooks, and not enough guidance counselors. Its facilities were outdated. Few students leaving Garfield went on to attend college; many were not able even to get skilled work. Many of the boys were part of a growing gang population.

Two of the "East Los" high schools, Garfield and Roosevelt, were built in the 1920s to house about 1,000 students each. They each now housed several thousand. More than half of the children under the age of eighteen lived in poverty; more than fifty percent of the adults over twenty-five years old did not have a high school diploma. Some of the families had recently arrived from Mexico. Many of the families were large, with several children, and a large percentage spoke only Spanish in their homes. At the time of Escalante's arrival at Garfield, more than 75 percent of Latino children scored in the bottom half of standardized achievement tests nationwide.

In 1968, six years before Escalante's arrival, hundreds of Chicano students from several high schools in East Los Angeles, including Garfield, began a political campaign protesting poor quality education, overcrowded conditions, and racist curriculums. In early March, they walked out of their classes. They called the protests "blowouts." In the end, city education officials offered a few token responses to the protests. They developed courses in Chicano studies, for example. But overall the city did little to change conditions. When Escalante arrived at Garfield, an atmosphere of resistance and bitterness still pervaded much of the school population. For the newest addition to the faculty at Garfield, it was, indeed, a challenging time.

When Escalante came to Garfield High in 1974, the Western Association of Schools had threatened to revoke its accreditation. Order and discipline had disintegrated at the school to the point that teenage gang members were setting up turf boundaries on the campus. Teachers faced problems that seemed almost insurmountable—drug use, violence, and ever-growing indifference.

Escalante's first day at Garfield was not encouraging—and this was the day before the students arrived. At a teacher's meeting the day before the school year opened, he soon realized the difficulties that he was confronting. He had been hired to teach computer science. He had spent much of the summer carefully designing materials to introduce the students to computers. But now, a day before the classes were to begin, he learned that the school did not have any computers. The school administration had asked for computers, but, like many of its requests, had been turned down.

Instead, Escalante suddenly prepared to teach math with outdated textbooks. As he walked into the classroom for the first time, he looked around to see litter, walls and desks covered with graffiti, and a restless group of teenagers, many wearing gang colors. It took several minutes just to produce a semblance of quiet and order.

After the first few classes, Escalante realized the magnitude of the problem. He did not blame the motley group of students he saw in front of him; he blamed a system that had utterly failed to provide anything in the way of a decent chance for them—from ignorance and apathy of parents, cultural dislocation, language barriers, poverty, teacher weariness, and school facilities that appeared to be several decades behind. The school did not foster a culture of learning but merely one of survival. It was overwhelmed by social forces and a spirit, not of moving forward and of opportunity, but of disillusionment. Most of all, he reasoned, the students did not learn in this environment because so little was expected of them.

Escalante was not one to back down from a challenge. After all, his own life story attested to his grit and determination. But even for him, the situation he saw at Garfield was more daunting than he ever imagined. Escalante was so discouraged by the first few days at the school that he actually called the Burroughs Corporation about returning to his old job. Nevertheless, as the days went on, his spirit revived. He began with the classroom. If this was the place for achievement, he thought, it had to look like it. He enlisted the help of some of the students in scraping off the ancient, encrusted paint and graffiti from the walls and desks and repainting them. He asked the class about their heroes. Soon, posters of athletes graced the walls. Escalante added his own posters: "Mission Possible" and "I'll Be a Success." But posters alone, he knew, would do little. The students needed discipline and goals.

Early on, he decided that the chaos he encountered in his first days at the school was intolerable. He simply would not accept it. He refused to allow late students into the class. He sent scores of students to the principal's office for what had in earlier years been considered minor disruptions. He made certain that students had the right textbooks and that they did not mutilate them, as almost all of them had done before.

He tried as best he could to enlist the aid of the parents. It helped greatly that he was Latino, could speak their language, and knew first-hand their economic struggles. But he infuriated more than one parent with calls at 5:00 A.M. in the morning. He wanted to make sure, at least at that hour, that he would be able to contact them. But all of it—the pressure on both students and parents—had Escalante's touch of effervescent temperament, optimism, and quick humor. He could be intimidating and rough; he could also be charming and understanding.

He gave the students nicknames, such as "Lieutenant" to a boy who walked stiffly and "Fingerman" to a boy who counted on his fingers. The students gave him a nickname—"Kemo Sabe," the name given to Lone Ranger by his sidekick Tonto. The name meant "wise one." He chided them, bantered with them, and prodded them to rise to the challenge. He even kept a soft, red velvet pillow at the ready to gently bop on the head any student whose eyes seemed in the process of glazing over.

His swirl of classroom antics, from the simple motivational sayings to the jokes and quips, was all designed to keep them moving forward, to make them realize their individuality and potential. He often told them they were "gifted," a term that few of these children had ever been called before. He used every angle he could think of to motivate the students. To some of the campus athletes, Escalante offered a challenge. Meet him on Saturday morning on the handball court, he said. Escalante would take on the student at handball using either hand the boy demanded. In addition, Escalante would give his opponent points. If the student beat Escalante, the teacher said, he would get an "A." If Escalante won, the student would complete a difficult homework assignment. A number of students challenged. None of them won. All of them, however, learned more mathematics.

On one occasion, the students entered the class to find Escalante dressed in a chef's hat and white apron that he still had from his days at Van de Kamp's restaurant. To the startled and amused group, the teacher pulled out a thick meat cleaver and began splitting apples into various sections on a cutting board. Some of apples were cut into thirds, others into fourths, and others into fifths. He passed out some of the apples and told the students to dig in. After one of the students had eaten one of the pieces of her apple, Escalante asked what percentage she had left. He did the same thing with several other students. When one boy began to answer the question after eating one of the pieces of his apple, Escalante quickly scooped up one of the pieces and gulped it down. The boy had to quickly revise his figure. To all of these students, fractions were now more than figures on a paper; they had seen a demonstration they would never forget.

Progress was slow in the first couple of years, but Escalante could see a steadily upward progression. Some of his students agreed to take algebra courses far beyond the mathematical level at which any of his students had been the day he walked into Garfield.

In 1976, Escalante and Fabiola took their two sons to visit relatives in Bolivia. Escalante had not been home in twelve years. As the family made the rounds visiting his mother, who was convalescing in the hospital, and other members of the family, they went back to the markets, to the lakes, and to the restaurants they had enjoyed years before. Although the pleasant memories flooded back and although family members could not understand why this trip was temporary, why Escalante would not move back to Bolivia, he did not hesitate to return to Los Angeles. Room 233 awaited him.

PREPARING STUDENTS FOR A SPECIAL TEST

In 1978 Escalante seized on an idea that on its face seemed almost preposterous. He would find enough students at Garfield to compose a team; its goal—to prepare to take the advanced placement calculus exam. This was a national, college-level preparatory examination taken by only three percent of the senior high school students across the country who planned to enter a college or university the next year.

Garfield's administrators opposed the grand idea, which was not surprising. Indeed, during his early years at the school, one assistant principal threatened him with dismissal for acting outside the school's fixed hours and methods. He came to school too early, he said, left too late, and was introducing concepts and practices not within the structured curriculum. Escalante was also, in the eyes of some of his fellow teachers, simply a nuisance. He did not hide his contempt for those he felt were not giving their best to the students. On some occasions, he reported what he saw as laziness and incompetence to school officials and asked that they insist on better teaching performance.

The tenuous relationship between Escalante and his superiors improved dramatically, however, with the arrival of a new principal, Henry Gradillas. A veteran teacher in inner city schools including Garfield, Gradillas saw Escalante much differently from how many of the teachers and supervisors did. Here was a teacher, Gradillas believed, who understood how to connect with these children more directly than any other teacher he had ever seen.

When Gradillas took over the reins at Garfield, he not only eased the pressure on Escalante to conform, he encouraged the innovation. Gradillas overhauled the mathematics curriculum at Garfield, reducing the number of basic math classes and requiring that the students taking basic math also had to take algebra. He denied extracurricular activities to students who failed to maintain a C average and new students who failed basic skills tests. He was determined that Garfield would no longer be on the edge of losing its accreditation. And as for Escalante's idea for fielding a team of students to take the advanced placement calculus exam, Gradillas was all for it.

It was not as though Escalante wanted to find just one student at Garfield who would accept the challenge. That achievement, itself, would have been remarkable, given the academic levels at which most students at the low-income, inner-city school performed. But Escalante had something else in mind. The concept of a team, of a group of individuals who had each others' backs, a group motivated to beat the odds and the expectations, might be just crazy enough, just brash enough, to pique their interests.

Escalante saw the math test as a perfect tool to unite the students in a team effort. "Their focus easily shifts to other more pressing problems, particularly when they are living in poverty," Escalante later explained. "The [advanced placement] test provides the formidable outside 'opponent' that galvanizes the students and teacher in a united charge...."[9]

It was an in-your-face kind of gesture that, in a startling and marvelous way, sparked a flurry of talk around the school. Soon, a number of students came to Escalante wanting to know what kind of commitment it would take and what kind of chance did they actually have of succeeding. He did not disguise or soften the challenge. This was bases loaded, bottom of the ninth kind of stuff. This was stuff, he said, that would make the papers, that would make the parents and kids over at Beverly Hills High School wonder what in the world had happened.

He would be the coach. His friend Ben Jimenez, another teacher at Garfield, would be his assistant coach. This would normally be a four-year process, at the least. Before students could take calculus they would have to gain the necessary background knowledge, from algebra to trigonometry. Yet Escalante was determined to make an impact almost immediately. He tried to persuade the school to allow him to teach a summer school course that would lay the foundation for calculus. The budget made that request impossible. He looked without success to local colleges.

Undeterred, he managed to find fourteen Garfield students who agreed to meet before and after school and on Saturdays to gain the necessary background to take calculus. Within two weeks, seven had dropped the class. Two left shortly thereafter. The team now had only three girls and two boys. The students and Escalante worked relentlessly. When the time approached for the students to take the examination, they organized car washes and sold candy apples to pay for the administrative fees. In May 1979, four of the five students passed the test, the first students in the history of Garfield High School to pass an advanced placement calculus exam.

The word got around Garfield. With the success of the four students, others with a facility for mathematics were not as intimidated by the prospect of joining Escalante's team. Suddenly, at Garfield, calculus did not seem like some foreign or interplanetary phenomenon. With hard work and dedication, others began to think that perhaps they could also pull off what seemed only a year before an impossible feat.

By the second year, the small group of students increased from five to ten. He tried to make them like a group of athletes training for the Olympics. Constantly emphasizing the idea of team and competition, Escalante even gave jackets to the members with their names on them and the words "Advanced Placement" on the backs. Beginners wore white jackets, second-year members wore red, third-year members wore blue, and the seniors wore black. The give and take in the classroom had the aura of a team meeting. He often opened the sessions like a pep rally. From inside Escalante's room, the sounds of Queen's rendition of "We Are the Champions" began with his signal:

> Thump, thump, Clap.
> Thump, thump, Clap.

With the entire room now thumping feet in unison, they built the sound to a crescendo—"We will rock you!"—and then started a wave row by row as if they were in a stadium. "Yip, yip, yipeeeeeeeeeeeeeeeeeeeeeeyyooooouuu," Esclante would shout.[10] And the jargon was always about sports. Escalante explained: "For example, I introduce the concept of illegal defense—that in mathematics you cannot divide by zero. So I want this to be clear, and I put a zero denominator and the whole class they shout 'illegal defense!' And I ask them, you're going to have to help me out. If somebody comes and asks, 'What's illegal defense?' They going to say, 'You can't divide by zero.' With each new concept I have to do exactly the same thing; I have to use some toy or something for the concept itself. So from that you start."[11]

Of the ten students who took the advanced placement tests in the second year of the program, eight passed. Team "Advanced Placement" was maintaining its 80 percent success rate.

The following year, Escalante involved the parents to a greater degree in the effort. He devised "contracts" between himself, the students, and the parents for all to sign. The students agreed to adhere to the study and attendance schedule, parents agreed to participate, and Escalante agreed to teach them everything they needed to know to pass the tests. The results for 1981: Of the fifteen students who joined the team, fourteen passed. The success rate had progressed even higher.

To some of the teachers and administrators at Garfield, Escalante's unusual pedagogical methods were a form of showmanship. He was mostly a loner and grandstander, they complained, attempting to gain publicity. Others, however, quickly became convinced that the middle-aged, Latino math teacher was on to something big. Those students, now numbering twenty-three in the third year of the program, had achieved a level of accomplishment never before realized in any public school they had ever heard of, much less in an inner-city school racked by the usual deprivations. They felt his passion for achievement and shared it.

LEARNING, NOT CHEATING

In 1982, Escalante and the calculus program he founded at Garfield faced a crisis. The story of that year at Garfield and the resolution of the crisis would become national news. It would inspire a movie. It would have much to say to educators, parents, school systems, and to all who assumed that lower-class Latino children could not perform academically as well as children from other economic and cultural backgrounds.

Escalante's calculus team was now as much a part of Garfield as its athletic teams. Each year the number of students attempting the challenge had increased; each year the team achieved astonishing success rates.

The early spring of 1982 was tough on Escalante. During one of the classes, a sharp pain racked his side. Leaving the room to try to get a drink of water, he began to walk down the stairs and fell, hitting his head. At the hospital, they treated his head wound and, at first, were concerned that he may have had a heart attack. Later tests revealed gallbladder difficulties. Undeterred, he returned to the classroom a few days later. The incident demonstrated to Escalante the high regard in which he was held by the students. They rallied to his side. Realizing that he always gave to them his best effort, they would give the same to him.

And now, on May 19, in Room 411 of Garfield's main building, a team of eighteen students prepared to take the test. Andreda Pruitt, the head counselor at Garfield, spread the desks across the room and closely monitored the examination as required by the Educational Testing Service (ETS). The eighteen students, many of them quite tired from anxiety, lack of sleep, and extra studying, opened their booklets and began.

As the students first looked at the test, several felt a sense of relief. They soon realized how Escalante's teaching had made the problems seem routine. They had practiced similar problems late at night and at times during the days when other kids were doing the many other things that kids do. They had put in the time, made the sacrifices, and now realized the reward. As they began filling the circles on the computerized answer sheets with their number 2 pencils, as they scribbled notes on scratch paper, they moved swiftly through the questions. Most of them finished early. Although they would have to wait the usual two months before learning the results, many felt not only relieved that the test was over but even confident.

Escalante was also confident. This had been an enthusiastic and disciplined group. Nevertheless, when he heard the results from the Garfield counselor that summer, his spirit soared. All eighteen students had passed. This kind of performance was not only unusual for a school in the inner city; this was unprecedented for any high school. A jubilant sense of victory surrounded the announcement of the scores. All along, Escalante had emphasized that this was a team. He had stressed teamwork, had pushed and pushed the players in their practice and drills, and had given them the sense that they were all on a mission to defeat an opponent. The opponent was the test and they had won, resoundingly.

They did not have long to savor the moment. Soon, fourteen of the eighteen students opened letters sent by certified mail from the ETS. The letters were not congratulations on a major achievement. The letters gave the stunning news that a board of review for the testing organization had "found close agreement of your answers with those on another answer sheet from the same test center. Such agreement is unusual and suggests that copying occurred. The Board doubts that the grades are valid...." In other words, the ETS accused the students of cheating.[12]

On a Saturday afternoon in late July at the family house on Orange Avenue in Monrovia, Escalante answered the phone. On the line was one of the eighteen students, Elsa Bolado. Hurt, angry, confused, she read to Escalante from the letter. Soon, Escalante heard from other students. They all had the same stories. When Escalante questioned them regarding the accusation, they told him there was no way any of them could have cheated, even if they had tried. They all reported that the monitor, Mrs. Pruitt, had nearly hovered over them while they worked.

At the ETS, readers had noticed that several of the papers from the class at Garfield had similar incorrect answers to one of the questions and that the methods at arriving at those answers had striking similarities. After discussions with a number of reviewers, the ETS had decided that the coincidence had been too great, that the only conclusion they could draw from the similarities was that fourteen of the eighteen students among the Garfield class had copied each other.

Escalante was just as baffled as any of Garfield's administrators and the eighteen students involved as to what the next step should be. The ETS asked the fourteen students to take the test over again. Should Escalante fight the demand, claiming that the bureaucracy had once again let down an inner-city school? Or should he ask that the students swallow their hurt and anger, and prove to the ETS and to the world that the Garfield team was made up not of cheaters but of kids who had worked hard, learned the material, and deserved to be commended, not condemned.

One of the fourteen students, Fernando Bocanegra, wrote to ETS explaining what might have happened in Room 411 two months earlier. "Our instructor did not accept any other method of solving problems than his own," Bocanegra said. "Consequently, our steps in solving calculus problems were obviously similar if not the same." Other students gave much the same response to ETS in attempting to explain the similarity in answers and methods.[13]

The story about the calculus students at Garfield soon began to generate publicity in the Los Angeles area. A number of prominent Latino organizations and activists charged that the ETS had singled out Garfield. They charged that bias had clouded the judgment of ETS and that the idea that all eighteen students from one inner-city class could conceivably pass the test was just too much for them to accept.

After some angry exchanges with ETS administrators, Escalante decided to advise the students to retake the test. With the story gaining momentum, he believed, a refusal to retake the test might lead the general public to believe that the accusations were true. Escalante had enough confidence in the abilities of the students to believe that they not only passed the test the first time around but could do so again.

He asked the fourteen students to gather in Room 233 to reach a decision. He suggested that it would be best if they agreed to take the test. He then left the room for them to decide. Although convinced they had been unfairly treated, twelve of the fourteen students agreed to take the test. When they gathered together again, smiles broke out. They were doing this for Escalante, they said—for the dedication he had shown toward them. The team would take on yet another challenge.

On August 31, 1982, they again sat for the test. This time, two administrators from the ETS acted as proctors. On September 13, ETS reported the results to Gradillas: All of the students passed. When word reached the local community that the Garfield students had all passed the test, it was as if the entire neighborhood had won some sort of championship.

Many mathematics teachers at other high schools were astonished. After all, it had been two months since the original examination. The students had been engaged in various summer activities and, for the most part, had put calculus far out of their immediate thoughts. To respond the way they did reflected not only their own abilities, determination, and will, but also the remarkable teaching influence of Escalante.

The story even reached Bolivia. As Escalante's sister, Olimpia, was listening to the radio on La Voz de America (Voice of America), she heard a short report about a class of Latino students in Los Angeles who had been accused of cheating on an examination. The announcer went on: "but Señor Escalante had them take the test over again and they all passed... a wonderful moment for a very good teacher." A tearful sister called her mother to tell her the news.[14]

STAND AND DELIVER (1988)

Over the next few years Escalante's program grew at a phenomenal pace. Each successive year, the number of students on the team grew. In 1983 both enrollment in his class and the number of students passing the advanced placement calculus test more than doubled, with thirty-three student taking the exam and thirty passing it. In 1987, seventy-three Garfield students passed the test, and another twelve students passed a new, accelerated version of the test.

The 1982 story about the charges of cheating and the vindication of the students became a local legend that drew the attention of educators around the city. Many asked to sit in on Escalante's classes. But the story was now about to reach an international audience. Film producer Tom Musca and director Ramón Menéndez became convinced that the students' scores would not have been questioned by ETS if they had not been from a predominantly Latino community. This story of triumph over prejudice, they reasoned, had an unquestionable heroic element that would play well on the big screen. They approached Escalante about his willingness to participate in the making of a film.

At first skeptical about the venture and, as ever, extremely pressed for time, Escalante was at first cool to the idea. Nevertheless, when the filmmakers were able to land the heralded actor Edward James Olmos to play Escalante in the film, the teacher became increasingly interested. Olmos himself had grown up in East Los Angeles. Like many of Escalante's students, he had overcome tough odds to succeed. A unique talent, Olmos not only gave back to the community of his origins, but he aggressively worked to improve its conditions. His off-screen activities to help the poor and disadvantaged had distinguished him as much as his respectable movie career. Escalante, with the support of Garfield's principal Gradillas, agreed to allow Olmos to accompany him eighteen hours a day for one month to prepare for the role.

Written and directed by Ramón Menéndez, starring Olmos as Escalante, Lou Diamond Phillips as student Angel Guzman, and Andy Garcia as a representative of the ETS, *Stand and Deliver* was released by Warner Brothers Pictures in 1988. Unique in subject with a brilliant acting performance by Olmos, the film was a box office success and won several awards.

The hours Olmos spent listening to Escalante in the classroom translated profoundly and directly to the screen. In the film, when Escalante first meets his class of Latino students he declares,

> There will be no free rides, no excuses. You already have two strikes against you: your name and your complexion. Because of those two strikes, there are some people in this world who will assume that you know less than you do. Math is the great equalizer.... When you go for a job, the person giving you that job will not want to hear your problems; ergo, neither do I. You're going to work harder here than you've ever worked anywhere else. And the only thing I ask from you is *ganas*.[15]

Looking back on the performance, Olmos said, "The film is really about the triumph of the human spirit.... It's about something we've lost—the joy of learning, the joy of making our brains develop."[16]

After the release of the film, Olmos enlisted the help of several major corporations in a project to place a copy of *Stand and Deliver* in every school, library, prison, hospital, youth organization, and other groups that he thought could benefit from the message of the film. Through the film, the world came to know of Escalante's work. Suddenly, he was an international figure, a heroic figure at a time when questions about education and race and immigration swirled in contentious debate. He had demonstrated that a group of so-called underprivileged children could not only succeed but excel, given the motivation, encouragement, and a simple chance.

The film earned Escalante an invitation to the White House to meet President Ronald Reagan. Vice President George Bush visited Garfield High in the spring of 1988 and even mentioned Escalante during one of his presidential debates with Bill Clinton. Escalante was soon hosting a Public Broadcasting Service series on math and science that won a number of broadcasting and education awards. Titled *Futures 1* and *Futures 2*, the shows demonstrated mathematical applications in careers, such as fashion, engineering, space exploration, and sports. They included guest appearances by celebrities. The series won a George Foster Peabody Award in 1990.

The publicity surrounding the noted math teacher translated into more than $750,000 in corporate contributions to Garfield. The world of Jaime Escalante had spiraled to a height of success that he could never have thought possible. Nevertheless, with fame and publicity came tensions and challenges. No longer would he work at his craft in relative obscurity, doing those things that made possible his remarkable achievements.

MOVING FROM GARFIELD

If Jamie Escalante had made his own personal mark in showing that inner-city children could compete in even the most difficult academic areas, his rise to fame had increased tensions among his fellow teachers. Garfield High School was now a spot on the national map, known not only to Los Angeles residents but now to casual moviegoers around the world. But for Escalante's colleagues, he had made their jobs more uncomfortable. He had raised the educational bar, and many felt he had done it at their expense and the expense of the majority of students.

Yes, some fellow teachers said, Escalante's unique methods and irrepressible personality had achieved near miraculous results with the calculus students. But they were a small percentage of the student body. His methods, they believed, would not work with the vast majority of students. His success, they reasoned, had much to do with his own unusual motivational techniques and a distinct personality that most teachers could not possibly imitate. They increasingly resented his fame and adulation.

He had never been close to most of the teachers at Garfield. He regarded many of them as incompetent and lazy and was not reluctant to relate that opinion to Principal Gradillas. He could not understand why his own prodigious energy could not be matched by others. When criticized for working outside school policy and for creating dissension among the faculty, he refused to back down.

The tensions between Escalante and most of the Garfield faculty continued to grow. Nevertheless, Escalante and his fellow math teachers, led by Ben Jimenez and Angelo Villavicencio, continued to take on a greater number of students who wanted to become part of the math team. In 1987, 129 of Garfield's math students took the advanced placement calculus tests. They achieved an above average 66 percent pass rate. The number of Garfield students taking the test that year was more than all but four high schools, private and public, in the entire United States. The program was also setting high marks in algebra and trigonometry.

By 1991, 570 students, ranging from beginning algebra to advanced calculus, took part. Escalante hoped that someday the program would involve more than a thousand students. But the hope faded away in bitterness and jealously. Increasingly isolated and fatigued, Escalante decided to leave Garfield in 1991. Most of the math enrichment teachers soon followed him.

A major reason for Escalante's final break with Garfield was his insistence on an open admission policy. Calculus grew so popular at Garfield that classes grew beyond the thirty-five-student limit set by the contract with the school and the teachers' union. Although Escalante would have preferred to keep the classes below the limit, he did not want to deny the opportunity to students willing to put in the time and effort that he demanded. In the end, the school simply did not have the number of qualified teachers or the resources to keep up with the growing demands of Escalante's powerhouse math program. Rather than compromise, Escalante decided to leave.

It was never the students at Garfield that Escalante resented, even though each was a special and sometimes very frustrating challenge. It was never the students that incurred his special wrath. It was the bureaucracy, the reluctance to break away from standard patterns and old thinking, and the weak-kneed acceptance of stereotypes that brought on his inner fury.

He was more than sixty-one years old now. His sons were already successful. Jaime, Jr., was an electrical engineer, and Fernando had almost finished his civil engineering program at California Polytechnic. He and Fabiola looked forward to starting over at a new place. They decided on Sacramento.

Escalante chose Hiram Johnson High School. Located in a working class section of the city, the school was ethnically diverse but far different from Garfield. In his years in Bolivia and at Garfield, Escalante's students had been almost entirely Latino. Here, the population was almost equally divided among European-American, Asian-American, African-American, and Mexican-American students.

In 1990, only six students at Hiram Johnson had passed the advanced placement calculus exam. Escalante looked forward to putting together a new team of youngsters. Before long, the classroom at Hiram Johnson looked very much like the one at Garfield. Up went the posters with inspirational sayings along with the images of sports figures. He soon found money for a Saturday enrichment class. He soon had rolled out his pet phrases, his math tricks, and his repartee with the students. Within three years, the number of successful advanced placement students had tripled.

Escalante received the Presidential Medal for Excellence in Education in 1988. In the same year, the Organization of American States also honored Escalante with the Andres Bello Award by the Organization of American States, named after the esteemed Venezuelan poet and scholar regarded as an intellectual father of South America. Escalante also continued his indefatigable outside work, writing a calculus workbook and appearing on television and as a speaker at schools and companies. He returned often to Los Angeles to seek out the other math instructors and students with whom he had worked so closely. In the summers, he taught classes in Bolivia.

Finally, in 2001, at age seventy-one, after his enormous successes in the United States, Escalante decided to retire from his gruelling, self-imposed teaching rigors and to return to Bolivia. He and Fabiola moved from Sacramento to Cochamba, Bolivia, Fabiola's hometown. Even in retirement, Escalante maintained a part-time teaching schedule at a local university.

WHAT HE STOOD FOR AND DELIVERED

Jaime Escalante's program was not magic. His teaching prowess, although substantial, was also not magic. So what made it all work?

Recent studies point to simple conclusions. Escalante understood what so many educators and the public failed to grasp decades after his experience at Garfield. The success of the students rested with the challenge and their motivation to take on the challenge. It was not only honor roll students who benefited from attempting the advanced placement and international baccalaureate courses but average students as well.

Data from Texas schools in 2004 suggested that the experience for all students who attempted the advanced placement and international baccalaureate courses benefited them in the long run, regardless of whether they passed the tests. Students who went through the process, even with low grade point averages, who put in the time and effort, who were exposed to the degree of difficulty demanded in the tests, were substantially more likely to advance to a college degree than those students who did not try.

Jay Mathews, a reporter for the *Washington Post* who wrote a biography on Escalante, read the study and had this advice for every advanced placement and international baccalaureate teacher in the country:

> Copy that Texas chart, blow it up to 3-by-4-foot size and tape it to the wall of his or her classroom. And every parent and every student in every high school that restricts access to advanced placement and international baccalaureate courses should wave the chart at the principals, school superintendents, school board members and other thick-headed people refusing to open the doors to those courses for everyone who wants to take them. Escalante, enjoying a happy retirement in Bolivia, isn't around to stick his fingers in people's faces anymore, so we are going to have to do it for him.[17]

Escalante once said:

> The important thing is the kid has to be ready to learn, willing to learn. Otherwise, it's difficult for us. The minds of the kids are on basketball, music, or copying those funny haircuts, and so on. In order to motivate them, we have to touch those points they will remember. We have to use that to reach kids in different ethnic groups ... pull some examples from the Hispanic community, the Black community, the Anglo community, the Vietnamese community here, and so on, to motivate.[18]

Most of all, Escalante showed that there can be tremendous untapped genius in ordinary people. Inspired to release their own intellectual energy, children have a fighting chance. That genius was in his students. Many went to college, and quite a few went on to successful professional careers, a number of them putting to use the mathematics and physics skills they learned in his classes.

Armando Islas, dentist and surgeon, was the first in his family to go to college. Educated at Harvard University, University of California San Francisco Medical Center, and other institutions, he said of Escalante, "He let you experience different things. He told you, 'You can do anything you want to do and nobody can put a ceiling on how high you can go.'"

Angel Navarro, an attorney with the Office of the Federal Public Defender in Pasadena, California, said, "There isn't a day that goes by that

I don't think about the lessons we learned in Mr. Escalante's class. We apply those every day in my job as an attorney."

Juanita Gutierrez, now a director of public relations at a major bank, says that the experience with Escalante's program "changed my life forever." After leaving high school, she received a master's degree in Comparative Politics from the London School of Economics and a bachelor's degree from Wellesley College in Massachusetts.

Sergio Valdez became a Senior Mechanical Engineer at the Jet Propulsion Laboratory (JPL). The JPL is managed for the National Aeronautics and Space Administration by the California Institute of Technology. It is the leading U.S. center for robotic exploration of the solar system. Valdez is one of several of Escalante's students who have worked for JPL. Valdez designed the imaging instruments for the earth-orbiting Active Mirror Telescope. He said, "In the work we did in the classroom he just basically lowered the barriers. He brought on the work and we responded."[19]

NOTES

1. Sam Miller, "Still delivering his message: Renowned math teacher Jaime Escalante offers math and career tips to students in Mission Viejo," The Orange County Register, February 24, 2006, http://www.ocregister.com/ocregister/news/atoz/article_1015711.php.

2. Miller.

3. "Excellence: Do It Right The First Time: An Interview With Jaime Escalante," http://www.govtech.net/magazine/visions/feb98vision/escalante.php.

4. "Excellence...."

5. Jay Mathews, *Escalante: The Best Teacher in America* (New York: Henry Holt & Company, 1988), 28.

6. Jaime Escalante and Jack Dirmann, "The Jaime Escalante Math Program," *The Journal of Negro Education*, Summer, 1990, 407–423.

7. Matt Meier, *Notable Latino Americans* (Westport, Connecticut: Greenwood Press, 1997), 126–7.

8. Mathews, 52.

9. Escalante and Dirmann.

10. Mathews, 258.

11. "Excellence...."

12. Mathews, 17.

13. Mathews, 160.

14. Mathews, 173–4.

15. "Memorable quotes for Stand and Deliver (1988)," http://www.imdb.com/title/tt0094027/quotes.

16. Hispanic Heritage Biographies, Gale Resources: Edward James Olmos, http://www.gale.com/free_resources/chh/bio/olmos_e.htm.

17. Jay Mathews, "See, If Pushed, Kids Deliver," *Washington Post*, December 5, 2004, http://www.washingtonpost.com/ac2/wp-dyn/A34111-2004Dec3?language=printer.

18. "Interview with Jaime Escalante," *Technos Quarterly*, Spring *1993*, http://www.ait.net/technos/tq_02/1escalante.php

19. Last four quotes from "Jaime Escalante's Students: Where Are They Now?" http://www.thefutureschannel.com/jaime_escalante/jaime_escalante_students.php

SUGGESTED READING

Escalante, Jaime, and Jack Dirmann. "The Jaime Escalante Math Program." *The Journal of Negro Education*, Summer, 1990, 407–423.

"Excellence: Do It Right the First Time: An Interview with Jaime Escalante." http://www.govtech.net/magazine/visions/feb98vision/escalante.php.

"Jaime Escalante's students: Where Are They Now?" http://www.thefutureschannel.com/Jaime_escalante/jaime_escalante_students.php.

Jesness, Jerry. "*Stand and Deliver* revisited: The untold story behind the famous rise—and shameful fall—of Jaime Escalante, America's master math teacher" *Reason Online*, July 2002, http://www.reason.com/news/show/28479.html.

Mathews, Jay. *Escalante: The Best Teacher in America* (New York: Henry Holt & Company, 1988).

Mathews, Jay. "See, if pushed, kids deliver." *Washington Post*, December 5, 2004, http://www.washingtonpost.com/ac2/wp-dyn/A34111-2004Dec3?language=printer.

Gordo, Speedy Gonzales, Dora the Explorer, Baldo, and La Cucaracha

Funny, captivating, clever, often able to overcome difficult circumstances and terrible odds, the heroes of newspaper comic strips, comic books, and animated cartoons have entertained readers, movie goers, and television viewers through the years. But cartoons and comic strips are much more than simple stories of heroes and evildoers. The images have deeper meaning—they reflect the times in which they were created and also the prevailing attitudes and stereotypes.

Since World War II, a number of Latino cartoon and comic characters have frolicked and schemed through the pages of comic books and on film—from a lazy, sleepy Mexican bean farmer (Gordo) and a superhero mouse (Speedy Gonzales) to an adventuresome girl (Dora the Explorer) and a hip teenage boy (Baldo). All of them, in their own time and in their own way, were icons that reflected an emerging Latino culture in the United States.

GORDO—1941

Cartoonist Gus Arriola (1917–) never crossed the Mexico border until he was an adult, although both of his parents were born in Mexico. Arriola grew up in Arizona and Los Angeles and graduated from Manual Arts High School in Los Angeles where he took many art courses. He got his start in the newspaper cartoon business in 1936 when he took a job at the Charles Mintz Studio, whose productions included Krazy Kat and Barney Google.

Soon, Arriola moved to Metro-Goldwyn-Mayer, the giant company that was setting up a cartoon division. He began to work on a character called "The Lonesome Stranger." Arriola later reflected,

> In those days, the terrible stereotyping of characters were always Orientals or Mexicans, Arabs or something. So I designed this bad-looking, big, fat Mexican bandit with a black beard, and like I said I'm not too proud of it. But I kept playing with that character, and later on I cleaned him up and thought maybe I could make him a poor bean farmer and see where that leads me.[1]

And so, Arriola added some weight to the Mexican character's midsection and named him Perfecto Salazar "Gordo" Lopez, or simply Gordo (Fatso). When a newspaper syndicate decided in November 1941 that a cartoon strip featuring the chubby Mexican bean grower could be a hit, *Gordo* was born. The strip appeared in a number of newspapers across the country shortly before the Japanese attack on Pearl Harbor and the beginning of major U.S. involvement in World War II.

Even if Arriola had "cleaned up" his main character a bit, as he said, Gordo was anything but a favorable Mexican role model. Gordo had little energy and liked to take exceptionally long siestas, many lasting most of the day. He spoke in broken English and was a lovable if clownish and stereotyped buffoon. In many newspapers across the country, Gordo now took his place alongside such cartoon icons as detective Dick Tracy, housewife Blondie, and a plucky, redheaded youngster named Little Orphan Annie.

Gordo's sidekicks included his young nephew Pepito; his best friend Paris Juarez Keats Garcia, better known as "The Poet;" Artemisa Gonzalez, a middle-aged widow whose major goal in life was to marry Gordo, much to his consternation; Senor Dog, Gordo's pet chihuahua; and assorted animals who shared Gordo's home. The animals could speak with each other but not with Gordo and other humans.

Long accustomed to seeing the Latino image defiled in Hollywood, many Mexicans suddenly took an interest in the bean farmer. At least he was not a killer or an alcoholic or just plain mean. The comic strip soon drew praise from prominent educators, Mexican government officials, and others for helping to promote understanding between various American countries. But less than a year after he had launched the strip, Arriola suspended the publication after joining the U.S. military to work on training films. The comic resumed publication shortly after the war.

Arriola's strip, although perpetuating impressions of Mexicans as lazy and unproductive, was never mean-spirited, violent, or evil. The characters, in over their heads, silly, and capable of outrageous mistakes and misunderstandings, mostly bumbled and grumbled through life bounding from one humorous situation to another.

In the early years of the strip, *Gordo's* characters were mostly Latinos. Many U.S. citizens reading the strip learned for the first time in their lives the meaning of such Spanish words as *tortilla* and *tamale*. As the series progressed, Ariolla introduced a few characters from the United States. One was Mary Frances Sevier, who Ariolla named after his wife. With a thick Southern accent and flirty manners, she became romantically involved with Pepito. Another major character also appeared in the strip later in the series. A housekeeper named Tehuana Mama was of advancing age but her lap became a favorite meeting place of many of Gordo's animals. She also became the most important love interest of his life. Not all of the characters in the strips were of flesh and blood. One was an old bus. It was called La Cometa Halley after the spectacular comet that flashes in the skies every seventy-five years or so. The strip was infused with puns and comical wordplay. Arriola often signed individual strips with such titles as "Alla Twitter" and "Bea Aware." The strip was whimsical and, to some extent, poetic.

As *Gordo* gained increasing popularity and readership, running in nearly three hundred newspapers nationwide, Arriola became more aware that his strip was the only mass-circulation vehicle that regularly portrayed the Mexican people. Realizing that the crowd of characters in the strip were mostly shiftless, even if non-threatening, he began to think of ways to make the strip more useful, more thoughtful as a means of communicating some of the Mexican culture that flowed in his own blood lines.

For the first time in his life, Arriola traveled to Mexico, trying to soak up some folklore, history, and art. When he returned, the character of Gordo took on a new role. He would no longer be a bean farmer. Laid off by his landlord, Gordo left the farm and began to use his faithful automobile, La Cometa Halley, to embark on a new career as a tour guide.

Arriola's characters now showed less stereotypical behavior. Their clothes began to reflect more of what their creator had seen in his own travels in Mexico—a combination of fashion worn by people on both sides of the border. Gordo himself started wearing clothes that could be seen on the streets of Los Angeles.

Gordo was now earning his living showing tourists from the United States the cultural attractions in Mexico, telling the visitors some of its history as he understood it, and about some of its traditions and celebrations. Because of the animals in the strip and also the cartoon insects, Arriola was even able, on a number of occasions, to be a voice for environmental concerns. He was one of the earliest cartoonists to speak out on the issue.

The early *Gordos* were very stereotypical, and the dialogue was very broken English....

> So little by little I began clearing up the dialogue and cleaning up the characters myself in order to appeal to a wider audience. When you do a humorous story strip based on human interest you can't help but make social commentary. As I did different stories and introduced new characters I discovered that some of them were going to have to be a little brighter than my main characters. Gordo changed through the years, as I did, and got a little more information.

Once Gordo became a tourist guide, Arriola gave the chubby main character a bit more sophistication—but not too much.

> When you work on a strip the way I did for forty years, it's bound to change and so do the characters. The more erudite commentary I would put in the mouths of, say, Bug Rogers, the spider, or the owl, or the worms. I found it easier to make them express ideas than the human characters. It is much easier for animals to comment on the foibles of humans than for humans to do it.[2]

From the inception of the *Gordo* comic strip in 1941 until the last of the drawings in 1985, the strip was by far the most visible of any with a Mexican setting and characters. The other was *Little Pedro* drawn by William de la Torre, which ran from 1948 to 1974 but had only minor circulation nationwide.

To most readers in the United States, *Gordo* had a faintly exotic feel, these foreign characters with an accent in a strange land. During most of the strip's run, most Americans north of the border were acquainted with Mexico and its people mostly through the exploits of the television hero, the Cisco Kid. The Cisco Kid, however, was like any other cowboy legend, fighting off the bad guys against seemingly insurmountable odds. *Gordo*, on the other hand, especially after Arriola introduced some Mexican customs and ceremonies, was much more of a lesson on the people and manners with whom most of the readers had little or nothing in common.

But *Gordo* held the interest of readers and the admiration of other cartoonists and critics during its entire run. Although at the beginning of the series Arriola had never intended the strip to be about ethnic pride or heritage, *Gordo's* emphasis on the human foibles of his characters seemed to ring true. In this sense, readers in the United States, in the dilemmas faced by Gordo and his buddies, could see the same kinds of challenges they faced themselves. The strip leaped over cultural boundaries.

San Francisco Chronicle columnist Herb Caen said:

> We all need families, our own and at least one other. For more years than I care to think about, my other family has been the singular creation of Gus Arriola—Señor Gordo and his extended menagerie of diverting humans and spectacular animals. Haven't we all wanted to live as Gordo does? One can only envy him his charmed life: the perfect village, the adorable senoritas, the easily survivable hangovers and heartbreaks, and the marvelous array of animals that give the comic strip—a term that seems inadequate—its several dimensions....[3]

Arriola won a number of awards for *Gordo*. He received the National Cartoonists' Society's certificate for Best Humor Strip in 1957, the first year it was given, and he won again in 1965. The California State Legislature took the extraordinary step of voting a resolution honoring Arriola's professional accomplishment and expressing gratitude for his work in promoting inter-ethnic understanding. Cartoonist Eldon Dedini said, "Ecology and race relations were Gus's concerns long before they appeared in other strips.... He brought a sensitivity and insight to his cartoons that existed in no other strip. Unique. People knew it and felt it. And they honored him for it."[4]

Looking back on *Gordo*, Arriola said, "As a funny strip that had some heart and soul, because that's what I poured into it. Something that was unique in its time, which it was because it was the only one in the paper that had a definite ethnic background. Gordo was a Mexican from Mexico."[5]

SPEEDY GONZALEZ—1953

Speedy Gonzalez was the fastest mouse in all of Mexico. He sported an oversized yellow sombrero and a bandana around his neck as he zipped away from trouble at a blinding pace, shouting "Arriba! Arriba!" at his pursuers. Of all the Latino cartoon characters in history, Speedy was unquestionably the most famous.

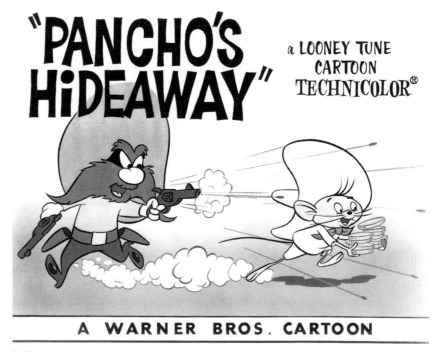

© Warner Bros.

Unlike Gordo, a newspaper comic page creation, Speedy was a movie sensation. In 1953, Warner Brothers' Bob McKimson created Speedy. The rapid rodent made his first appearance in a short called "Cat-Tails for Two." Decked out in his outrageously Mexican attire, he outwits and outsmarts a couple of evil but brain-challenged pussycats named Benny and George who are looking for something to eat. Although the tiny mouse would have been much less than a full meal, the cats try various means to entrap Speedy, only to make total fools of themselves.

Like many cartoon characters, Speedy changed appearance after his initial debut. In the "Cat-Tails for Two" episode he is rather scrawny and bucktoothed. Soon, the animators made his image more likable and cute, with a sparkling, mischievous smile.

Although the series did not take off immediately as a huge success, Fritz Freleng of Warner Brothers took the original idea of the mouse a step further in 1955. Speedy's archenemy became Sylvester, the "Greengo Poosygato." It was not so much that Sylvester was totally stupid or irrational; it's just that all of his schemes to take down Speedy, the mouse with the supersonic speed, were doomed to failure. At the end of each of the episodes, Sylvester is the one who suffers all manner of embarrassment and humiliation—from accidentally consuming large amounts of hot sauce to getting caught in mousetraps set to catch Speedy. For many Americans of Latino descent, this was the first time that a cartoon or comic strip character that represented their side of the cultural divide continuously humiliated the forces arrayed against them.

Michael Guillen, a child of migrant laborers who worked the harvest fields of the Imperial Valley of California to the valleys of Southern Idaho, remembered Speedy fondly. He did not see the character as a stereotype or view the series as a generally negative portrait of Mexicans; he saw Speedy as a hero. It was Speedy, the Mexican mouse, who continually outwitted Sylvester, the representative of all that attempted to put down the hero.

Guillen recalled a day with his mother in Twin Falls, Idaho, when they walked into a store that displayed the sign "No Mexicans or dogs allowed" and the owner of the store indignantly pointed to the sign when the two walked in. For Guillen, when Speedy defeated Sylvester the Cat, he was winning out over people like the store owner. It is important to note that Speedy spoke with a Mexican accent; Sylvester, on the other hand, had no such accent. Guillen wrote:

> As a little Chicano boy I *loved* Speedy Gonzales. Not so much because he was an *accurate* portrayal of my ethnicity—nothing of the sort—but because he was *all I had* in a world where my ethnicity was not allowed, let alone visible, and because he was quick and clever and made a fool of *El Greengo Poosygato* (aka Sylvester) time and time again, cartoon after cartoon, all the time joyfully and unabashedly shouting, "*¡Arriba! ¡Arriba! ¡Ándale! ¡Ándale! YEEHAH!*"[6]

Much like the western heroes in early television such as Roy Rogers, Gene Autry, and the Cisco Kid, Speedy had a sidekick who had just the opposite characteristics from those of the hero. Speedy's cousin, Slowpoke Rodriguez, was there to offer Speedy encouragement and companionship but little more. Invariably, Rodriquez, "the slowest mouse in all Mexico," gets into all sorts of difficulties from which only Speedy can help him escape.

Like many other Warner Brothers cartoon figures, including Bugs Bunny, Speedy was an example of what folklore students call "trickster figures." The hero is pursued by evil villains; through brain power and cleverness, the hero confounds and confuses his enemy. Br'er Rabbit in the Uncle Remus stories, for example, begs not to be thrown in the brier patch when he is caught. For most creatures the brier patch would be a painful and undesirable location in which to be thrown. For the rabbit, however, it is home. When he is thrown in the patch, he has won, gaining his triumph through trickery.

The 1955 film short "Speedy Gonzales" won an Academy Award for Best Short Subject (Cartoons). It involved a number of starving mice attempting to get cheese from a cheese factory and falling victim to the evil Sylvester. This was the first film to pit the mouse against his constant tormentor. Despite Sylvester's attempts to bring down the fastest mouse using nets, land mines, and dynamite, Speedy acquires the cheese, saves his fellow mice, and defeats the bad pussycat. The cartoon set the pace and tone for dozens of

Speedy cartoons that followed, including three more that were nominated for Oscar awards: *Tabasco Road* (1957), *Mexicali Schmoes* (1959), and *The Pied Piper of Guadalupe* (1961).

Freleng and McKimson worked together for the next ten years directing the series of Speedy productions. In *Tabasco Road*, Speedy tries to protect two drunken, belligerent friends who keep challenging cats to "combato." The film has much fractured English-language dialogue, many Mexican characters of less than sterling personal character, and other stereotypes that some viewers over the years would find offensive to Latinos. In the film short Pablo and his drinking buddy Fernando are swilling drinks in the El Tio Pepe Cantana. One of the songs called *La Cucaracha*, which deals with cockroaches, added to the stereotypes.

In the film short called *The Pied Piper of Guadalupe*, a flustered Sylvester goes on a verbal attack. All that the little cheese thieves like Speedy can do, Sylvester asserts, is steal and then run, run, run. To some viewers in the mid-1950s this was just further confirmation of views they already held about Mexicans as cowardly thieves. There is little question that many viewers in the United States had some sympathy for the addled Sylvester and shared his opinions.

Yet the Speedy films remained popular to a wide assortment of readers for nearly two decades. They were nominated for a number of Academy Awards. Regardless of the social and cultural implications in the characters, they made people laugh. If Mexican stereotypes were everywhere in the series, few people, Latino or otherwise, complained about Speedy Gonzales. Speedy himself was a heroic figure, capable of magnificent athletic prowess and devoid of any antisocial behavior. He was never pictured smoking or drinking. Indeed, in only a couple of the cartoons are Speedy's neighbors or friends intoxicated. In those films, Speedy intervenes, persuading them to stop drinking and then escorts them home. "To many people, he was a hero," said Virginia Cueto, associate editor of Hispanic OnLine, a Web site based in Miami. "He is seen by many Hispanics as a positive role model. This guy is a winner."[7]

By the 1960s Speedy became Warner Brothers' most prominent caricature. He appeared in nearly thirty cartoons. In one called *The Wild Chase* Speedy appears alongside the Roadrunner and his own personal enemy, the Coyote. It was as if two Olympian sprinters, Speedy and the Roadrunner, had a magic moment together.

In the 1965 film short *Assault and Peppered* (many of the Speedy cartoons carried titles with such puns), Daffy Duck declared war on the starving mice in his community because they lowered the values of his property. He and Speedy do battle. Over the years Speedy came in contact with an assortment of other animal characters such as a Buzzard named "El Vulturo, the Bandito Bird." For the remainder of his career as a cartoon figure, Speedy was always paired with Daffy. The last cartoon in which either character appeared was *See Ya Later Gladiator* (1968).

The story of Speedy did not end with his last cartoon creation. By the 1980s, Speedy's popularity on television showings and on video reproductions was nearly as great as Bugs Bunny. The cable network Nickelodeon, which featured heavy programming for children and had obtained the rights to Warner Brothers' animation, often ran Speedy cartoons as part of its "Nicktoons" series. But the social turbulence of the 1960s and the assertion of Chicano pride brought greater sensitivity regarding the images of Latinos that cartoonists and animators produced in comic books, comic strips, and in films.

Were the cartoon characters portrayed in the Speedy films outdated and offensive stereotypes that had no business being shown in the television markets of a more modern period when cultural pride demanded fair treatment? Or rather was the Speedy characterization actually a positive role model of fighting back against all sorts of unfair and unjust odds? Two decades after the last Speedy film was produced, television network officials and others would argue their cases.

CARTOON CONTROVERSY

In 1999, an unlikely controversy swept the television industry. Nickelodeon dropped their showings of all Warner Brothers cartoons and sold the rights

A Cartoonist, a Scholar, and a Cartoon History

The cartoon can be an invaluable tool in communicating much more than humor or satire. It can enliven stories; it can help make history come alive.

In 2000, cartoonist Lalo Alcaraz, whose strip *La Cucaracha* had gained increasing popularity, teamed with esteemed teacher and scholar Ilan Stavans in creating *Latino USA: A Cartoon History*. The work uses four main narrators to tell the story of Latinos in the United States. The narrators include Calavera (the skeleton-icon from Mexican Day of the Dead decorations), a schoolteacher named Maestra, Toucan, a figure from magical-realism novels, and Stavans himself.

Lively and entertaining, the book is packed with controversial clashes of historical interpretation as well as revealing insights into the point of view of Latino figures in the course of U.S. history. In these pages, the Alamo takes on a new meaning.

This book, along with the cartoon strips and cartoons now appearing from Latino creators and writers about historical events and cultural themes, are valuable for readers of Latino background. But they are especially valuable for Americans who are not Latinos, not only for learning about events that might be new to them but also for the point of view. From such wider perspective comes understanding.

to Cartoon Network. A year later ABC Network did the same. Thus, Cartoon Network became the only television channel to show classic Warner Brothers cartoons.

Media mogul Ted Turner, the owner of Cartoon Network, and other executives of his company, whose productions reached many international venues, were especially sensitive about any material that might create cultural misunderstanding. They were determined not to show cartoons, regardless of the times in which they were created, that directed ricidule at any group of people.

Soon after securing the rights to *Speedy Gonzalez*, the company decided that Speedy was no longer appropriate for children. Program directors indicated that in test audiences Speedy did not fare well. They also cited concerns about the stereotypes of lazy, drunken, Mexicans that were portrayed in the series. They were not talking about the character of Speedy himself, they made clear, but of his friends, especially Slowpoke Rodriguez and some of the other roughnecks who drank excessively and smoked heavily. And so the mouse who had been one of Warner Brothers' biggest animated stars alongside Bugs Bunny would not get air time, even though, according to a company spokeswoman, Speedy Gonzales remained "hugely popular" on stations that carried The Cartoon Network Latin America.[8]

When word got out that the mouse had been axed from the coming year of network cartoon shows, the outcry was immediate. Soon there was a movement. Organizers called it "Free the Mouse." The protests did not come from Anglo viewers who delighted in Speedy's antics; it came from Latino viewers who had grown up looking at Speedy as a hero.

Gabriela Lemus, Director for Policy and Legislation for the League of United Latin American Citizens in Washington, D.C., declared that Speedy was a motivator who always beat the bad guys. She and her friends, said Lemus, did not consider the character of Speedy as a negative stereotype but a positive role model. "Some of the other mice were not the best of all characters," she said, "but Speedy always chastised them for being lazy and he always told them to get your act together."[9]

The organization called on the cable channel to show Speedy Gonzales cartoons because "Speedy's a cultural icon. He's a good mouse," said Lemus. She and her organization, she said, wanted their mouse back—not Mickey Mouse but Speedy.[10] Soon, other Latino organizations joined the fray. The Latino Web site Hispanic OnLine was soon receiving 100,000 hits a month in their own "Save the Speedy" drive.

"It's been silly not to have Speedy on the air because people watch him in Latin America, and they love him," Virginia Cueto said, "Thousands of Hispanics and others have logged onto Hispanic Online's message board to voice their support for Speedy's return."[11] The postings on the online site were nearly unanimous in support of the mouse. "I am thirty years old and have found myself saying, 'Arriba, Arriba, Ole, Ole' many times throughout my life," one fan said. "The little guy is in me. I have a small stuffed version of him in the back window of my car as I fly through the Houston highways!"[12] Another wrote,

> If you ask me, the cartoons depict "gringo" society (those crafty American cats …) as a not-too-bright, conniving species that exploits anyone who happens to be handy. The Mexican mice are always content in their own pueblos, doing their own thing, and here come the gringos into Mexican turf, interfering and looking out for their own interests. And Speedy always wins! So who is being depicted negatively here?[13]

Yet another called Speedy "more of a positive symbol. He always brings down that Daffy Duck to the point that the latter finally started respecting Speedy. People like Speedy."[14]

Cueto agreed, saying "many Hispanics view Speedy as a positive ethnic reflection because he always outsmarts the 'greengo' cat Sylvester." Unlike other animated characters that did draw criticism from Latino groups, especially the Frito Bandito, the gun-toting bandit who stole chips in Frito-Lay commercials, Speedy was just the opposite, she said—he broke negative stereotypes.[15]

Cueto was right about other stereotypical cartoon characters that Latino groups had attacked. In 1971, community organizing by Chicano activists, along with the work done by the National Mexican-American Anti-Defamation Committee, succeeded in banishing Frito Bandito, the Mexican cartoon hustler for corn chips, from the airwaves. The Frito-Lay company wisely chose another mascot. In addition to the Frito Bandito, other caricatures such as Bucky & Pepito, an animated cartoon series that appeared in the late 1950s, came under fire. The Taco Bell chihuahua dog was another character attacked by Latino groups as demeaning to their culture. The dog was soon dropped. The reason given by the company had nothing to do with stereotypes. The dog, company spokesmen said, was not selling enough tacos.

For many Latino groups, then, the Speedy Gonzales matter was entirely different. Although the sentiment was certainly not unanimous among Latino viewers and cultural observers, a large portion of the community saw Speedy in a positive light and they wanted the network to run the cartoons. By June 2002, the pro-Speedy forces had won out. The press releases and online petition drive led The Cartoon Network to change its mind. Speedy Gonzales was back on television.

And that was not all. To many the victory seemed like a cultural triumph. When the docmentary film titled *The Bronze Screen: 100 Years of the Latino Image in American Cinema* premiered in 2002, Latino actor Cheech Marin celebrated as his own positive Latino image that of Speedy Gonzales persevering against all kinds of obstacles in his path throughout the years.

In addition, the famed mouse again become commercially appealing. From Auburn Hills, Michigan, in 2006 came word that the manufacturer of Volkswagen had decided to use the cartoon icon to promote its Volkswagen GTI MkV. Blending animation with actual footage of the automobile, Volkswagen's advertising agency created its own Speedy cartoon. Two Volkswagen engineers take the new GTI MkV for a test run. At the same time, Speedy goes out for a cheese run. Somewhere in the middle of the desert the two ride alongside each other. The advertisers called the beginning episode of the television ad campaign "Speedbump." Kerri Martin, director of brand innovation for Volkswagen, said that both Speedy and the car permeate pop culture. Both can accelerate at great speeds. Both have loyal and passionate fan bases, and both have achieved iconic levels. Speedy, said other company spokesmen, communicates to Latino viewers such qualities as intelligence, confidence, and resourcefulness.

DORA THE EXPLORER—1999

In 1999, a seven-year-old animated character with dark-brown hair, big brown eyes, light-brown skin, and unmistakably Latina features became a fixture in children's cable television. Named Dora Marquez, she was the cartoon world's first Latina heroine, and she and her friends experienced adventures in jungles, beaches, and rainforests. The cartoon series based on these adventures, Dora the Explorer, was designed for children from ages two to five.

© CBS

Created by Chris Gifford, Valerie Walsh, and Eric Weiner, the Dora the Explorer show used the research of a team of teachers and other consultants with the express purpose of involving children in a bilingual experience. Many of the youngsters watching the series on Nickelodeon would be exposed for the first time in their lives to Spanish words. They would also see a young, virtuous character with exceptionally positive attributes interacting with other young friends to solve problems and face challenges. It would also expose young preschoolers to Latino culture and make the world of computers and technology a part of the cartoon world.

The show premiered in August 2000 on Nickelodeon and in twenty-two Latin American countries. It was the network's first series to open simultaneously in other parts of the world. Soon, it debuted online on a Web site that featured a translator tool that allowed children to hear words spoken in both English and Spanish.

In less than a year, the animated television show became the top-rated series for preschoolers in commercial television. Shown weekday mornings on Nickelodeon and Saturday mornings on CBS, the success of Dora led to a line of toys and apparel much sooner than it normally takes to develop a market for such products. Soon, teachers and parents began to appreciate Dora as a role model for their students and children, and Dora merchandise began to out-sell products featuring Barbie, Winnie the Pooh, and dolls created to look like Snow White and Sleeping Beauty. Her popularity spread. *Dora the Explorer Live*, a musical stage show based on the cartoon series, began a national tour in 2003 at the Palace Theatre in Louisville, Kentucky, including a ten-day run at New York City's famous Radio City Music Hall.

The Television Critics Association nominated *Dora the Explorer* for an Outstanding Achievement in Children's Programming award. Herb Scannell, president of Nickelodeon, was euphoric. "It's a very special show. I'm very proud of it," he said. "At Radio City Music Hall we had 5,000 kids yelling 'salsa'—that's special. There's a celebration of a language and a culture that is rich." The pint-size Latina heroine had become something of an icon.[16]

The concept of the series *Dora the Explorer* was simple enough. The episodes recount the adventures of Dora, a spirited youngster who constantly takes on various quests, all of them involving difficult challenges. In each episode, Dora asks the viewers to help her in the adventure, either by helping her find clues or evidence on the screen or by helping her find which way to go using a map. The origin of Dora's name is the Spanish word *exploradora*, which means "female explorer."

When Dora succeeds in her efforts with the help of her friends, she ends each episode with a victorious song called "We Did It." In the early episodes of the series, Dora actually lived in a computer, an attempt to introduce young viewers to the magic of technology. Later, the artificial story device was changed and Dora was shown to reside in a jungle with her family.

Her roots are never exactly explained, although it is clear that she is Latina. She uses such words as *vamanos* (let's go). In some of the episodes, there are suggestions that one or both of her parents were from Puerto Rico. The jungle portrayed in the series most closely resembles those of Costa Rica or perhaps a tropical area of southern Mexico. One of the characters in the series is a Spanish-speaking squirrel named Tico. Residents of Costa Rica are called *ticos*. Dora's best friend is a monkey called Boots, given that name because of the bright red shoes he wears. Boots accompanies Dora on her adventures; he helps her solve riddles and puzzles and helps her gain insight into clues. In one episode, Dora and Boots help a *coqui*, a small frog from Puerto Rico, return to its native island so it can sing again.

Almost every show features a villainous fox named Swiper. The nefarious creature constantly steals or attempts to steal items and clues that would benefit Dora in helping solve mysteries. Although Dora constantly admonishes the pesky fox, he often manages to sneak away with items before Dora can intervene. When he succeeds, he gloats, often saying "You're too late," or "You'll never find it now." Interestingly, Swiper has a New York accent. Although annoyed by Sniper's actions, Dora always remains focused, never reduced to threats or attempted violence. And when the fox himself gets into trouble, Dora is always there to help him out, despite his annoying behavior.

Diego is Dora's cousin, an adventuresome young animal rescue worker. So popular did the character of Diego become on *Dora the Explorer* that Nickelodeon introduced a separate children's show with the animal rescue worker as the hero. *Go, Diego, Go!* premiered in 2005.

The series also included a singing group called Fiesta Trio, composed of a grasshopper, a snail, and a frog. Assorted other creatures cross paths and befriend Dora, including Isa the Iguana and Benny the Bull. The show also featured a number of objects that speak, such as Dora's purple backpack, a magical wonder that can quickly produce items that Dora needs immediately in her adventures such as ladders and space suits. In some episodes, trees, automobiles, boats, and walls talk.

The voice of Dora was that of Kathleen Herles, the sixteen-year-old daughter of Peruvian immigrants. Using Herles reflected a growing trend among children's television to have Latino actors play Latino characters. Within a few years of the show's inception, Nickelodeon sponsored Hispanic Heritage celebrations in New York, Los Angeles, Chicago, and Miami. The creators of Dora were determined to make the series a contribution to cultural exchange and saw the cartoon as a direct move against the stereotypes that had plagued Latinos in the media for so many years, both in motion pictures and on television. They also sought to involve the viewers, the young preschool children, in the learning process.

In 2007, Herles told *TV Guide* interviewer Matt Mitoich that she believed the popularity of the character had to do with the interaction with the viewers. "Dora makes them a part of what she's doing and she always asks for their opinion and for their help," said Herles.[17]

In a major way, *Dora the Explorer* plowed new ground, showing that the old stereotypes were not only unfair and inaccurate but also crude. Cultural organizations such as the National Council of La Raza saw the *Dora the Explorer* series in the forefront in altering public perception of Latinos as lazy, addicted, lawless, and dangerous. In series such as *Dora the Explorer*, children now would see Latino children just as other children—eager, wide-eyed, ready to take on the world. They would see Latino families as dedicated to each other, generally religious, and hardworking.

Dora the Explorer has been dubbed into many languages all over the world. Because the creators of the series had from the beginning wanted its format to help youngsters learn words in more than one language, *Dora the Explorer* was especially suited for dubbing into various languages other than Spanish and English. The series has appeared in France and a number of other countries.

Leslie Valdes, one of the show's writers, attributed the show's success not only to the fact that it combined play with learning but also because it gave Latino children a sense of connection. "We are influenced by all the things we see and read," he said. "A lot of it is taken from Spanish culture and history and kids' fables. We often combine a Latino character with a fable character. But really, it's all a legacy of imagery." Valdes, along with the other writers, admired the character of Dora. For Valdes, the experience of creating the series was inspiring. "It's been great," he says. "You have the heroine who's a very can-do character. She's indefatigable—she can't be stopped." Valdes kept thinking of the great motto from the movement of the farm workers led by Cesar Chavez—"Si, se puede." (Yes, it is possible). Dora, said Valdes, "cannot take no for an answer. I take confidence from her."[18]

BALDO—2000

A year after preschool viewers met Dora the Explorer and her band of friends, comic strip readers across the country met another Latino comic hero. His name was Baldo, and he was a teenager living in the United States. Created by Héctor Cantú and Carlos Castellanos, *Baldo* was the first nationally syndicated cartoon to feature a Latino character and his family and friends. The Universal Press Syndicate comic strip debuted in about 100 newspapers in the United States including the *Washington Post, Philadelphia Inquirer, Boston Herald*, and *Chicago Tribune*.

"He's a typical teenager," said Castellanos, the strip's illustrator. "He's into low-riders, soccer, and the prettiest girl who is brown-skinned and has dark hair."[19]

AP Photo/Terry Renna

Cartoon character Baldomero Bermudez lives with his father, his little sister, Gracie, and his aunt, Tia Carmen, who looks over Baldo and the family with her kindly but old-world ways. Baldo is the modern Latino teenager, hip and conscious of fitting in with his peers, but also short on knowledge of the cultural ways and practices of those of his Latino ancestry. Tia Carmen and other relatives are there to educate and remind him and the readers of the comic strip of that culture.

Cantu said that the idea for the comic strip was a simple one. He wanted to write about those things that he knew best, about growing up as a Latino in Texas. Cantu's parents were Mexican Americans; Castellanos was Cuban-American. Baldo's specific Latino heritage is not apparent. The strip is geared to show the common experiences of a Latino family in the United States. Castellanos talked about focusing on those aspects of life that all Latinos living in the United States would likely experience and those feelings that many of them would share. The challenge, both creators acknowledge, is appealing directly to the diverse cultures of their Puerto Rican, Cuban, Mexican, and Dominican readers.

The strip often emphasizes the humorous aspects of Baldo's youth, things such as Tia Carmen's near obsession with candles. But the strip also tackles the critical issues of the time, from a humorous slant. "We hit important issues in a funny way," Cantu said. In one strip, for example, Baldo serves as a translator for relatives and family friends in a hospital. Because Baldo's Spanish is limited and awkward, he often incorrectly translates words and phrases, thereby confusing and occasionally scaring patients. Through this comic interaction among the characters the strip's creators deal with the important issue of bilingualism in the setting of hospitals and other health care facilities.

Although Baldo is principally English-speaking, he often uses Spanish idioms and phrases. In this way, the strip, much like the children's television cartoon series *Dora the Explorer*, acts as something of an educational tool in introducing readers to at least bits and pieces of a new language. In the strip, Daddy Bermudez often speaks about how important it is to him that his children speak Spanish.

Baldo often speaks directly to the question of what it is to be Latino in the twenty-first century. In a December 2007 strip, Gracie asks her father whether their family is "literally Hispanic." Reading his newspaper, the father casually says that he does not know, that it depends on what the word means to different people. He explains that someone should not use the word if they do not know its exact meaning. Puzzled, Gracie asks again whether the family is Hispanic. Her father, now truly on the wrong track, says to Gracie that he thought the word she was talking about was "literally."

Cantu, a newspaper editor at the *Dallas Morning News*, created his first newspaper cartoon when he was only twelve years old. From his earliest years, he said, he always wrote comic book stories and always hoped to get them published. For a time he worked at *Hispanic Business* magazine until he hooked up with Castellanos, an illustrator based in West Palm Beach, Florida, who had also from his early childhood drawn cartoon characters and began as a freelance illustrator in 1981 while attending college.

With *Baldo*, Castellanos and Cantu broke down a barrier in the comic-strip industry. *Baldo* became the only comic that focused on a Latino character and family. From the beginning of their partnership, the two were concerned that the issues about stereotypes would be handled gracefully and that the series would accurately reflect the experiences of a group of Latinos. Cantu and Castellanos also realized early on that the challenge of the creator of a comic strip is not only to be humorous but also to appeal to a mass audience. With *Baldo*, they were able leap a tall hurdle, to fashion a strip that deals with the little, everyday victories and defeats as well as the foibles and challenges of contemporary life. The strip had to remain mainstream to be read and had to phase in the aspects of ethnicity and culture, which was a major goal of creating Baldo and his family in the first place.

Cantu said, "We were just talking about a sequence where Baldo's great-great-grandmother comes to visit." "Carlos and I started talking about his great-grandmother, who is like a hundred years old, and he was telling me all these funny stories about her. I said, 'Yeah, that's how it would be in my family.'"[20]

In one episode, Great Grandma Zoraida arrives at the Bermudez family household for a visit. A few days after her arrival, the wise old lady grabs her clipboard and walks around the house beginning a family inspection and test. The first test is for Baldo himself. She asks him to get her a glass of water, not cold but not hot either. Also, the water is to be in a cup, not a glass and is to be stirred with a spoon. Baldo carefully follows the instructions. In the kitchen, Great Grandma Zoraida snares another family member for testing. She corners Gracie and says that someone should make empanadas, a staple dish of the Latino culture. Gracie is not fazed in the slightest. She merrily prepares the ingredients and gets to work. Great Grandma Zoraida, with a smile on her face, tallies the scores for the Bermudez family. It is a resoundingly excellent tally—respect for elders: A+; retaining family traditions; also A+.

The fact that Latinos can see someone of their own ethnicity in a comic strip is a breakthrough, Castellanos said with much satisfaction. Fans across the country and from Latin America ask the two creators about Baldo mugs, T-shirts, and calendars. "It's almost like a pride thing," said Castellanos. "I've got two kids; Hector's got three kids. We see the difference that it makes for kids to see other kids that speak Spanish, whether it be on TV or comic books or comic strips. All of a sudden their family isn't so odd, you know what I mean?"[21]

LA CUCARACHA—2002

In 2002, the comic strip *La Cucaracha* became Universal Press Syndicate's newest addition to a growing number of efforts to bring Latino characters and cultural interests to newspaper readers across the country. Lalo Alcaraz, the strip's creator, had actually drawn versions of the strip for a relatively limited readership in the *Los Angeles Weekly* since 1992. Alcaraz began creating editorial cartoons for his college paper, San Diego State's *Daily Aztec*, in the late 1980s. Some of his work occasionally appeared in such publications as *The New York Times*, *The Village Voice*, and *The Los Angeles Times*. But now *La Cucaracha* was ready to take off.

Gordo and *Baldo* and other, less successful cartoon strips drawn by Latino artists and cartoonists had generally been light and humorous, offering glimpses into the nagging and irritating circumstances facing everyday individuals. Mostly, the strips were in no way hard-edged or politically contentious. Their message was that of inclusion. See, look at this character and his friends and relatives. Yes, they are Latinos, but look at the similar crosses they have to bear in life. Look at the roadblocks and misadventures they face, just as you and I. The strips also offered insights into a cultural

AP Photo/Damian Dovarganes

background quite foreign to most U.S. readers. Yes, Christmas is also an important holiday among Latinos, but here are other ways in which we celebrate. Here, child, hit the *piñata*!

La Cucaracha was different. The sketches were far edgier. For example, in his strip, Alcaraz berated the Immigration and Naturalization Service's processing program that greatly favored highly talented individuals over those who were uneducated, poor, or with no extraordinary skills. In another instance, the Statue of Liberty invites to the United States not the tired, hungry, huddled masses longing for freedom but the entertainers, athletes, scientists, and business executives. *La Cucaracha* was cutting and biting, an irreverent look at American society from the point of view of a poor Latino trying to succeed.

The son of Mexican immigrants, Alcaraz grew up bicultural and bilingual in San Diego, California, near the border and Tijuana, Mexico. "I grew up a little Mexican kid," he said. "I was born a poor brown child. I remember reading Mexican comics and watching Mexican wrestling movies in Tijuana on the weekends and … Batman at night at home—so I really did split my time."[22]

But when he turned on the television, he saw the character Adam on the western series "Bonanza" and wondered whether he was Mexican. He looked in vain for Latino characters that had class and distinction and saw only goofy sidekicks, drunken thugs, and lazy bums. He did in his early years enjoy the strip *Gordo*. Only later did he realize that the chubby bean farmer who spoke like "dees" was also a stereotype.

Alcaraz earned a master's degree in architecture at the University of California at Berkeley. While at Berkeley, he helped create the satirical magazine

Pocho—named after a derogatory term some Mexicans use against Mexican Americans who speak Spanish poorly. Through his use of satire, Alcaraz and the other student contributors of the magazine turned the term that was normally used as an insult into a term of pride. Alcaraz later formed a comedy team called the Chicano Secret Service that performed skits at campus protests.

When he turned to a career in creating cartoon strips, Alcaraz kept his sharp satirical focus. *La Cucaracha* defiantly took on the stereotypes that had been for so long directed at Mexican Americans. He did it so aggressively sometimes that even his Latino reading audience failed to see the dark humor. The main problem he faced with his cartoons, Alcaraz said, was that some Latinos "take things literally," and sometimes misunderstood what he was attempting to convey. But Alcaraz persisted, "doing my bit to promote the image that [Latinos] are real people."[23]

La Cucaracha follows the lives of Mexican-American Eddie, his girlfriend Vero, his friend Cuco Rocha and Eddie's brother Neto. Alternating between a kind of hip look at the relationships of the characters to biting political satire, the strip owed a major debt to the work of cartoonist Garry Trudeau in *Doonesbury*. So influenced was Alcaraz by Trudeau that Alcaraz often referred to his own strip as "Doonesbarrio." In one strip titled "Army of Juan," Eddie and his friends look warily at an Army recruitment poster that depicts an Iraqi enemy that in his appearance looks stunningly Latino.

Alcaraz's often paid tribute to Gus Arriola, the creator of *Gordo*, as a major inspiration, although Arriola's work was far less political than that of Alcaraz. Arriola himself admired the young cartoonist. "I had to be a little more subtle in my day," he said, "But now, he can come right out and say things that none of us could have said thirty years ago. I envy him the ability that he has now of doing that and having editors accept it."[24]

In characterizing his work on *La Cucaracha*, Alcaraz said, "You might not like it. Hopefully you'll laugh and maybe become educated—and maybe the cucaracha will get your attention."[25]

In a similar if much shorter replay of the Speedy Gonzales cancellation protest a few years earlier, *La Cucaracha* sparked its own drama in 2007. *The Los Angeles Times* suddenly decided to drop *La Cucaracha* from its comic pages to make room for other features. The decision, in a city with such a large Latino readership, proved to be a big mistake. Suddenly, there was an outpouring of protest led by several Web sites. Calls flooded the *Times* offices. Lalo Alcaraz had known nothing of the plans of the *Times* to drop the series and said he was dumbfounded when he opened the paper and saw no sign of his Chicano hipster Cuco Rocha and his barrio friends.

The decision by the *Times* lasted exactly one day. With a brief apology, *La Cucaracha* was reinstated. One Web site reported: "There was joy in "Roachville" on Wednesday as the edgy, Latino-themed comic strip *La*

Cucaracha returned to the *Los Angeles Times* after a swift, Internet-driven protest."[26]

NEW LATINO CARTOON IMAGES

By the turn of the twenty-first century, fans of cartoons and comic books could find many images of Latinos, from the long-familiar characters of sloth and violence to new characterizations that looked inside family life, traditions, celebrations, and other cultural aspects. A century's worth of mostly damaging profiles had at last found counterparts in such children's programming as *Dora the Explorer* and comic strips such as *Baldo* and *La Cucaracha*.

Latino artists and animators had begun to make their mark in an industry formally dominated by men and women not closely familiar with the lives and culture of Latinos. The portrayals of stupidity and wretchedness that had so dominated cartoons and comics still remained, the stereotypes engrained in the field of work just as it remained engrained in the motion picture industry and other media forms. Nevertheless, much new material was now there to paint the broader canvas of Latino life.

Today, illustrated and animated Latino characters often speak both English and Spanish. Individuals and families of Latino characters wrestle with life's challenges in ways that are sometimes humorous and thus entertaining, do foolish things, joke and play pranks, are smart and not-so-smart, good and not-so-good. In other words, they are just like other Americans. New artists are beginning to make a solid mark in the cartoon and comic strip fields. Peter Ramirez grew up in a Brooklyn barrio in New York City. One of six children raised by a single mother among the tough streets, Ramirez escaped by reading comic books and the newspaper funny pages. He was the first person in his family to graduate from college and as a senior began developing his artistic talents and passion for creating comics as an intern working under cartoonists Bill and Bunny Hoest, creators of *The Lockhorns*.

In 1986, he became a New York police officer but was forced to retire in the spring of 1991, when he was injured while trying to arrest an alleged drug dealer. Ramirez found himself at home, raising his infant son while his wife continued her career. It was in this situation that Ramirez created *Raising Hector*.

Ramirez named the semi-autobiographical comic strip after a fellow police officer who was killed in the line of duty. It involves three generations of the Sanchez family, a middle-class Hispanic family. Antonio and Maria are steeped in the cultural values of their Mexican parents and grandparents, still celebrating family traditions. Their son is Hector who has two children born in the United States, P.J. and Melissa. Hector is in the middle of the cultural tug-of-war between his parents on the one side and the new ways of his children, pulled by their own peers, on the other side.

Ramirez described his main character, Hector, as a man much like himself: "A middle class guy who thought he could make the transition from 'macho cop' to "stay at home dad' but who is obviously in way over his head. Hector is 'Mr. Mom' with a dash of hot sauce and, like any good cop, he likes to improvise when the going gets tough. Unfortunately, his street savvy short cuts usually only makes things worse!"[27]

As a greater number of Latino men and women ply their skills as creators of cartoons and comic strips, the caricature world of Latino life reflects a real-world quality far different world from the images of a half century ago.

SELECTED MOVIES AND TELEVISION

SPEEDY GONZALES

Looney Tunes: Golden Collection, Volume One. Directed by Robert McKimson, Friz Freleng, and Robert Clampett. Warner Home Video, 2003. DVD.

Looney Tunes: Golden Collection, Volume Two. Warner Home Entertainment, 2004. DVD.

Looney Tunes: Golden Collection, Volume Three. Directed by Rudolf Ising, Robert McKimson, and Chuck Jones. Warner Home Video, 2005. DVD.

Looney Tunes: Golden Collection, Volume Four. Directed by Chuck Jones and Frank Tashlin. Warner Home Video, 2006. DVD.

DORA THE EXPLORER

Dora's Ultimate Adventure Collection. Directed by Arnie Wong, Sherie Pollack, George S. Chailtas, and Gary Conrad. Nickelodeon, 2004. DVD.

Animal Adventures. Directed by Arnie Wong, Sherie Pollack, George S. Chailtas, and Gary Conrad. Paramount, 2006. DVD.

Puppy Power! Directed by Arnie Wong, Sherie Pollack, George S. Chailtas, and Gary Conrad. Paramount Home Video, 2007. DVD.

Undercover Dora. Directed by Arnie Wong, Sherie Pollack, George S. Chailtas, and Gary Conrad. Nickelodeon, 2008. DVD.

NOTES

1. John Province, "Gus Arriola, Interview," *Hogan's Alley*, http://cagle.msnbc.com/hogan/interviews/arriola/home.asp.

2. Province.

3. History of Pioneering American Comic Strip about Mexican Milieu," http://www.rcharvey.com/gordo.html.

4. History of Pioneering.

5. Arriola.

6. Michael Guillen, "Fritz Freleng Blogathon – Speedy Gonzales (1955), August 21, 2006, http://theeveningclass.blogspot.com/2006/08/friz-freleng-blogathonspeedy-gonzales.html.

7. Lucio Guerrero, "Speedy Gonzales: Back in a flash?" *Chicago Sun-Times*, April 3, 2002, http://findarticles.com/p/articles/mi_qn4155/is_20020403/ai_n12461252.

8. Ed Driscoll, "SPEEDY GONZALES UPDATE," April 3, 2002, htttp://www.eddriscoll.com/archives/2002_04.php.

9. Driscoll.

10. Driscoll.

11. Sam Francis, "The Secret of Speedy Gonzales: Hispanic Race Consciousness," *VDARE,* July 4, 2002, *VDARE,* http://www.vdare.com/francis/hispanic_race.htm.

12. Tom Kuntz, "Adios, Speedy. Not so Fast," *New York Times,* April 7, 2002.

13. Kuntz.

14. Francis.

15. Francis.

16. Eunice Sigler, A Girl Named Dora," *Hispanic,* September 2003, 42–45.

17. Matt Mitoich, "¡Hola! *Dora the Explorer* Previews Her New TV-Movie," TVGuide, November 4, 2007, http://www.tvguide.com/news/dora-explorer-herles/071104-01.

18. Sigler.

19. Isis Artize, "Building Characters," *Hispanic,* October 2000, 36. http://www.hispaniconline.com/hh04/culture/buildingcharacter.html.

20. Vanessa Jones, "Drawing on culture: A growing number of cartoonists are helping Latinos see themselves in the funny papers," *Boston Globe*, July 3, 2001, http://www.cartoonista.com/about/article/bostonglobe.html.

21. Jones.

22. Mandalit del Barco, "'La Cucaracha' Goes Nationwide," National Public Radio, "All Things Considered," January 1, 2003, http://www.npr.org/templates/story/story.php?storyId=882141.

23. Artize.

24. del Barco.

25. del Barco.

26. "Protest resurrects Latino-themed comic 'La Cucaracha,'" http://www.hispanictips.com/2007/03/08/protest-resurrects-latino-themed-comic-la-cucaracha.

27. "Raising Hector by Peter Ramirez," http://www.raisinghector.com/bio.php.

SUGGESTED READING

Artize, Isis. "Building characters." *Hispanic,* October 2000, 36, http://www.hispaniconline.com/hh04/culture/building_character.html Latino.

Francis, Sam. "The secret of Speedy Gonzales: Hispanic race consciousness," *VDARE,* July 4, 2002, http://www.vdare.com/francis/hispanic_race.htm.

Guerrero, Lucio. "Speedy Gonzales: Back in a flash?" *Chicago Sun-Times*, April 3, 2002, http://findarticles.com/p/articles/mi_qn4155/is_20020403/ai_n12461252.

Harvey, Robert, and Gus Arriola. *Accidental Ambassador Gordo: The comic strip art of Gus Arriola*. Jackson, MS: University Press of Mississippi, 2000.

Jones, Vanessa. "Drawing on culture: A growing number of cartoonists are helping Latinos see themselves in the funny papers." *Boston Globe*, July 3, 2001, http://www.cartoonista.com/about/article/bostonglobe.html.

Province, John. "Gus Arriola, Interview," *Hogan's Alley*, http://cagle.msnbc.com/hogan/interviews/arriola/home.asp.

Sigler, Eunice. "A Girl Named Dora," *Hispanic*, September 2003, 42–45.

"Speedy Gonzales, Arriba, Arriba!," *Xispas*, November 28, 2006, http://www.xispas.com/blog/2006/11/speedy-gonzales-arriba-arriba.html.

"Stereotypes in Drawn Media," http://www.umich.edu/ac213/student_projects05/las/index.html.

AP Photo/Dave Hammond

Dolores Huerta

PURSUING JUSTICE

Dolores Huerta is one of the most productive social activists of the twentieth and twenty-first centuries, co-founder with Cesar Chavez of the United Farm Workers, prominent feminist and labor leader, and a tireless campaigner on the front lines of pickets and boycotts aimed at making life a little more fair for those on the bottom. So connected was Huerta to *La Causa* (The Cause) and its fight for equal rights that many in the farm workers' movement referred to her as Dolores "Huelga," Spanish for strike. The recipient of countless awards from community service, labor, Hispanic, and women's organizations as well as the subject not only of murals but also of *corridos* (ballads) and poetry, Huerta remains a greatly admired Latino figure.

At the corner of Nostrand and Greene Avenues in the Bedford Stuyvesant neighborhood of Brooklyn, New York, a giant, 3,300-square-foot mural celebrates women in U.S. history who have made a profound difference in the struggle for human rights and justice. Unveiled in the fall of 2005, the mural is the work of a collaboration of artists and includes the images of such activists as civil rights pioneer Fannie Lou Hamer, anarchist Emma Goldman, and Congresswoman Shirley Chisholm. The mural itself is in the congressional district represented by Chisholm in her years in the U.S. Congress. One of the panels on the mural captures the image of Huerta. Arts administrator Jane Weissman, one of the creators of the mural, said, "It is a celebratory mural and people feel good when they see it. But it is also true that while it celebrates what we've done, it reminds us how much organizing and political work we still have to do for women's equality and social justice to become real."[1]

Those exact words could have been spoken by Huerta herself. Organize! Organize!

FROM NEW MEXICO TO CALIFORNIA

Huerta was born in 1930 in Dawson, New Mexico, a small coal-mining town established at the turn of the century. The scene of a number of coal mine tragedies, Dawson was populated in the 1930s mostly by immigrant Italian workers and their families. Two decades later, when the Phelps Dodge Corporation closed down operations, Dawson became a ghost town.

The family of Juan Fernandez, Huerta's father, had emigrated from Mexico early in the twentieth century. He was born soon after the family arrived. Fernandez worked both in the mines and as an agricultural worker in Dawson. The family of Huerta's mother, Alicia Chavez, had lived in New Mexico for two generations. Dolores was the second child and only daughter of Juan and Alicia Fernandez.

When Huerta was six years old, her parents, struggling under the strains of financial trouble during the Great Depression, divorced, and her mother moved the children—John, Dolores, and Marshall—to Stockton, California.

For a time Alicia Fernandez worked two jobs, as a waitress and cannery worker, to keep the family afloat financially. She relied on her father, Herculano Chavez, a widower, to watch the children much of the time. Although constantly struggling to pay the bills, the family was close and loving. Dolores' mother tried very hard to give her children the extra incentives to spark their interests. Dolores took violin, piano, and dance lessons, and she was an active member of the Girl Scouts. She joined church groups and sang in a church choir.

Huerta was particularly close to her grandfather, who patiently entertained the children with stories and spent more time with the youngsters during these years than their mother. Early on he could see the inquisitive and garrulous nature of his granddaughter. "My grandfather used to call me seven tongues," Huerta wrote, "because I always talked so much."[2]

The young Huerta followed, as much as she could, the progress of her father after the move to California. Juan Fernandez stayed in Dawson only briefly, joining the migrant work force that traveled from Colorado to Wyoming for the beet harvests. His experience as a migrant worker fired his spirit concerning labor issues. He had seen enough of the terrible wages, frequent accidents, and wretched working conditions in the labor camps and decided to fight all of it as a labor organizer. He served as an official of a local union at the American Metals Company. Eventually, he became secretary-treasurer of the Las Vegas, New Mexico, chapter of the Congress of Industrial Organization. By 1938, using the predominantly Latino union in Las Vegas as a base of operations, he leaped into politics, running for the state legislature on a program to promote labor benefits.

"My father was very intelligent, very intelligent," Huerta said, "He had a very strong personality, a very handsome man. He looked very Indian, in fact I look like my father, but he had green eyes. So he had a very striking appearance and he had a very good way with words and I can see my father as an organizer. In fact, my dad, wherever he went he was a very strong union man." She talked about her father's strong dedication to the rights of workers and his skill in gathering people together to unite in a common cause. "He organized the government employees union at the government facility where he was working," said Huerta. "He was very strongly devoted to the cause of unionism. He felt very strongly about that. I would hear stories about them organizing the union when I was small, around my dad."[3]

Fernandez won the election and served one term. Although his career was short-lived, mostly because of his outspoken stands and fiery temper, he made a lasting impression on his daughter living in Stockton. She would come to share his abhorrence of the suffering and inequities of the migrants. She would share his enthusiasm for battle, for conquering long odds. He made it from the beet fields of Wyoming to the state legislature on his own grit and guts. She took his example as inspiration.

Huerta spent her school years in a diverse neighborhood. She wrote,

> We had on the left hand side an Italian family. They were recent Italian immigrants.... Our neighbors on the right hand side were an African-American family, the Smiths. We had around the corner Filipinos. These were all new immigrants, right? A Filipino family. There were Chinese and Japanese, Native Americans, Greeks. People that had come in from Oklahoma, the Okies as they were called... in Stockton, California. So it was just this very poor neighborhood, but it was so wonderful because we had all of these—all of our friends were from all these different ethnic groups. That made it so, to me, that was a preparation. A universal preparation for the world.[4]

She recalled the Filipino pool hall, the Mexican drug stores and bakeries, and the variety of food establishments. The ethnic mix, she believed, broadened her understanding of the diverse cultures and backgrounds of those who had ended up in this one small part of the planet at this place and time. Even though she had fond memories of the ethnic blend of friends and neighbors living around her, she later remembered her years in public school as difficult, most of the problems surrounding the issue of racism. "They were always punishing the Latino kids and the African-American kids," she recalled, "so by the time I reached my senior year most of the Latino kids had dropped out. We had a very clean group of kids that we hung out with. We didn't do dope. We didn't drink, you know, but they were just always investigating us."[5]

During World War II, the family fortunes in Stockton improved. After Alicia and Juan Fernandez divorced, Alicia remarried to a man named James Richards. The two were able to purchase a small hotel in Stockton located on the fringe of skid row that catered to the migrant workers who moved in and out of the town during the harvest seasons. The hotel had become available after the U.S. government began to establish relocation camps of Japanese-American citizens during the war. The hotel had belonged to one of those families. Alicia Fernandez, James Richards, and the children moved into the hotel. The children worked part-time helping as janitors and maids. Huerta often said later that this experience helped her understand even more intensely the character and fortitude of the field workers who lived on the economic edge of American society.

Huerta believed her mother was a true feminist of her generation. "My mother was a strong woman," she said, "This was after the Depression. She was a business woman, she had a restaurant and hotels, she owned a business. So that was my role model growing up. I was not taught that women were subservient to men and women were not second-class citizens. My role model was my mother. I think it was a learned behavior in a way to say, 'Wait a minute, I'm not supposed to serve the man.' And that is not the way

Virgin de Guadalupe: A Symbol

The image of the Virgin de Guadalupe appeared at rallies of farm workers in the 1960s and, many years later, at immigration policy protest marches in 2007. It appears on the windows and doors of homes of Latinos throughout California and other states in Southwest.

It is said in Mexican culture that the image appeared on the cloak of an Aztec named Juan Diego in 1531. It became the patron and symbol of Mexico, representing the fusion of the Aztec and Spanish cultures. It is a strong image of Latino culture in the United States that has powerfully affected U.S. Latino identity. The feast day of the Virgin de Guadalupe is December 12, already one of the Catholic calendar's three most popular churchgoing days in Los Angeles and in other heavily Mexican dioceses in the country. Every year on that day, mariachis serenade her at dawn. Immigrants have carried the image with them as they have settled in various parts of the country, and so the symbol has expanded well beyond its ethnic base.

I grew up. My brothers and I were raised equally. My brothers had to clean and wash the clothes. I never had to serve my brothers, you know, cook for them and iron. And of course in the Latino culture that is not the way it is."[6]

Dolores remembered her mother as a kind of Renaissance woman, one who believed in culture and learning and the arts. She bought the children season tickets to symphony performances when they were teenagers, and often the children and their friends would join caravans of cars to drive to San Francisco to hear Charlie Parker and Dizzy Gillespie. Their life during these years was not only about making it through the monthly bill cycle but also saving enough money to go to the Bay area to hear great musicians.

After her graduation from high school, Huerta held a variety of jobs. She managed a small neighborhood grocery store that her mother purchased. She got a job at the Naval Supply Base. She began taking night courses at Stockton College in hopes of becoming a teacher. In 1950, shortly before her twentieth birthday, she married a manual laborer named Ralph Head. The brief marriage produced two children, Celeste and Lori, but the relationship was stormy and the two soon divorced.

During the marriage, Huerta temporarily abandoned her educational efforts and worked briefly for the sheriff's office. After the divorce, she returned to college, graduating with a teaching certificate from Delta Community College of the University of the Pacific. Huerta then found a job teaching elementary school in Stockton. Dealing with the lack of resources, seeing the frustration and weariness of the children of migrant laborers, she soon became disillusioned and dubious about being able to accomplish much to alleviate their condition. "I realized one day," she said, "that as a teacher I couldn't do anything for kids who came to school barefoot and hungry."[7] She soon decided that she could do more for them by engaging in social work and in organizing farm workers to ensure that those children no longer had to walk around shoeless and malnourished. She felt that there must be a more effective way to fight poverty and inequality.

THE COMMUNITY SERVICE ORGANIZATION AND ORGANIZING

Huerta met a California activist and organizer named Fred Ross in 1955. She later remembered him showing her pictures of workers in Los Angeles whom he had helped mobilize six years earlier into an organization called the Community Service Organization (CSO).

A grassroots organization of workers volunteering their time, the CSO worked to end segregation and racism against Mexican Americans in California. Like other Mexican-American community organizations, or *mutualistas*, the CSO promoted self-reliance and provided a variety of services including low-cost medical care and job referral. It acted to help ensure that children of Mexican descent could receive a decent education. It also worked for civil rights issues and was active in encouraging Mexican Americans to vote. Huerta later remembered her excitement upon learning about the health clinics that the CSO had helped build in the city. She was impressed with the fact that a number of local Hispanic leaders active in the CSO had actually entered the political arena. But she was particularly fascinated with the story of Ross and his commitment to helping farm workers.

When the acclaimed novelist John Steinbeck wrote *Grapes of Wrath* in 1939, a riveting story of the tribulations of the Joad family, a group of migrants from Oklahoma who traveled west to California looking for a way out of destitution, he modeled a federal migrant labor camp in the novel after the Sunset Camp near Bakersfield, California.

Shortly after Steinbeck left the area, it was Ross, a young graduate from the University of Southern California, who became the camp's director. At the camp in Bakersfield, confronting the poverty and deplorable working conditions facing the workers, Ross decided to do something about them. His heart was in organizing. He earned the trust and respect of the migrants by instituting a form of self-government for the camp. Every day he went from cabin to cabin encouraging residents to band together as a large force to help improve the conditions and to fight for concessions from those who held power. He prodded people to speak up for their interests, to fight through the fear of confrontation, and to be heard.

When Ross left the migrant camp, it was to take on another organizing project. Joining the Friends Service Committee, he worked to help Japanese Americans who had been herded into internment camps during World War II find jobs. After the war, he returned to southern California and joined with social activists in helping blacks and Mexican Americans fight against segregation in housing and education. In Arizona, he helped Yaqui Indians acquire medical facilities, streets, and other basic needs.

Ross, who was learning Spanish from flash cards, met small groups of Mexican Americans in their homes. The groups then branched out into the community, creating new groups and establishing footholds. The Los Angeles CSO became highly successful in registering new voters and in establishing citizen involvement in social issues. By building Mexican-American voter strength, Ross believed, politicians would have to pay attention, would be forced to improve services, streets, parks, sewage systems, garbage removal, and, especially, schools. They would be, after all, their constituents.

And now Ross wanted Huerta to join him. The CSO was organizing chapters in a number of other California localities. The organization, Ross told Huerta, would soon be the most forceful Mexican-American civil rights organization in California. Impressed by Huerta's passion and outspoken nature, he saw her as a community organizer. Huerta was sold. Here was an organization, she thought, that could actually make a difference at the grassroots level. Here was an organization into which she could pour her energy and passion. She agreed to help Ross organize a Stockton chapter of the CSO. Huerta's mother also joined the organization.

In Stockton, Huerta became a key CSO organizer. Attractive, dynamic, full of enthusiasm that could rouse the lethargic to action, Huerta took on the work of the CSO with a passion Ross had seldom observed. She helped run the CSO civic and educational programs in Stockton. Soon, she was taking an active political role for the organization, pressing local government leaders for improvements in the barrio, organizing fundraising drives and local and regional meetings for the CSO. Because of her gregarious and energetic manner, she was sent to Sacramento, the state capital, to lobby state government leaders on behalf of the CSO agenda, including old age security benefits for first-generation Mexican Americans, even if they had not been citizens, and the expansion of state disability assistance to agricultural workers. She also lobbied for laws that required voting and driver's license tests be given in Spanish as well as English.

During this time, she met and married her second husband, Ventura Huerta, who was also a community activist and member of the CSO. This relationship produced five more children (Fidel, Emilio, Vincent, Alicia, and Angela).

Despite increasing domestic demands, Huerta continued her all-out activism in the CSO in the late 1950s. Her intense involvement led to strong disagreements with her husband who had not assumed that Dolores, with a growing family, would continue to work as vigorously as an activist as she had in the past. She had not been comfortable in the role of the traditional wife, she later told friends. She prevailed on her mother and other friends to help stay with the children. Without her mother's financial help and moral support, Huerta's career would have been far less likely. Huerta later admitted that she had not leveled with her husband about the expectations each had for the relationship. The marriage, constantly battered by arguments over her work, tottered for several years through several trial separations, and then failed. She was now a single mother with seven children.

During this period, Huerta joined the Agricultural Workers Association (AWA), a community-interest group founded through a Catholic church to help agricultural workers. The AWA later merged with the Agricultural Workers Organizing Committee (AWOC), a group that undertook efforts to generate self-help programs for farm workers and was sponsored by the American Federation of Labor and Congress of Industrial Organizations (AFL-CIO). Although a fledgling, underfunded group, the AWOC early on entertained the idea of attempting to organize a strike against local growers. For a time, Huerta served as secretary-treasurer of the AWOC.

But Huerta soon became unhappy with the organization, whose leaders, she thought, did not understand fully the needs of the farm workers and who did not have the fire to take on the growers and their contractors. The migrant workforce, she realized, was easily intimidated and manipulated. It would take much more than the type of activity promoted by the AWOC to make an impact. While working for the CSO, Huerta met the man who would change her life and propel her career into the national arena: Cesar Chavez.

WORKING WITH CESAR CHAVEZ

As a boy Chavez had worked the fields in Arizona and California as a migrant worker. He had seen and felt first-hand the injustices meted out to his family and other laborers, those on the lowest rung of America's economic ladder. Small and stocky in stature, with jet-black hair, and quiet, Chavez had served a brief stint in the Navy and then had married and started a family. But his spirit was in doing anything he could to change the conditions under which individuals such as those in his own family had been forced to endure—the agonizing, stooped labor for a pittance of wages, the deplorable living and sanitation facilities provided by the growers, the lack of leadership, and total lack of political muscle of an entire group of American workers.

Like Huerta, Chavez had seen much good in the work of the CSO. Like Huerta, he had helped Ross form a CSO chapter, this one near Chavez's home in San Jose. Huerta had heard of Chavez from a number of friends, including Ross. From their talk about his prodigious energy, his gift for organizing, and his vision for bettering the conditions of migrant workers, she had envisioned a dynamic individual, with flair and a gift of oratory. When she met him, she was at first taken aback. He seemed almost shy and retiring. Yet, in conversation, she picked up what everyone else who had met and worked with Chavez had come to recognize—an intense dedication, a keen intelligence, and a seeming lack of fear in tackling problems that seemed to most so intractable.

Huerta and Chavez both began to envision the formation of a union of farm workers, those impoverished and marginal individuals with whom Chavez had worked and whom Huerta had befriended at the hotel in Stockton and in her work with the AWOC. They talked with Ross and others at CSO, asking whether the organization would be willing to sponsor an effort to organize agricultural laborers, to enlarge its current vision beyond helping those in urban areas.

Although Ross and others at CSO shared the belief that some kind of activism was necessary to improve the lot of the migrants, they would not agree to lead the organization in that direction. They seriously doubted, as they should have, the possibility that that kind of work force could form a union. Since the early efforts of the Industrial Workers of the World to organize migrant workers and other unskilled laborers, there had been aborted attempts through the years to help agricultural workers—but nothing on the scale envisioned by both Chavez and Huerta.

In 1962, after the CSO Board of Directors turned down his proposal to organize a pilot project toward creating a union of farm workers, the determined Chavez resigned. He packed up his belongings from the CSO headquarters and headed north to Delano, California, the hometown of his wife, Helen. He had little money, no property, and no job. He had only a burning wish to form a union. He soon asked Huerta to join him, and she accepted.

CREATING A UNION

When Chavez met Huerta, they began a lifelong friendship, often turbulent, but always with shared ideals and goals. Huerta later said, "When Cesar told me, 'I'm going to start my own union,' I was just appalled, the thought was so overwhelming. But when the initial shock wore off, I thought it was exciting."[8]

Huerta was going through her second divorce and had seven children and no financial assets. Yet, it was Huerta whom Chavez asked to be his partner in this organizing adventure with very long odds. After she made the decision to help Chavez, she said, she opened her door one morning to a surprise. Someone left a big box of groceries on the porch. She would need all the groceries she could get.

If Chavez and Huerta were to create enough support to start a union movement, they would also have to overcome a problem of expectations. First, the workers themselves had endured the injustices for so long and knew the reprisals that had been dealt to others who had challenged the system that they expected the treatment and the system to continue. The workers were largely illiterate, extremely poor, and divided culturally from mainstream America. They did not usually remain very long in one locality, making stability and communication highly dubious.

On the other side, the growers and the rest of the community also fully expected the system to continue as it had. Workers knew their place, did the work they were expected to perform; if not, all the local institutions, from the police to business owners and political leaders, could be expected to react defensively, protecting the status quo and what they considered the usual way of doing things. Most labor leaders privately believed that the goal of creating the first successful union of farm workers in U.S. history was close to impossible.

Nevertheless, Chavez, Huerta, and others settled in Delano to try to make American labor history. With the help of friends and relatives, they survived financially in the early months as they traveled from house to house attempting to interest workers in the idea of union. Gradually, their earnest and persuasive arguments won over an increasing number of laborers who suddenly found an outlet for their frustrations, a hope of bettering their condition.

On Sunday September 30, 1962, in an abandoned movie theater in Fresno, California, approximately 200 workers gathered to show their solidarity. Calling the new organization The Farm Workers Association, they adopted a union motto: "Viva la causa!" (Long live the cause!). Chavez showed the new union members a flag designed by his brother Richard and sewn by his cousin, Manuel Chavez. It bore the symbol of an Aztec eagle, emblematic of pride and dignity. As Manuel pulled a cord to unveil the flag, Chavez declared that when the eagle flies, the farm workers' problems will be over.

At their constitutional convention in Fresno in January 1963, the farm workers presented a constitution. The preamble, drafted by Chavez, declared in part, "We the Farm Workers of America, have tilled the soil, sown the seeds and harvested the crops. We have provided food in abundance for the people of the cities, and the nation and world but have not had sufficient food to feed our own children.... We have been isolated, scattered, and hindered from uniting our forces."[9]

It was now the work of Chavez, Huerta and others to forge that unity. They gathered together a close knit set of "co-fanatics," as they called themselves, including Julio Hernandez, a cotton picker from nearby Cocoran, California, who had already had a bitter experience with a union organizer who had abandoned him at the beginning of a strike; Gilbert Padilla, a CSO veteran and former agricultural laborer like Huerta and Chavez; and Jim Drake, a graduate of Occidental College and Union Theological Seminary and now a director of the California Migrant Ministry, an organization of Protestant ministers dedicated to helping the farm workers.

When Chavez, Huerta and the others began local tours of the homes of farm workers to recruit members, Drake was soon at their side. The farm workers were not organized in large gatherings but one by one, in cars on the way to labor commissioner meetings or while driving to meet other workers. "Whatever the need was, Jim was there," Huerta said of Drake. "He had a very, very big heart."[10]

From the earliest days of their collaboration, Huerta and Chavez worked closely together. With Chavez in the organization's base in Delano and Huerta working in Stockton, they fanned out across the rich agricultural valleys of northern California. Although the relationship was often contentious and rancorous, it was always from a base of mutual respect. If some of Chavez's lieutenants were sometimes reluctant to criticize certain steps that Chavez planned for the union, Huerta had no such reservations. She was a critical sounding board, blunt and honest. As she reminded Chavez during one of their disagreements, she was never the quiet or long-suffering type.

In the formative months and years of the National Farm Workers Association (NFWA), as the organization came to be known, the union leaders slowly gained recruits. Chavez and Drake held town meetings. Huerta began to take charge of administrative matters. Padilla took jobs picking cherries and peeling peaches so he could secretly pass out cards to workers in the fields. Manuel Chavez, a vigorous organizer, decided to give up a permanent, well-paid job as a car salesman in San Diego to join his cousin and the cause.

Nevertheless, progress was painstakingly slow. Workers would agree to join and then change their minds. Many were not in the area long enough to be of any help to the union. For the organization's leaders, finding ways to feed their families and at the same time organize an infant union was next to impossible. Although the first few years were arduous and frustrating, the determined leadership of the union persevered. The number of members slowly began to increase. By 1964, they had signed up more than 1,000 families. The NFWA was even able to create its own credit union and provide services such as immigration counseling and voter registration.

Chavez and his lieutenants looked forward to the time when the union could seriously challenge the growers with a strike. Nevertheless, they did not feel that the time had yet arrived. Faced with demands by workers, Chavez knew, the companies would use a number of ruthless strikebreaking strategies that the union would have to overcome. The companies would approach the courts for rulings to prevent the union from boycotting or picketing. They would hire goons from other parts of the valley to come in and beat up strikers. They would bring in undocumented foreign workers to help replace picketing workers. They would enlist the efforts of police to arrest picketers and protesters for causing mayhem. They would plant stories in the media that the strikers were violent, un-American, and probably

communists. Union leaders knew well the tactics they would face. They figured it would take at least another couple of years for the union to have the
money, the numbers of members, and the experience necessary to take on
that kind of power. As Chavez and his lieutenants also knew, however,
events often change plans. In the spring of 1965, they suddenly found themselves at a fateful moment in the infant life of the union.

THE DELANO GRAPE STRIKE

As the summer of 1965 drew to a close near Delano, California, migrant
laborers arrived to begin picking the ripening grapes, expecting to make
$ .90 an hour plus $ .10 a basket. However, led by members of the AWOC,
the group that Huerta had helped create years earlier, a small group of
workers, mostly Filipinos, decided to begin a strike to demand an increase
in wages. They decided to ask Chavez, Huerta, and the other leaders of the
Farm Workers Association to help in the strike.

On September 16, 1965, the members of the union gathered at a church
in Delano. Local disc jockeys on Spanish radio announced that an important decision would soon be announced. Chavez explained to the membership what a strike would entail. He knew in his heart how the members
would respond. Around 500 workers and their leaders, voted unanimously
to join the strike. From the church, the cry sounded: *Viva la huelga!* (Long
live the strike!)

From the outset of the strike, Chavez preached the message of nonviolence. He had seen Martin Luther King, Jr., and other black civil rights leaders use the tactic successfully. Like King, Chavez was deeply religious. The
union often held religious services, and Chavez surrounded himself with
Christian leaders from various denominations. One minister who joined the
strike said, "I'm here because this is a movement by the poor people themselves to improve their position, and where the poor people are, Christ
should be and is."[11]

Like Martin Luther King, Jr., Chavez also read and deeply respected the
teachings of Mahatma Gandhi. Indeed, it would be Chavez himself who
would use the fast, as Gandhi had in India, to attempt to motivate social
change.

Striking workers began to march in front of the vineyards where growers
wanted them to work for miserly wages. Huerta, who seemed born for such
clashes, coordinated the picket lines, entreating those who grew tired to
keep up the pressure. She was tough-minded, focused, and, in the eyes of
many, indefatigable. In the Delano strike, Huerta would join workers in jail
for violating local ordinances and orders from police. It would be the first
of more than twenty arrests over the course of her career. She would see the
arrests as badges of honor.

"We had been on strike for a few months and the growers were bringing in strike-breakers from Mexico," Huerta recalled. "They went and got court injunctions limiting us to five people per field. Can you imagine five pickets on a big thousand-acre field? So we were kind of stymied in terms of trying to keep the people from breaking the strike." At one point, Huerta traveled to Juarez, Mexico, to spread leaflets to Mexican workers pleading with them not to help break the strike in Delano.[12]

Faced with increasing pressure, the union leaders decided to broaden the attack. They called for a boycott of grapes. Young volunteers who had shown up in Delano to help picket were soon sent on the road to spread the word. With little money, they hitchhiked to New York, Chicago, St. Louis, and other major cities, carrying signs imploring people not to purchase products produced by the Schenley Company, the union's first major target in the strike.

Strike leaders then decided to publicize their cause with a long march, as the civil rights leaders had done on a number of occasions. They would march from union headquarters in Delano to Sacramento, the state capital. On March 17, 1966, about one hundred individuals began the march in Delano. Followed by the press, curious onlookers, and members of the Federal Bureau of Investigation looking for links between the strikers and communism, the marchers headed down Highway 99 toward Sacramento. Along the way, they picked up additional marchers. They carried banners emblazoned with the Virgin of Guadalupe, the patron saint of Mexico. The carried union flags. They wore crosses. They sang.

On April 3, 1966, a week before the marchers were due to reach Sacramento, Chavez received a call from a representative of Schenley Vineyards. Already damaged by the publicity generated by the union and hurt economically by the strike and boycott, the company decided to cut its losses. They decided to enter into negotiations with the union for a contract. Anxious to settle before the marchers reached Sacramento and before the inevitable landslide of publicity that the event would produce, the company signed a preliminary agreement. Huerta drew up a full contract that would be finalized in ninety days.

The company agreed to recognize the NFWA as a bargaining partner. This was the first time in the history of the United States labor movement that a farm labor union had received such recognition. In negotiating the contract, Huerta also was able to strike a deal for wage increases and improvements in working conditions. After this negotiation and a few others, word spread among some of the growers that Dolores Huerta, as tough a labor negotiator as many had ever seen, was "The Dragon Lady."

As the grape strike continued against other companies, Huerta successfully negotiated more contracts for the farm workers. Some of them even established health and benefit plans for farm workers, an unheard of development. She set up hiring halls for workers, administered the contracts, and worked on behalf of many workers on grievance procedures. The strike had brought Schenley and some other companies to the table. Other companies held out. There was still much work to be done.

NONVIOLENCE AND FASTS

The union stayed on the attack. In the spring of 1966, it launched a boycott against DiGiorgio Fruit Corporation, a major grape-growing company near Bakersfield, California. Known for its innovative tactics against organized labor and its ruthless strikebreaking methods, DiGiorgio had a new strategy to use against the farm workers union.

DiGorgio's officers turned to the International Brotherhood of Teamsters Union, whose leadership was open to the idea of incorporating farm workers among its membership. DiGorgio knew that the Teamsters would be a much less demanding organization with which to deal than the upstart but spirited NFWA. The grape grower and the Teamsters would try to use each other to defeat Cesar Chavez and his union. DiGiorgio invited the Teamsters to organize company workers. The agreements would not include job security, seniority rights, and other benefits for which the NFWA pledged to fight. The tactic did not work. In the ensuing months, the workers at DiGiorgio turned away from the Teamsters to the NFWA. The new union had won another fight.

Later that summer, with union membership reaching over 8,000 members, many of whom resided outside of California, the leaders turned their sights on Giumarra Vineyards Corporation, the largest producer of table grapes in the United States. Huerta told a newspaper reporter, "If we can crack Giumarra, we can crack them all." A Giumarra official dismissed the union as a "socialist civil rights movement" aided by "do-gooder elements, beatniks, and socialistic-type groups."[13]

As the national media focused more intently on the struggle and the stakes rose higher, so did tensions and anger. With little or no money and beset by hired thugs, the strikers became increasingly restive and were barely able to continue their nonviolent methods. In a number of cities, fights broke out. In some cases, protesters roughed up a number of individuals suspected of being company spies.

To demonstrate his commitment to nonviolence and also to bring greater attention to the needs of the farm workers, Chavez decided to conduct a public fast. On February 14, 1968, Chavez stopped eating. Immediately, the national press began covering the unusual event occurring in the small farming community of Delano. A number of other individuals close to Chavez also decided to show support by going on their own fasts, including Huerta and Chavez's brother, Richard.

From Martin Luther King, Jr., and from Senator Robert Kennedy of New York, now in the race for President of the United States, came words of support. As far as generating publicity and support, the fast gained remarkable attention. Chavez took Communion every day. He asked that daily mass be held at union headquarters each day. His wife Helen became increasingly concerned about his health. Some of his closest supporters not only worried about his health but about the tactic itself.

Huerta, who was in close contact with labor leaders and organizers around the country, later said, "Well you can imagine what these tough, burly labor leaders from New York thought when we told them our leader, our president, was fasting. 'What's wrong with him? Is he crazy?' I mean they were just—they went ballistic. Because in New York, especially during that time, they'd go into a place and wreck it up. They would wreck it all up to get a contract and here we had our leader who was *not eating*. All he would do was take Holy Communion every day."[14]

Although Huerta and others had been dubious about the fast as a tactic, they soon began to realize that it had become one of the most effective organizing tools they could have used. Money began arriving at the headquarters. Letters came in from around the country. Most important, the fast energized the workers who began to see again what the movement was all about. Only through a nonviolent course could they prevail.

For twenty-one days Chavez fasted, losing thirty-five pounds. On March 10, 1968, he finally gave in to the pleadings of those closest to him. A crowd of several thousand watched as Chavez, seated with his wife and mother, broke bread with Senator Kennedy. But the next few months would be filled with horror and sadness. Two towering national figures would lose their lives to assassination: Martin Luther King, Jr., in Memphis, Tennessee, before a rally on behalf of sanitation workers, and Robert Kennedy in Los Angeles, California, on the night of his victory in the California presidential primary election. Huerta and others of Senator Kennedy's supporters stood on the stage at the Ambassador Hotel that evening, moments before his death.

The union carried on. Huerta was working mostly out of New York as the director of the table-grape boycott for New York City, the nation's primary distribution center for grapes. "When we got to New York," she vividly remembered, "it was something like four or five degrees above zero." Relentlessly, Huerta was determined to mobilize and organize and turn the heat on the grape growers.[15]

Huerta mobilized other unions and political activists. She visited Latino associations, religious groups, peace organizations, and consumers across racial and ethnic lines, demonstrating the common cause toward which these various individuals and groups could work. She was especially effective in training farm workers who had left the fields and traveled all the way to New York to help. For the young women who had made the trip, Huerta was a mentor, guiding them in interpersonal relations both within the group and in public and giving them a first-hand experience in social activism. In return, they gave the union growing strength, solidarity, and a youthful, infectious exuberance.

Throughout 1969, shipments of table grapes slowed dramatically in most large cities. Even in some British ports, dockworkers refused to unload grapes. On July 29, 1970, with the growers feeling a severe economic effect from the boycott, more than twenty companies, led by Giumarra, signed a historic labor agreement with the union. It increased wages and included new safety requirements on the use of pesticides and a health plan.

They celebrated in Delano. It had been five years since the infant union had dared take on the grape growers. This was a day for which the union leaders had labored for so long, a day for the *campesinos*, the field workers, many with their backs bent by years in the fields, their hands roughened and skin weathered like leather. Today, as they met in Delano, many of their eyes filled as Chavez, along with the growers, signed the contract that gave their union formal representation.

By 1971, the union, which became known as the United Farm Workers of America (UFW), had won pivotal contracts. Huerta had bargained a very favorable contract from InterHarvest, a lettuce and vegetable giant with ties to Central America. Not only did the increase in wage to $2.10 far exceed anything that the Teamsters had been able to offer farm workers, but Huerta also negotiated an agreement by the company to eliminate the use of DDT and other dangerous pesticides that Chavez and the union had denounced.

In 1973, the UFW began a nationwide consumer boycott not only of grapes not covered by contracts, but also of lettuce and other products. Once again, Huerta acted as the director for the East Coast, bringing together community workers, religious groups, women's organizations, and others to the cause. The boycott resulted in the California table-grape growers signing a three-year collective bargaining agreement with the UFW.

In 1975, California Governor Jerry Brown signed the Agricultural Labor Relations Act, the first bill of rights for farm workers ever enacted in America. The new law gave workers the right to secret ballot elections to choose a union and required growers to bargain with unions that won those elections.

During the late 1970s, Huerta became the director of the UFW's Citizenship Participation Department (CPD), a newly established political arm of the UFW. As she was at the negotiating table across from the company representatives, Huerta was persuasive and relentless in fighting for every inch of political advantage she could claim. She lobbied the California state legislature especially hard to protect the new farm labor law.

Later, she took on another trailblazing assignment—the establishment of Radio Campesina, the radio station of the farm workers. For the first time, UFW had a means to reach its membership and supporters.

With the Republican ascendancy to power both in California and nationally, the UFW faced a fearsome challenge to maintain its momentum. Indeed, there would setbacks and a decline in membership, but the farm workers union was now an established player on a much larger stage than the fruit and vegetable valleys of California. Especially in the large cities such as Los Angeles and Chicago, young Mexican Americans now followed closely the drama being played out in the fields of California. A new generation of young people looked to reclaim the pride and heritage of their culture. They began to use the name "Chicano," a term once used as a racial slur by non-Mexican Americans, as a gesture of political defiance and ethnic pride.

BALANCING FAMILY AND CAREER

In the early 1970s, Huerta began a personal relationship with Richard Chavez, Cesar's brother. In the succeeding years, the two produced four children: Juanita, Maria Elena, Ricky, and Camilla. Huerta now was the mother of eleven children. Often criticized, even by her own father, for the choices she made in her personal life in the midst of a demanding and dangerous career, Huerta often looked back with some regret that she had not had enough time to spend as a mother. In many ways, Huerta's own mother and her associates in the union acted as surrogate parents.

It had been a high-wire balancing act. Nevertheless, she maintained her dogged pursuit and devotion to *La Causa*, traveling to all parts of the country, negotiating contracts, lobbying state and federal officials, even testifying before Congress. On some occasions, some of the children would accompany her; at other times they did not. As the children grew older, she enlisted them in the struggle and tried to pass on her own sense of urgency and commitment in improving the lives of farm workers. Several of them joined her on picket lines and in other organizing activities.

Looking back, she said of her children, "They had a lot of hardships—we were very poor and never had any money. Working for the union, all we had were our subsistence rent and food. They never had good clothes or toys. I do regret not being able to provide them with music lessons. My son Ricky's very talented, but I was never able to give him any music lessons. I did have violin and dancing lessons growing up. I regret that, but at the same time it makes me feel very strongly that, as women, we need to fight for support systems. We need to be activists; women need to be in decision-making roles."[16] She recalled an incident while she was in jail, one of the more than twenty times over her career that she was incarcerated. "This group of college kids came to meet outside the jail," she recalled. "One of them handed me a note and it was from my fifteen-year-old daughter, Angela. The note said, 'Mom, sorry I can't meet you when you come out of jail, but I'm knocking on doors to register people to vote.' That was a big gift for me."[17]

Several of her children over the years have expressed some resentment and bitterness about their early lives, about some of the things they missed because of their mother's activities. Most of all, they missed the presence of their mother for long periods of time. "Like most working women, you have guilt complexes," Huerta said, "You do it without thinking about it, because if you think about it, you can't do it."[18]

All of her children recognized her dedication to *La Causa*. Huerta herself took great pride whenever her children chose to be involved. She told a story about her daughter, Juanita.

> When she was three years old we were doing a training session for organizers. She was walking in and out with her dolls. When we got back to our boycott house in New York City, she was on the line with her play telephone. I said, 'What are you doing?' She said, 'I'm calling the people.' I said, 'Are you calling them to picket?' [She said,] 'They're not ready to picket; they're just going to leaflet.'[19]

BECOMING A FEMINIST

Dolores Huerta became a national figure on two fronts because of her gender. On the one hand, as the farm workers union's first contract negotiator, she gained instant notice among those in the labor movement and among the business leaders she confronted. The sight of this Latino woman across the table in contact negotiations made an immediate impression on many savvy veterans of the labor wars.

Her influence on another front was even more conspicuous. Because of the sudden appearance of a woman in a position usually filled by a man, she achieved immediate status in the feminist movement. While in New York, she became personal friends with Gloria Steinem, writer and founder of *Ms. Magazine*, and with other activists.

With an increased consciousness raised by the feminist movement against gender stereotypes and discrimination, she began to speak out against the treatment of women and to encourage the greater involvement of women outside of the normally prescribed gender roles. She lamented the absence of women in leadership positions in all areas of American life. She talked of her admiration of Eleanor Smeal, director of the Feminist Majority Foundation. In a compliment from Huerta that could have no greater impact or personal stamp, she compared Smeal's vision and innovative drive with that of Cesar Chavez. "In the '60s and '70s, many of us were working hard for La Raza, not for women," said Huerta. "We should have been doing more for women at the same time. We've had to do a lot of catching up."[20]

She began to speak out on sexual harassment issues, lobbied hard for federal and state legislation favorable to welfare mothers, and pushed for laws prohibiting discrimination against women in the workplace. She dedicated time to helping Smeal's Feminist Majority Fund's campaign to recruit women to run for political office. Huerta traveled to many parts of the country encouraging Latino women to enter the political arena.

In 1993, Huerta learned of sad news from Arizona. Cesar Chavez, her long-time close friend and founder of the UFW had passed away. He died, as he had lived almost all of his life, fighting for farm workers. He had gone to Arizona, at the border in Yuma, close to where he had been born sixty-five years earlier, to testify on a labor suit. In her eulogy, Huerta, his close partner, said that his death, at Easter time, would bind the union together once again. Her remarks echoed the religious symbolism that had characterized the movement from its beginning, from the ever-present flag of the Virgin of Guadalupe to the union's anthem, *De Colores*. They sang the anthem at Chavez's burial with renewed faith that his movement would live on.

BATTERED BUT NEVER BEATEN

In September 1988, outside the Sir Francis Drake Hotel on Union Square in San Francisco, Huerta was once again in a picket line. This time she was demonstrating against the policies of the Reagan administration and of presidential candidate George Bush, the Republican nominee for the 1988 election. Specifically, she and others were protesting the administration's lack of support in banning the use of various pesticides that had been proven to be injurious to the health of field workers.

In a scuffle with police, Huerta, now fifty-eight years old, was clubbed by a policeman wielding a baton. She collapsed on the sidewalk and was soon rushed to a hospital. Many of those close to Huerta during the incident witnessed the brutal severity of the blows and feared for her life. Huerta underwent emergency surgery. She suffered several broken ribs and a spleen so badly damaged that it had to be removed. Captured on film by local television crews, the beating eventually led to a string of lawsuits that forced the San Francisco Police Department to change some of its practices regarding crowd control and police discipline. The video footage was also the key piece of evidence that led to a significant court judgment against the police. Huerta donated the money to the cause of the farm workers.

After years on the picket lines, after numerous periods behind bars, after receiving many death threats, and after enduring personal insults and highly critical statements in the press, Huerta had taken on all that the opposition could give. As the legal teams arrayed against her in union negotiations had said, she was "The Dragon Lady." But somehow this was different—she had nearly given her life. The beating affected Huerta as no other event had ever done and taught her something primal, she said, about human courage.

"It's not only the physical disability," she recalled, "but also the emotional disability. I found that I was so emotional that during our board meetings ...

I told them, 'I'm not going to be able to fight with you like I usually do.' I'd just start crying right away. It took a long time to get my emotional stability back after that beating. It just did something to me. I couldn't be in crowds, I'd just panic. The physical disability healed in months, but my emotions took about a year and a half. That made me understand a lot about people, when you ask them to come and they're not ready."[21]

Recovering from her injuries, Huerta resumed a hectic pace, addressing a wide variety of groups, always turning over to the union her honoraria and speaking fees. She kept herself in the front lines on labor issues, women's rights causes, and in political campaigns. She lamented the fact that many business leaders and political organizations still seem rooted in a mindset of the last century, still chafing against progress toward human rights issues, still unwilling to come to grips with the problems of poverty, racism, immigration, and the rights of workers. Always aggressive, never backing off, she made her herself increasingly visible in the national spotlight, endorsing political campaigns, railing against the policies of political administrations. She endorsed and worked for Al Gore's presidential campaign in 1992.

In 1993, Huerta was inducted into the National Women's Hall of Fame. In the same year she also received the American Civil Liberties Union Roger Baldwin Medal of Liberty Award, the Eugene V. Debs Foundation Outstanding American Award, and the Ellis Island Medal of Freedom Award.

In 1995, the UFW launched a major strike on behalf of 20,000 California strawberry workers. Beset with low pay, no benefits, wretched working conditions, and sexual discrimination, the strawberry workers rode the back of the UFW in demanding change. Huerta charged that strawberry workers made an average of $8,000 a year with no health insurance or other benefits. Such conditions, she intimated, amounted to something close to slave labor.

In late March 1996, the UFW organized marches in New York City, San Antonio, San Francisco, Los Angeles, and Chicago to demand workplace rights for California strawberry workers. In the front line of the marchers in New York and San Francisco were familiar faces from the early days of the farm worker movement such as former California governor Jerry Brown and Richard Chavez, brother of Cesar Chavez.

But now there were new supporters, thanks to the contacts built by Huerta. In the front lines were Gloria Steinem and Patricia Ireland, president of the National Organization for Women (NOW). The UFW now had the official support of NOW in its campaign against the strawberry growers. It also had the support of the civil rights and religious organizations. Despite intense industry resistance, the UFW won contracts with two of the nation's largest berry producers.

In 1998, Huerta was one of three *Ms. Magazine's* "Women of the Year" and one of the *Ladies' Home Journal's*, "100 Most Important Women of the 20th Century." In 1999 President Bill Clinton presented Huerta with the Eleanor Roosevelt Human Rights Award. In 2004, Huerta won a $100,000 Creative Citizen Award from the Puffin Foundation. She donated the entire amount to starting a foundation for training young activists in how to continue the work that she and others began during the 1960s. Its mission was "to build active communities working for fair and equal access to health care, housing, education, jobs, civic participation, and economic resources for disadvantaged communities with an emphasis on women and youth."[22]

The eminent black historian Vincent Harding, a close friend of Martin Luther King, Jr., and a prominent figure in the civil rights movement, worked with Huerta and others on a project in 2004 to bring the lessons and teachings of social reformers and other leaders into focus for young students. Harding had not met Huerta until the project began, but he was immediately impressed by her intellect, commitment, wit, and dedication to young people. They shared stories about the African-American freedom movement and the drive for the rights of farm workers, and they spoke of the connections between the two, especially the emphasis on nonviolent protest.

Later, Harding wrote of the impact that Huerta's life and work had on the students.

> They were especially moved by her willingness to sacrifice on behalf of the well-being of others, and by the time the retreat was over they had taken up the Farm Workers' declaration: "*Sí, Se Puede!*"—believing in their own potentials so fully that some were saying, "We are strong. We can work for change...." By then they were prepared to carry the spirit of Dolores Huerta back to their high school, along with a list of proposed changes they would present to their principal—and a list of promises they were making to themselves, and to their African-American fellow students—and perhaps to the Virgin of Guadalupe who means so much to Dolores?

Harding was touched by Huerta's own words, those of the crusader never willing to hang back, always hopeful in the face of great challenges, always moving forward. "I think," she said, "we have a renaissance of sorts happening with the young people. *Si, se puede.*"[23]

Two years later, at a conference on education, Huerta declared:

> Education is so important. You know, Cesar Chavez only went as far as the eighth grade, but he always had a book under his arm. He was always learning and always promoting education. A farm worker's daughter told me that when she was a girl, her father went to a Farm Workers rally and heard Cesar say, 'Your children need to go to school. They don't belong in the fields, take them out.' The next day, her father sent all his children to school. Today, that daughter is a community college president.[24]

Looking back over her career, Huerta said that her hope was that she would be remembered, above all else, as an organizer:

> ... that I have passed on the miracles that can be accomplished when people come together, the things they can change. And I look at ... when we passed the pension bill, the voting in Spanish, the getting driver's licenses in Spanish— all these bills we've passed. The fact that you can build and you can make non-violent change through organization; that's what I would want my legacy to be. And hopefully we'll see the day when we don't have discrimination against women, against minorities, against workers. And working for a just world.[25]

In July 2007, Hillary Clinton joined a group of volunteers in Nevada to organize strategy for the state in her run for the presidency of the United States. Joining her, Clinton said, was "my friend, the legendary human rights activist Dolores Huerta, who is also the national co-chair for Hispanic outreach for my campaign.... I am honored to have Dolores Huerta's support!" At the age of seventy-seven, with a fighting spirit as robust as ever, Huerta declared, "Are we going to be able to get out there? Are we going to be able to recruit a lot of volunteers? Are we going to win the state of Nevada for Hillary Clinton? In [the United] Farm Workers [Union] we say, "Yes, we can," and in Spanish that's '*Sí, se puede!*'"[26]

NOTES

1. Eleanor Bader, "When Women Pursue Justice," *Z Magazine* Online, April 2006, http://zmagsite.zmag.org/Apr2006/bader0406.html.

2. Margaret E. Rose, "Dolores Huerta: Passionate Defender of La Causa," http://216.239.51.104/search?q=cache:pbZz_vGA-voJ:chavez.cde.ca.gov/ModelCurriculum/Teachers/Lessons/Resources/Documents/Dolores_Huerta_Essay.pdf+dolores+huerta+interview&hl=en&ct=clnk&cd=12&gl=us#13.

3. The Veterans of Hope Project: Excerpts from an Interview with Dolores Huerta, http://www.veteransofhope.org/show.php?vid=51&tid=46&sid=79.

4. Veterans of Hope.

5. Veterans of Hope.

6. Southwest Research and Information Center, "Voices from the Earth, An Interview with Dolores Huerta," October 29, 2003, http://www.sric.org/voices/2004/v5n2/huerta.html.

7. Rose.

8. Carol Larson Jones, "Dolores Huerta: Cesar Chavez' Partner in Founding the United Farm Workers Union in California," http://www.csupomona.edu/~jis/1997/Mullikin.pdf.

9. Jones.

10. "A Rare, Unheralded Champion of American Workers, February 22, 2004, http://www.epinions.com/content_3786842244.

11. Dick Meister, "La Huelga Becomes 'La Causa,'" *New York Times Magazine* November 17, 1968, 92.

12. Veterans of Hope.

13. "Farm Union Pins Its Hopes on Victory in Coast Grape Strike," *New York Times,* October 2, 1967, 43.

14. Veterans of Hope.

15. Rose.

16. Rose

17. Rose.

18. Rose

19. Lobaco.

20. Rose.

21. Lobaco.

22. The Dolores Huerta Foundation, http://www.doloreshuerta.org.

23. Veterans of Hope.

24. "Respect, Spanish, and Unemployment Insurance," *NEA Today,* May 17, 2006, http://www.nea.org/neatodayextra/huerta.html.

25. Lobaco.

26. *My Grito,* July 4, 2007, http://www.mygrito.com/profile.php?sub_section= blog&id=2833.

SUGGESTED READING

"Dolores Huerta," *Notable Hispanic American Women,* Gale Research, 1993.

Dunne, John Gregory. *Delano: The Story of the California Grape Strike.* New York: Farrar, 1976.

Griswold del Castillo, Richard, and Richard A. Garcia. *César Chávez: A Triumph of Spirit.* Norman, OK: University of Oklahoma Press, 1995.

Jones, Carol Larson. "Dolores Huerta: Cesar Chavez' Partner in Founding the United Farm Workers Union in California," http://www.csupomona.edu/~jis/ 1997/Mullikin.pdf.

"Let Them Eat Grapes," *National Catholic Reporter,* September 30, 1988, 12.

Lobaco, Julia B. "Dolores Huerta: The Vision and Voice of Her Life's Work," AARP SegundaJuventud, Fall, 2004. Available at: http://www.segundajuventud.org/ english/presence/2004-oct/dolores_huerta.htm.

Rose, Margaret E. "Dolores Huerta: Passionate Defender of La Causa," http:// 216.239.51.104/search?q=cache:pbZz_vGA-voJ:chavez.cde.ca.gov/ModelCurri culum/Teachers/Lessons/Resources/Documents/Dolores_Huerta_Essay.pdf+ dolores+huerta+interview&hl=en&ct=clnk&cd=12&gl=us#13.

Southwest Research and Information Center. "Voices from the Earth, An Interview with Dolores Huerta," October 29, 2003, http://www.sric.org/voices/2004/v5n2/ huerta.html.

The Veterans of Hope Project. "Excerpts from an Interview with Dolores Huerta," http://www.veteransofhope.org/show.php?vid=51&tid=46&sid=79.